Véronique Lacoste, Jakob Leimgruber, Thiemo Breyer (Eds.)
Indexing Authenticity

linguae & litterae

Publications of the School of Language & Literature
Freiburg Institute for Advanced Studies

Edited by
Peter Auer, Gesa von Essen, Werner Frick

Volume 39

Indexing Authenticity

Sociolinguistic Perspectives

Edited by
Véronique Lacoste, Jakob Leimgruber, Thiemo Breyer

DE GRUYTER

ISBN 978-3-11-034347-2
e-ISBN [PDF] 978-3-11-034701-2
e-ISBN [EPUB] 978-3-11-038460-4
ISSN 1869-7054

Library of Congress Cataloging-in-Publication Data
A CIP catalog record for this book has been applied for at the Library of Congress.

Bibliographic information published by the Deutsche Nationalbibliothek
The Deutsche Nationalbibliothek lists this publication in the Deutsche Nationalbibliografie;
detailed bibliographic data are available in the Internet at http://dnb.dnb.de.

© 2014 Walter de Gruyter GmbH, Berlin/Boston
Typesetting: epline, Kirchheim unter Teck
Printing: Hubert & Co. GmbH & Co. KG, Göttingen
∞ Printed on acid-free paper
Printed in Germany

MIX
Papier aus verantwor-
tungsvollen Quellen
FSC® C016439

www.degruyter.com

Contents

Section I: Indexing local meanings of authenticity

Section 2: Indexing authenticity in delocalised settings

Section 3:
Authenticity construction in other mediatised contexts

Véronique Lacoste, Jakob Leimgruber and Thiemo Breyer

Authenticity: A view from inside and outside sociolinguistics[1]

What does it mean to be 'authentic'? Can authenticity ever be achieved? Is it a fundamental property of some entities or is it rather an element of attribution? How can sociolinguistics, which has tended to leave this issue out of its main considerations, best define what it means to be authentic in language production and perception? What properties can one assign to socio-linguistic authenticity and from whose perspective is it evaluated? Whether it is planned or not, it may be legitimate to present authenticity as an assumedly common enterprise whose social functioning is a driving force of each individual's behaviour and is evaluated according to cultural contexts and mediated by and expressed in language. Conversely, 'inauthenticity' would manifest itself as a failure to display a person's true self in terms of their sociolinguistic individualities and/or to reject conventionalised speech behaviours which are not *truly* their own. Originally from Greek *authentikós* (*autós*, self), this concept has been taken to mean something that is genuine, proven to be original (also, *authéntes*, author, originator, initiator). The semantic field of authenticity itself is rich and detailed and its set of related words can be applied to various contexts. As semantically related words, one may find features associated with 'realness', 'genuineness', 'naturalness', 'originality', 'individuality', 'credibility', 'expressivity', 'immediacy', 'truthfulness', 'faithfulness' and so on. Authenticity may be argued to be a relational concept which accounts for the many ways in which a speaker or agent can be authentic in a given situation in relation to a particular aspect of his or her environment. Having this in mind, however, as Straub (2012: 10) has recently put it, authenticity "comes with a warning that one should not buy into it without some good insurance".

1 The present volume is based on a conference that was organised on the theme of sociolinguistic authenticity by the authors in Freiburg in November 2011. We are extremely grateful to FRIAS (Freiburg Institute of Advanced Studies) and more particularly to Peter Auer for the generous grant which we won in the context of the FRIAS annual Junior Research Group Competition 2011.

1 Authenticity: Some theoretical considerations

The concept of authenticity has received a lot of attention from numerous scientific perspectives. In the vast philosophical literature, the issue of authenticity is often treated from a binary and static viewpoint, usually by comparing 'the original' to 'the copy' in terms of mimetic features, that is, by asking whether an interpretation sticks to the author's intentions or whether or not it is true to the original historical, social or cultural context (Kant 1999 [1791]). This view of authenticity equates the latter with a property of things and/or people. For instance, an essential view exemplifies a static perspective on authenticity in being intrinsic to the object or the person, for instance through an expressive quality of an artefact or the mode of being of a personality (Heidegger 1927). A relational view as discussed by Sartre (1945) portrays authenticity as being constituted in relation to something or someone else, for example standards, values, groups, etc., but it remains relatively fixed in the ways in which it manifests itself. One could also argue that authenticity is a dynamic process and/or a result of authentication and validation. In this view, a methodical approach to authenticity regards the latter as being measurable with certain scientific tools especially considering the validation of a particular age or material, for instance a Ming vase. From an attributional point of view, authenticity is rather in the eye of the beholder, for instance whether a spectator feels emotionally affected or not. Finally, an interactional and thus dynamic view of authenticity is one which suggests that authenticity is created through the complex interplay of producer, product and recipient (Gadamer 1960). Both the static and dynamic views of authenticity may lead us to claim that authenticity is at least at some levels 'constructed'. We may distinguish between three different modes of authenticity construction: firstly the *canonical mode*, which relates to a construction via conventionalised power, that is when authenticity of a given object is determined by an authority; secondly, the *explanatory mode* by which authenticity is methodically investigated on the basis of knowledge about sources – here we refer to a reconstruction of authenticity via the plausibility of evidence; and thirdly, the *performative mode* where authenticity is staged by creating 'reality effects', that is an enactment via credibility of performance and content. These various views and modes of authenticity share common features to some extent insofar as authenticity can be seen as a state of adequation between at least some of the following elements (Table 1).

The rapport between these different elements, which pertain to a particular 'type' of authenticity, perhaps only makes sense if they are coherent over time, since, we would argue, authenticity is also a characteristic feature of certain types of diachronic processes, for instance regarding the *persistence* of a feature or set of features. As an example, take the famous German Leibniz Butterkeks, which

Element 1	Element 2	Authenticity type
object/person	its/her/his nature	ontological/essential
being	what should be	deontic
fact	description	descriptive
intention	action	intentional/behavioural
mind	world	epistemic
object	reproduction	medial

Table 1

is "nur echt mit 52 Zähnen", i.e. the Leibniz butter biscuit, which is "real only with 52 'teeth'", as it says in the advertisement slogan. Here, the viability of the authenticated feature is accepted by a particular group of language users. The *consistency* of attitudes, patterns of behaviour and ideas according to established sets of codes, values and norms (e.g. 'never trust your neighbour'), is part of the uniformity principle. Still, what happens to more ephemeral authenticities, as in the question: 'What's happening in this moment'? How can one produce authenticity only temporarily? We will leave this question open at this stage.

Beside the temporal aspect of authenticity, Lévi-Strauss (1976) distinguishes *levels of authenticity* in anthropology which have a constitutive function for all forms of social life. Being authentic describes types of (inter-) personal contact that is direct and emergent in face-to-face interaction, but is not governed by social institutions or forms of media. Arguably, all individuals seek for some forms of authenticity at different points of their lives. The role of the 'context' in human interaction, whether it is social, cultural or stylistic in nature, is crucial in producing or failing to produce authenticity. Coupland makes a point about this quest of individuals for authenticity: "Authenticity matters. It remains a quality of experience that we actively seek out, in most domains of life, material and social. [...] We value authenticity and we tend to be critical of pseudo-authenticity" (2003: 417). Authenticity does matter, but more importantly the question may be "how and where authenticity matters most" (Coupland, this volume). Traditionally, anthropology was concerned with small-scale communities in local settings based on which Lévi-Strauss submitted his view on authenticity. From Lévi-Strauss onwards, an anthropology of globalisation has developed in which some sociolinguists such as Blommaert (2010) or Coupland (2001) have tried to define authenticity for speakers living in a globalised world. Clearly, the size of the communities investigated and the degree of mediation in human communication differ between Lévi-Strauss and sociolinguists interested in globalisation, but one may assume that there is a similar underlying structure that is functioning independently of the size or the type of speaker group. The quest for some aspects of authenticity seems to be a prominent (if not anthropologically universal) feature of people's social behaviour. If the individuals of a society were not 'authentic' in a minimal sense to the different domains and levels of the social system and the web of cultural meanings (Geertz 1973), various forms of cultural learning and mimetic practices, the conservation of traditional values and norms as well as the prediction of the behaviour of social agents would not be possible (Strathern 2004). For sociolinguists, an important question is how the social functioning of authenticity as a driving force of individuals' behaviour and its evaluation according to socio-cultural contexts is mediated by and expressed in language. But is authenticity an important explanatory factor for the analyst and for lay people themselves? A clarification for the latter question might be an eminent task for research in sociolinguistics at present, especially since, with few exceptions (Coupland 2010, 2003; Bucholtz 2003; Eckert 2003; Blommaert & Varis 2011; Gill 2012), the problem of authenticity has not been a thorough part of sociolinguistic theoretical discussions, although it was considered "ripe for critical consideration" some time ago (Eckert, at the 31st NWAV conference, 2002). However, it is well-known to philosophers, historians, scholars in the cultural sciences, and has recently been a concern within linguistic anthropology (Bucholtz & Hall 2004; Ochs 2004), language and communication (van Leeuwen 2001), research on mediated experience (Montgomery 2001), literary studies and the visual arts (Straub 2012; Scannell 2001). It should be noted that contributions in this volume treat the concept of authenticity not simply as an import for convenience definitions from the above fields into their sociolinguistic analyses but deal with the question in an effort to problematise the 'authentic speaker' as a reflection of a complex, dynamic, deployment of socio-linguistic and socio-pragmatic resources.

In light of this, this volume seeks to pose a number of questions such as the following: What are the local meanings of authenticity embedded in large cultural and social structures? What is the meaning of linguistic authenticity in delocalised and/or deterritorialised settings? How is authenticity indexed in other contexts of language expression (e.g. in writing or in political discourse)? The following concern formulated by Coupland echoes the issues that the present work raises about linguistic authenticity: "To what extent is it tenable to think of language use as being constrained by people's (authentic) membership of social groups (what Eckert called 'ingrained behavior'), as opposed to the social construction of personal, relation and social meanings in discourse?" (Coupland 2010: 1). Coupland also asks in this volume "how do discursive accounts stand as evidence of authentic experience"? Some sociolinguists recognise the importance of the many ways in which authenticity can be assigned to speakers or groups of speakers. As Coupland states elsewhere: "To be authentic, a thing has to be original in some important social or cultural matrix" (2003: 419). We argue that the layers of such a matrix are addressed by speakers in various situationally embedded ways and on various *orders of indexicality*, as explained in the next section. The volume begins with Nikolas Coupland's examination of the place of authenticity in sociolinguistic work. In his chapter, "Language, society and authenticity: themes and perspectives", Nikolas Coupland offers a critical update of the issue of authenticity and the role it has played in the field of sociolinguistics, first by revising his own views on the matter and then by critically discussing the other contributions of this volume. His chapter provides a refreshing look at the various social meanings of authenticity expressed in language production, which, to a certain degree, are discussed in the context of the indexicality framework. The volume as a whole investigates the concept of authenticity from various sub-disciplines of linguistics, various social practices and different types of mediatisation. As we have shown in this section, there are many ways of approaching or defining authenticity outside the field of sociolinguistics (and within sociolinguistics). The reader will discover different approaches to authenticity as provided by the contributors that satisfy the aims of their respective analyses and thus diverge from each other to some extent. We take these different approaches to the intricate functions of sociolinguistic authenticity to be an exciting tension that we hope will enliven current debates on authenticity in sociolinguistics and beyond.

2 Indexicality and local meanings of authenticity

Indexicality, in linguistics, is the property of linguistic elements to index (to point to) certain non-linguistic entities. There is referential indexicality, which can best be illustrated with deixis (of person, time, place, etc.). Thus in the sentence *We'll meet again here in two hours* the words *we*, *here*, and *in two hours* are all dependent on actual situational context for their pragmatic meaning to be clear. More interesting from a sociolinguistic point of view, however, is non-referential indexicality, which links indexes with social meanings (stances, politeness, identities, etc.). In sociolinguistic terminology, these indexed entities are social meanings, indexed by sociolinguistic variables. The concept, initially proposed by Peirce (1932), has been extended notably by Silverstein (2003). Silverstein, taking an anthropological linguistic approach, conceptualises several orders of indexicality: a first-order pragmatic level, a second-order metapragmatic level, and even higher-order, conventionalised discourse levels. An example would be that of the so-called T/V distinction (the use of two separate second-person pronouns when addressing someone, as in French *tu* and *vous*, German *du* and

Sie, Italian *tu* and *Lei*, etc., see Silverstein 2003: 204–211). Here the traditional dimensions of solidarity and power (Brown & Gilman 1960) are simply first-order indexicals, in that reliance on these dimensions of deference indexicality alone are not enough to explain how such a binary choice is made. A second-order, metapragmatic indexicality is needed, titled "enregistered honourification" by Silverstein, which, essentially, has T index 'informal' and V 'formal'. An example of higher-order indexicality in T/V-usage is seen in 17th century Quaker communities, who, in an attempt at levelling out social differences within the community, established a norm of V-avoidance, which became the "enregistered norm", a system of "counter-honourification" (Silverstein 2003: 211).

Extensions of the basic indexicality framework include Eckert (2008), who proposes an indexical field that covers the range of social meanings that a particular linguistic variable indexes. Her illustration is that of word-final /t/-aspiration in American English, which covers a range (a 'field', in her term) of social meanings. These meanings can be momentary 'stances' taken by speakers (e.g. formal, polite, annoyed), 'permanent qualities', i.e. stances taken repeatedly by the same speaker (e.g. educated, articulate, prissy), and 'social types', enregistered categories of speakers seen to be marked by this particular index (e.g. British, nerdy girl, school teacher). This field shows how a single variant can index a wide range of social meanings, dependent on co-textual and contextual setting. Other approaches include Johnstone & Kiesling (2008), where local-dialect stereotypes are recast in the indexicality framework. Their example is that of the pronunciation of the diphthong in words like *house* as a monophthong [aː] by residents of Pittsburgh. This feature, often described as distinctly local, is here shown to be perceived with a much wider array of attitudes than traditional sociolinguistic approaches would suggest: the disjunction between individual production and perception, coupled with speakers' own reflections on the variable, offer insights into the layered nature of indexical processes operating in spoken interaction, as well as into the multiplicity of social meanings indexed by a same variable. Elsewhere, Johnstone et al. (2006) recast Silverstein's orders of indexicality in Labovian terms, equating first-order indexicality with indicators, second-order indexicality with markers, and third-order indexicality with stereotypes.

Sociolinguistic research within the indexicality framework can be seen as being situated in the 'third wave' of sociolinguistics, in that it is interested in stylistic variation as a 'resource for the construction of social meaning' (Eckert 2005). This is certainly what Johnstone and Kiesling (2008) did for Pittsburghese, but it also happened much earlier, when Ochs (1992) similarly drew on the concept in her analysis of gender in American and Samoan society. Blommaert (2007) brought indexicality to discourse analysis, and Ewing et al. (2012) even to the field of advertising and its strategic use of language choice. If authenticity has to be created in language production with reference to some extra-linguistic reality, one theoretically fruitful way to describe this may be in terms of indexicality. Johnstone & Kiesling (2008) is particularly relevant to the indexing of authenticity with respect to locality. In traditional sociolinguistics, local-dialect stereotypes are typically taken for granted as universally recognised. This was shown, in the Pittsburgh study mentioned above, as being an oversimplification, with respondents assigning different meanings to /au/-monophtongisation. Thus while one Pittsburgher may indeed use the variable to index 'localness', another may use a different variable, and hearers (whether themselves 'authentic' Pittsburghers or not) may or may not recognise the social meaning 'localness' ostensibly indexed. Some papers in this volume combine the linguistic findings on such indexing with the 'shifting contexts' (Strathern 1995) thematised in anthropological accounts of the relationship between local, global and medial in specific socio-cultural settings in order to develop a better understanding of the concept of 'place' in the production of (linguistic) authenticity. For instance, in her chapter "The trouble with authenticity", Penelope Eckert provides a critical view of the authentic speaker as it has been discussed in the field of sociolinguistics and problematises the issue of authentication within a group of preadolescents, making particular reference to Silverstein's theory of indexical order. Lauren Hall-Lew's chapter "Chinese social practice and San Franciscan authenticity" explores the indexical complexity and the local authenticity of linguistic and social practices among Chinese people in San Francisco, paying particular attention to narratives of youth styles collected in schools in the 1990s. In the following chapter entitled "Being more alternative and less Brit-pop: the quest for originality in three urban styles in Athens", Lefteris Kailoglou compares different subcultures in Athens and their quest for authenticity. He shows that this quest can be analysed by looking at the linguistic practices, rather than at the conceptualisations of authenticity by the speakers themselves. In "'100% authentic Pittsburgh': sociolinguistic authenticity and the linguistics of particularity", Barbara Johnstone explores the discursive construction of Pittsburgh identity (specifically as portrayed on a souvenir T-shirt), which also draws on linguistic stereotypes that are represented by respellings. The chapter entitled "'Oh boy, ¿hablas español?' – Salsa and the multiple value of authenticity in late capitalism" by Britta Schneider focuses on the construction of authenticity in relation to collective ideals in times of globalization. In communities of practice such as groups of salsa dancers, she investigates different levels of indexical meanings. In the last chapter of this section, "The commodification of authenticity", Monica Heller considers linguistic minority movements and their use of language in indexing 'authentic' ('indigenous') identities in targeting 'outsiders', thus using linguistic resources, among others, for marketing purposes.

3 Authenticity construction in delocalised contexts

Any form of authenticity, be it intra-speaker or inter-speaker, is subject to evaluation and implies a certain degree of approbation. Performed authenticity, for instance, involves the perspective of a speaker as the original author or performer of their communicative intentions, while an interpreted authenticity would represent an act of speech evaluated by an external source. The use of stylistic resources is closely connected to this issue of authenticity: whether performed or interpreted, speech is faithful to formal (or standard) vs. informal (or non-standard) contexts. Clearly, authenticity expresses itself in language use, similar to what Coupland calls "the discursive construction of authenticity and inauthenticity" (2010: 6). Authentication as the performative dimension of authenticity, then, is "a discursive process, rather than authenticity as a claimed or experienced quality of language or culture, [which] can then be taken up analytically as one dimension of a set of intersubjective 'tactics', [and] through which people can make claims about their own or others' statuses as authentic or inauthentic members of social groups" (Coupland 2010: 6). Surely, people must find strategies to construct and deconstruct their identities in communication as well as 'stage' them. They may own, inhabit or reject others' original, authentic sociolinguistic behaviours and identities. Authenticity thus is "negotiable" (Eira & Stebbins 2008: 24), though certainly not always purely discursive. It also resides in the physical representation, construction, experimentation and performance of personal and socio-cultural identity and style. As Jaspers put it, "all speech is constructed, styled to the occasion" (2010: 191). Taking the chav subculture as an example, Blommaert and Varis (2011) show that there exists a wide breadth of features which are solicited to display a certain authenticity, and which can be reflected in various semiotic representations. However, interestingly, they argue that not all features of a given identity are needed in order to "pass as 'authentic' to someone" (2011: 6), despite the rules that one needs to observe to be(come) an 'authentic chav' and be recognised as such by the other members of the chav group. According to the authors, a "homeopathic dose of resources" would suffice to exhibit at least some aspects of the expected distinctiveness of an authentic character (i.e. the "defining ones" as they call them), for instance, a Burberry cap for a 'chav'. They propose that "the dose can be small, but the only thing that is required is that it is *enough* – enough to produce a recognisable identity as an authentic someone" (2011: 8). From this argument, we understand that any given entity possesses a prototypical member which stands for the most credible member of the category, itself associated with a number of 'less authentic' members which are lightly dosed or enough to signal genuineness or fidelity to the intended identity. We also infer that all members of an entity may be subject to constant update or change due to ever evolving experiences with that entity, implying that the prototypical member may also shift to being a non-core member and be replaced by a new one which, in turn, more authentically embodies the new experience.

Furthermore, as we argued earlier in this introduction, authenticity is often closely linked to the notion of 'place', which leads us to ask another question: What is the meaning of linguistic authenticity in delocalised and deterritorialised settings? Arguably, there is the traditional, 'natural', local environment, but also other non-geographical loci such as media communication, online chat forums, etc. One could claim that any geographical context in which languages were 'born' is the place where the most authentic languages are generated and conserved. This is reminiscent of a classic assumption within variationist sociolinguistics that vernacular speakers are the best representatives of linguistic authenticity. Blommaert states that sociolinguistics has tended to focus on "static variation, on local distribution of varieties" (2010: 1). In the Labovian sense, authenticity correlates with geographically and socially demarcated linguistic communities, in which authentic speech behaviour manifests itself along a stylistic continuum. However, linguistic authenticity can also emerge in non-territorialised loci, as in computer-mediated communication: "Language and discourses move around, but they do so between spaces that are full of rules, norms, customs and conventions" (Blommaert 2010: 80). With mobile languages, norms must be re-localised too and re-interpreted in relation to the required linguistic practices, communicative intentions and the speakers themselves. In both geographical and non-geographical contexts of language use, speakers belong to a community of practice inasmuch as they come together to fulfil the same communicative functions and language practices. What matters to both types of contexts are internal norms deployed (and shared) by the speakers, employing what Coupland calls "speech style as an anchor for solidarity and local affiliation" (2003: 420). Authenticity would be about deploying linguistic resources in many different (extra- or para-linguistic) contexts such as local, mobile, variable, and normative contexts, e.g. within the 'landscape' or the 'mediascape'. Linguistic authenticity then must be an adaptive and flexible concept relevant to any communicative constellation – oral vs. written, face-to-face/direct in tightly knit local communities vs. mediated/distant in loosely knit web forum communities for instance, all in search of "[local] meanings and categorisations" of linguistic resources (Jaspers 2010). It should be noted that a common view among the contributors of this volume is not to "track down authentic speakers" (Bucholtz 2003: 406) but to figure out how sociolinguistic features have become authentic in the sense of normalised and standardised by a relevant group of speakers and furthermore from whose perspective the speakers are evaluated as being authentic. Authenticity is not meant to be treated as a static label as some philosophical accounts would have it, but generally the focus is placed upon the "authenticating practices of language users" (Bucholtz 2003: 403), that is, any authenticity construction, be it discursive in nature or not, is part of an authenticating process while deconstructing one's (own) authenticity participates in a de-authenticating process. Strategies for both processes are manifold and the second section of this volume offers a fresh perspective on the issue of authenticity construction in various types of media discourse found in deterritorialised settings. Looking at the relationship between locality, dialects, and accents, Michael Silverstein offers a critical analysis of authenticity within the framework of indexicality. His chapter "The race from place: dialect eradication vs. the linguistic 'authenticity' of *terroir*" questions the 'natural' link between language and place and pays special attention to the ways in which language users evaluate discourses with their personal models of coherence and what counts to them as authentic. Graham M. Jones's chapter "Reported speech as an authentication tactic in computer-mediated communication" challenges the popular assumption that computer-mediated communication somehow hampers young users' development of 'real' (i.e. verbal/spoken) communicative abilities. Andrea Moll, in her chapter "Authenticity in dialect performance? A case study of 'Cyber-Jamaican'", examines how authenticity can be created and maintained in online interaction on the Internet. With the example of Jamaican Creole she demonstrates the types of ethnolinguistic repertoire used in cyber communication. In Theresa Heyd and Christian Mair's contribution "From vernacular to digital ethnolinguistic repertoire: the case of Nigerian Pidgin", spoken, face-to-face interaction is shown to be not the only 'authentic' mode of communication, with online forums a place for active negotiation of the indexicalities associated with language. Lastly, in "Hybridity as authenticity in Nigerian hip-hop lyrics", Akinmade T. Akande looks into the authenticity of creativity of Nigerian hip-hop music. He demonstrates how Nigerian artists in the hip-hop scene exhibit authenticity in its uniqueness but also as part of a more global scale, through various channels such as their accent, their syntax or their commitment to local matters.

A final question that we wish to address in the third section of this volume is that of authenticity in other contexts of language expression, e.g. in writing and in institutional or political domains. In this vein, "Authentic writing" by Florian Coulmas shows how authenticity in more 'classical' types of mediatisation is manifested in writing material, as in textual authorship, handwriting or signing, paying special attention to the rapport between writing and national-cultural sense of belonging. He argues that writing is at least on a par with speech and has a lot to reveal about how authenticity is expressed and validated. Analysing the discussion on English or Danish language use in Denmark, gathered in newspapers and universities, Anna Kristina Hultgren's chapter "Lexical variation at the internationalized university: are indexicality and authenticity always relevant?" takes a critical stance and aims to show how referential indexicality often trumps social meaning in such discussions. In his chapter "'Real communities', rhetorical borders: authenticating British identity in political discourse and on-line debate", Martin Gill investigates the issue of the nature of Britishness 'under threat' in a speech delivered on immigration to Britain by British Prime Minister David Cameron and also analyses English language requirements for immigrants in a corpus of posts stemming from the BBC online newspaper. Finally, in their chapter "What's in a *promesse authentique*? Doubting and confirming authenticity in 17th-century French diplomacy", Johanna Sprondel and Tilman Haug describe the development of the semantic field 'authentic/authenticity' from a historical perspective and trace back the notion of authenticity to French diplomacy in the 17th century and investigate the indexing and staging of authenticity in the political domain at that time.

To conclude, beside our faith in the highly welcomed discussions of the complex functions of linguistic authenticity offered by the contributors of this volume, we hope that this work stands as an invitation to continue research in the direction of a theoretically informed sociolinguistics which would actively participate in challenging the meanings of certain concepts, frameworks or theories that we use for our analyses, as well as questioning our own beliefs we may have for those concepts or frameworks which sometimes (not to say very often) have already been established in other scientific disciplines. We do not, however, suggest that the present work has exhausted the debate on linguistic authenticity although it might have generated some new thinking and ideas around the issue, which is, to say the least, not at all a primarily sociolinguistic matter but probably one which concerns us all to varying degrees.

References

Blommaert, Jan 2007: Sociolinguistics and discourse analysis: Orders of indexicality and polycentricity. *Journal of Multicultural Discourses* 2(2): 115–130.

Blommaert, Jan 2010: *The Sociolinguistics of Globalisation*. Cambridge: Cambridge University Press.

Blommaert, Jan & Piia Varis 2011: Enough is enough: The heuristics of authenticity in superdiversity. *Working Papers in Urban Language and Literacies, 76.* London: King's College.

Brown, R. & A. Gilman 1960: The pronouns of power and solidarity. In: T. A. Sebeok (ed.), *Style in Language*, 253–276. MIT Press, Cambridge, MA.

Bucholtz, Mary 2003: Sociolinguistic nostalgia and the authentication of identity. *Journal of Sociolinguistics* 7(3): 398–416.

Bucholtz, Mary & Kira Hall 2004: Language and identity. In A. Duranti (ed.), *A Companion to Linguistic Anthropology*, 269–289. London: Blackwell.

Coupland, Nikolas 2001: Stylisation, authenticity and TV news review. *Discourse Studies* 3(4): 413–442.

Coupland, Nikolas 2003: Sociolinguistic authenticities. *Journal of Sociolinguistics* 7(3): 417–431.

Coupland, Nikolas 2010: The authentic speaker and the speech community. In Carmen Llamas & Dominic Watts (eds.), *Language and Identities*, 99–112. Edinburgh: Edinburgh University Press.

Eckert, Penelope 2003: Elephants in the room. *Journal of Sociolinguistics* 7(3): 392–397.

Eckert, Penelope 2005: Variation, convention, and social meaning. Paper presented at the Annual Meeting of he Linguistics Society of America, Oakland, CA, USA, 7 January 2005. Available online at http://www.stanford.edu/~eckert/EckertLSA2005.pdf.

Eckert, Penelope 2008: Variation and the indexical field. *Journal of Sociolinguistics* 12(4): 453–476.

Eira, Christina & Tonya Stebbins 2008: Authenticities and lineages: Revisiting concepts of continuity and change in language. *International Journal of the Sociology of Language* 189:1–30. (Issue devoted to 'Authenticity and Linguistic Heritage in the Age of Globalization'.)

Ewing, Douglas R., Chris T. Allen & Randall L. Ewing 2012: Authenticity as meaning validation: An empirical investigation of iconic and indexical cues in a context of "green" products. *Journal of Consumer Behaviour* 11(5): 381–390.

Gadamer, Hans-Georg 1960: *Wahrheit und Methode*. Tübingen: Mohr.

Geertz, Clifford 1973: *The Interpretation of Cultures*. New York: Basic Books.

Gill, Martin 2012: Nativeness, authority, authenticity: the construction of belonging and exclusion in debates about English language proficiency and immigration in Britain'. In C. Percy and M. Davidson (eds.), *The Languages of Nation: Attitudes and norms*, 271–291. Bristol: Multilingual Matters.

Heidegger, Martin 1927: *Sein und Zeit*. Tübingen: Niemeyer.

Jaspers, Jürgen 2010: Style and styling. In Nancy H. Hornberger & Sandra L. McMay (eds.), *Sociolinguistics and Language Education*, 177–204. Bristol: Multilingual Matters.

Johnstone, Barbara, Jennifer Andrus & Andrew E. Danielson 2006: Mobility, Indexicality, and the Enregisterment of 'Pittsburghese'. *Journal of English Linguistics* 34(2): 77–104.

Johnstone, Barbara & Scott F. Kiesling 2008: Indexicality and experience: Exploring the meanings of /aw/-monophthongization in Pittsburgh. *Journal of Sociolinguistics* 12(1): 5–33.

Kant, Immanuel 1999 [1791]: *Critique of Pure Reason*. Ed. Paul Guyer & Allen W. Wood. Cambridge: Cambridge University Press.

Lévi-Strauss, Claude 1976: *Structural Anthropology*. Vol 2. New York: Basic Books.

Montgomery, M. 2001: Defining authentic talk. *Discourse Studies* 3(4): 397–405.

Ochs, Elinor 1992: Indexing gender. In Alessandro Duranti & Charles Goodwin (eds.), *Rethinking Context: Language as an Interactive Phenomenon*, 335–358. Cambridge: Cambridge University Press.

Ochs, Elinor 2004 Narrative lessons. In A. Duranti (ed.), *A Companion to Linguistic Anthropology*, 269–289. London: Blackwell.

Peirce, Charles S. 1932: Division of signs. In Charles S. Peirce et al. (eds.), *Collected Papers of Charles Sanders Peirce*. Cambridge, MA: Harvard University Press.

Sartre, Jean-Paul 1945: L'être et le néant. Essai d'ontologie phénoménologique. Paris: Gallimard.

Scannell, Paddy 2001: Authenticity as experience. *Discourse Studies* 3(4): 405–411.

Silverstein, Michael 2003: Indexical order and the dialectics of sociolinguistic life. *Language and Communication* 23(3): 193–229.

Strathern, Marilyn (ed.) 1995: *Shifting Contexts. Transformations in Anthropological Knowledge*. London: Routledge.

Strathern, Marilyn 2004: *Partial Connections*. Oxford: Altamira Press.

Straub, Julia 2012: Introduction: The paradoxes of authenticity. In Julia Straub (ed.), *Paradoxes of Authenticity: Studies on a Critical Concept*. Transcript Verlag: Bielefeld.

Van Leeuwen, Theo 2001: What is authenticity? *Discourse Studies* 3(4): 392–397.

Nikolas Coupland

Language, society and authenticity: Themes and perspectives

In between reading drafts of the stimulating new material compiled for this book, I re-read two sources which were important stimuli for my own interests in language and authenticity[1]. The first is Lionel Trilling's (1972) treatise *On Sincerity and Authenticity*. It is, initially, a critical commentary on how considerations of personal sincerity – the moral principle of 'to thine own self be true' in the words of *Hamlet*'s Polonius – came to prominence as a motif in major international works of literature. Trilling goes on to distinguish sincerity from authenticity, taking authenticity to represent 'a more strenuous moral experience' (1972: 11) and a fundamental concern in artistic representations of humanity. He shows us that critical inquiry into authenticity opens up complex, profound and often unsettling perspectives on selfhood, interpersonal relations, culture and art. He traces the interplay between truth and representation, and between the commonplace and the performative[2], in literature and in life. Trilling is no sociolinguist, but he provides copious insights into the tantalising interfaces between language, society and authenticity.

The other source is a thematic issue of the journal *Discourse Studies* edited by my former colleagues Joanna Thornborrow and Theo van Leeuwen (2001), under the title *Authenticity in Media Discourse*. While the emphasis in Trilling's book is mainly historical, Thornborrow and van Leeuwen introduce a forward-looking perspective, starting from their belief that, at least in the institutions and practices of broadcast media, authenticity is 'in crisis'. They point to how producers and presenters of television and radio programmes have developed techniques for projecting sincerity and intimacy, but in a cultural climate where media consumers are often sharply aware of the devices and implications of mediation pro-

1 I am grateful to Sari Pietikainen for helpful comments on an earlier version of this paper, which has also benefited from extensive discussions of language and authenticity with Misty Jaffe, Helen Kelly-Holmes and Sari in the context of our shared project on Peripheral Multilingualism, funded by the Finnish Academy. Further helpful input came from a research seminar series at the University of Copenhagen, convened by Marie Maegaard and colleagues. Shortcomings in the chapter are my own.
2 I use the term 'performative' in this chapter in a general sense, relating to performance rather than specifically to the pragmatic theory of speech acts and later extrapolations from it, e.g. by Judith Butler (1997).

cesses. Papers collected in that journal issue[3] therefore address the discursive construction of authenticity, and the implications of this apparent paradox. They ask how it might, or might not, be possible for authentic meaning to survive and transcend mediation. Can radio and television, for example, provide audiences with any sort of authentic experience? What can authenticity mean in a wider, *mediatised* world where so many facets of social life are subject to mediation (Androutsopoulos in press; Livingstone 2009), even outside of the broadcast media themselves?

These two sources are sufficient, I think, to suggest that sociolinguistics (using that term in its broad contemporary sense) needs to engage seriously with the challenge of authenticity and inauthenticity. We need confident theory and robust empirical investigations organised in relation to it, and the present book makes strong and welcome contributions in each of these respects. But across the literature as a whole there are also unreconciled differences of stance and interpretation. For some, authenticity is a conceptual error in earlier research that we can now set aside, a misguided and under-analysed assumption about speech and speakers standing as 'authentic' members of their speech communities. Authenticity as a term is commonly quote-marked (as in my previous sentence), but more resolutely, perhaps to imply that it is a pseudo-concept, one that doesn't stand up to critical scrutiny, or one that somehow reflects badly on its user. Some researchers write about authenticity 'effects', implying that authenticity itself is unreachable or even illusory. Others (like Trilling) hold on to a notion of authenticity as a crucial reference point for personal, social and cultural identity. There are different targets of authenticity: what exactly do we want to interrogate? Authentic language, the authentic speaker, authentic experience, authentic actions, authentic community, authentic social belonging? Does authenticity have some specific resonances in relation to different social formations – ethnicity, class, gender or age? Is authenticity absolute or relative, singular or plural? Is inauthenticity a quality of local experience encountered in exceptional cases, or is it a defining characteristic of the late modern age?

Basic questions need to be reconsidered, and in that spirit, in the next two sections, I start by reconsidering my own earlier accounts[4] of (1) what authenticity might mean, in and of itself, and (2) what might be meant by authentic language. In later sections, and informed by the many excellent chapters of this book

---

3 The contributing authors were Ian Hutchby, Martin Montgomery, Paddy Scannell, Joanna Thornborrow, Andrew Tolson, Theo van Leeuwen and myself.
4 The relevant sources are Coupland 1985, 2001a, 2001b, 2001c, 2003, 2004, 2007, 2009, 2010a, 2010b, 2011a, 2011b.

as well as by other important sources, I try to reach an understanding of (3) how authenticity is at issue in indexical meaning (this book's main focus), and (4) how it can be seen not only as a casualty of discursive construction but actually as an achievement of social action, and particularly (and perhaps paradoxically) of performance.

1 Meanings of authenticity

In an earlier effort (Coupland 2003) I suggested that the term authentic is applied to some target when some particular attributes are in place, in five dimensions. I labelled the five dimensions *ontology*, *historicity*, *systemic coherence*, *consensus* and *value*. I do not mean to suggest that authenticity can be atomised into five 'components', only to suggest that the notion of authenticity – which can often strike one as too totalising and too hegemonic to use – commonly implicates clusters of attributes that are in themselves relatively easy to detect.

The simplest case to consider – and it is a very traditional and traditionalising one – might be when the authenticity of a written text or work of art is at issue. Trilling (1972: 93) in fact says that the provenance of the term authenticity 'is the museum, where persons expert in such matters test whether objects of art are what they appear to be or are claimed to be, and therefore worth the price that is asked for them… or worth the admiration they are given'. Martin Montgomery and Theo van Leeuwen (in their contributions to Thornborrow and van Leeuwen 2001) have made similar observations about the origins of authenticity. It happens to be the case that, as I write this, British media are reporting that a portrait of Rembrandt van Rijn, held by the National Trust at Buckland Abbey in England, has recently been assessed to be 'a genuine Rembrandt', a self-portrait by the Dutch Master. The portrait is signed in his name and dated appropriately (1635), although it was previously thought to have been painted by one of his pupils. The painting is of course a material object, but the *ontology* issue here is its state-of-being as 'a Rembrandt' – whether or not it has secure existence within that and related categories. The BBC's online account[5] mentions that the painting had previously been 'shrouded in mystery', a mysteriousness from which it has now emerged, the report says, as 'an actual Rembrandt'. A National Trust spokesperson is quoted as saying 'We never dared think it might actually be an original, and many of our visitors will have just passed by it in what is sure to be a real contrast

---

5 See http://www.bbc.co.uk/news/entertainment-arts-21827478, last consulted 29th October 2013.

to the attention it is now going to receive'. Through the process of authentication, the ontological status of the painting changes; in its 'actually being' a Rembrandt, it becomes a more consolidated object of gaze and cultural recognition.

The four other dimensions of the authentic are also very clearly in play in this example. The portrait is authenticated as to its date of composition, and the belief, held 'for decades', that it was painted by a pupil has been shown to be wrong. The recent reassessment of the painting has re-written history, and it is *historicity* – the time-depth of the story and the idea that the painting has survived intact since 1635 – that largely underpins its *value*. Value here is multi-dimensional: most obviously it is financial (the BBC story suggests the painting is now worth 20 million pounds). But we can also think of news values; mass media interest in the episode confirms that the painting's change of status is deemed highly newsworthy. There is also cultural value, the painting's symbolic value as a cultural icon. While the technical aspect of authenticating a painting is a matter of confirming the circumstances of its production, its socio-cultural significance has to do with re-evaluation. Authenticity claims are always claims to high or deep values in some specific ideological matrix.

The fourth quality of the authentic, *systemic coherence*, refers to matrices of this sort. The newly authenticated painting takes its place within specific familiar, culturally-known and coordinated structures of value. To be 'a portrait by a Dutch Master' and to be 'a Rembrandt' is (in each case) to be aligned with and to be inducted into systems of cultural recognition (for example, the BBC text quotes the National Trust as saying that the painting has now become 'one of our most important works of art'), backed up by technological systems that validate the painting's status and guarantee its authenticity (the account mentions testing done by 'a leading expert', involving X-ray, infrared and tree-ring analyses). These are the bases on which a *consensus* has arisen, initially a small one among 'experts', about the painting's authenticity. Media reports, including the BBC's coverage of the story, then become active in lobbying for that consensus and actively building it. Just as historicity is implicated – overtly or covertly – in authenticity claims, so are coherence and consensus. This is not to say that people always agree about what is and is not authentic; authenticity is commonly contested, and contests of wider sorts are often focussed around competing claims to authenticity. But a successful authenticity claim is one where the target and its value are rendered coherent with known priorities in some known normative framework. As Mary Bucholtz (2003) says, authenticity often arises out of a 'desire for origins', which we might gloss as the ambition to find valued consensual coherence about existence in history.

These five dimensions are of some analytic value if they help us orient to how authenticity claims and disputes are staged in discourse. The Rembrandt example is almost uniquely uncomplicated and transparent, where the focal issue of the painting's authenticity is determined through physical tests on a material object. But this institutional process connects with much wider aspects of local, individual and community experience in which authenticity is still relevant (even if authenticity is in crisis in other ways). If we find a painting beautiful, this might be an authenticating experience of some sort, where we recognise a value-set that holds for us in our understanding and appreciation of the social world, coherently with the evaluations of some other people. The institutional process of authenticating the painting is relatively cut-and-dried, based in an established assessment regime that is beyond the reach of most people. But we can assume that regimes like this have come about in recognition of the aesthetic and cultural value of known classes of fine-art production. In Trilling's conception, works of art sometimes express values that are authentic because they give us glimpses of what it means to be human. All the same, we should note how discursive processes are fundamentally implicated in the projection and evaluation of authenticity, even in the Rembrandt case. The painting's authenticity has to be *accounted*. Its status as 'a Rembrandt' is achieved performatively via an act of declaration. In many other cases, including most of the cases considered in the other chapters of this book, authenticity claims, counter-claims and denials are *wholly* discursive, because the target is abstract rather than material. What is at issue is some aspect of an identity – personal, group-salient, national, ethnic, and so on – or some aspect of a mode of practice as being authentic or not, and how that status is asserted, exploited, challenged or recontextualised, more or less authoritatively. As we shall see in the next section, authenticity can be said to sit in several particular relationships to language, not least because authentication and deauthentication are social processes that are negotiated through discourse.

Like paintings, linguistic texts can be institutionally scrutinised for their authenticity. In this volume Florian Coulmas comments on aspects of writing (e.g. handwriting and signing, textual authorship and plagiarism) that connect to authenticity in a direct and again a material sense – whether a text is in fact authored by a purported author, whether it is the original or a copy, and so on. But the importance of authenticity extends well beyond material targets and bureaucratic procedures of 'rubber stamping'. Writing's association with what is considered 'standard' in spoken language lies at the basis of authenticity claims and counter-claims in this area. Proponents of standard languages tend to argue that they are authentic phenomena, whose value is underpinned by historicity, consensus, coherence and so on. A standard variety of a language is held to be 'the best' variety, but this means much more than just a preferred variety; it is held to be a variety (in fact *the* variety) that has been repeatedly credentialised over time and which binds together the values of the cognoscenti. Sociolinguists have tended to argue the direct converse, that *vernacular* language is authentic, for precisely the same reasons (see Coupland 2003; Coupland & Kristiansen 2011). Coulmas also explains how writing itself can, less directly but more deeply, confer a sense of national heritage and cultural belonging, and it is in these emotional and identity-salient dimensions that authenticity claims and disputes are of most significance.

To say that authenticity matters is close to tautological, because value is one of the defining dimensions of the authentic. But it is important to ask how and where authenticity matters most, whose interests it serves, and how it can be brought into play. In the domain of personal identity, and however unfashionable it sounds in an intellectual climate where identities are said to be contingent, hybrid and socially constructed, we all have some serious investment in assessing and reassessing 'who we really are'. My point here is not that identities are *not* socially constructed – they clearly are – but that a social construction perspective should not imply that identity is a matter of inconsequential discourse play. Authenticity also surfaces at the interface between personal and social identities, in our relationships with others and in our allegiances to groups and communities, at whatever level of generality. Most people do invest trustingly in (at least some of) their social relationships; even in a fast-globalising world, many people do feel authenticated by their local, national or other allegiances[6]. There is huge variability in who is most likely to make these assessments, with what level of intensity, at what life stages and under what conditions, and being *in*authentic in relation to an attributed or assumed identity can have many attractions too. Sensing that one's identities are unstable or contextually variable may well be a condition of the late modern age, related to increasing transnational/global mobility and increasing cultural complexity and reflexivity (Beck, Giddens and Lash 1994, Castells 2010). But these social changes do not simply banish authenticity. They force us into new alignments with authenticity, and they demand new ways of managing it discursively.

Writing before the current wave of globalisation had established itself, Trilling (1972: 93) said that authenticity is 'a word of ominous import', and there have been plenty of deeply 'ominous' cases to consider. One context in which discourses of authenticity have surfaced is when repressive political regimes have made strong inclusionary and exclusionary claims about individuals' authentic membership of groups. In such cases, being inauthentic, and more precisely

---

6 See Lacoste and Mair (2012) for an excellent collection of studies on authenticity in relation to creole languages and cultures.

being deauthenticated or discredited relative to normative criteria, can have catastrophic consequences; totalitarianism has notoriously made play of ethnic and national authenticities (Hutton 2005). In less extreme but still highly concerning cases, political appeals to cultural authenticity can be exclusionary and prejudicial. Martin Gill (in this volume), for example, critiques a senior British politician's rhetorical designs that construct a sense of authentic Britishness prejudicial to mobile groups. In data of this sort we see how the different dimensions of authenticity are worked into an apparently benign ideology that centres traditional Britishness, but which decentres and excludes others. Britta Schneider describes how ethnic and class meanings circulate around the use of Spanish in Australian salsa classes, how they are dislocated from their most traditional values, but still manage to serve the interests of particular members of the group.

As Trilling also says, authenticity 'is implicitly a polemical concept' (1972: 94), which is partly to acknowledge that authenticity inevitably features in a dialectical relationship with inauthenticity. An authenticated target holds its quality of authenticity at the expense of other targets, but there are also ways to claim authenticity in particular dimensions by acknowledging inauthenticities on other dimensions (a point I come back to later). Authenticity's tendency to exclude and to essentialise is without doubt an important factor in academic tentativeness in engaging with the concept in constructive ways. If we are uncomfortable with the concept of authenticity it is probably because, as above, it can easily be a privileging concept, one that endorses one individual's or one group's value and excludes others. This moral stance explains contemporary resistance to the suggestion that human experience is, even potentially, grounded in the way that the concept of authenticity seems to imply. That is, and although I want to argue the contrary position later in this chapter, sociolinguistic engagement with authenticity is liable to be dismissed for its apparent failure to respect the tenets of not only social constructionism but of liberal democracy too. Critical theory is full of radical postmodern refutations of social reality (Belsey 2005 gives an excellent overview), although one consequence of its stance is to close off empirical engagement of any sort with the negotiation of authenticity.

In any event, there are some severe misunderstandings lurking in the stances mentioned in the previous paragraph and in blanket resistance to, or denial of, or flight from authenticity. Critical engagement with authenticity is *anything but* the endorsement of authenticity's hegemony. As in Gill's analysis, we need to expose the workings of authenticating discourses, where they are prejudicial, in order to assess their social and political implications, and in order to resist them. It is the contestation of authenticity under conditions of mobility that we need to have most in mind (Blommaert 2010). Social change generates instability whereby authenticity cannot be based in any simple way in historical certainties and consensus, and this creates new opportunities as well as new pressures. In this spirit, when Thornborrow and van Leeuwen suggest that authenticity is in crisis, it is not to wallow in moral relativism about media and meaning, but to encourage researchers to build more nuanced accounts of how authentic experience *may well* be achievable via mass media, but in less direct ways that we have previously assumed. The fact that authenticity is discursively constructed does not diminish its force as an organising principle for self-identity and cultural belonging.

Trilling's perspectives, then, still have some relevance. He was primarily interested in the human quest for authentic meaning in social life, and in the potentially disruptive consequences of that quest. It can sound impossibly grandiose, but Trilling insisted that authenticity is a concept that needs to be entertained on the same scale as beauty, truth or 'the sublime' (Belsey 2005: chapter 8). These are concepts established at the intersection of philosophy, aesthetics, ethics and phenomenology, and it would be unsurprising if sociolinguists felt that the idea of authenticity was stretching the usual range of sociolinguistics. But what could be a better sociolinguistic question than how language mediates our worldly experiences and our understandings of who we and others really are? The present volume shows that sociolinguists are meeting this challenge and that they do have resources to interrogate authenticity in coherent and revealing ways.

2 Perspectives on authentic language

Following Charles Hockett's list of the design features of human language, John Lyons (1977: 83–85) discusses 'prevarication' – the linguistic capacity for feigning, dissimulating and deceiving. In Benjamin Lee Whorf's (1956) view, languages shape our perception of social reality as much as vice versa. In popular discourse, speech is sometimes held to be 'cheap' and unreliable relative to physical action ('actions speak louder than words'; 'put your money where your mouth is'). In English, some people challenged about the accuracy of something they have just said can try for a curious form of redress by saying 'I was only saying'! For reasons like these, language in itself can never be said to be authentic, but there are ways in which language can be and has been associated with authenticity. In an earlier paper (Coupland 2001a) I suggested six associations of this sort:
1. Attested and attestable language
2. Naturally occurring language
3. Language encoding fact and truth
4. Fully owned, unmediated language
5. Language expressing personal authenticity
6. Language expressing authentic cultural membership

Each of these associations is far from straightforward and open to severe challenge, and perhaps for that reason the set of six might be helpful in shaping more
critical perspectives on language and authenticity. I will comment briefly on the
first four here, then discuss the fifth and sixth in the next section, because they
are concerned with authenticity as indexed meaning.

The first and second points in the list are familiar to us, partly from peda-
gogic applied linguistics, where the importance of exposing language learners
to authentic language – attested linguistic usage – has been widely debated.
Authentic in this sense means language that has actually been spoken or written,
presumably by competent language users (whoever they might be defined as
being), under what are taken to be natural conditions (whatever those might
be defined as being), rather than constructed or 'made up', e.g. by people who
prepare language teaching materials. If we want to access authentic language
data of this sort, we can presumably just capture instances of 'ordinary language'
in use, perhaps by audio-recording dinner time conversations at home or service
encounters at travel agencies, by collecting articles published in the newspapers of the relevant country, and so on. But the assumptions embedded in these
authenticity claims need to be (and have already been) carefully critiqued, not
least because they tend to privilege so-called native speakers over others. It is
difficult to make a convincing case that native speakers, if we can identify who
they are in the first place, have particular social and linguistic attributes that cre-
dentialise them as authentic language users (Blackledge 2005). There is also the
important problem that the notion of naturalness trivialises the account of social
context.

However, we should note that an explicit conception of naturalness has
persisted in some sociolinguistic traditions, for example in the canonical variationist account of style (see discussion and critique in Coupland 2007), but also
in Conversation Analysis, where researchers have tended to put their trust in
the authenticity of 'mundane' conversational data (cf. critical commentaries in
Bucholtz 2003: 405–406; Montgomery 2001: 401–402). Sociolinguists originally
extolled naturalness in order to mobilise arguments against the idealisation of
(intuited) linguistic data in theoretical linguistics, and that critique still has relevance. Current enthusiasms in corpus linguistics are also based on the view that
large corpora of real, natural language data produce significant accounts of what
language is really like. So, although linguistic naturalness remains a tricky and
reductive concept, it might have some utility in specific contexts of debate. We
might see it as a form of strategic essentialism.

What can be more productive is to get inside the gross distinction between
natural and unnatural language, to explore local circumstances under which
language does emerge as either more or less authentic. While to (attestably) say

something is clearly no guarantee of any sort of authenticity, there are circumstances of linguistic performance under which speakers are conventionally heard to be being sincere or insincere and/ or to be telling or not telling some kind of truth (which is the third association in the above list). Issues of this sort are explored by Graham Jones (in this volume) who examines the belief, which he shows to be false, that face-to-face conversation is inherently a more authentic mode of communication than computer-mediated communication. Jones shows that polyphonic (multi-voiced), performative language, for example through use of the BE+LIKE quotative in English, is characteristic of both face-to-face and interactive new media exchanges, where it has the potential to dramatise participants' stances and interpersonal relationships in very vivid ways. Several other chapters in this book demonstrate the affordances of electronically mediated communication in related ways.

So what should we say about the authenticity of vividly dramatised constructed dialogue? It doesn't meet the criteria that underpin the third type of authentic language in the list above, 'language encoding fact and truth'. Or at least (and as Jones explains), we already know that constructed dialogue is indeed a discursive (re)construction of earlier episodes of social action (what someone said, or might have said, to another, or what the speaker thought, or might have thought), and to that extent we have to see it as a simulation of prior talk. (The authentic is often contrasted with the simulated, *realia* versus *simulacra*, although, as van Leeuwen [2001] suggests, the contrast of often not that simple. See also Jaffe 2011 on 'verisimilitudes', conventionalised representations of the real[7].) In constructed dialogue we can easily attest the recreative act, but in most circumstances not the original act, so there is (to put it negatively) some deficit of fact and truth. If we also invoke the criteria attaching to the fourth type of authentic language, 'fully owned and unmediated language', we could challenge the authenticity of constructed dialogue on further grounds. The design principle of quotativity is based in mediation, in a narrator voicing a prior utterance in current talk, and this is mediation in the sense of a stylistic orchestration of voices and their inter-relationships.

If we go back again to Trilling, we see that he escalates this critical standpoint to extreme proportions. He associates narrative in all of its manifestations

---

7 In this source Jaffe provides an extensive review of critical approaches to authenticity in mass media, focussing on processes of mediation and mediatisation. She shows how television, in particular, is replete with devices and resources for attributing and denying both authenticity and authority to targets, and how we as audience members are generally competent in reading these conventionalised resources.

with inauthenticity, saying that 'there is something inauthentic for our time in being spellbound, momentarily forgetful of oneself, concerned with the fate of a person [a narrative protagonist] who is not oneself but who also, by virtue of the spell that is being cast, is oneself' (Trilling 1972: 135). He is suggesting that narrative is not only a distraction from the fundamental demand of perpetually assessing one's own personal authenticity (which is certainly a 'strenuous moral experience'), but a device that dupes us in to seeing ourselves in and through the constructed personas of others. Because, as language users, we are all orchestrators of narratives and sociolinguistic performances, and involved in the construction and deployment of personas and stances in discourse (Coupland 1985, 2007; Jaffe 2009; see below), we must all confess to being both deceivers and deceived. Indeed, Trilling concludes that 'we are all inauthentic' (1972: 102).

Yet there is a different sense in which vividly dramatised polyphonic narrative (and not all narrative) can generate a sense of authenticity, and we might broaden the discussion to consider whether there is a wider class of modes or formats of spoken language that have this quality. In his discussion of broadcast media and authenticity Martin Montgomery (2001) explains the appeal that spontaneous talk has for the broadcasting institutions. Broadcasting is often and obviously an arena in which language use is scripted and staged, and this means that it tends to be denied the positive values that are commonly associated with spontaneous talk, which Montgomery says are 'egalitarianism, informality, intimacy, greater possibilities for participation, and so on' (2001: 398). In this list we can see traces of the authentic as I discussed it in the previous section, in that we might expect informal, spontaneous talk to reflect a consistency of participants' evaluative stances over time (systemic coherence, historicity), and an egalitarian footing for interaction to allow for degrees of personal integrity and the building of shared perspectives (ontology, consensus). Montgomery reminds us of Erving Goffman's (1981) related idea of 'fresh talk', which Goffman says arises from congruence among the roles of *principal* (the original source of ideas expressed), *author* (the composer or entextualiser of the ideas), and *animator* (the person who articulates the ideas in a given instance). In broadcasting, these three roles are commonly not congruent, e.g. when newsreaders (as animators) read aloud from texts that have been scripted by others (authors) to reflect overarching institutional standpoints (principals). Goffman was well aware that fresh talk in broadcasting is often not as fresh as it might appear, but the *ideal* of fresh talk is precisely what is implied by the fourth type of authentic language in the list, 'fully owned, unmediated language'.

But is spoken language ever fully unmediated, even when it is not subject to editorial and scripting intrusions? The view of language as performance suggests not, because there are always elements of intertextuality at work in language framed as performance (Bauman 2004; Briggs & Bauman 1992). All the same, it is interesting to consider that some sort of authenticity can emerge from speech as opposed to writing (see again the chapter by Coulmas), from lay as opposed to institutional practice, from autonomous as opposed to authoritative agency, and from spontaneity as opposed to historicity. There are good grounds to believe that, in order to locate the authentic, we do *not* need (as Trilling suggests we do) to turn away from performative dimensions of narrative, art and discursive construction. In a fourth section I will put the case that performance talk opens up specific opportunities for authentication as well as deauthentication.

3 Authenticity and indexical meaning

The expression 'indexing authenticity' might be an oxymoron. As we have seen, and at least at first blush, the concept of authenticity challenges us to make Trillingesque categorical decisions about real and essential being, whether people, things and actions are or are not authentic. If we entertain indexicality – processes of 'pointing to' a social category, where the meanings of linguistic features or styles are indirect and depend on ideological norms and conventional associations (Agha 2007; Ochs 1992; Silverstein 2003) – then we have already failed to meet authenticity's most stringent principles of inclusion and exclusion. From this point of view, indexed authenticity makes as little sense as 'an effect of beauty' when what is at stake is whether we experience an image as beautiful or not. We know, however, that the social and discursive world does not work this way, and that we have to accept more relativist and more dialogic approaches.

We sometimes come across metacultural texts (texts that express cultural meanings, while also being part of a culture) that assert fully paid-up, authentic belonging, but they tend to be ironic to a degree or we find them unconvincing. One of them is part of the t-shirt text that Barbara Johnstone takes as her starting point for a 'linguistics of particularity' analysis (in this volume): '100 % authentic Pittsburgh'. Johnstone's analysis of the shirt's text is grounded in a theory of indexical relations precisely because the text cannot be taken at face value as an authenticity claim. The t-shirt displays that I have studied in Wales (Coupland 2012) are rather different and metaculturally more oblique, to the extent that I considered them to be stylisations of Welsh cultural identities. They pose interpretive puzzles about language and culture to people who see them being worn, challenging them to make inferences about what the text might refer to, and then about why the wearer has chosen to display that text and what the 'ownership' of the text might be (in Goffman's terms). So once again, indexicality theory gives us good tools to analyse public displays of this sort, although there is a residual tension between the absolutism of authentic meaning and the contextuality and obliqueness of indexical relations.

In 2003 Penelope Eckert triggered a productive debate about the status of informants as authentic speakers in sociolinguistic variation studies. She said that the authentic speaker was construed as a 'spontaneous speaker of pure vernacular [who functioned as] the dialectological poster child – our direct access to language untainted by the interference of reflection or social agency' (Eckert 2003: 392). Eckert's account of this idealised character refers to several of the presumed characteristics of authentic language that we have been considering – above all, naturally occurring speakers and speech (whose naturalness is not critically examined in variation research, but is assumed to be dictated by their socio-demographic and geographical locations). But there is also the criterion of full ownership of speech style, if speakers are assumed to be prototypical exemplars of their social categories; and historicity, if it is assumed that authentic membership is static over time. But Eckert also shows how the authentic speaker in variation research was most commonly presumed to be working class and male, echoing Trilling's observation that, in literature, 'the person who accepts his class situation ... as a given and necessary condition of his life will be sincere beyond question ... sincere *and* authentic' (1972: 115, with original emphasis). Orienting to women as inauthentic relative to men, e.g. the idea that women are pragmatically more indirect and polite, or that their speech is less closely tied to vernacular norms, has some history in sociolinguistics (Bucholtz 2003), although this tendency also positioned men more resolutely at the bottom of some social hierarchies, closer to the soil.

In her chapter for the present volume Eckert extends the critique of the authentic speaker in variation research and argues that authentic group membership, premised simply on demographic classification, 'becomes moot' once we adopt a more dynamic view of social meaning and become more sophisticated in our understanding of indexical processes, inspired by Michael Silverstein's theoretical contributions, in a 'third wave' of variationism (cf. Eckert 2012)[8]. As Eckert

---

8 From a non-USA standpoint the linearity of Eckert's three phases of variation research, culminating in the 'emergence of meaning', is hard to recognise. The study of style in textual and interactional meaning-making has a long European history in general stylistics, for example, and critical approaches to discourse, context and ideology were well embedded in the 1970s, often under the influence of Michael Halliday's theoretical work (e.g. Halliday 1978). Allan Bell's influential, variation-focussed model of style as audience design (Bell 1984) and Howard Giles's theory of speech accommodation (Giles & Powesland 1975) both implicated the active construction of social meaning at the level of interpersonal and intergroup relations, and these initiatives (in which I took part) were present in the early years of what Eckert calls the first and second waves.

says, a dynamic view locates social meanings in social practice rather than in a pre-existing social structure, and is sensitive to more local and more differentiated meanings for speech. So, in Eckert's perspective, a problematic implication of authenticity is erased from the variationist perspective when it goes indexical and when it is overtaken by membership claims and associations made more locally and more contingently by speakers. In her present chapter Eckert gives the example of Linda, whose Chicano-sounding pronunciation indexed a cool persona that was highly valued in her school community of practice, rather than indexing Chicana ethnicity itself.

Mary Bucholtz takes the same critical line on the history of variationism in her contribution to the (2003) *Journal of Sociolinguistics* collection of papers on language and authenticity. Like Eckert, she argues against the variationist assumption that individuals whose speech characteristics locate them, on statistical criteria, in the middle of a demographic group's normal range are authentic speakers. She makes it clear, though, that if this perspective amounted to a variationist theory of identity, it was only an implicit one. Indeed there is no direct discussion of authenticity in classical variationist research on speech communities, and the tendency for both William Labov and Peter Trudgill to distance themselves from considerations of social identity in general in their most recent work has been noted (see some discussion of this in Coupland 2010a). With Kira Hall, Bucholtz has reasserted the relevance of authenticity in the sociolinguistics of identity in proposing that a dimension of authentication-to-denaturalisation is negotiated in social interaction as a key resource in the tactics of intersubjective discourse. They suggest that 'speakers make claims to realness and artifice' as people's alignments with identity categories are verified or disrupted (Bucholtz and Hall 2005: 601). In another dimension, identities can be either authorised or cast as illegitimate, which addresses more institutionalised bases of (de)authentication.

When Michael Silverstein (in this volume) reviews Labov's seminal study of speech variation in the Lower East Side of Manhattan, he returns to Labov's idea that speakers of the New York vernacular were prone to 'linguistic insecurity' (Labov 1972). This concept is perhaps the closest that Labov has come to suggesting that, for some New Yorkers, their own speech style was culturally deauthenticating. Labov's empirical procedures imply that 'the vernacular' is the most authentic style (it is modelled as a structurally regular and psycholinguistically unmonitored base-line from which style-shifting happens in an 'upwards' direction). The idea of covert prestige similarly pointed to a gap between externally expressed and internally held ideological beliefs about the meaning and value of speech style – a theme that has been taken up in extensive empirical research on language attitudes in Denmark by Tore Kristiansen (e.g. Kristiansen 2009) and his colleagues.

In his chapter Silverstein reports, from his analysis of newspaper readers' reactions to a published feature about New York speech, that the main trend is for readers to express a pro-New York City, 'anti-homogenization' [of speech] standpoint, professing their support for New York-accented speech and for local speech more generally. He interprets this as a second-order indexical relationship, a popular alignment with New York cultural values, where New York voice functions as a positive emblem of place. Linguistic insecurity is not strongly evident in these responses, and some respondents convey not only a sense of alignment but what looks like a sense of authentic belonging through voice; one respondent says: 'Treasure who you are, New York!'. Some of these evaluative discourses do clearly recognise an essentialising function of New York voice, or as Silverstein puts it, 'an ideologically naturalized – if not natural – fact about inner identity'. And as Johnstone argues in relation to her own data, authenticity claims of this sort are not restricted to people who actually speak the local variety. They feature in conventionalised accounts of what is distinctive about local speech, once a speech style has come to people's awareness through the process of enregisterment (Agha 2007).

But this again raises questions about methodological orientations to authenticity that are of fundamental importance (and which I discuss further in the next section). If we followed Trilling, we would have to see authenticity as a pre- or ultra-discursive phenomenon, located in people's unspoken and even unspeakable understandings of themselves and their socio-cultural embeddedness. Indeed Trilling suggests that grief, love and terror are quintessentially authentic emotions – the emotions that are capable of rendering people speechless. The less radical question is how discursive accounts stand as evidence of authentic experience. The view from indexicality theory is that social interaction is a progressive, real-time process of closing meaning-gaps, between macro-level identity categories and possibly local instantiations of them, indexed through speech. It is a matter of communicators coming to good-enough, 'predictable-as-true', act-of-faith metapragmatic understandings of what is going on in the immediate pragmatics of social exchanges (Silverstein 2003: 202). From this perspective, interactional meaning is the outcome of an authenticity quest, and one that is never fully resolved. But there is a risk of overplaying the constructedness and graduatedness of authenticity, just as there is a risk of underplaying these aspects (as in Trilling's stance). There has to be room to investigate the different degrees of individual and social coherence and validity that have provided the agenda for so much of sociolinguistics, and that have motivated all chapters in this book.

A key socio-political theme – and a classically sociolinguistic one – is that authentic belonging is not exclusively under the control of the self. Independently of how we might experience or account our own experiences of belonging, our belonging (or otherwise) to social formations is sometimes legislated by others, and this brings us back to the macro-politics of authenticity (as analysed in Gill's chapter). Even if authenticity is ultimately a universal human quest for meaning and validation, and if authenticity is always potentially at stake in interaction, key dimensions of authenticity are not only manipulated by, but also occasioned by, political structures. As Monica Heller explains (in this volume), the conception of being an authentic member of a national community is made possible and relevant by nationalist ideology, which sets the terms of (and drives the discourse of) national authenticity – belonging to a nation. Language is often a potent theme in nationalist discourse, particularly when national boundaries or even the viability of a nation is at stake. In contemporary Wales, for example, language planning discourse constructs authentic Welshness as being reliant on the Welsh language and bilingualism. Efforts to promote the Welsh language are, to a large extent, appeals to national authenticity through language. The following short extract is from an influential planning document of the Welsh Assembly Government titled *Iaith Pawb* ('Everyone's Language', see Coupland in press).

> We want Wales to be a truly bilingual nation, by which we mean a country where people can choose to live their lives through the medium of either Welsh or English and where the presence of the two languages is a visible and audible source of pride and strength to us all.

The phrase 'truly bilingual Wales' neatly brings ideas of language, nation and authenticity into the same frame of reference. It also associates the Welsh language with national 'pride' – the affective dimension in which, according to nationalist ideology, national authenticity is presumed to be experienced by national citizens (cf. interpretations of 'pride and profit' Duchêne & Heller 2007, 2012).

In her present chapter Heller is concerned with what happens to the ideology of national authenticity under changed market conditions, particularly when 'profit' (the economic exploitation of linguistic and other sorts of indexed localness) displaces, or rather appropriates, 'pride'. In her Canadian data she is able to trace how corporations exploit the use of French, for example in the marketing of cheese, trading off indexical associations that had been previously forged in Quebec between French and local food production. She says that, in the same economic conditions, smaller cheese-making enterprises can promote themselves in equivalent ways, but as artisanal (and presumably then, more credibly local) businesses. Heller refers to this shift as 'the commodification of French Canadian authenticity', although it is interesting to ask what is and is not authentic, for whom, in its earlier (old economy) stage as well as in its later (New Economy) stage. Given that nationalist ideology is itself acknowledged (at least by critics) to be romanticised and romanticising, we have to be wary of attributing authenticity too readily to earlier-stage lifestyles, economic and linguistic practices. Following Anderson (1991) and Hobsbawm and Ranger's (1983) highly influential accounts of imagined communities and invented tradition in the context of nationalism, dominant inter-disciplinary accounts of nationalist ideology stress its inauthenticity, and of course its potential to move beyond 'banal' and routine flag-waving (Billig 1995) into 'hotter' and more aggressive forms.

If we consider the social and sociolinguistic circumstances of artisanal, small-scale cheese-manufacturing, French-speaking workers in pre-globalized economies, we might expect individuals themselves to have rather low reflexive awareness of the authenticity (if this is what it was) of their lifestyles and language. It is heightened social reflexivity, entailed in increased geographical mobility, mediatisation, cultural comparison and so on, that creates conditions under which cultural (in)authenticity becomes meaningful, and starts to provide a basis for authenticity disputes and for cultural and sociolinguistic commodification. The same might be said for second-order indexicality (see chapters by Johnstone and Silverstein), which is a process we would expect to be made especially salient when metacultural awareness rises. Once appeals to authenticity begin to be made (for example in the rise of nationalist discourse in struggles to create and sustain nation-states), we might say that whatever authenticity had existed (probably unbeknown to its incumbents, and therefore difficult to locate) has inevitably started to lapse – authenticity ought to be ineffable. When New Economy markets seek to promote localness of language and culture as commodities, when cultural values are strategically worked into patterns of semiotic display and lose touch with the matrices of meaning and practice in which they arose, this further discredits their authenticity. If anything that we can call authenticity survives, it survives only inauthentically, on marketers' terms and in consumers' compliance.

Once again we have reached a point in critical interpretation where authenticity needs to be considered in highly nuanced ways. In Wales, for example, we see widespread commodification of Welsh language and Welshness, e.g. in the names of advertised Welsh-themed products (including cheese, in fact) and commercial establishments. But people's engagement with Welsh on these terms, productively or receptively, seems to be neither wholly cynical nor naively accepting. A valued sense of place and cultural distinctiveness can survive commodification, and in complex, commercially saturated cultures we become tolerant of muted or partial authenticities. As critical consumers, and much like the acculturated readers of mass-mediated 'realness' (Jaffe 2011), we expect to discover authenticity in less direct, more heavily contextualised ways. We also expect to experience authenticity at new intersections between social categories, under conditions that are usually called hybrid (but see below).

In this volume Akinmade Akande explains how 'keeping it real' in Nigerian hip hop means staying true to at least two different authenticating ideals – the originating values and performance styles of African American hip hop, but also the realities of Nigerian life and language. There is also a blending across the two modes of authenticity discussed in the previous section – between the authenticity of continuity and the authenticity of freshness and creativity. It is this sort of creativity that underpins the quest for authentic identity that Lefteris Kailoglou analyses among subcultural groups in Greece, innovatively styling themselves in opposition to each other and to mainstream cultural norms. Theresa Heyd and Christian Mair show how Nigerian Pidgin is rehabilitated and celebrated in diasporic digital communication, and how conventional sociolinguistic meanings of vernacularity shift and evolve in this process. Vernacularity goes global in their data, and this challenges us to reassess the sociolinguistic account of 'the vernacular'. As I noted earlier, authenticity has often been claimed for vernacularity, not so differently from how it has been claimed for standardness (Coupland 2003). But mediation potentially makes vernacularity spectacular, and lifts it out from its older associations of social class and stigma (Coupland 2011b). An online discussion forum proves to be facilitative in rather similar ways in Andrea Moll's detailed analysis of performances of Cyber-Jamaican. The forum provides a platform both for hyper-vernacular performances and for evaluative discourses, renegotiating indexical values associated with the Creole (cf. Lacoste & Mair 2012). Lauren Hall-Lew documents the evolution of fob style in San Francisco, and the blending of Chinese and American cultural norms and forms, which is another instance of fusing the local and the global.

All the above studies are concerned with social change, increasing indexical complexity and the crossing and blending of older categories in new social and semiotic configurations under globalisation. The term 'hybridity' has some resonance here, and seems to imply a deauthenticating of traditional language-society relations in favour of looser, more open, more mixed ones. But the studies have all also documented a process of reauthentication – a *re*-centring of new semiotic practices – in Nigerian hip hop, Nigerian Pidgin online, Cyber-Jamaican and in Chinese America. We have to ask whether sociolinguistic changes of this sort are actually experienced as hybridity, or whether we are just tapping into processes of change and re-embedding that are quite general, in type if not in degree. Lilie Chouliaraki and Norman Fairclough make the point that, although hybridity is often seen as a characteristic of the postmodern, the social processes it points to are not a matter of moving from pure to hybrid states. They say that 'hybridity…is inherent in all social uses of language. But particular social circumstances create particular degrees of stability and durability for particular articulations' (Chouliaraki & Fairclough 2001: 13). New articulations, new ways of speaking and meaning, express new, changed social realities and relations, and they reflect how people fashion new sorts of authentic experience for themselves in the context of mobility and change.

Alastair Pennycook's (2010) mantra that language is always and inevitably 'a local practice' captures this alternative viewpoint very well. To talk of hybridity (or hybridities) is to persist in thinking in terms of old and static categories, which are in fact always lapsing and being replaced under specific contextual circumstances. We should similarly say that authenticity has to be an emergent quality of whatever discourses are locally available, and defined in relation to local contingencies. Jan Blommaert (2010) makes the point that, in an increasingly mobile world of circulating people and circulating semiotic resources, values and social meanings attaching to ways of speaking often have to be radically renegotiated in new environments. As Anna Hultgren surmises (in her chapter for this book), we might have to get used to hybridity (which might perhaps be better referred to as a process of dynamic decentring and recentring) being the unmarked norm.

4 Authenticity, style and performance

Contributors to this volume base their arguments in analyses of data of very different sorts – song lyrics, ancient manuscripts, t-shirt inscriptions, ethnographic observations and notes, interviews, audio-recorded speech data, political speeches, web forum discussion threads, online instant messaging texts, questionnaires, policy documents, newspaper articles, and so on. This range is impressive, and it illustrates a widening of sociolinguistic methods and orientations to data. But in this section I would like to review arguments for approaching authenticity through discourse analysis of performance events, which has been the approach I have taken in several earlier studies. This might seem rather perverse, if we take the view (discussed above) that authenticity can be equated with naturalness and absence of mediation, neither of which is a quality of performance.

I would argue from a different starting point, presuming that authentic meaning is elusive and difficult to access, in three different respects. Firstly, as we saw in discussing indexicality, the agentive, meaning-producing speaker who projects indexically meaningful personas into social arenas has rather little security. As Eckert, Ochs, Silverstein and others have suggested, the styling of a social identity has to rely on indirect indexical relations between particular linguistic features or styles and arrays of potential social meanings. Interactional sociolinguistics has emphasised dialogic processes of projection and inferencing (Gumperz 1982, LePage & Tabouret-Keller 1985). These general considerations suggest that insecurity and inauthenticity are endemic risks in the pragmatic quest for indexical meaning. Speakers are not in any simple sense authentic practitioners, and neither is language itself, so that speaking is strategic social action to conjure identities, even in the most benign of social circumstances. Even 'being yourself' is a constructive representational act, reliant on the activation of relevant sociolinguistic norms and ideologies in particular contexts.

Then, secondly, as we saw in the previous section, there are countless more particular circumstances – and this is the home-ground of critical sociolinguistics – where projectable identities are disallowed or discredited by macro-level social processes, or when (as in Bucholtz and Hall's model of intersubjective processes) interactants work to discredit others' identities. These are circumstances when inauthenticity becomes much more than a technical systemic and metapragmatic issue, when individuals or groups struggle to assert and to embed legitimate identities. This often arises (as we see in many chapters here) in relation to ways of speaking and groups that are minoritised in different ideological regimes. My own studies of authenticity in performance have mainly centred on vocal constructions of Welsh identities, and on reframings of social class and ethnic/national identities, both of which are very active symbolic dimensions in Wales (Coupland & Coupland in press).

The third consideration has to do with what Joanna Thornborrow and Theo van Leeuwen (see above) mean by authenticity being in crisis. In globalised and mediatised late modernity our social identities seem to be less securely rooted in the social structures that we inhabit. We are less confident of what it means to be of a certain social class, gender, age-group or ethnicity, and of the predictive power of sociolinguistic indexicalities. We are more reflexively aware and less trusting. Sociolinguistic variation research has moved to distance itself from presumed authentic speakers, I suspect, partly because a more adequate theory has evolved (as Eckert argues here), but also partly because the predominantly young people who feature in contemporary community-of-practice studies are actually less socio-structurally determined by their inherited demographics than their grandparents were. Ben Rampton's research on multi-ethnic British young people's crossing between ethnically-linked and class-linked speech styles to achieve particular local footings for their interpersonal relationships is a paradigmatic instance of the same shift (Rampton 2006). The explosion of studies of crossing over the last 15 years suggests social change as well as a change in critical sociolinguistic thinking. Blommaert and Rampton (2011) talk of the need for a radical paradigm shift in sociolinguistic theory and method to maintain purchase on a world where mobile superdiversity has overtaken diversity, as we have understood it to be.

If we take the view that authenticity is indexically relevant, but on several grounds precarious, then we arguably need to look beyond 'straight' modes of indexical meaning, at more deeply contextualised and more strategic modes. And why not look at *mass*-mediated performances, which are where we know we will find layers of mediational management (again see Jaffe 2011) that allow media performers to skip along the boundaries between the real and the unreal. If we can presume that one or more layers of inauthentic self-representation exists in many contexts, and that it is expected to do so by an increasingly reflexively-aware population, then we can look at how presumedly inauthentic identities play out 'on stage' (more or less literally) in performance (in the senses of Bauman 1977 and Goffman 1974), and how the dialectics of authenticity and inauthenticity are discursively framed there and to what effects.

There are some nice ironic aphorisms that express (but, appropriately enough, overstate) this viewpoint, and the best of them are attributable to Oscar Wilde. For example:

- A little sincerity is a dangerous thing, and a great deal of it is absolutely fatal.
- Consistency is the last refuge of the unimaginative.
- The first duty in life is to be as artificial as possible. What the second duty is no one has as yet discovered.
- Man is least himself when he talks in his own person. Give him a mask, and he will tell you the truth.

I have suggested elsewhere that performance needs to be thought of as existing on a scale of intensity or 'stagedness'. At one end we have what we might call ordinary performance which, following Goffman, is arguably the general design-frame for being and 'acting' in the social world, and which has its own variation between relatively staged and relatively unstaged frames and episodes. At the other end we have full or high performance, where social action is institutionally managed (and usually named) as performance. But across this range there is the same potential for authentic experience to rise through the layers of mediation. One intriguing instance is the performance of sincerity in popular singing that, as Paddy Scannell (1996: chapter 3) shows, was actually made possible by the invention of microphone technology.

'The truth' (in Wilde's last aphorism, above) and authentic experience do not, of course, simply and necessarily crystallise out of performance, but some sorts of metacultural performance do manage to put cultural forms and tropes on display, often in hyperbolic forms of representation, and make them available for reflexive reconsideration. Are they real? Should we take them as such? What do we think of them? Should we perpetuate them or change them? These questions relate to the sorts of dialogic construction and inquiry that were foregrounded in Mikhail Bakhtin's (1981, 1986) writings about heteroglossia and stylisation. In my own interpretation, stylisation can be seen as a particular performance frame that self-consciously ambiguates the ownership of voices and invites or requires critical reflexive decoding of an unusually intense sort on the part of audiences (Coupland 2001a, 2001b, 2007). It is through this heightened interpretative activity that indexical meanings of voice come up for re-examination (we might say re-enregisterment), and where the potential for sociolinguistic/ language-ideological change resides.

In his detailed examination of the relationship between performance and ritual, Rampton (2009) is concerned that over-emphasising the sociolinguistic functions of performance might deflect attention from the importance of ritual, and he sees ritual function in crossings and stylisations in his own data. A distinction that he recognises between performance and ritual is that performance leads audiences away from the ordinary world, where it can be seen differently, while ritual registers the exceptional but leads audiences past it, back to ordinary life. This is a productive distinction, although I would see both ritual and performance qualities in the sorts of data I have examined, which are more heavily and more institutionally framed as (high) performance events in the first place: radio DJ talk, television news reframed as banter, TV comedy and theatrical pantomime (see sources cited in note 2). Audiences select themselves into these events *as* audiences, and their expectations of performative role-play and characterological extravagances are not disappointed. The often stylised personas that they encounter include pastiche representations of known cultural types and relationships, and the semiotic demand on audiences is to find boundaries in the voiced performances that are put in front of them between the culturally authentic and the simulation. It seems entirely reasonable to theorise these interactions as oscillations between performance (centrifugal) and ritual (centripetal) functions in Rampton's senses.

5 Conclusion

In the process of this overview I have canvassed some quite contradictory views on the nature and even the possibility of authenticity, and different stances, overt or covert, on whether and how to pursue the interface between authenticity and language. As yet there is no consensus among sociolinguists on how to approach authenticity – reputedly a former elephant in the room that some might say we have sent on its way. Others, myself included, would say that the elephant has not only become visible, but has grown and reproduced itself. The 'ominous' quality that Trilling saw in authenticity can be analysed into three types of fear: first, a fear of the inherent grandiosity of the concept; second, a fear of the restrictions some people experience on their autonomous agency in expressing their own valued authenticities; third, a fear of losing touch with authentic experience in a complex and semiotically overloaded social world. But as we see in several of the new studies in this book, there are important new platforms, including in the less institutionalised domains of interactive new media, for rediscovering and reasserting authenticities of place, style and identity that constitute the sociolinguistic orders of our lives.

'Language' has itself meant different things in this review, with perhaps two main alternative foci emerging. On the one hand there is interest in the meanings of linguistic forms and styles that might index group belonging in more or less consolidated and authenticity-conferring ways. On the other hand there is interest in the discourses through which authenticity and inauthenticity are described, claimed, discredited or performed. But there is also considerable and growing overlap between these two broad sociolinguistic perspectives. As we have seen, researchers have become more committed to exploring how indexical meanings for features and styles emerge from and circulate through social environments, where they may (as second-order or higher-order indexicals) become topics of metalinguistic debate. In performance-based studies, there is no alternative to a holistic approach that examines not so much the distribution of features and styles, but their social and discursive embedding. Similarly, the authentic or other status of languages as objectified codes needs to be established not only in evaluative discourses (which are certainly part of the ideological constitution of variation) but in contexts where such codes may be actualised and performed. Having one's voice heard is perhaps the most obviously authenticating sociolinguistic experience (Hymes 1996).

References

Agha, Asif 2007: *Language and Social Relations*. Cambridge: Cambridge University Press.
Anderson, Benedict 1991: *Imagined Communities: Reflections on the Origin and Spread of Nationalism*. London: Verso.
Androutsopoulos, Jannis (ed.) in press: *Mediatization and Sociolinguistic Change*. FRIAS Linguae & Litterae series. Berlin/Boston: De Gruyter.
Bakhtin, Mikhail 1981: *The Dialogic Imagination*. Austin: Texas University Press.
Bakhtin, Mikhail M. 1986: *Speech Genres and Other Late Essays*. Austin: University of Texas Press.
Bauman, Richard 1977: *Verbal Art as Performance*. Prospect Heights: Waveland Press.
Bauman, Richard 2004: *A World of Others' Words: Cross-Cultural Perspectives on Intertextuality*. Malden, MA: Blackwell Publishing.
Beck, Ulrich, Anthony Giddens & Scott Lash 1994: *Reflexive Modernization: Politics, Tradition and Aesthetics in the Modern Social Order*. Stanford: Stanford University Press.

Bell, Allan 1984: Language style as audience design. *Language in Society* 13: 145–204.

Belsey, Catherine 2005: *Culture and the Real*. London: Routledge.

Billig, Michael 1995: *Banal Nationalism*. London: Sage.

Blackledge, Adrian 2005: *Discourse and Power in a Multilingual World*. Amsterdam: John Benjamins.

Blommaert, Jan 2010: *The Sociolinguistics of Globalization*. Cambridge: Cambridge University Press.

Blommaert, Jan & Ben Rampton 2011: Language and superdiversity: A position paper. *Working Papers in Urban Language and Literacies* 70, King's College London. Available at http://www.kcl.ac.uk/innovation/groups/ldc/publications/workingpapers/70.pdf

Briggs, Charles L. & Richard Bauman 1992: Genre, intertextuality and social power. *Journal of Linguistic Anthropology* 2(2): 131–72.

Bucholtz, Mary 2003: Sociolinguistic nostalgia and the authentication of identity. *Journal of Sociolinguistics* 7(3): 398–416.

Bucholtz, Mary & Kira Hall 2005: Identity and interaction: A sociocultural linguistic approach. *Discourse Studies* 7: 585–614.

Butler, Judith 1997: *Excitable Speech: A Politics of the Performative*. New York/London: Routledge.

Castells, Manuel 2010: *The Power of Identity* (second edition). Malden: Wiley-Blackwell.

Chouliaraki, Lilie & Norman Fairclough 2001: *Discourse in Late Modernity: Rethinking Critical Discourse Analysis*. Edinburgh: Edinburgh University Press.

Coupland, Bethan & Nikolas Coupland in press: The authenticating discourses of mining heritage tourism in Wales and Cornwall. *Journal of Sociolinguistics*.

Coupland, Nikolas 1985: 'Hark, hark the lark': Social motivations for phonological style-shifting. *Language and Communication* 5(3): 153–172.

Coupland, Nikolas 2001a: Stylisation, authenticity and TV news review. *Discourse Studies* 3(4): 413–442.

Coupland, Nikolas 2001b: Dialect stylisation in radio talk. *Language in Society* 30(3): 345–375.

Coupland, Nikolas 2001c: Language, context and the relational self: Re-theorising dialect style in sociolinguistics. In P. Eckert and J. Rickford (eds.) *Style and Sociolinguistic Variation*, 185–210. Cambridge: Cambridge University Press.

Coupland, Nikolas 2003: Sociolinguistic authenticities. *Journal of Sociolinguistics*. 7(3): 417–431.

Coupland, Nikolas 2004: Stylised deception. In A. Jaworski, N. Coupland & D. Galasiński (eds.) *Metalanguage: Social and Ideological Perspectives*, 249–274. Berlin/New York: Mouton de Gruyter.

Coupland, Nikolas 2007: *Style: Language Variation and Identity*. Cambridge: Cambridge University Press.

Coupland, Nikolas 2009: Dialect style, social class and metacultural performance: The pantomime Dame. In N. Coupland and A. Jaworski (eds.) *The New Sociolinguistics Reader*, 311–325. Palgrave: Macmillan.

Coupland, Nikolas 2010a: The authentic speaker and the speech community. In Carmen Llamas and Dominic Watts (eds.) *Language and Identities*, 99–112. Edinburgh: Edinburgh University Press.

Coupland, Nikolas 2010b: Language, ideology, media and social change. In K. Junod and D. Maillat (eds) *Performing the Self*, 127–151. Tübingen: Gunter Narr Verlag.

Coupland, Nikolas 2011a: The sociolinguistics of style. In Rajend Mesthrie (ed.) *The Cambridge Handbook of Sociolinguistics*, 138–156. Cambridge: Cambridge University Press.

Coupland, Nikolas 2011b: Voice, place and genre in popular music performance. *Journal of Sociolinguistics* 15(5): 573–602.

Coupland, Nikolas 2012: Bilingualism on display: The framing of Welsh and English in Welsh public spaces. *Language in Society* 41: 1–27.

Coupland, Nikolas in press: Wales and Welsh: Boundedness and peripherality. In Dominic Watt and Carmen Llamas (eds.) *Language and Borders*. Edinburgh University Press.

Coupland, Nikolas & Tore Kristiansen 2011: SLICE: Critical perspectives on language (de) standardisation. In Tore Kristiansen and Nikolas Coupland (eds.) *Standard Languages and Language Standards in a Changing Europe*, 11–35. Oslo: Novus.

Duchêne, Alexandre & Monica Heller (eds.) 2007: *Discourses of Endangerment: Ideology and Interest in the Defence of Languages*. London: Continuum.

Duchêne, Alexandre & Monica Heller (eds.) 2012: *Language in Late Capitalism: Pride and Profit*. London: Routledge.

Eckert, Penelope 2003: Elephants in the room. *Journal of Sociolinguistics* 7(33): 392–397.

Eckert, Penelope 2012: Three waves of variation study: The emergence of meaning in the study of sociolinguistic variation. *Annual review of Anthropology* 41: 87–100.

Giles, Howard & Peter Powesland 1975: *Speech Style and Social Evaluation*. London: Academic Press.

Goffman, Erving 1974: *Frame Analysis*. Harmondsworth: Penguin.

Goffman, Erving 1981: *Forms of Talk*. Oxford: Blackwell.

Gumperz, John J. 1982 *Discourse Strategies*. Cambridge: Cambridge University Press.

Halliday, M. A. K. 1978: *Language as Social Semiotic: The Social Interpretation of Language and Meaning*. Maryland: University Park Press.

Hobsbawm, Eric & Terence Ranger (eds.) 1983: *The Invention of Tradition*. Cambridge: Cambridge University Press.

Hutton, Chris 2005: *Race and the Third Reich: Linguistics, Racial Anthropology and Genetics in the Dialectic of Volk*. Cambridge: Polity Press.

Hymes, Dell 1996: *Ethnography, Linguistics, Narrative Inequality: Toward an Understanding of Voice*. London: Taylor and Francis.

Jaffe, Alexandra (ed.) 2009: *Stance: Sociolinguistic Perspectives*. Oxford: Oxford University Press.

Jaffe, Alexandra 2011: Sociolinguistic diversity in mainstream media: Authenticity, authority and processes of mediation and mediatisation. In Helen Kelly-Homes and Tommaso Milani (eds.) *Thematising Multilingualism in the Media* (Special issue of *Journal of Language and Politics*.), 562–586.

Kristiansen, Tore 2009: The macro-level social meanings of late-modern Danish accents. *Acta Linguistica Havniensia* 41: 167–192.

Labov, William 1972: *Sociolinguistic Patterns*. Philadelphia: University of Pennsylvania Press.

Lacoste, Véronique & Christian Mair (eds.) 2012: *Authenticity in Creole-Speaking Contexts. Zeitschrift für Anglistik und Amerikanistik* 60: 3.

Le Page, Robert B. & Andrée Tabouret-Keller 1985: *Acts of Identity: Creole-based Approaches to Language and Ethnicity*. New York: Cambridge University Press.

Livingstone, Sonia 2009: On the mediation of everything. *Journal of Communication* 59(1): 1–18.

Lyons, John 1977: *Semantics* (Volume 1). Cambridge: Cambridge University Press.

Montgomery, M. 2001: Defining authentic talk. *Discourse Studies* 3(4): 397–405.

Ochs, Elinor 1992: Indexing gender. In A. Duranti and C. Goodwin (eds.) *Rethinking Context: Language as an Interactive Phenomenon,* 335–358. Cambridge: Cambridge University Press.

Pennycook, Alastair 2010: *Language as a Local Practice.* London: Routledge.

Rampton, Ben 2006: *Language in Late Modernity: Interaction in an Urban School.* Cambridge: Cambridge University Press.

Rampton, Ben 2009: Interaction ritual and not just artful performance in crossing and stylization. *Language in Society* 38(2): 149–176.

Scannell, Paddy 1996: *Radio, Television and Modern Life: A Phenomenological Approach.* Oxford: Blackwell Publishers

Silverstein, Michael 2003: Indexical order and the dialectics of sociolinguistic life. *Language and Communication* 23: 193–229.

Thornborrow, Joanna & Theo van Leeuwen (eds.) 2001: *Authenticity in Media Discourse.* Thematic issue of *Discourse Studies,* Volume 3, Issue 4.

Trilling, Lionel 1972: *On Sincerity and Authenticity.* Cambridge, Mass.: Harvard University Press.

Van Leeuwen, Theo 2001: What is authenticity? *Discourse Studies* 3(4): 392–397.

Whorf, Benjamin Lee 1956: *Language, Thought and Reality: Selected Writings of Benjamin Lee Whorf,* edited by. J. B. Carroll. New York: Wiley.

Section I:
Indexing local meanings of authenticity

Penelope Eckert
The trouble with authenticity

1 Introduction

Authenticity has long been an elephant in the room in the study of sociolinguistic variation. It is embedded in the notion of the vernacular, in our relation to the rest of the field of linguistics, in our field methods, and in prevalent understandings of the nature of the indexical nature of variation. The vernacular emerged early on in the study of variation as the holy grail of language study – as the authentic production of the authentic speaker, the natural object of scientific investigation. Labov (1972) defined the vernacular as the speaker's most automatic linguistic production, directly produced by, and reflective of, the speaker's grammar. This production, free of interference from conscious processes, could be witnessed only in the most unreflective, spontaneous, speech untainted by the corrective forces of standard norms. The ultimate inauthentic speaker emerged as the middle class speaker, seen as suppressing the vernacular in response to the demands of the standard language market (Bourdieu and Boltanski 1975). Labov (1972) characterized middle class speech as more self-conscious and contrived than working class speech, and Kroch (1978) suggested that the socioeconomic stratification of variation results from stratified resistance to vernacular innovation. In other words, class emerges as a cline of (in)authenticity. Equally inauthentic are speakers who do not produce the language of their assigned population group, such as middle class Nathan B., whom Labov eliminated from his New York City (Labov 1966) sample for his consistent use of a working class pattern. In other words, authenticity in this tradition is based on conformity to membership in enduring structural categories, and linguistic authenticity entails using the patterns of variation associated with those categories. Authenticity, then, is something the analyst bestows on speakers and their speech performances.

Over the years, though, leading up to the current Third Wave of variation studies (Eckert 2012), we have come to view variation as a more robust and dynamic indexical system. Correlations with abstract demographic categories such as gender and class are not the source of indexicality, but the outcome, resulting from patterns of activity that constitute those categories. In turn the broader structure acts as constraint on those patterns of activity so that there is a continuous reproductive relation between structure and practice. Variation enters into stylistic configurations as speakers construct personae in the moment and through time – personae, needless to say, that may inhabit the broader categories into which they fit, but also personae that don't quite fit the categories, that push the envelope and bring about change. And just as new concepts require new words (e.g. *software, metrosexual*), ever-changing social dynamics require ever-changing indexical resources. The mechanism for indexical change is what Silverstein (2003) has called *indexical order* in which, for example, a linguistic variant associated with a social category comes to index some salient quality associated with that category. The continual extension of indexical potential creates – and continually modifies – an array of potential meanings, or an indexical field (Eckert 2008). Thus, for example, depending on context, an aspirated /t/ can index such things as formality, prissiness (Podesva 2004), nerdiness (Bucholtz 2011) or even anger.

This more dynamic view of variation as integral to social practice, and as constructing as well as reflecting social categories, makes the structural notion of authenticity moot. Authenticity cannot be a state of possession of qualities that define an enduring category; rather, it is something that people claim. And more importantly, at the same time that it is a claim about the individual's possession of those qualities, it is a claim about what those qualities are. In other words, the claim to authenticity ties the construction of the self to the construction of the categories one aspires to. Bucholtz and Hall (2004, 2005), on the basis that identity is inherently relational, point out (2005: 605) that a claim of similarity to another or to others is never total, but always partial, "... produced through contextually situated and ideologically informed configurations of self and other." In other words, when people strive to identify with chosen others, they claim not global similarity, but similarity with respect to selected qualities. They refer to this claim to selected qualities as *adequation*, and the process of adequation itself reinscribes those selected qualities as definitive. Indeed, the desire to claim authenticity arises from some assessment of the qualities of that entity that make it desirable, and this assessment – to the extent that it is shared by numerous others – reflects back on, and changes, the category. To the extent that a linguistic variable is deployed in an authenticity claim, the process of adequation will contribute to its ever-changing indexical field.

2 Authenticity and variation

Labov's study of Martha's Vineyard (Labov 1963) was the first clear study of variation and authenticity. The diphthongs PRICE[1] and MOUTH had conserved the historical central pronunciation [ɐj] on Martha's Vineyard, as on islands along the Atlantic coast of North America more generally (Wolfram & Schilling-Estes 1998), while on the mainland, this nucleus had lowered to [a]. For some years, Vineyard speakers had been following the mainland trend to lower the nucleus. But Labov found that some speakers were reversing this lowering trend, in an apparent move to recapture one of the most salient features of the distinctive island dialect. Led by the English ethnic fishing community whose control over the local economy was under threat from the mainland-controlled tourist industry, this revival of a 'traditional' local pronunciation constituted a claim to island authenticity. "It is apparent that the immediate meaning of this phonetic feature is 'Vineyarder.' When a man says [rɐjt] or [hɐʊs], he is unconsciously establishing the fact that he belongs to the island: that he is one of the natives to whom the island really belongs." (Labov 1963)

This indexical move was a textbook example of indexical order. A feature that had simply marked a speaker as a Vineyarder came to be used stylistically within the island to index a particular kind of Vineyarder, making salient a particular aspect of island identity. The simple association of the centralized diphthongs with the general Vineyard dialect, hence with membership in the native "Vineyarder" population, constitutes an "nth" order indexical. Any link between a linguistic form and a population opens the potential for the form to become linked in turn with associations with that population. In the Vineyard case, the fishing population's claim to authenticity led them to claim the linguistic form as indexical of their particular authentic status. In this case, Vineyard authenticity did not simply distinguish islanders from mainlanders: the English-descent fisherfolk who engaged in this linguistic move were laying claim to greater island authenticity than other islanders as well. Kiesling (2005, 2009) has argued that variables take on indexical value as speakers take stances in interaction, and although Labov gathered his data in one-on-one interviews, it is probable that this new pronunciation moved onto the public stage in authenticative, legitimating moves, as people took stances in conversations that involved island issues and particularly the fate of the island. This linguistic move constituted simultaneously a claim to personal legitimacy and an ideological position. And it did not simply claim authentic membership in a pre-existing category, "the Vineyarder,"

---

[1] I refer to vowels using the system developed by Wells (1982).

but reinscribed that category as embodying a specific island ideology and as peopled by a new version of an old authentic persona. It placed this persona, and the issues that distinguished it from past personae, into the indexical field associated with this particular linguistic form.

Indexical moves of this sort don't occur randomly, but at junctures that are sufficiently important to motivate a collaborative ideological move. It has been said that linguistic change accelerates during times of social upheaval, and we can see this in the case of the quiet upheaval that was taking place on Martha's Vineyard at the time of Labov's study. This is not to say that all change requires upheaval, but the propagation of a change involves indexical moves, and indexical moves are useless if they don't create some kind of distinction. Archeologist Ian Hodder, based on studies of style in archeological artifacts, links stylistic moves in material culture to the need for legitimation:

> decoration and shape distinction may relate not so much to the existence of social categories but to a concern with those categories .... Where social groups are threatened or contradicted, or are otherwise concerned with self-legitimation, 'stylistic behaviour', in the form of numerous contrasts and variations in pottery, stone, metal and other types, may be most marked. Stylistic behaviour is ... linked directly ... to ideologies and strategies of legitimation. (Hodder 1982: 193).

3 Ethnicity and the crowd

Perhaps the social category that has proven the most resistant to a fluid perspective on variation has been ethnicity, and most particularly the linguistic varieties associated with racialized ethnic groups. In the US, the "ethnolects" associated with African Americans and Latinos have been viewed as separate from the co-territorial white Anglo dialects, and as indexing, purely and simply, ethnicity. The emphasis has been on difference or divergence and, occasionally, on the extent to which speakers participate in regional (i.e. white Anglo) sound changes (e.g. Bailey & Maynor 1987; Labov & Harris 1986). Bucholtz's study (1999, 2011) of white boys appropriating features from African American Vernacular English, though, shows just the kind of indexical claims discussed above. These boys are not laying claim to African American ethnicity, but to what they perceive as the special coolness associated with African Americans. Coolness, indeed, is a powerful notion in youth cultures, and plays an important role in indexical fluidity. And coolness itself is as diverse as the people seeking it.

In what follows, I will examine the complex indexicality of the ethnic variety known as *Chicano English*, in a preadolescent population in Northern California, and will consider what it can mean to claim Chicano authenticity. The study unfolds in two schools, Steps and Fields, which serve adjacent but very different catchment areas. Steps serves a poor neighborhood, and its student body is diverse. Eight percent of the students are white Anglos, and the majority are Latino and Asian American. There are also a small number of Pacific Islanders and African Americans. Fields serves a solidly middle class population. Its student body is eighty-two percent white Anglo, and the remaining eighteen percent mirror the non-white Anglo ethnic makeup of Steps. The differences between the dominant speech patterns at Steps and Fields are generally heard as ethnic differences, with Chicano English being the unmarked variety at Steps, and White Anglo English being the unmarked variety at Fields. But this is an oversimplification. Neither dialect is monolithic, and neither simply indexes ethnicity. Indeed, to some extent, the indexical complexity of both dialects arises in the same conditions, and for the same purposes. And it is this similarity that brings together their indexical fields.

My ethnography followed an age cohort in both schools through fifth and sixth grades, and into middle school in seventh grade[2]. During this time, the kids were moving from childhood towards adolescence, collaboratively reorganizing themselves into a peer-based social order. At the center of this movement in both schools was the emergence of a "popular crowd" that led the cohort into adolescent practices. Crowd activity centered above all around the pairing up of boys and girls as heterosexual couples, which lasted anywhere from a few hours to a few weeks, rarely months. The pairing was not so much about relationships between the individual boys and girls who made up the couples, but about the crowd itself. The crowd arranged the pairings, and the couples generally spent little time together. Rather, the constant turnover of couples created a social market, as individuals accrued value on the basis of whom they were paired with, and of their role in pairing up others. The activity, in other words, was not about heterosexuality so much as about creating social structure and specifically a status system. The crowd stood out in a variety of ways – by its sheer size in contrast with other kids' smaller friendship groups and its concomitant domination of space and visibility; by its transformed gender relations, not only in the heterosexual pairing but in the collaborative enterprise behind it; and by its general claim to cultural leadership in the move to adolescence. The crowd's size, status and visibility facilitated symbolic domination, as crowd members collaboratively performed cool on the stage offered by the captive audience of their classmates.

2 Christi Cervantes joined me in the ethnographic work at Fields. I am eternally grateful to Christi for her great field skills and excellent insights. This research was supported by The Spencer Foundation.

The crowd defined coolness in all stylistic matters from clothing to activities to language. And while coolness looked very different in the two schools, its relation to the emerging social market and to the language that indexed this market was strikingly similar.

At Fields, the popular crowd was more powerful than that at Steps, because of the relative homogeneity of the student population. At Fields, the crowd was dominated by white Anglo kids, but involved a minority of Chicano, Asian American, and African American kids. The ethnic diversity at Steps yielded greater diversity of practices and orientations to school and to peer relations, particularly between the predominant Asian American and Latino populations. The public heterosexual market, though, was predominantly Chicano, and involved a minority of African American, Asian American, and Anglo kids, and prided itself on its diversity. The dominant ethnic group in each crowd determined the "ethnolect" that provided shared ways of talking for the crowd. Thus in both schools, features that function at a higher social level to index ethnicity, index social status, and particularly crowd status, at the more local level. In what follows, I will focus on two features – the white Anglo fronting of back vowels, and the Chicano wholesale backing of the TRAP vowel.

The fronting of GOOSE and GOAT is a highly salient marker of California Anglo English, and figures prominently in imitations of the popular gendered stereotypes of laid-back affluent Californians, Valley Girls and Surfers. Quite possibly because of these specific associations, these two vowels remain quite far back in prototypical Chicano English. In a study of Chicano speech in Los Angeles, Carmen Fought (1999) found that most young Chicanos, most particularly those who are gang-oriented, tend not to front the GOOSE vowel, while those who are more engaged in mainstream culture do. The Anglo character of this fronting shows up clearly in the differences between Fields and Steps – most kids at Fields front this vowel at least to some degree, most kids at Steps do not[3]. The same is true of the fronting of the GOAT vowel. Kids at Fields front both GOOSE and GOAT more than kids at Steps, as measured by the second formant ($p < .001$). It is no doubt the association with a trendy ethnic stereotype, the Valley Girl and the Surfer, that makes fronting unpopular at Steps and popular at Fields. GOOSE fronting is stereotypically associated with surfers in the stereotypic exclamative *dude!* (Kiesling 2004). GOAT fronting is highlighted in the quotative *go,* which is socially salient not only because it is a reasonably trendy quotative, but also

---

3 In the case of GOOSE, all speakers front to some extent following coronal consonants, although Fields speakers front these occurrences more than Steps speakers. The most socially salient occurrences of fronting are those following non-coronals.

because direct quotation is an important element of the talk in which teenage norms and status are negotiated. Indeed, occurrences of this vowel have been found (Eckert 2011) to be significantly more fronted in occurrences of this quotative than in other occurrences of the verb *go*. It should not be surprising, then, that those most engaged in the negotiation of norms and status should show the most fronting of this vowel. At Fields, the members of the crowd lead their peers in the fronting of the GOOSE vowel ($p < .05$) and the GOAT vowel ($p < .0015$). In other words, a feature that indexes California White youth in a global sense also indexes crowd status more locally. This does not make the crowd "whiter" or more "Anglo" than their peers, but more trendy.

In the western United States, Anglos raise the TRAP vowel before nasal consonants (e.g. *stand*), in what is commonly referred to as the *nasal pattern*. This nasal pattern is enhanced in California Anglo speech by a concomitant lowering and backing of non-nasal occurrences of TRAP, leaving a considerable split between the two sets of occurrences. This nasal split is shown in Figure 1, an F1–F2 plot of occurrences of the TRAP vowel in the speech of Rachel, a prominent member of the crowd at Fields. In Chicano English, however, there is no nasal pattern, and all occurrences of the TRAP vowel are relatively low and considerably back. This Chicano pattern is shown in Figure 2, an F1–F2 plot of occurrences of the TRAP vowel in the speech of Selena, a prominent member of the Steps crowd. This Chicano pattern is commonly heard as a "Spanish" accent, and indeed it may have been retained in the Native English of Chicanos for its Spanish indexicality. Almost all kids at Fields show the nasal pattern, while many at Steps do not. And overall, the split, as measured by the distance between the means of nasal and non-nasal occurrences, is significantly greater ($p < .001$) at Fields than at Steps.

And in each school, there is a relation between participation in what one might reasonably identify as the local ethnic pattern, and local social status. At Fields Elementary, as in the case of the fronting of GOAT and GOOSE, the crowd members show a significantly greater nasal split than non-crowd members ($p < .001$). Meanwhile, at Steps, the magnitude of the split correlates inversely with crowd membership, with non-crowd members showing a greater split than crowd members ($p < .001$). In fact, no member of the crowd, regardless of ethnicity, shows a significant height difference between nasal and non-nasal occurrences, while most non-crowd members, once again regardless of ethnicity, show a split with a significance ranging from $p < .05$ to $p < .001$. Indeed, one Chicana who is on the outs with the crowd shows a highly significant nasal split at $p < .001$.

These cases all indicate that linguistic features that are associated with ethnicity are linked to local status within the community. But this is not simply ethnic status – the members of the crowd at Steps are not "more Chicano" or even claiming to be "more Chicano" than their non-crowd Chicano peers. (In

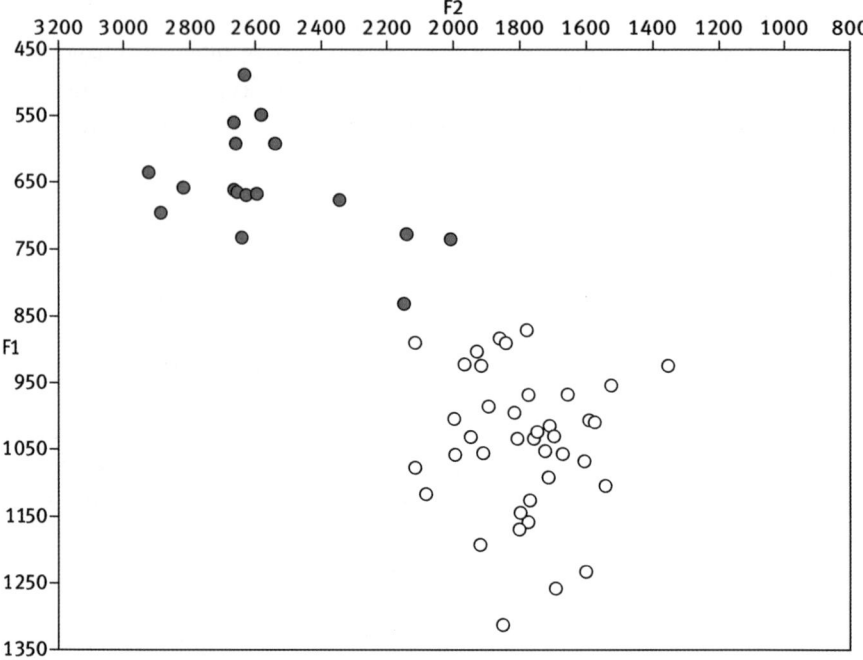

Figure 1: The Fields Pattern: Rachel's TRAP (Black=pre-nasal; White=non-pre-oral)

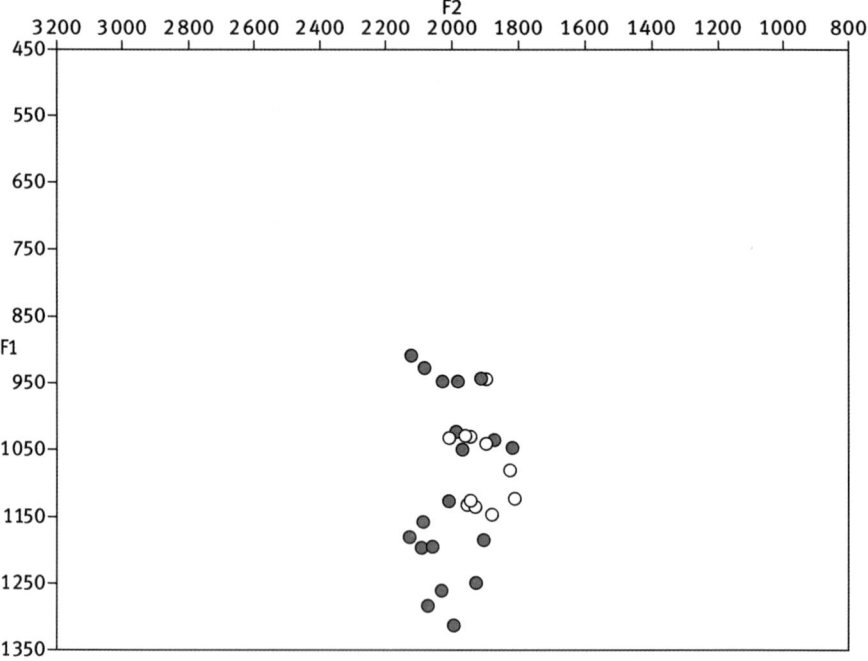

Figure 2: The Steps Pattern: Selena's TRAP (Black = pre-nasal; White = non-pre-oral)

fact, one Asian American member of the crowd who, like the rest of the crowd shows no nasal split, could on occasion be quite militant about her ethnicity). Specifically, in each of these schools, phonological features that distinguish the ethnic community are deployed to index social status within the community. The Asian, African American and Anglo members of the Steps crowd are not using Chicano features to lay claim to status as Chicanos. And the Chicana who is a prominent member of the Fields crowd is not using Anglo features to lay claim to Anglo status. Rather, in each school, locally current features are embraced by those laying claim to central local status. And as the following example suggests, this central status is more specifically a claim to coolness – to being a player in the heterosexual market.

4 Linda and the crowd

Linda was a member of the Steps cohort. She had one Chicano parent, and admired her older Chicano cousins for their coolness. She had marginal status in the crowd at Steps, and while being Chicana was not a requirement for crowd membership, she resented the fact that her ethnic status was always in question. She was not paired up with any boys, and was not considered particularly cool. But things changed at the end of elementary school, when she began to partic-ipate in the heterosexual market beyond her school. One day early in seventh grade, she said I should come with her with my recorder, because she had some-thing she wanted to tell me. Her friends rolled their eyes and said that I definitely had to hear what she had to tell me. As we walked to a quiet place to talk and record, she said she'd gotten into some serious and exciting stuff – she'd been "messing with" guys. And she particularly wanted to tell me how she'd hooked up that weekend with a guy at a quinzeañera (the traditional celebration of a girl's coming of age at her fifteenth birthday). Particularly noticeable in this long narrative was the importance of the audience to her actions. The guy himself, beyond the fact that he was a cholo and "so fine," was not the center of the story – rather, the story was built around the series of events that drew others' atten-tion to the fact that she was sexually engaged. She took on a completely differ-ent persona in this narrative – a "player", in stark contrast to the marginalized member of her sixth grade crowd. Her speech suddenly showed a broad range of Chicano features, and sounded radically different from her speech on other recent occasions. Figure 3 compares her pronunciation of the TRAP vowel in this conversation (black circles) with her pronunciation of the same vowel in a con-versation a few months earlier (empty circles), when she was still in sixth grade. As this figure shows, her pronunciation of this vowel shows a dramatic difference

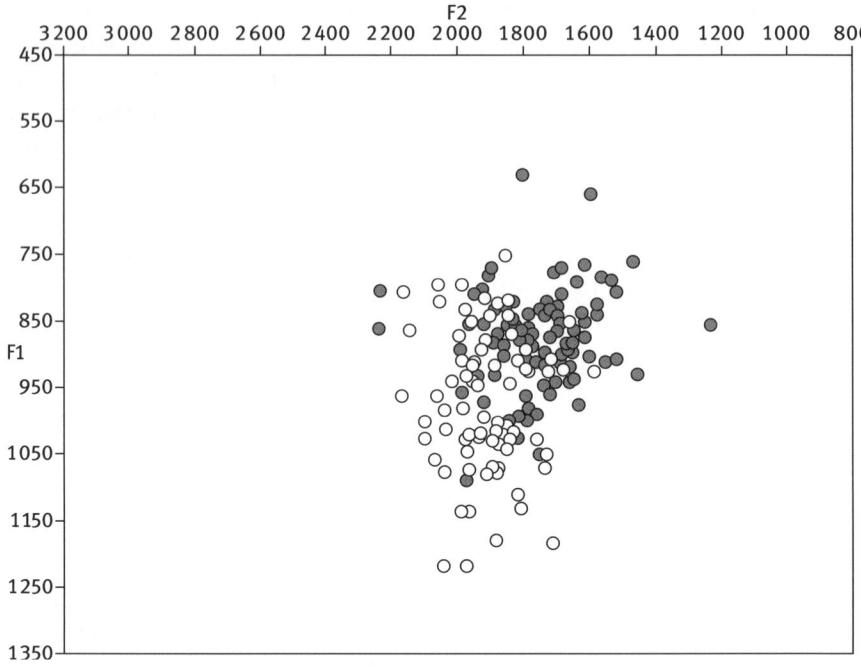

Figure 3: Linda's TRAP in Sixth (white) and Seventh (black) Grades

between these two events, with her "player" pronunciation both farther back (p < .001) and higher (p < .001) than in sixth grade.

While Linda's speech conformed more to the Chicano pattern while telling of this adventure, and while the events took place in a saliently Chicano context, the persona she is presenting is not laying claim to Chicana ethnicity so much as "player" status. One might be tempted to say that Linda became "more Chicana" between sixth and seventh grade. But if she wanted to be accepted as Chicana, it was for the sake of being a "player" in a Chicano-defined social market. In this case, she was no more Chicana than the Chicanas who were on the outs with the crowd in her elementary school. Indeed, she was not interested in a non-cool Chicana identity, and one might say that Chicano authenticity had no use to her if it was not the way to be cool.

5 Conclusions

In her actions at the quinzeañera, and in recounting the narrative to me, Linda was making an authenticative move. But she was not simply claiming authentic status in the category that "owns" the dialect features she was using. Or to the extent that she was making a claim to Chicana status, she was also making a claim to a particular Chicana persona – a "player". In doing so, she contributed to the indexical field that highlights this persona as part of the definition of *Chicano*.

We miss the relation between linguistic and social practice if we focus on demographic categories. Indeed, there is a statistically significant relation between ethnicity and one's use of linguistic variables such as the nasal pattern, but a focus on such correlations leads to a kind of essentialism that associates dialects passively with birthright. The Chicanos at Steps Elementary who show the nasal pattern are no less Chicano than those who do not. One could not reasonably say that they have become more "mainstream" than their peers in the crowd, or even that they have more Anglo friends. Rather, they are not engaged in the indexical work that associates Chicano features with coolness – perhaps, indeed, they associate these features with completely different traits and practices. Nor can you say that kids at Fields are claiming Anglo-ness when they front their back vowels or raise TRAP before nasals. They are, however, claiming aspects of the privilege that comes with their ethnicity. It is this indexical fluidity that makes variation a robust system for the construction of social meaning, and that gives variables an indexical field rather than "a meaning". The history of the study of variation has connected the notion of authenticity to invariant social meaning based on supposedly enduring census categories. But if census categories endure, they also vary across social space, and they change over time. And authenticity is always a claim – whether a claim made by the researcher who assigns speakers to analytic categories, or a claim made by speakers as they define, and orient to, their own categories. The speaker's claim expresses desire, and is transformative both of the speaker and of the category on the basis of which he or she claims authenticity.

References

Bailey, Guy & Natalie Maynor 1987: Decreolization? *Language in Society* 16: 449–473.
Bourdieu, Pierre & Luc Boltanski 1975: Le fétichisme de la langue. *Actes de la recherche en sciences sociales*, 2–32.
Bucholtz, Mary 1999: You da man: Narrating the racial other in the production of white masculinity. *Journal of Sociolinguistics* 3: 443–460.
Bucholtz, Mary 2011: *White Kids: Language, Race, and Styles of Youth Identity*. Cambridge/New York: Cambridge University Press.
Bucholtz, Mary & Kira Hall 2004: Theorizing identity in language and sexuality research. *Language in Society* 33: 469–515.
Bucholtz, Mary & Kira Hall 2005: Identity and interaction: a sociocultural linguistic approach. *Discourse Studies* 7: 585–614.

Eckert, Penelope 2008: Variation and the indexical field. *Journal of Sociolinguistics* 12: 453–476.

Eckert, Penelope 2011: Language and power in the heterosexual market. *American Speech* 86.

Eckert, Penelope 2012: Three waves of variation study: The emergence of meaning in the study of variation. *Annual Review of Anthropology* 41: 87–100.

Fought, Carmen 1999: A majority sound change in a minority community /u/-fronting in Chicano English. *Journal of Sociolinguistics* 3: 5–23.

Hodder, Ian 1982 *The Present Past*. London: Batsford.

Kiesling, Scott F 2004 Dude. *American Speech* 79: 281–305.

Kiesling, Scott 2005: Variation, stance and style. *English World-Wide* 26: 1–42.

Kiesling, Scott 2009: Style as stance: Can stance be the primary explanation for patterns of sociolinguistic variation? In Alexandra Jaffe *(ed.) Sociolinguistic Perspectives on Stance*, 171–94. Oxford: Oxford University Press.

Kroch, Anthony S. 1978: Toward a theory of social dialect variation. *Language in Society* 7: 17–36.

Labov, William 1963: The social motivation of a sound change. *Word* 18: 1–42.

Labov, W. 1966: *The Social Stratification of English in New York City*. Washington, DC: Center for Applied Linguistics.

Labov, William 1972: The logic of nonstandard English. In William Labov (ed.) *Language in the Inner City*, 201–240. Philadelphia: University of Pennsylvania Press.

Labov, William & Wendell Harris 1986: De facto segregation of black and white vernaculars. In David Sankoff *(ed.) Diversity and Diachrony*, 1–24. Amsterdam/Philadelphia: John Benjamins.

Podesva, Robert 2004: On constructing social meaning with stop release bursts. Paper presented at Sociolinguistics Symposium 15. Newcastle upon Tyne.

Silverstein, Michael 2003: Indexical order and the dialectics of sociolinguistic life. *Language and Communication* 23: 193–229.

Wells, J.C. 1982: *Accents of English 3: Beyond the British Isles*. Cambridge: Cambridge University Press.

Wolfram, Walt & Natalie Schilling-Estes 1998: *American English*. Malden/Oxford: Blackwell.

Lauren Hall-Lew
Chinese social practice and San Franciscan authenticity[1]

1 The Chineseness of San Francisco

This chapter explores the possibility that Chinese social and linguistic practices are available resources for place authentication in contemporary San Francisco. The analysis draws on ethnographic observation and a content analysis of retrospective narratives about youth styles in neighborhood schools in the 1990s. The emergence of new indexes of place authenticity is seen as a result of the transnationalization of San Francisco and the emergence of neighborhoods known as New Chinatowns (Laguerre 2005). In contrast to earlier periods of American history, these neighborhoods have become sites of new hybridities and the local authentication of what were previously the most exotic and foreign of social practices.

As one of the first neighborhoods ever established in the city, San Francisco's Chinatown might be considered locally authentic by virtue of its clear *historicity* (Coupland 2003: 418). But as a segregated ethnic enclave, and as a diasporic beacon for new immigrants, Chinatown's position vis-à-vis mainstream San Franciscan culture has long been marginal, and at times in the past, actively targeted for removal and destruction. Chinatown was the site for the earliest discursive construction of 'Chineseness' as the canonical American Oriental – that which was most exotic, most foreign, and most threatening. In part because of the poor living conditions in Chinatown at the time, the neighborhood was subject to intense stigma. Irish/Chinese relations were especially infamous for being the most antagonistic. While the Irish began to lay claim to early San Franciscan authenticity (Hall-Lew under review), the Chinese were subject to intense marginalization.

The neighborhood's first shift in authenticity came after the 1906 earthquake and fire; buildings were razed and reconstructed with a new vision. In a process of *museumization* (Relph 1976), Chinatown shifted its economic goals to satisfy

1 Earlier versions of this paper has benefited from the thoughtful and generous comments of Graham M. Jones, Laura Staum Casasanto, members of the *Language in Context* research group at the University of Edinburgh, the New York University Linguistics Department, and the Departments of Linguistics, East Asian Languages & Literatures, Asian American Studies, and the Institute for Chinese Studies at The Ohio State University. All remaining faults are, of course, my own.

the tourist gaze, to "suit the taste and imagination of...the American public" (Chen 1952: 89, cited in Light 1974). Residents re-imagined their neighborhood as a space for the consumption of an exotic aesthetic in a comfortable American environment. "Chinatown chambers of commerce began to regulate the architecture on main thoroughfares so that a uniform, pagoda-styled decor replaced ramshackled predecessors" (Light 1974: 391). This "other-directed architecture" (Jackson 1956) and its Oriental aesthetic gained a kind of local authenticity, iconicizing a style known as "San Francisco Chinese" (Sinclair 2004). By the 1950s, San Francisco Chinatown had achieved a new kind of hybrid authenticity: still 'authentically foreign', but firmly situated in the American landscape. In 1957, Herb Caen, a writer for the San Francisco Chronicle, called it the "city's most fascinating and authentic foreign colony" (50). Chinatown's localized exoticism helped construct San Francisco's international reputation as a cosmopolitan urban center. However, as a truly 'San Franciscan' social identity, its scope was still limited; Chinatown residents remained largely confined to working menial jobs and living in over-crowded, substandard housing (Yung 2006). Chinatown's 'San Franciscanness' was merely ornamental.

In the following decades, Chinatown cemented its identity as one of San Francisco's major tourist attractions and culinary hotspots. Meanwhile, local changes in fair housing legislation opened up the rest of San Francisco to upwardly mobile Chinatown residents. This resulted in a dramatic change in the wider cultural and linguistic landscape. In 1957, Herb Caen called this change the 'Hongkongization' of San Francisco (Caen 1957; cited in Ong 1999). By the 1980s, some formerly European (American) neighborhoods came to be seen as 'New Chinatowns'.

> The appellation "New Chinatown" is multi-vocal, as it carries diverse meanings depending on the interpretive actor or analyst. It is projected by Asian Americans as a non-ghettoized enclave since Chinese immigrants can live wherever they want in the city and since it is a mixed neighborhood of white and non-white residents; it is identified by Anglo Americans as a Chinese business district and middle class residential quarter; and it is seen by tourists simply as an exotic immigrant enclave outside its presumed natural niche. The adjective "New" is used in contrast to "Old", because it invokes the free choice that immigrants have to settle in this community, the location of the enclave outside of the downtown area, the on-going interaction with the homeland for communicational familial, religious, and business purposes, and above all, its status as a microcosm of the Old Chinatown and the homeland. (Laguerre 2005: 41)

Despite a Chinese plurality, the New Chinatown is a multiethnic, transnational, "global neighborhood" (Laguerre 2005: 42); gone are the days of segregated ethnic enclaves. At the same time, 'Chinese identity' in San Francisco became more complex, multidimensional, and diverse. Crucially, it also became less exotic. Ang (2001: 8), describing her visit to San Francisco in the mid-1980s, notes how "San Francisco has long had a large and highly visible Chinese-American population, so being Asian was nothing exceptional." Despite this growth and diversification of the Chinese heritage community, 'Old' Chinatown remained associated with first-generation immigrants, perpetuating views of the neighborhood as inherently 'foreign'. Despite the indexical relationship (Silverstein 2003) between 'Chineseness' and 'San Franciscanness' evident in tourist encounters (for example), and despite the neighborhood's legitimate historical claims to San Franciscan authenticity, Old Chinatown is still arguably viewed as Caen's "foreign colony," where residents are still positioned as the "forever foreigner" (Tuan 1998). Ironically, then, it is in the New Chinatown neighborhoods where Chinese social practice has come to index local authenticity.

I argue in this paper that these neighborhoods have been witness to a major shift away from exoticism and stigma and towards normalcy and even prestige. In arguing that Chinese cultural and linguistic practices have become an integral, 'typical' part of San Franciscan life, I also argue that they are increasingly available as resources for local authentication (Bucholtz & Hall 2005). 'Chineseness' has undergone a shift of indexical valence, from 'authentically foreign' to 'authentically San Franciscan', and the recency and rapidity of this change complicates how young people, in particular, construct a San Franciscan identity. Non-Chinese adolescents are increasingly orienting to formerly 'Chinese' social practices; this alone is evidence of a radical shift away from a long history of stigma against Chinese in North America. The New Chinatown context means that young white San Franciscans confront the challenges of cultural hybridity in a manner comparable to that described elsewhere for Asian Americans (Lowe 1996; Ang 2001; Louie 2006).

However, while such practices are gaining place-based meanings, they are not shedding their ethnic meanings, and as such, processes of authentication and denaturalization are highly complex. For adolescents of Chinese heritage, while these symbolic resources may allow greater access to constructing a local identity, the interaction between multiple orders of indexicality (Silverstein 2003) can also lead to ambivalence or even rejection of those very same Chinese practices that are gaining currency among non-Chinese. Optimistically, the rise in prestige of the New Chinatown symbolic market seems to offer an American context where Chinese are neither "forever foreign" nor "honorary white" (Tuan 1998). However, while white San Franciscans can begin to draw on Chinese practices to construct a cosmopolitan, transnational-yet-local identity, Chinese San Franciscans are restricted full access to these higher orders of indexicality precisely because of the constraints of their ethnic and racial identity.

This study is part of a larger exploration of linguistic variation in a New Chinatown neighborhood (Hall-Lew 2009). The analysis is based on interviews and participant observation in public spaces and private homes in San Francisco's Sunset District. Here, I focus on narratives of reminiscence produced by a small subset of Sunset District public (state) who attended the interviewees schools in the 1990s. Schools are microcosmic sites of community shift, and an individual student's experiences shape their particular subjectivity with respect to community identity. Through content analysis of these ethnographic interviews, I focus on how young white women[2] and young Chinese American women[3] experienced the rise of the New Chinatown landscape, in different ways. Descriptively, these narratives demonstrate the consequences of major social change at the individual level. Analytically, they point to the emergence of a higher indexical order for Chinese social and linguistic practice, from ethnic meanings to local, place-based meanings.

2 A San Franciscan neighborhood

All of the San Franciscans quoted here were raised in the Sunset District. The neighborhood is known throughout the city for having a particularly high proportion of Chinese[4] residents, even relative to an already large proportion across the city in general. In 2008, when asked how the Sunset District "had changed over the years," the most frequent answer was that it had become more Chinese (1). When asked about what the neighborhood was 'known for', one of the first things that San Franciscans mentioned was the large Chinese (or Asian[5]) population (2); residents interviewed in 2012 confirmed this same impression (3).

---

2 The community term is either 'white' or 'Caucasian'.

3 The community term is usually 'Asian' (or sometimes 'Chinese').

4 'Chinese' and 'Chineseness' are, of course, essentializations. Sunset residents of 'Chinese' heritage are distinguished by "very different and largely unconnected histories" (Ang 2001: 91). However, unlike Ang's depiction of 'Chinese' in Australia, those differences are not cited in San Franciscan discourses nearly as often as homogenizing references to 'Chinese' culture, people, and language.

5 'Asian' is a complex referring term in relation to 'Chinese'. By US Census figures, San Francisco's 'Asian' population is over 65% Chinese; Filipinos constitute less than 14% of that population, and all other groups less than 5% each. The clear majority of Chinese ethnicity means that terms 'Chinese' and 'Asian' are used nearly interchangeably, even to the extent that San Franciscans will, for example, talk about "whites, Asians, and Filipinos," discursively placing Filipinos outside of the category 'Asian'. The indexical shifts discussed here have different consequences for non-Chinese Asians, and will likely be widely variable depending on factors such as specific national and ethnic identification.

(1) Sal[6] (b. 1963, male, Chinese American)
  LHL:How's it changed?
  Sal: How has it changed? Um, I mean, definitely a lot more Chinese.

(2) Monica (b. 1992, female, Chinese American)
  LHL: What do you think the Sunset's known for?
  Monica: … Definitely for being safe, um, ((and)) for having a lot of Asian people! [laughter]

(3) Marina (b 1997, female, white)
  Marina: The Sunset District is definitely very, a very Asian district. … Definitely my neighborhood ((has)) lots of Chinese stores.

In San Francisco's Sunset District, the term 'New Chinatown' is most often applied to the neighborhood's commercial corridors (Figure 1). Chinese language business signs indicate a cultural dominance over the local economy and suggest the regular use of spoken Chinese in public interactions (Landry & Bourhis 1997). Bilingual signs on libraries, churches (Figure 2), and other community spaces add to the perception of a linguistic landscape that is predominantly Chinese. The New Chinatown label is then discursively extended to encompass the neighborhood as a whole, which is largely residential.

The Sunset District became a New Chinatown around the 1980s. Chinese settlement in the Sunset District was initially led by native San Franciscans moving out of the Chinatown area, "to mark their middle class status and to take advantage of the amenities that could be found there and not in the Old Chinatown" (Laguerre 2005: 45). This 2008 comment (4) confirms this:

(4) Cindy (b. 1966, female, Chinese/Singaporean American)
  Cindy: The friends that we hung out with who had lived close to Chinatown moved out to the Sunset District. So it's like if you could get out of Chinatown, you were in the Sunset District if you could afford a place.

New Sunset District residents have also arrived directly from Asia, part of larger immigration trends stemming from a wide range of national and international factors such as the Immigration Reform Act in 1965, the Vietnam War, and Hong Kong's reunification with China, among many others (Fong 2008).[7] For over a decade, the contemporary ethnic demographics of the Sunset District have been, on average, just over 50% Asian and just under 40% non-Hispanic white,[8] and a majority of those Asian residents speak a LOTE (Language Other Than English) at home.

---

6 All names given here are pseudonyms.
7 Note how the socioeconomic differences between immigration motivations foster the existing class distinctions between New Chinatowns and the old Chinatown (Ong 1999; Laguerre 2005).
8 More sociohistorical details about the Sunset District are given in Hall-Lew (2009; 2010).

Figure 1: Noriega St., one of the Sunset District's commercial streets

Figure 2: The Sunset Church, a bilingual church in the neighborhood

The Sunset District's schools, particularly the public (state) schools, are also associated with Chinese ethnicity. For example, the two large public high schools, Lincoln High School and Lowell High School, have large student bodies and are both predominantly Chinese American. Lincoln is the most requested public high school in San Francisco (Blackstone, p. c.); it is centrally located in the Sunset District and has a particularly high proportion of neighborhood students. Lowell requires a high academic standard for entry and is nationally famous for its long legacy of academic excellence. This academic prestige is further associated with its large Chinese American population, a powerful instantiation of the 'model minority' stereotype which precipitated a 1983 court case in which the San Francisco Unified School District succeeded in establishing race-based criteria to limit Chinese Americans' entrance to Lowell. Although these criteria were in effect until 2005, Lowell nonetheless remained majority Chinese throughout the period. In 2008–2009, 53 % of the student body was Chinese, and no other single ethnicity represented more than 15 %.

Explicit hostility toward this rapid demographic shift was readily apparent in the 1980s and into the 1990s. The following quote comes from a sociolinguistic interview conducted by Birch Moonwomon in the Sunset District in 1991:

"There's just too many Orientals. … Cause they own everything, and they're taking over San Francisco. I mean, you may as well call it China, the amount that – that are here. [ ] I mean my dad said that when he was a child, there were … twenty kids on the block to play with, just on your block. And now, you don't see kids playing in the streets, for one thing. And, if you do, they're always Chinese and every house on the block you might see um [one] Caucasian family, per block. And they own everything. They get money from the government. They live … twenty million people in one house so they can all save up money and buy another house. I mean, it, it amazed me the amount of Oriental people. I mean, it's terrible to be racist but it amazes me on the amount of Oriental people that will, um … have brand new Mercedes, brand new BMWs … and you wonder how they get that money. I mean, and not even speak English (laugh). That's what gets me, they should be able to, they should speak English if they're in our country." (22-year-old working class female; Moonwomon 1992: 423)

Sentiments such as these that so clearly expressed a stigmatization of Chinese residents were very hard to come by in 2008[9]. In less than two decades, Chinese bilingualism, or even Chinese monolingualism, had come to be perceived as a 'normal' part of the linguistic landscape a defining feature of the neighborhood. One day during my fieldwork in the spring of 2008 I was introduced to a middle-aged white woman who had grown up in the Sunset District neighborhood. The friend introducing us said that I was conducting a research project in linguistics and that I was "looking for accents in the Sunset." To this, the woman replied: "Oh! It must be either Cantonese or Toisanese, right?" She went on to explain that she was a local kung fu teacher, and that her students' language use "has certainly affected my speech!" My interlocutor's reaction suggested that

---

9 Moonwomon is not of Chinese heritage, whereas I am of mixed Chinese and European heritage. While this may have influenced this finding, most interviewees expressed surprise at the end of their interview when they learned of my Chinese background.

Chinese ethnicity and Chinese language use were so strongly associated with the neighborhood that the concept of 'accentedness' did not refer to variation in English, but to variation in Chinese (or, perhaps, varieties of English influenced by specific varieties of Chinese). For her, Chinese linguistic practices had become an index of resident identity in the Sunset District. Her comment that her own speech has been "affected" by her students' suggests local linguistic accommodation toward this new linguistic landscape.

The increased valuation of 'speaking Chinese' is the clearest example of changes in linguistic capital in San Francisco, California. Elsewhere, I consider how features of Chinese-influenced English, particularly L-vocalization, may be increasingly available resources, as well (see Hall-Lew & Starr 2010; Hall-Lew & Fix 2012). In addition to these examples, the following analysis examines changes in the circulation and use of a single lexical item from Asian American discourse: *FOB*.

3 *Fob* style in the Sunset District

In the 1990s,[10] a new style emerged in neighborhood's public schools that reimagined the symbolic value of Chinese immigrant and transnational identities: the *FOB* style. Since my fieldwork was in 2008, and in people's homes rather than their schools, what follows is not a complete account of this style, but rather an exploration of differing subjective reminiscences towards it. Here, I focus on how *FOBbiness* is framed by second-generation Chinese American adults, in contrast to how it is framed by adults of European heritage. The original term, *FOB*, is an acronym for *Fresh Off the Boat*, referring to recently arrived migrants. For much of its life, *FOB* has been a highly loaded and contested in-group slur, "widely used in Asian diasporas, especially in the context of post-1965 Asian migration, to differentiate new arrivals from those who have learned requisite cultural and linguistic codes" (Shankar 2008:270). The use described here, however, does not seem to (primarily) signify recency of arrival. Furthermore, there also appears to be some use, or at least awareness of its use, among San Franciscans of non-Asian heritage. On the one hand, the retrospective comments by the Chinese Americans quoted here highlight complex shifts in second-generation identities over time, as individuals experience new life stages with differing valuations of ethnic identity. On the other hand, one non-Asian perspective offers additional, but starkly different, evidence for the valuation of FOB identity, one that is clearly positive. And while this amelioration of FOB

---

10 Or perhaps earlier; the data are limited.

identity among non-Asian adolescents is strong evidence that Chinese cultural practices are increasingly available for local authentication, the perseverance of ethnic indexicality limits access to that local value for those same adolescents. I suggest that both are consequences of the rise of New Chinatowns and the subsequent changes in the local semiotic space.

Previous studies on *FOB* style have focused almost exclusively on representations of *FOB* in youth discourses, showing how "FOB is commonly used by second-generation Asian American youth to distance themselves from the perceived negative attributes of first-generation or 1.5 generation youth" (Shankar 2008: 270). Jeon (2001) discusses how American-born students in a Korean-English dual-immersion program resist speaking Korean because doing so indexes the undesirable *FOB* label. The clearest example of *FOB* as an in-group slur comes from Talmy's (2004) analysis of an ESL classroom in Hawai'i, where "ESL students ... particularly the long-term US-resident, or 'generation 1.5' students ... derisively referred to this Other as 'FOB' – 'fresh off the boat' – a noxious label signifying a recently-arrived, monumentally uncool, non-English-speaking rube of mythical, and for some, hilarious proportions" (Talmy 2004:150). In short, most previous work shows that *FOB* is a stigmatizing, Other-directed term that indexes recent immigrant status.

One exception to this is an analysis of *FOB* identity among South Asian youth in San Jose, California (Shankar 2008, 2011). Here, *FOB* is found to not index immigrant status directly: "FOBby teens were not the new arrivals for whom the term FOB is usually reserved. They nonetheless earned this label from populars and other youth who thought that they performed linguistic and cultural attributes of speech, dress, and self-presentation linked to newly arrived immigrants. Youth who displayed FOBby styles made ample use of the attributes populars avoided, including gangsta elements and a preference for appearing and sounding tough" (Shankar 2011: 650).

Like the South Asian youth analyzed by Shankar (2008, 2011), Chinese (American) youth in San Francisco's Sunset District in the 1990s also appear to have used *FOB* to refer not to immigrant status primarily, but rather to a particular, hybridized youth style, only indirectly related to immigrant identity, if at all. Relatedly, the term was not necessarily used as a pejorative slur. In fact, unlike the case described by Shankar (2011), the narratives analyzed here suggest that the Sunset District's *FOB* style gained circulation beyond Asian diasporas as a coveted, "cool" identity. While Shankar (2011) discusses a local contrast between the *FOB* style and the "popular" style, the prestige of the *FOB* style in San Francisco calls this dichotomy into question. Furthermore, the fact that this prestige is most evident among residents of non-Asian heritage means that its circulation is limited in interesting ways.

In fact, I first learned of the *FOB* style while interviewing Aubrey, a white woman born in 1951 whose children had gone through the local schools in the 1990s. In (5), Aubrey refers to a friendship group that her daughter, Mary, had had in middle school.

(5)   Aubrey (b. 1950, female, European [white] American)
      Aubrey: And there's, what is it, 'fresh off the boat'? That's what ((Mary)) would say. Some of
      her friends changed their clothing habits to look as though they were 'fresh off the boats'. ...
      They're Asian American, but they changed to – they changed their language and their
      clothing in order to associate with the new Asian community.

In (5), Aubrey recounts the existence of a particular adolescent group, members of which were American-born, of Asian descent, and self-styling towards a "fresh off the boat" or "new Asian" aesthetic and away from (presumably) 'American' "language and clothing." The fact that this report came from someone outside the relevant social group with respect to both age and ethnicity speaks to the salience of a *FOB* style beyond the beyond the middle school limited market middle school market, itself. In a separate interview in 2008, as Mary is describing the various social groups that were part of her middle school experience, she also mentions the existence of this 'new Asian' style:

(6)   Mary (b. 1979, female, Irish American)
      Mary: ... you know, and there's – um, there – there's a lot more. Like, 'fresh off the boat',
      kind of, you know there's like the 'Russian posse', and there's the – everything, you know,
      there's all kinds of things. And there was a –, the *FOBs*, when I was there, um, which was
      the reappropriation of 'Fresh Off the Boat' and was 'Fresh Oriental Boyz'.

What Aubrey meant in saying that "they changed their language and their clothing," is still unclear; Mary's description here does not elaborate on the elements of the style itself. But what is interesting about her quote in (6) is the act of reappropriation she describes. Not only did this particular social group ameliorate the value of *FOB*, but they reacronymized it, in effect reappropriating the elements within. The first element plays on the polysemy of *fresh*, playing down connotations of immigration status and playing up connotations of hip-hop culture (Brathwaite 1992; Labov 1992). The second element reappropriates the use of *Oriental* from explicitly racist discourses such as those documented by Moonwomon (1992). Note that the 1990s also mark the period of transition both in San Francisco and across the United States, in general, away from the use of the term *Oriental* to the more prevalent term *Asian* refer to Chinese Americans. Lastly, the third element in *FOB* is the change from 'boat', indexing immigrant status, to 'boyz', indexing youth and gender. Given the nature of the data, the spelling of 'boyz' by members of this particular social group is, of course, entirely unknown, but the non-standard 'z' is used here because it is categorically used in circulation of the same acronym on internet.[11] If we take the rendering of standard 's' as 'z' to index orientations to hip-hop culture (Smitherman 2006), this may provide some insight into the stylistic composition of the Sunset District *FOB* style.

These two quotes from Aubrey and Mary were two of the four mentions of *FOB* in my 2008 interviews. The other two (spoken by a middle-aged Filipino American man and a young Chinese American man) used *FOB* in its original sense, to refer in an unambiguously pejorative way to recently arrived immigrants. In wondering how the use of *FOB* related to the rise of New Chinatowns in San Francisco, in 2012 I conducted ten follow-up interviews that investigated Sunset residents' awareness of a *FOB* style. Of the ten interviewees, only Mary was specifically familiar with the 'fresh oriental boyz' reacronymization, and no one older than Mary was familiar with *FOB* as a youth style. However, those who were younger than Mary, and Chinese American, recalled using the term '*FOBby*' to describe a salient middle/high school style. In fact Vicky, in (7), used the term spontaneously to describe the social distinction between the students at her former high school, Lowell, and the students at the other neighborhood school, Lincoln.

(7) Vicky (b. 1986, female, Chinese American)
   LHL: When you were at Lowell, what did people think about Lincoln?
   Vicky: I mean, I think people just thought, oh, it's just the local, like, Sunset school, lots of Asian people, and the kind of Asian people who are more *FOBby*? I guess? [laughter] I don't know. [laughter] Yeah.

In (7), Vicky invokes *FOBby* as the most immediately available descriptor for "the kind of Asian people" who attended "the local Sunset school." *FOBby* functions as an enregistered (Agha 2003) resource for indexing the ideological associations between ethnic identity, neighborhood identity, and certain orientations to immigrant identities. However, it does not denote immigrant identity directly; while ethnicity and place are specifically mentioned here, the "fresh off the boat" meaning is not made explicit. Indeed, as shown in (8) and (9), these young Chinese Americans from the Sunset District appear to not use *FOBby* to refer, primarily, to recent immigrants.

(8) JoJo (b. 1982, female, Chinese American)
   JoJo: Um, and I understand that the term is 'fresh off the boat' [laugh], and they're not fresh off the boat but it's a very, um, it's a very. Asian. Thing. To do, to cut your hair like that. And so I guess associating that with being Asian, and associating Asian with being a *FOB* [laughter].

---

11 E. g., http://www.myspace.com/freshorientalboyz; http://www.myspace.com/fobzdancecrew

LHL: So these were people that were born in California?
JoJo: I'm assuming, yeah.
...
LHL: So what about people who are immigrants. Are they also *FOBby*?
JoJo: I don't know that I ever use that term for recent immigrants. I mean you can, sometimes you can obviously tell, someone who has arrived recently, but I don't think I'd necessarily associate the term, *FOB*, with them.

JoJo's description suggests that *FOB* style primarily indexes ethnicity; indeed, it may not index immigrant status at all. It is possible that this newer meaning of *FOB* is only possible by virtue of a reassignment in reference value, from 'recent immigrant' to 'Asian style'. However, the latter nonetheless emerges from the former, and the interrelationship is surely complex. If the formation of *FOB* style here is at all similar to that described by Shankar (2008) among South Asian adolescents in the south San Francisco Bay Area, then this is a style that pulls from a wide range of ethnic and Californian linguistic and aesthetic elements. Elements of young Asian immigrant styles are picked up and reinterpreted, situated in the New Chinatown context and restyled locally, simultaneously becoming available for consumption and participation by American-born Chinese adolescents. Vicky elaborates on this in (9),

(9) Vicky (b. 1986, female, Chinese American)
Vicky: And, um, they don't necessarily have to be literally 'fresh off the boat'. I mean, I think there's some who are literally fresh off the boat and then speak whatever language that they were- that's their native tongue, and others are ABCs or American Born Chinese kids who just happen to dress really *FOBby*. [laughter]

In (9), Vicky echoes JoJo's formulation that the identifying factor in the *FOB* group membership was Chinese ethnicity, which was shared, rather than immigrant status, or language use, which were not. Furthermore, her description of the Chinese American participation as "kids who just happen to dress really *FOBby*" highlights not only the (unsurprisingly) central role of physical presentation, but furthermore the status of *FOB* as an aesthetic style on par with other aesthetic styles, which she elaborates on in (10).

(10) Vicky (b. 1986, female, Chinese American)
LHL: So how would you describe what it referred to?
Vicky: I think it's a look, just like when you think about *hipsters*? That image immediately flashes in your mind of somebody in plaid, and skinny jeans and the messed up disheveled hair, and they talk about very, like, esoteric things and, like, you know, kind of- music that's very indie. I think it's a certain look, aesthetic? And I think, for *FOBs*, I used to think of it as, um, somebody really dyed; hair. [laughter] Um, [pause] dressed in black, lot of black, with a souped up car. ... Just like other cliques, people talk about the *skater group* in high school. ..

I think there always is, just, like, a *FOB* group, and you find your way into it and then you end up dressing or being like that.

In (10), Vicky positions *FOB* as a style of the same semiotic status as other well-known styles, in that it's "a look, just like" *hipster* and *skater*. Her further comment that "there always is, just, like, a *FOB* group" again highlights the New Chinatown experience and the possible completion of a shift towards Chinese or 'Asian' styles being viewed as unmarked or 'typical'.

Note also that the similarity in the sartorial features mentioned for the components of *FOB* style, across unacquainted Chinese American interviewees, is striking. For example, compare JoJo's description in (11) to Vicky's in (10).

(11) JoJo   (b. 1982, female, Chinese American)
    JoJo: Back in high school, middle school, I just remember the boys had all these bangs, like, hang((ing)) in front and we always associated that with being *FOBby*.
    LHL: Anything else besides the hair?
    JoJo: Oh, well, the dyed hair, the brown streaks? ... Actually this was not too long ago when I think my friend wanted to dye her hair or streak her hair just have some highlights, and she was like "I just hope that it doesn't come out *FOBby*!" Cuz we just remember the days, back in the days when you, girls, even guys, would have this huge this huge brown streaks down their hair, um, and we associate that with being *FOBby*. Um, I also remember ... Souped up cars, low riders.

In (11) JoJo enacts a moment of reported speech "not too long ago" that suggests that *FOBby* is not a desired quality. So, although *FOB* was a youth style on par with other youth styles, it does not have high symbolic value for her. Although in (12) she describes a context in which its use might be relatively more positive, in (13) Vicky is quite clear that the *FOBby* style is not and never has been an attractive one for her.

(12) JoJo (b. 1982, female, Chinese American)
    LHL: So how insulting would it be if somebody said you were *FOBby*?
    JoJo: Well it really depends, when you're in high school it's almost like you don't want to associate with being *FOBby*, but as you transition through, at least for me when I transitioned to college, there's more more- it's almost like I want to be associated more with my Asian culture. ... So if someone called me *FOBby* in college I'm like, "Great! I'm doing something right!" you know? [laughter] I'll take it as a positive compliment almost. [laughter]

(13) Vicky (b. 1986, female, Chinese American)
    LHL: That's actually- that concept is something that I really want to talk to people about, so, um-
    Vicky: Of, like, *FOBbiness*? Really?

LHL: Yeah, like, do you still use that term? Or when's the last time, like is that still- I mean, what do you associate that with?
Vicky: I think I don't talk about that anymore cuz it's just not part of my life anymore? I think you kind of grow out of it. But I do remember talking about it when I was like immersed in it. I wasn't immersed in *FOBbiness* itself, [laughter] But- yeah. I kind of thought of it as "eeuh" [::shudder::]. But I do remember talking about it, say, in middle school and high school.
...
LHL: But clearly for you it was not an attractive-
Vicky: No. [laughter]

Even JoJo's hypothetical context for a 'positive' interpretation of *FOBby* is hedged: "a positive compliment almost." What's more, her retrospective description of high school valuation is clearly negative, but again hedged, "it's almost like you don't want to associate with being *FOBby*." Her conflicted attitudes appear to stem from her representation of *FOBbiness* as a locus of ethnic authenticity, and variability in her attitude towards her own ethnic identity. She rationalizes this variability by representing it as a contrast between two life stages, high school and college, and the differing political economies of each (see Erikson 1968). Because of the direct association with ethnicity identity, *FOB* becomes an available frame of identification. For Vicky, however, the value of *FOBbiness* is almost viscerally negative, remaining specifically associated with marginalized adolescent styles (e.g., Talmy 2004). Between these two second-generation Chinese Americans, then, perspectives vary; the *FOB* identity is met with some ambivalence in one case and aversion in the other.

One additional observation about the use of *FOB* among contemporary Chinese Americans in San Francisco is that, generally speaking, there seems to be a general reluctance to talk about the term. The frequent laughter in Vicky's and JoJo's quotes may serve as a contextualization cue (Gumperz 1982) to this reluctance. *FOB* may be an example of Herzfeld's (2005: 3) "cultural intimacy": "the recognition of those aspects of a cultural identity that are considered a source of external embarrassment but that nevertheless provide insiders with their assurance of common sociality." This is especially the case when *FOB* is used to refer not to adolescents but to the traditional referent, the elderly immigrant. For example, in the case of the website "My Mom is a Fob",[12] the use is similar to a term of endearment. The co-occurring and contrasting possibilities of reference make the use of the term *FOB* additionally complex.

In short, Chinese American orientations to *FOB* style are diverse. Given the social landscape of the Sunset District's public schools, where some Chinese

---

12 http://mymomisafob.com/

American adolescents were members of the *FOB* group while others (probably most) were not, this diversity of orientation is hardly surprising. Both Vicky's and JoJo's opinions reflect their positionality as hybrid subjects (Lowe 1996; Ang 2001) whose adolescent years entailed navigating the local, rapidly changing shifts in local symbolic value. So, while JoJo's differing valuation of *FOB* as an adult versus as an adolescent may be due to the difference between social distinction and ethnic identity in high school versus college, it may also be aided by changes in the value of Chinese practices across the Sunset District.

Their experience is particularly striking in contrast with an experience like Mary's, a fifth-generation Irish American San Franciscan, whose perspective was that the *FOB* style was an unambiguous carrier of positive symbolic value within the adolescent heterosexual market; that it was the style of "the crowd" (Eckert 2008; this volume). According to Mary, the experience of a frustrated adolescence marked by an unachievable *FOB* aesthetic is an experience that today unites some middle-aged white San Franciscans, at least those who grew up in the New Chinatowns of the Richmond or the Sunset Districts. Mary describes this in her 2012 interview:

(14) Mary (b. 1979, female, Irish American)
Mary: You know, I talk a lot with the other woman who leads my team, she grew up in the Richmond, she came from Russia when she was five, we talk a lot about … ((How)) we both, like in middle school, wanted to be five-foot-tall Asian girls who could dance and like write in bubbly letters [laughter]. There's like this distinct 'girl' who's like part of this group who had like the perfect high bangs and like all of these things that just didn't work, um-
LHL: So this is a [type of] girl who hung out with the 'Fresh-'
Mary: Yes, '((unintelligible)) Oriental Boyz,' the girl version. Um, and they all had Hello Kitty stuff and had really cute writing and [laughter] like glittery pencils and like stuff like that [laughter]. You know, the middle school cool stuff.
LHL: Would you call those girls 'FOBby'?
Mary: Um- it was really- I mean for my experience of it, it was a self-reflective [sic.] term. So it wasn't- it was basically like, "Oh, they're gonna be going out with the *FOBs*."

Mary describes the female *FOB* style with none of the same features mentioned by JoJo and Vicky, and she goes into much greater detail, citing dance, penmanship, and evidence of conspicuous consumption. Her greater attention to stylistic detail, in addition to her expression of "wanting to be" part of this group, reflects a much stronger valuation as "cool" of the *FOB* style for Mary than was seen for the Chinese Americans.

Not only was *FOB* style clearly valued and yet unattainable for Mary, the term *FOB* itself was not even available for her to use, except (it seems) in reference to the name of the group. The adjectival form *FOBby*, which was the most commonly used form in JoJo's and Vicky's interviews, seems to be off-limits to Mary. Unlike mainstream processes of cultural appropriation of Asian commodities by white, middle-class Americans, the market value of the *FOB* aesthetic appears to have been produced by Asian(-American)s themselves, within a local economy, and desired by, but unavailable to, non-Asians. This production of symbolic capital marks a crucial turning point where Chinese and other Asian (American) social practices begin to index local belonging. Furthermore, as Asian practices acquire place-based meanings, older indexes of authenticity begin to index that past era, rather than local belonging. They come to construct the subject as old-fashioned or nostalgic; they come to index a time, rather than place. Young Sunset District residents with a birthright to that older model of authenticity, such as Mary (a fifth-generation San Franciscan of Irish Catholic heritage), therefore struggle against the confines of that birthright, attempting to adapt in order to stake claims to local belonging. Mary's avoidance of the adjectival, *FOBby*, indexes her inability to fully align with new forms of local authenticity.

The physicality of the *FOB* style, particularly as it relates to racialized or ethnicized bodies, is central to Mary's descriptions. In (14), Mary describes the physical aspects of the *FOB* style as "all of these things that just didn't work." She begins by citing height, a stylistic feature that is the epitome of unalterable if the valued height is a shorter one. Height appears to be the most salient feature for her; she mentions it in both 2008 and again in 2012, both times using the exact phrase "five-foot-tall" (approximately 1.5 meters) as the remembered ideal. The ethnic quality of the *FOB* style thus gets expressed through a larger discursive frame of Asian bodies being short and European bodies being tall, particularly for women. The relevant distinction for the *FOB* style is, again, not immigrant-versus-American, as the original source of the acronym might imply, but rather Asian-versus-European. This point is highlighted by Mary's reference to her colleague, who came to San Francisco as a Russian immigrant, but who was also excluded access to the valued *FOB* style. In (15), Mary recounts an expression of solidarity through a reported speech moment in which the colleague 'jokes' about the undervaluation of their European bodies:

(15) Mary (b. 1979, female, Irish American)
> Mary: The 'pretty girls' were always these like tiny, tiny girls. And I was this tall- I'm five-ten, I was five-ten at thirteen. [laughter] But ((name of colleague)) and I joke about it all the time, she's like, "Anywhere else in the country, you're a five-foot ten blond who weighs like a hundred and thirty pounds, and you're stoked! [laughter]. But here it's like "uh::: [groan of resignation]." [laughter]

In (15), Mary's experience becomes locatable in her community, a place that gains distinctiveness by virtue of being in contrast to "anywhere else in the country." Mary's experience of frustration around her inability to adapt to the symbolic market of her middle school thus becomes a resource for constructing a very local kind of white American experience. The bounds of this constructed place are not always clear – her narrative is explicitly about her middle school and her colleague's middle school, however our interview is explicitly about the Sunset District, and her colleague's school was in the Richmond District (the 'other' New Chinatown), so both of these neighborhoods may be included in the scope of place identification. Whatever the bounds of her constructed place, Mary's experience is framed as crucially local. I take this locality to be relevant wherever the New Chinatown appellation applies. The rise in authentication of what were previously exoticized and stigmatized Chinese social practices, and the loss of prestige of what were previously authenticating European social practices, is a key feature of an individual's lived experience in the New Chinatown context.

While these narratives reveal a new use of a particular referring term, with some mention of the sartorial elements that accompany that use, they say little about the linguistic elements that accompanied the style. Aubrey's description in (5) suggests *FOB* stylization involved a change in "language," and the following excerpt from her daughter's interview in 2008 hints at the nature of those linguistic features.

(16) Mary (b. 1979, female, Irish American)
Mary: You get to pull like, anything you want out of the different influence[s] you had growing up, and it comes off natural. ...I was about as cartoonishly, you know, upwardly-mobile-white-girl as you get, but I could slip into how I talked when I was in middle school and people were like 'Whoa, how do you know how to talk like that?' you know and I was like, 'Oh [laughter] all I wanted to be when I was thirteen was a five-foot-tall Asian girl who could breakdance!' [laughter]

In (16), Mary links her youthful bids for *FOBby* identity to a contemporary skill for linguistic style-shifting. She re-enacts an interactional moment of recognition by her contemporary interlocutors to claim a certain fluency in the code associated with that target youth style. At the same time, she again frames her thirteen-year-old bids for identity as aspirations rather than direct reflections of her friendship network. Her description that her use of this linguistic style "comes off natural" effectively strikes a balance between parody and farce on the one hand ("comes off") and authenticity on the other ("natural"). The linguistic style, "how I talked when I was in middle school," is framed in two different ways: first, as directly contrasted with the persona of the "upwardly-mobile-white-girl," and second, as equivalent with the linguistic style appropriate to someone wanting to be "a five-foot-tall Asian girl who could breakdance." The specific citation of breakdancing, combined with tentative insights from internet representations of the 'Fresh Oriental Boyz' reacronymization discussed earlier, minimally suggests an alignment with the *FOB* style and hip-hop styles more generally. With respect to race and class, 'Asian' links through hip-hop culture to African American identities and away from upward mobility and traditional associations of whiteness. Despite the lack of any empirical data, we have reason to suggest that the linguistic features of *FOB* style in the Sunset District in the 1990s would have drawn on features of Hip-Hop Nation Language (Alim 2004b). Indeed, several accounts of English language variability in other parts of the US have documented the use of African American linguistic practices among Asian American youth for the construction of non-white identities (Chun 2001; Reyes 2005). Work on youth styles in other parts of the San Francisco Bay Area also strongly support this analysis (Bucholtz 1999, 2011; Alim 2004a; Paris 2009), including work looking specifically at Asian youth (Bucholtz 2004) and *FOB* style (Shankar 2008, 2011).

As the referent of *FOB* sheds its associations with immigrant status and gains local ethnic meanings, it simultaneously enters into wider American tropes of ethnicity, i.e., race: the *FOB* style indexes not only 'Chinese' or 'Asian' identities but, crucially, *non-white* racial identities. In this context, Mary's inability to fully attain her desired place in the peer social order is blocked on multiple semiotic levels, of which height is only one (which is perhaps the most frequently cited one because it is less contentious than skin color). The *FOB* style presents a strong example of how the challenges of late-modern hybridity can be just as palpable for white subjects in the San Francisco context as for Asian subjects in other North American contexts (Lowe 1996; Ang 2001; Louie 2006; Shin 2012).

4 Discussion

The retrospective narratives presented above paint a picture of variable orientations to the rise of New Chinatown symbolic markets in San Francisco, California. As retrospectives, they represent hindsight accounts of a period of particularly dramatic social change by those individuals who were in adolescence at the time of that change. I take these accounts to represent a window into San Franciscan society at the historical moment when the city becoming an increasingly transnational space. At one level, these changes echo similar shifts across North America, as the 1990s witnessed a rise in the global exchange of commodified symbolic resources. However, the unique position of San Francisco as the historical (and, in many ways, contemporary) center for Chinese American culture encourages a further interpretation of these processes as crucially local, as well. In particular, I suggest here that white San Franciscans' positive orientation to *FOB* style is best understood in terms of local authentication, rather than illegitimate appropriation.

Bucholtz and Hall (2005) define *authentication* in contrast to its opposite, *denaturalization*. The former "focuses on the ways in which identities are discursively verified," whereas in the latter, "by contrast, such claims to the inevitability or inherent rightness of identities is subverted" (Bucholtz & Hall 2005: 601–602). At its most basic, the adoption of a *FOB* style – presumably comprised of elements of Chinese and African American social practices – by an Irish American is, itself, a prime example of denaturalization. Discursively, Mary's recognition of her inability to use the adjective, *FOBby*, is recognition of that fact. This process operates at the first order of indexicality (Silverstein 2003), in the realm of ethnic meaning and ethnic identity. The ease with which JoJo and Vicky use the adjectival (or, even more obviously, speak in Chinese) would be an example of authentication of the first order.

However, the ethnographic evidence suggests that processes of social change in San Francisco have resulted in the emergence of higher orders of indexicality. Specifically, indexes of ethnicity are now (also) indexes of place authenticity. This second order meaning has different consequences for different ethnic subjects, resulting in something of an inversion of authentication. To the extent that her practices are successfully ratified (and the evidence for this does appear to be variable), Mary's engagement with *FOB(by)* social and linguistic practices may authenticate her position as a San Franciscan. This authentication operates along two tracks, one drawing on the historicity of the Chinese presence in San Francisco, the other drawing on San Francisco's transnational identity and centrality in the political economy of the Pacific Rim (see Ong 1999). However, access to this place-based level of authentication is more difficult to access for people like JoJo and Vicky, whose bids for place-based authenticity are more likely to be interpreted as authentications of ethnicity. This perspective helps to reconcile Mary's account of self-stylization toward *FOB* style with JoJo's ambivalence and Vicky's aversion toward the same.

The narratives presented here only represent a small sample of the full scope of lived experience, and they provide only a retrospective account of a style that is now two decades in the past. There are a large number of unanswered questions about the composition of the *FOB* style and the position of the *FOBz* in the broader symbolic marketplace. The most glaring omission in the present analysis is a consideration of narratives produced by the *Boyz* themselves, or in fact any male perspectives on the value of *FOB* style, at all. In fact, the present discussion has not been able to give space to equally frequent descriptions of race-based conflict that reached a violent peak during this same period, the 1990s, in this same location, the Sunset District. Narratives of this violence typically come from, and concern, adolescent males, which in itself casts doubt on the likelihood that the *FOB* identity was prestigious among non-Asian male students at

Mary's middle school. If the local valuing of Chinese and other Asian social practices were indeed limited according to gender, this raises compelling questions about the intersectionality of indexing authenticity.

5 Conclusion

This chapter explores the possibility that Chinese social and linguistic practices are available resources for contemporary San Franciscan authenticating. This authenticity is grounded in historicity, for Chinese Americans today can claim a San Francisco nativeness that is just as old as any (non-Hispanic) European American claim. In areas like the Sunset District, a Chinese plurality is now the norm for schools, businesses, and other community spaces. While some may lament the radical restructuring of the ethnic landscape, for an increasing number of residents, the New Chinatown is the norm. This chapter explores how young San Franciscans, those who have experienced this demographic shift directly, have understood and navigated local belonging in a hometown that became increasingly Chinese over the course of their adolescence. Their perspectives suggest that social practices that previously only indexed Chinese ethnicity have undergone a shift in indexical value. They cite instances of Chinese Americans self-styling with elements of Chinese immigrant-oriented styles, and of non-Chinese Americans coveting those same elements. This superficially unusual context follows logically from an emergent indexical order in which non-Chinese Americans can index local place authenticity via Chinese social practice, unlike Chinese Americans, whose engagement with those same practices is more often interpreted as indexing only ethnic identity.

Of course, San Francisco is a highly complex city, and Chineseness is but one part of this picture of 'glocalization' (Robertson 1995, a. o.). The meanings indexed by the Chinese practices discussed here co-exist with innumerable other indexes of authenticity available to San Franciscans, ones beyond the scope of this paper. However, 'Chineseness' is a particularly interesting case for detailing the emergence of authentication because its historical trajectory is rooted in characterizations as quintessentially foreign. Understanding how authenticity may emerge from such profound indexes of exoticism, and how the two might paradoxically co-exist in the present day, may shed light on the nature of authenticity, itself. Despite a long-standing pattern of racial and linguistic discrimination, the consequences of New Chinatown glocalization point to the ability for 'non-native' practices to come to index particular kinds of 'native' authenticities. From this perspective, Chineseness in San Francisco is but one example of a remarkable shift in indexical value, from 'foreign' to 'local', from Oriental exoticism to a new American authenticity.

References

Agha, Asif 2003: The social life of cultural value. *Language & Communication*, 23:231–273.

Alim, H. Samy 2004a: *You Know My Steez: An Ethnographic and Sociolinguistic Study of Styleshifting in a Black American Speech Community*. Durham: Duke University Press.

Alim, H. Samy 2004b: Hip Hop Nation Language. In Edward Finegan and John R. Rickford (eds.), *Language in the USA: Themes for the Twenty-first Century,* 387–409. Cambridge, UK: Cambridge University Press..

Ang, Ien 2001: *On Not Speaking Chinese: Living Between Asia and the West*. London/New York: Routledge.

Blackstone, Cammy: Personal communication. May 11, 2012.

Brathwaite, Fred 1992: *Fresh Fly Flava: Words & Phrases of the Hip-Hop Generation*. Stamford, CT: Longmeadow Press.

Bucholtz, Mary 1999: You da Man: Narrating the Racial Other in the Linguistic Production of White Masculinity. *Journal of Sociolinguistics* 3(4): 443–460.

Bucholtz, Mary 2004: Styles and stereotypes: The linguistic negotiation of identity among Laotian American youth. *Pragmatics* 14: 127–147.

Bucholtz, Mary 2011: *White Kids: Language, Race, and Styles of Youth Identity*. Cambridge: Cambridge University Press.

Bucholtz Mary & Kira Hall 2005: Identity and interaction: A sociocultural linguistic approach. *Discourse Studies* 7(4–5): 585–614.

Caen, Herb 1957: *Herb Caen's Guide to San Francisco*. Garden City, NY: Doubleday.

Chen, Wen-hui Chung 1952: Changing Socio-Cultural Patterns of the Chinese Com- munity in Los Angeles. Ph.D. dissertation, University of Southern California.

Chun, Elaine W. 2001: The Construction of White, Black, and Korean American Identities through African American Vernacular English. *Journal of Linguistic Anthropology* 11(1): 52–64.

Coupland, Nikolas 2003: Sociolinguistic authenticities. *Journal of Sociolinguistics* 7(4): 417–431.

Eckert, Penelope 2008: Where do Ethnolects Stop? *International Journal of Bilingualism* 12: 25–42.

Erikson, Erik 1968: *Identity, Youth, and Crisis*. New York: W.W. Norton.

Fong, Timothy P. 2008: *The Contemporary Asian American Experience: Beyond the Model Minority*. Upper Saddle River, NJ: Pearson Education.

Gumperz, John J. 1982: *Discourse Strategies*. Cambridge, UK: Cambridge University Press.

Hall-Lew, Lauren under review: "I went to school back East… in Berkeley": San Francisco Identity and San Francisco English. In H. Samy Alim, Patricia Baquedano-Lopez, Mary Bucholtz & Dolores Ines Casillas (eds.), *Vox California: Cultural Meanings of Linguistic Diversity*.

Hall-Lew, Lauren 2009: Ethnicity and Phonetic Variation in a San Francisco Neighborhood. PhD Dissertation, Stanford University, Stanford, CA.

Hall-Lew, Lauren 2010: Ethnicity and Sociolinguistic Variation in San Francisco. *Language & Linguistics Compass* 4(7): 458–472.

Hall-Lew, Lauren & Sonya Fix: 2012. Perceptual coding reliability of (L)-vocalization in casual speech data. *Lingua* 122: 794–809.

Hall-Lew, Lauren & Rebecca L. Starr 2010: Beyond the 2nd Generation: English use among Chinese Americans in the San Francisco Bay Area. *English Today* 26(3): 12–19.

Herzfeld, Michael 2005: *Cultural Intimacy: Social Poetics in the Nation-State*. New York: Routledge.

Jackson, J. B. 1956: Other Directed Houses. *Landscape* 6, reprinted in Ervin H. Zube (ed.) 1980 *Landscapes: Selected Writings of J. B. Jackson*, 55–72. Boston: University of Massachusetts Press.

Jeon, M. 2001: Avoiding FOBs: An account of a journey. *Working Papers in Educational Linguistics* 17(1–2): 83–106.

Labov, Teresa 1992: Social and language boundaries among adolescents. *American Speech* 67: 339–366.

Laguerre, Michel S. 2005: The globalization of a panethnopolis: Richmond district as the New Chinatown in San Francisco. *GeoJournal* 64: 41–49.

Landry, Rodrigue & Richard Y. Bourhis 1997: Linguistic landscape and ethnolinguistic vitality: An empirical study. *Journal of Language and Social Psychology* 16: 23–49.

Light, Ivan 1974: From Vice District to Tourist Attraction: The Moral Career of American Chinatowns, 1880–1940. *The Pacific Historical Review* 43(3): 367–394.

Louie, Vivian 2006: Growing Up Ethnic In Transnational Worlds: Identities among second-generation Chinese and Dominicans. *Identities* 13(3): 363–394.

Lowe, Lisa 1996: *Immigrant Acts: On Asian American Cultural Politics*. Durham, NC: Duke University Press.

Moonwomon, Birch 1992: Sound Change in San Francisco English. PhD dissertation, University of California, Berkeley, Berkeley, CA.

Ong, Aihwa 1999: *Flexible Citizenship: The Cultural Logics of Transnationality*. Durham/London: Duke University Press.

Paris, Django 2009: "They're in My Culture, They Speak the Same Way": African American Language in Multiethnic High Schools. *Harvard Educational Review* 79(3): 428–447.

Relph, Edward 1976: *Place and Placelessness*. London: Pion.

Reyes, Angela 2005: Appropriation of African American slang by Asian American youth. *Journal of Sociolinguistics* 9: 509–532.

Robertson, Roland 1995: Glocalization: time-space and heterogeneity-homogeneity. In M. Featherstone, S. Lash & R. Robertson (eds.), *Global Modernities,* 25–44. London: Sage.

Shankar, Shalini 2008: Speaking like a Model Minority: "FOB" Styles, Gender, and Racial Meanings among Desi Teens in Silicon Valley. *Journal of Linguistic Anthropology* 18: 268–289.

Shankar, Shalini 2011: Style and Language Use among Youth of the New Immigration: Formations of Race, Ethnicity, Gender, and Class in Everyday Practice. *Identities: Global Studies in Culture and Power* 18(6): 646–671.

Shin, Hyunjung 2012: From FOB to cool: Transnational migrant students in Toronto and the styling of global linguistic capital. *Journal of Sociolinguistics* 16(2): 184–200.

Silverstein, Michael 2003: Indexical order and the dialectics of sociolinguistic life. *Language and Communication* 23: 193–229.

Sinclair, Mick 2004: *San Francisco: A Cultural and Literary History*. *Cities of the Imagination*. Oxford: Signal Books.

Smitherman, Geneva 2006: *Word from the Mother: Language and African Americans*. New York/ London: Routledge.

Talmy, Steven 2004: Forever FOB: The Cultural Production of ESL in a High School. *Pragmatics* 14(2–3): 149–172.

Tuan, Mia 1998: *Forever Foreigners or Honorary Whites? The Asian Ethnic Experience Today*. New Brunswick, NJ: Rutgers University Press.

Yung, Judy 2006: *San Francisco's Chinatown. Images of America*. San Francisco: Arcadia Publishing.

Lefteris Kailoglou
Being more alternative and less Brit-pop: The quest for originality in three urban styles in Athens

According to Coupland (2003: 417), "authenticity matters", and he calls for sociolinguistics to "play a role in the analysis of how we engage with authenticity". The approach I would like to take here is to investigate how people lay claim to authenticity through their speech rather than trying to define the 'authentic speaker'.

Descriptive studies of urban speech in Athens have been until recently rather rare. This is probably due to the diglossic situation that characterised Greece until 1976 and the ensuing debate concerning the 'Language Problem', which succeeded the 'Language Question' (Mackridge 2009). The discussion had, until then, been focused around the Dhemotiki/Katharevousa struggle and its repercussions. In the last 25 years, a new wave of descriptive grammars (Mackridge 1987; Holton et al. 1997) and dictionaries of Modern Greek have been published. Similarly, closer attention was paid to the ways people actually speak (for instance Androutsopoulos 1997). The first *Reader in Greek Sociolinguistics* was published in 2001 (Georgakopoulou & Spanaki) which included one of the first studies on teenage language in Modern Greek by Iordanidou & Androutsopoulos. They described a list of features that not only constituted what is widely regarded as slang, but suggested that this forms 'part of a wider vernacular'. They also found that several suffixes can be combined with unusual bases (as happens in slang in other languages) and they suggested that there is a relation between slang usage and adolescent networks and specific subcultures. My own research (Kailoglou 2010) confirms these findings. Moreover, linguistic divergence is not only achieved by morphological innovations but through the use of novel metaphors. Here I will discuss how such linguistic choices (of linguistic creativity) are linked to specific subcultures and how they are essentially a quest for authenticity.

1 Metaphors

A rather general definition of metaphor refers to the phenomenon whereby we talk and, potentially, think about something in terms of something else (Semino 2008: 11). From a rhetoric point of view, Keith and Lundberg (2008: 62) talk about figures (creative arrangements of words in phrases or sentences that catch the audience's attention and focus it on one's key ideas) and tropes (2008: 65). With the latter, they refer to a substitution of a word or phrase by a less literal word or phrase. The difference between tropes and figures is that the former "invoke images by moving beyond simple reference or description". Figurative language then consists of tropes (metonymy, synecdoche, and metaphor). Figures and tropes are means to make "new, creative and inventive meanings". This similarity in function is the reason they have been grouped together here, under the umbrella term "metaphor" as in the general definition above.

Research on metaphors in the previous three decades has been focused on the large numbers of highly conventional metaphorical expressions in language (Semino 2008: 5). The fact that they are conventional means that we are often not consciously aware of their metaphoricity. As Lakoff and Johnson (1980) showed, "many related sets of conventional metaphors ... are not simply ways of talking about one thing in terms of another, but evidence that we also think about one thing in terms of another" (Semino 2008: 5). For Lakoff (1992: 202), the locus of metaphor is not in language at all, but in the way we conceptualize one mental domain in terms of another. Consequently, the word *metaphor,* he argues, has come to mean a cross-domain mapping in the conceptual system. Conceptual metaphors, then," are seen as constituted by sets of mappings between the source and the target domains" (Kövecses 2010a: 11). Within contemporary theory, metaphor is primarily *conceptual*, *conventional*, and part of the ordinary system of thought and language (Lakoff 1992: 202). These are exactly the points where, according to Semino (2008: 9), the originality of the Conceptual Metaphor Theory (CMT) lies.

The emphasis on the cognitive aspect of metaphors led to "a general lack of consideration for the textual manifestations of metaphor and for the authenticity of the linguistic data that is adduced as evidence" (ibid.). Hence she sets out to explore the use of metaphor in authentic discourse. This is done by distinguishing between metaphorical expressions in language (the noun "battle" in "a battle of metaphors") and conceptual metaphors (e.g. ARGUMENT IS WAR). Within CMT the former are realisations of the latter. When deciding what counts as a metaphor, she follows the Metaphor Identification Procedure (MIP) proposed by the Pragglejaz Group (2007), focusing on a lexical unit "even if metaphorically used words often occur as part of multiword expressions rather than singly" (2008: 12). Part of the process involves the discovery of the basic meanings of words. For me this distinction is not of primary importance as what I investigate is the function of metaphorical words *or* phrases in interaction. She warns though (2008: 14) "that metaphoricity is a matter of degree, and that the boundary between metaphorical and non-metaphorical expression is fuzzy"; hence, relying on one's intuitions can be problematic. Nevertheless, this applies mostly on conventional and systematic metaphors used in everyday speech. On the contrary, the examples drawn from my data are mostly marked instances; that is they are unusual/ unconventional metaphors.

An analogous approach is adopted for similes, which are "explicit statements of comparison between two different things, conveyed through the use of expressions such as "like", "as", "as if" and so on"(2008: 16). She mentions that "within CMT, they are indeed seen as a type of linguistic realisation of cross-domain mappings" or, simply, as a way of talking of one thing in terms of another (ibid.). Semino expresses her concerns about some specific cases of the use of "like" and acknowledges studies which have pointed out some differences between similes and metaphors (e.g. Chiappe et al. 2003; Genter & Bowdle 2005). Still, these concerns are mostly cognitive while the interactional function of these forms as an in-group marker does not vary. Cameron (2006: 47) claims that "in post-cognitive times, when working with metaphor as it is actually used in discourse ... metaphor can be identified without evidence that users intended or invoked metaphorical processing". This shifts the interest from the (cognitive) production of metaphors to the function they perform, which is the aim of this analysis.

2 The three squares

When I first looked on teenage slang in Modern Greek in 2002, an emerging trend was observed in the interviews with various teenagers. The styles people used in the recordings had many of the features listed by Iordanidou & Androutsopoulos (2001). This raised the question what is slang and what is simply informal speech (what they called 'wider vernacular'). Young people used morphological innovations in informal words (slang or not) as well as a number of novel metaphors. This was especially the case for people that had 'non-mainstream' music tastes suggesting a link between subcultural affiliation and forms of linguistic creativity. By 'non-mainstream' I refer to people who were not fans of pop-music as presented by the channel MTV. This term will be discussed in more depth below.

This observation formed the basis for my investigation of in-group language later on. Young people, who listen to specific music genres, also follow similar dress codes and hang out in similar places. In other words, they belong to similar subcultures which are organised around music preferences. However, they include much more than that. What we are looking at here is a set of practices which has been called a 'lifestyle'. Lifestyle is linked to consumption practices; these practices can take the form of collecting artefacts, cds, vinyls, clothes, ornaments etc., but are also related to a variety of places where cultural events take place. Concerts, music clubs and cafes are places one visits as a reification of one's belonging to a subculture. Hence, nightlife consumption spaces are not ideologically neutral. They are places one visits as a confirmation of one's identity as a member of a certain subculture; consumers are not passive receivers. Instead, they engage actively in processes of identity construction. Nightlife consumption spaces have their norms, such as a required dress code, and these are judged not only by peers, but also from the gatekeeper, who either recognises and accepts a person as 'fitting in' and allows entrance or turns them away.

Nightlife consumption places are, according to Chatterton & Hollands (2003), divided into 3 categories: mainstream, alternative and residual. My research in Athens involves mostly the first two categories, which were located at the centre of Athens and attracted a clientele from all around the city. Residual cafes and clubs are predominantly 'mainstream' and are not of concern here, as their main characteristic is their local character. What is very interesting is that three of the main central squares in Athens are each linked with a different music subculture. These squares are located within walking distance of each other and they each symbolise a different lifestyle.

Exarheia Square, located close to the Polytechnic School of Athens, has been linked to rebellion and antiauthoritarianism since the student uprising against the Colonel' Junta in 1973. In the years that followed, the numerous cafes in the square and the surrounding area have been the meeting place of anarchists, students, leftists and rockers. It is the symbol of opposition to the mainstream and the establishment. The area has been repeatedly linked with riots and clashes with the police.

Kolonaki Square, is only a twenty minute stroll to the direction of Syntagma, where the Parliament, various ministries and embassies are based. It has long symbolised the upper classes and the elite. The phrase 'Laos kai Kolonaki' (the People and Kolonaki) captures this perceived differentiation between ordinary folk and the privileged inhabitants and patrons of Kolonaki, and has been the title of a movie and a song. Today, the various cafes, clubs and restaurants of the area around the square are frequented by politicians, business people, artists, intellectuals, journalists, celebrities etc. The British Institute is located centrally in the square. Kolonaki stands for the opposite of what Exarheia does.

Mavili Square is situated next to the American Embassy, the target and ending point of numerous demonstrations, and the Athens Concert Hall. There are a few cafes and bars around the square, and one of its trademarks has been the hot-dog canteen that operates there during the night. At some point, in the early '00s, many people who were mostly patrons of Exarheia started gathering at the square to sit around either the water fountain or in one of the cafes and bars (mostly during the warmer months of the year). These people belonged to an 'alternative' subculture, listened to music played by Rock Fm or Best Radio, and many of them sported what was known in Greece as the 'Brit-Pop' look. The patrons of the square were a mixture of students, rockers, fans of electro music and other 'alternative' trends.

In a mainstream/non-mainstream axis, Mavilli square and Exarheia are both located on the opposite side of the mainstream Kolonaki square. This is the main distinction. Nevertheless, the non-mainstream subcultures are not unified and mono-dimensional. There are further distinctions, and these distinctions evolve around issues of authenticity. People who gradually (albeit not exclusively) shifted from Exarheia to Mavilli square in essence rejected what they saw as the commercialisation or gentrification of Exarheia and ventured elsewhere to claim an authentic space. Between 2004 and 2009, there was another shift. This was in the form of a gradual increase in the popularity of the district of Metaxourgheio, in the city centre, as it became a hotspot for 'alternative' youths who wanted to stand out of the crowd. This quest for differentiation is negotiated between members of various groups and different people perceive differently what it means to belong to a certain subculture and to be authentic.

The role of the media as well as the perception of free choice is important here. Authenticity is about 'not trying too much' to be something. People who are predominantly linked to Exarheia square can be seen in Mavilli square and vice versa. The extent to which one chooses to be integrated in a subculture is a matter of choice and of perception.

This means that people can choose to take elements from each subculture and to follow its norms more or less, if they wish so. People who visit cafes in Exarheia, may find themselves in Mavilli square, or (less likely though) in Kolonaki. People who visit alternative venues may occasionally choose a mainstream club for the night out. This does not entail that they automatically switch allegiance.

Blurring the limits and boundaries between different subcultures has often led to a belief that late modernity is really the end of subcultures. As Coupland (2003: 426) points out, in late modernity people's memberships to various 'communities' are increasingly complex, more contextualised and less well predicted by socio-structural facts".

Redhead (1990) explains that this is as a) subcultures are increasingly fragmented, and b) there can be no authentic subculture which is media-free. A subculture needs to be (or perceived to be) authentic in order to be endorsed by youth. Nobody wants to be seen as inauthentic. Or as Coupland (2003: 417) puts it: "We value authenticity and we tend to be critical of pseudo-authenticity. We dislike people who dissimulate or are 'above themselves'; we dislike tourist venues that vapidly promise to offer 'the authentic Welsh cultural experience'; and so on."

As for people visiting cafes and bars linked with various subcultures, as Chatterton and Hollands (2003: 84) say, "despite post-modern assertions that hybrid eclectic styles today make it more problematic for young people to distinguish between themselves and other youth cultures (Muggleton 1997: 199), many young people have no such difficulty in identifying varied nightlife spaces inhabited by different social groups". Moreover, youth cultures are not unified, they have internal hierarchies with claims to authenticity (Thornton 1996). These hierarchies are linked with the role of the media, and this is indeed the case for the group discussed in this paper.

3 Subculture and late modernity

The turning point for the Greek society can be found in the last decade of the 20th century. The introduction of lifestyle magazines had already begun (late 1980s): Nitro, Klik, Men etc. It is at the same period that private TV Channels (Mega Channel, Antenna, Star Channel) and many new radio stations also began to be established. Therefore, a new factor, private mass media, emerged with an audience that, until then, had only a limited choice of public stations. This happened at a period when the Greek society was undergoing changes and was turning from a 'society of need, to a society of consumption' (Karakousis 2006). Entry to the EEC (later on EU) was accompanied with generous economic packages of support from Europe, and the political processes of the period meant that many people showed an opportunity for social mobility. It is in this climate that the lifestyle magazines prospered and endeavoured to dictate the new lines of distinction separating the now predominantly 'middle-class population'.

The umbrella terms 'mainstream' and 'alternative' cover a range of different subcultures, positioned along a continuum of lifestyle choices, each one associated with different practices, clothing, music and film preferences etc. The term 'alternative' originally described a sub-genre of rock. The major rock radio station Rock FM 96.9 styled itself as 'the alternative radio of town'. In some instances, but not always, the term includes what is known in the UK as 'indie' music. By extension, the word alternative is juxtaposed to 'mainstream' music and culture. By mainstream, I refer mostly to pop music (Greek and foreign), MTV and radio stations with hit lists, and various dance sub-genres like urban music, mainstream hip-hop etc.

While the Greek term for 'alternative' ('enallaktikós') can be used to describe the music genre interchangeably with the English term, it cannot be substituted in other usages. For instance, 'alternative tourism' or 'alternative cultivations (agriculture)' are both using the Greek term. Interestingly, alternative tourism involves outdoor activities which bring the person close to nature. Thus, it is opposed to mainstream tourism, which is linked with mass consumption and is regarded as inauthentic, conventional and, often, marks the landscape with large hotel units. Similarly, alternative cultivations avoid the use of chemicals and, thus, offer a more environmentally friendly use of land, which is closer to the traditional ways of agriculture (aided by technological developments, that is), and produces high-quality, organic fruit and vegetables. Both examples describe activities which are not strange to a general 'alternative' lifestyle with strong claims to authenticity.

Returning to alternative music, the English term signifies a link between the global and the local. Similar to other terms describing music styles (electronica, urban, heavy metal etc.), the English term has an international taste and connotations, and this is the reason why the Greek terms are not exclusively used. Moreover, one needs to be careful when interpreting such international terms. Global subcultures are reified differently in local contexts (Chatterton & Hollands 2003; Pennycook 2010). Therefore, socio-cultural terms and subcultural classifications do not have the same meaning in different societies. For example, the terms 'alternative', 'hard-core', 'goth', and 'emo', describe music subcultures which have international appeal, but their local meanings may not be always identical (for example what exactly constitutes an emo or a goth, which music groups are typical of the genre and so on).

It is with this caveat that the terms are used here. Similarly, alternative (enal-laktikó), as opposed to mainstream, encompasses a range of different music genres of which alternative music is only one. So, the 'alternative' patrons of Mavilli square may be fans of alternative/indie music, Brit-Pop or electronica, each genre with a different place in the non-mainstream hierarchy and a different claim to authenticity. Another interesting point related to local reification of global cultures is the fact that while Brit-Pop began in the UK in the mid-1990s, in Greece it became very popular somewhat later, in the early 2000s.

Indeed, the dress code and hair styles which prevailed in the early '00s were mostly inspired by British bands like Blur, Oasis, James or Supergrass. Other typical features were the male hand-bags and glasses with square frames. This dress style was perceived as inauthentic by some (in the sense of trying too hard) and, hence, some people made a distinction between Brit-Pop and the 'real' alternative. One of the three groups I studied took this stance and, during an in-group disagreement, the statement of the title was uttered as an explicit condemnation of Brit-Pop norms and a call for a return to authenticity - that is, to the real alternative norms and values against dictated fashion and commercial music.

4 Lifestyle in late modernity

Lifestyle in late modernity is seen as a matter of choice and a way of self-identification. Giddens (1991: 81) defines lifestyle "as a more or less integrated set of practices which an individual embraces, not only because such practices fulfil utilitarian needs, but because they give material form to a particular narrative of self-identity". Further, Featherstone (2007: 84) explains that "the new heroes of consumer culture make lifestyle a life project and display their individuality and sense of style in the particularity of the assemblage of goods, clothes, practices, experiences, appearance and bodily dispositions they design together into a lifestyle". It is, therefore, the way one adopts, uses, combines and gives new meanings to existing signs that serves the purpose of one's claim to being authentic (in a cultural sense). Different people (and different groups of people) go to different lengths in trying to dissociate themselves from the 'mainstream' culture in order to construct this authenticity.

It was mentioned earlier that, according to Thornton (1996), subcultures have internal hierarchies. As Barker (2000: 339) points out, these hierarchies are a system of distinction, as described by Bourdieu (1984). He says: "Thornton follows Bourdieu (1984) in claiming that distinctions are never simply statements of equal difference. Rather, they entail claims to authority, authenticity and the presumed inferiority of others". The role of the media is inextricably linked to issues of authenticity; subcultures are not authentic since they are formed 'inside the media' (cf. Thornton 1996). As for the cultural hierarchies, they mostly consist of the following dichotomies: 'authentic' vs. 'phoney', 'hip' vs. 'mainstream', 'underground' vs. 'the media'. These hierarchies are constructed around different claims to authenticity. Widdicombe and Wooffitt (1995) interviewed members of subcultures who contrasted their 'deepness' and 'authenticity' to the claimed 'inauthenticity' and 'shallowness' of others. The issue of authenticity then is central to the way members of various subcultures construct and perform their identities.

On a socio-cultural level, the way to achieve this target is through what Thornton calls "subcultural capital". This is a term expanding Bourdieu's notion of cultural capital. Subcultural capital can be objectified "in the form of fashionable haircuts and well-assembled record collections (full of well-chosen, limited edition 'white label' twelve inches and the like)"; or embodied "in the form of being 'in the know', using (but not over-using) current slang and looking as if you were born to perform the latest dance styles". One may notice the emphasis on the way authenticity is here expressed through a calculated demonstration of naturalness. Or, as Thornton (1996: 11) puts it: "Both cultural and subcultural capital put a premium on the 'second nature' of their knowledges. Nothing depletes capital more than the sight of someone trying too hard". This knowledge is demonstrated through the enacting of a performance (Goffman 1990).

In the aforementioned description, subcultural capital is embodied in linguistic forms too. There is explicit reference on slang. The exact degree of appropriate use of slang is not the same for all members of all subcultures, as slang carries different indexicalities for different groups. Different groups belonging to different subcultures have different linguistic styles. The groups I will be discussing here claim their authenticity on a socio-cultural and linguistic level alike. Their social and linguistic practices are a quest for authenticity (in the way described above) which takes the form of originality. The language forms they use and the linguistic practices they employ are indexing each group's authenticity. The differences in the degree that they use these practices are due to the different degree that each group perceives something to be unique but natural, without trying too much. This degree, again, is a matter of the group's beliefs and convictions and the norms of the subculture with which they are affiliated.

5 Metaphor and slang

Occurrences of figurative language as a form of creativity (and consequently, authenticity) could be said to all perform the same function. For instance, Swan (2006: 6) refers to the example "leaf in the wind" as a type of figurative or metaphorical language. She links creativity to the way people use literary-like features in everyday discourse (including humour in the forms of creativity). Similarly Carter (2006: 34–35), looking at everyday creativity, distinguishes between two different sorts of practices: pattern-reforming and pattern-reinforcing. He claims that "in the case of reforming choices speakers play more directly and overtly with language" and speakers "who reform patterns can sometimes do so by radically displacing or deviating from existing linguistic patterns". This is the reason, as stated previously, that the unconventional metaphors are marked features (or as Carter puts it "... extended or newly minted metaphors ... are relatively self-conscious [acts of language use] and there are risks in the undertaking").

The risks are failures of uptake, the embarrassment of unsuccessful performances and lapsed "presentationality" (Carter 2006: 35). And as Cameron (2006: 47) states, agreeing with Carter, "we find that everyday talk does not make much use of novel metaphors ... since the communicative pressures of talk do not allow time to compose new and vivid metaphors". She continues, "instead, users make deliberate use of metaphors that they draw from a common stock available to members of the speech community" (ibid.). It is interesting then to see why unconventional, novel metaphors are so prevalent in the language use of the non-mainstream groups in Athens. Here, the emphasis is on the function of metaphors alongside other instances of figurative language.

Kövecses (2010b: 35) argues that "novel metaphorical expressions have their source in poetry or literature but unconventionalised metaphorical expressions do not only come from the realm of art, strictly conceived". There are, he says, many creative speakers who use novel linguistic metaphors based on conventional conceptual metaphors, and he mentions sports journalists, graffiti writers, writers of song lyrics and authentic users of slang as typical examples. Eble, too, recognises the importance of metaphor on slang linking it also to poetic usages (1996: 67–68). She explains that its abundance on slang is not surprising, since it is widely used in non-literary language anyway (Eble 1996: 69).

This is a point made by Adams as well who also sees slang as 'poetry', with the metaphor being 'dead center in slang' (2009: 44–45, 112–113). He provides a historic account of the relevant discussion of the relation between slang and poetics (and especially concerning allusion and metaphor), and he quotes Mencken (1936) who argued that "slang originates in the effort of ingenious individuals to make the language more pungent and picturesque- to increase the store of terse and striking words, to widen the boundaries of metaphor, and to provide a vocabulary for new shades of differences on meaning". A very interesting point is that concerning the use of metaphors, rhyme and alliteration, in slang, as he captures their meaning (Adams 2009: 119): "Rhyme, alliteration, and metaphor are all poetic devices. When everyday speakers turn mundane expressions into poetry by means of these devices, sometimes going so far as to speak in verse, they straddle the domains of poetry and slang. Both challenge the social and structural norms of language but also improve on ordinary speech- at least, slang speakers are convinced that ordinary speech expresses less than they mean, perhaps attitudes they prefer to express indirectly."

This is exactly what the speakers in my data were doing. They used metaphors and slang to index their divergence from the norm (linguistic and socio-cultural) in an ingenious and rebellious way. What can be considered 'normal' or 'conventional' is challenged linguistically in an act of linguistic distinctiveness. Metaphor is a likely means to achieve this for the reasons discussed above, but is not the only one (cf. Whitman 1885; Eble 1996 on indirection). Adams (2009: 157) argues that "even rhyming greetings and farewells [in slang] question the legitimacy of 'normal'."

The discussion on the relation between slang and metaphor, thus, shows that slang (with or without metaphor) and metaphor (in slang or poetry) serve a similar purpose. Summarising the effects of slang, Eble (1996: 16) says that, although language does not need slang to accomplish them, slang "changes the level of discourse in the direction of informality", "identifies members of a group" and "opposes established authority".

What I am arguing here is that the use of metaphors also changes the level of informality, serves as a group membership signal and opposes established authority. It is one of the means to index the authenticity of the group speakers as opposed to the directives of established authority (linguistically and socio-culturally alike). Moreover, an important attribute of slang is innovation and the same holds true for metaphors, especially unusual ones. This has been used in the literature. Adams (2009: 116) mentions Muriel Spark's The Ballad of Peckham Rye (1960) and explains that the hipster characters' speech is characterised by metaphors stretched to snapping point, which demonstrates their slang attitude.

Shannon (1992: 677) sees metaphor as a prime instrument for the creation of novelty, too, and argues that "metaphor confronts one with incongruence, with things that do not seem to go together, inviting one to view those things in a new light and to recognize conceptual distinctions that were inconceivable before". The incongruous element of metaphor is interestingly reminiscent of a typical feature of humour. It is, then, perhaps telling that the young groups in Athens use exactly these features in order to create their group styles and to deviate from the norm.

6 The three groups

The groups under discussion here are each associated with a different lifestyle. They are three communities of practice (Lave & Wenger 1991; Wenger 1998; Eckert & McConnell-Ginet 1992; Eckert 2000) consisting of people from various backgrounds living in various parts of the city. They meet up regularly and each group is associated with one of the three squares mentioned earlier. The data consists of approximately 20 hours of video and audio recordings which took place between the years 2005–2008. A total of 12 hours of natural speech (4 for each group) recordings has been analysed.

I call here 'Cavemen' the group that mostly visits Exarheia square. The reason is that they usually gather in a small flat in the area of Exarheia square that they call 'cave' ('spilia' in Greek), and they used this word in their online alias, too. I call the group of Mavilli square 'Parea' ('fellowship', 'company'), as this is how they call their group. The third group, I simply refer to as 'Trendy'. The group did not like this term, but they don't have a specific name to use and, nevertheless, they accepted that the activities that described them best could be labelled as mainstream. Actually, it was a common locus amongst the groups that they are against labels. This stands far from claiming that there are no differences between the groups, nor that they are not aware of these differences. They all seek to declare their distinctiveness. Labelling was perceived to be an indication of a lack of will-of-their-own, and appeared to compromise their authenticity.

An important factor that demonstrates the importance of style has to do with the very process of creating distinctiveness (Irvine 2001). So, although all groups recognise the difference between 'mainstream' and 'alternative' style, they prefer to demonstrate negative identification rather than positive. The starting point is what they are not. The mainstream group does not like the label of "mainstream", but they know very well that they are different from the 'alternative' ones. Similarly, the non-mainstream groups seek to declare their distinctiveness not only from the 'mainstream' but also from the ones who 'pretend' to be different to the mainstream. On the whole, this explains the common stance by all three groups towards labelling, whether this is 'mainstream' or 'non-mainstream'.

The characteristics of the three groups can be summarised as the following: The Parea are an 'alternative' group, up to 15 persons of mixed sex, male majority, aged 27 to 35 years old, at the time of recording. Their music preferences are towards electronic music, Brit-pop, as well as world music. They meet up occasionally in Exarheia square, but they would mostly visit Mavilli square. The clothing style is mixed, with a preference for outdoor activities' clothes, Adidas trainers and hippy clothes (salwar trousers, etc.). They are interested in 'alternative' medicine, Tai-chi, Shiatsu and Yoga. They choose off-the-beaten-track holiday destinations, such as the islands of Elafonissos, Gavdos and Nisyros.

The 'Cavemen' are a 'non-mainstream' group as well, consisting of up to 8 male persons. Their age was between 28 and 30 years old. They also try to differentiate themselves from what is considered mainstream, but, in comparison to the "Parea", they adopt more 'hard-core' stances and they mostly hang out in the area around the Exarheia square (although they could be seen in Mavilli square occasionally). Their preference is for rock music, ranging from 1960's garage to classic rock and heavy metal. This is reflected in the clothing style with sleeveless shirts, dark colours, military boots, trainers and leather jackets. They would also visit non-mainstream holiday destinations like the Parea.

The third group can be positioned at the other end of the spectrum. They are a mixed group as well, but of younger age (22–27 years old) and they would usually go out to areas like Kolonaki square. They consist of up to 9 persons, with a male majority. They are fans of pop music (Greek and International) and they like to visit dancing clubs for the Saturday night out. They wear designer clothes and sun-glasses, the men sport a 3-day beard, the women wear intense make-up, and they generally keep fit by training regularly. Adidas trainers are popular, too. The lively islands of Paros and Mykonos with their nightclubs are a favourite summer destination.

7 The linguistic styles

Androutsopoulos (1997: 563) mentions that it is often proved that many of the elements which are characterised as teenage slang are not actually restricted to a certain age group. Instead, they generally occur in the vernacular. This is also supported by Adams (2009) and Eble (1996). Slang is mostly a matter of practice rather than form. It is a practice of challenging social and linguistic norms. Nevertheless, it is not the only linguistic means to achieve this aim. The groups I studied used slang, but they also used other forms of linguistic deviation from the norm, like linguistic innovations (whether one would call them slang or simply informal constructions; cf. the relevant discussion on Adams 2009), taboo language and unusual metaphors. In addition, humour, often comprising all of the previous three, was employed to serve a similar function. These four features characterised the linguistic styles of all three groups, although there are differences between the groups. Each of these features should be seen in conjunction with the others in order to appreciate its discursive function. They all reduce the formality of speech and serve group-bonding functions, but they do so while bringing along different connotations.

Slang is a 'typical way' of signalling rebellion and, as such, it is used by all groups. Linguistic innovations (slang or not, in forms or meaning) are also used by all groups. Contrary to slang, these are instant creations (Hapax Legomena) and are predominantly used within a discussion of a given group, never to appear again or extending their life outside the group boundaries. Their importance lies on the creative practice rather than their form; indeed, the two non-mainstream groups used 33 and 32 different morphemes accordingly in their informal constructions and the mainstream one 13 in 4 hours of recording. Metaphors, as mentioned earlier, are also instances of creativity and novelty. Here, I use metaphor as an umbrella term for non-literal language use (e.g. including simile, metonymy, or synecdoche), as the emphasis is placed on the innovative practice. This is the reason why the metaphors which serve the quest for originality best are the unusual metaphors. Finally, humour facilitates group-bonding and rebellion through its incongruous nature. In real conversation, these features co-exist and this co-occurrence is what gives each group their own distinctive style.

The element of evaluation is often present in such usages. In the following example, the Parea are discussing the correct pronunciation of Va'tatzi Str.:

(1) They ... they are some *goat-calves* who say Vata'tzi.

Animal metaphors are not uncommon in derogatory use. The interesting thing here involves the choice of animals as well as the construction of a compound word. Compounding has been chosen in order to intensify the semantic load of the word and to emphasise the condemnation of the ignorant people.

Another neologism with an evaluative purpose, again from the Parea, occurs while two male members are watching the sports news and they are commenting on the presenters.

(2)   Gosh, they are both stupid, mate. *Anti-football-faces* that is. They are not human.

Evaluation is not only expressed through metaphors. In the same example, the discussion moves on to the female hostess of the show:

(3)   1.   V: What do you think about her /
      2.   P: Do not let it [the water] drip on the peanuts (V is eating)
      3.   V: Anna Karamanli (on the TV).
      4.   P: What? She's the reason I watch Sport Sunday (the name of the show)
      5.   V: You like those *right-wing*, *working-class* (women), you malakas. Who even pretend they are ladies
      6.   P: *I'd guess she lives in Papagou* (a traditionally conservative district where many retired army officers live)
      7.   V: I'd also guess she lives there

Still, the evaluation is expressed with non-literary language in the next examples:

(4)   V: (commenting on P.'s sun-glasses) Nice. You are *Matrix*. Neo (in English).

Or even concerning the weather:

(5)   1.   P: Oh, look what it pours down (it rains).
      2.   V: *Goat-cheese* (a lot)!

The exact link between the heavy rain and the cheese is not clear and P. laughs. What is very interesting is this persistence on trying to be innovative even on mundane things like commenting on the weather. This is where this shared practice by the group members is used as an index of authenticity and group membership alike.

The other non-mainstream group (the Cavemen) also makes extensive use of this practice. They use it for evaluation as well. In the following example, they are watching the Oprah Winfrey show on TV and they comment on the participants. This is what they say about the presenter: a) *Her face is like a mackerel*, b) *she hits her breasts like a baboon*, and c) *If she was green, she would be Hulk*. As for a participating woman who protests her innocence over an extra-marital affair: "She looks *like she has swallowed a U-Boat*. Where do you see the innocence?" In another example, they watch a documentary on large boats and they comment on an especially large one: 'We are talking about a *schizophrenic* size, when it [the boat] is loaded [with cargo and passengers]'.

Nevertheless, this practice is not restricted to the commentary of television. They use these metaphors extensively while they play a video game.

(6)   With all these arrows on you, *you have become a Christmas tree. You have grown roots*.

(7)   You are the worst because you have the *look of a cartoon 'I fucked you and now I'm getting bored, so I will fuck you again'*

(8)   I sneaked out of the corner *like the ferret*.

(9)   You sneak out and shoot *like they are ghostbusters*, as *if you had taken the water pipe to water the plants*, so to speak.

(10) 'Right, *Sir Vomit* entered (meaning 'someone who ruins the game').

(11) You have chosen the most difficult stage which is *dirty* (difficult).

(12) This stage is disgusting. *Pervert*.

(13) After that, I shall be sending you to buy me cigarettes [meaning 'I shall rule over you']

And, to be sure, even negative evaluations take the following form:

(14) 'Oh, malakas, you are crisps. Crisps. Simply, like that. Of such [poor] quality [you are], crisps.

Interestingly, the constant attempt to say something in an unusual way is apparent in their use of taboo language and swearing. In addition to using the common word *malakas* (literally 'wanker', but widely used as a friendly term of address, e.g. 'mate') and verbs relating to sex, they revert to the creation of new terms and phrases during their exchanges of insults.

(15) You look awful, you suffered lead poisoning.

(16) You have the psycho-synthesis of a transsexual, malakas.

(17) Do not breathe again. Never.

This sort of inventiveness does not occur in the mainstream group (concerning insults), who use the 'established' taboo words. It is a characteristic of the non-mainstream groups, and it serves to create an expanded notion of rebellion and originality, as the use of slang and established taboo words is acceptable but not sufficient. Throughout the recordings, there has been only one occurrence where the mainstream group makes use of metaphors in this way. Two males are arguing over being late for an appointment:

(19) G: I may be late as well but I give you a call and tell you that I am coming in five minutes. You sense that I am coming. You sense though that I am coming.

A: I told you not to lie.

G: No, you sense that I am coming. This is a different thing whether I am (really) coming.

A: How do I sense it, you malakas? What are you? *A period*?

In the above example, being late for an appointment is linked with the female monthly cycle, which is an unusual metaphor. Moreover, since it is related to bodily functions it is an instance of taboo language. It is no coincidence that no women were present in the room during this conversation. Actually, the women of the group did not use taboo language and obscenities, and they protested strongly when the men did. There was a clear gender differentiation within the group concerning these features. On the contrary, the women of the non-mainstream group employed the same stylistic features as their male counterparts. This can be seen in the following example where two women are discussing their summer holidays on a Greek island.

(20) I: Where did you stay? Does Nikitas have a house?

A: His godmother (does). Great. A little house ...

I: *Like an octopus*?

(They laugh.)

Here, the connection between the house and the octopus is not very clear and they laugh, as the men did in the example with the rain and cheese. The group practice of creating innovative expressions, metaphors and neologisms is also seen in the following examples. In one instance, one woman is being sympathetic to the other's personal problems and she wants to emphasise her allegiance and agreement. She says: "I agree ... *I give you my panties for that*... Cuz you have trusted the one, you have trusted the other". This is a very unusual way to express sympathy and it serves the purpose of innovation as bonding.

In another instance, they employ productive morphology to create a new verb. The word 'vinegar' is used in slang to mean 'cheap booze'. Here, a new verb was constructed based on this informal meaning, which would be translated as 'vinegarise' (essentially, 'got drunk'). The exchange includes the use of the slang idiom 'fuck them' which refers to a bad situation and could be translated as 'shit'.

(21) A: Vinegars ('booze')...We got *vinegarised* ('we drank a lot') the first day there...

I: I can imagine.

A: Fuck them ('shit').

8 Conclusion

In general, the Parea women use more innovations, unusual metaphors and obscene words than the Trendy women although they are 10 years older (in their 30s); in the Trendy Group, the women did not use a single obscene word throughout the recordings and only a handful of established slang words. In many respects, the Parea women are more innovative/'rebellious' than the male members of the Trendy Group. Slang, neologisms, humour and unusual metaphors can all break the conventional norms of language and, as such, they are employed by the three groups. Nevertheless, the two non-mainstream groups make extensive use of unusual metaphors in addition to slang words and neologisms, which is something that is not prevalent in the other group. This practice then occurs in the groups who mostly try to dissociate themselves from the mainstream lifestyle too.

The quest for authenticity takes the form of a quest for originality. What I have argued here is that the use of figurative language (e.g. metaphors) is a means employed by the group members as an index of authenticity, which is then linked to status negotiations within the group. Indeed, "in the peer setting the identities of participants are negotiated within and through talk" as roles are achieved rather than ascribed (Goodwin 2006: 3) and this could explain why speakers are engaged in this undertaking of innovations.

The group members recognise the need for originality and they construct novel expressions, words and metaphors throughout their conversation. These constructions are not always successful, as the previous examples showed. The awkwardness of failed innovations is resolved through laughter, which also signals the negotiation of the norm and the acceptance of the innovative practice. In the end, it is this practice which is important rather than the produced forms themselves. Innovation and creativity through the use of non-literal language is perhaps more subtle than the overt rebellion of slang and taboo language. This explains why it is mostly found in the linguistic styles of those who position themselves opposite the mainstream lifestyle. Moreover, it is not enough to widely use established means of challenging the linguistic standard, like slang, as it is not enough to oppose mainstream culture in order to be authentic. For this reason, the young Athenian asks his mates to be more alternative and less Brit-Pop.

References

Adams, Michael 2009: *Slang: The People's Poetry*, New York/Oxford: Oxford University Press

Androutsopoulos, Jannis 1997: Comparative youth language: Greek, French, German, Italian' [in Greek] *Studies in Greek Linguistics* 17: 562–576.

Barker, Chris 2000: *Cultural Studies: Theory and Practice*. London: Sage.

Bourdieu, Pierre 1984: *Distinction: A Social Critique of the Judgement of Taste*. New York/London: Routledge.

Cameron, Lynne 2006: Metaphor in everyday language. In Janet Maybin & Joan Swan (eds.), *The Art of English: Everyday Creativity*, 46–53. Basingstoke: Palgrave Macmillan.

Carter, Ronald 2006: Extracts from 'Common language: corpus, creativity and cognition'. In Janet Maybin & Joan Swan (eds.), *The Art of English: Everyday Creativity*, 29–36. Basingstoke: Palgrave Macmillan

Chatterton, Paul & Robert Hollands 2003: *Urban Nightscapes: Youth Cultures, Pleasure Spaces and Corporate Power*. Oxon: Routledge.

Chiappe, Dan, John Kennedy & Tim Smykowski 2003: Reversibility, aptness, and the conventionality of metaphors and similes. *Metaphor and Symbol* 18(2): 85–105.

Coupland, Nikolas 2003: Sociolinguistic authenticities. *Journal of Sociolinguistics* 7(3): 417–431.

Eble, Connie 1996: *Slang and Sociability*. Chapel Hill/London: University of North Carolina Press.

Eckert, Penelope & Sally McConnell-Ginet 1992: Think practically and look locally: Language and gender as community-based practice. *Annual Review of Anthropology* 21: 461–90.

Eckert, Penelope 2000: *Linguistic Variation as Social Practice: The Linguistic Construction of Identity in Belten High*. Oxford: Blackwell.

Featherstone, Mike 2007: *Consumer Culture and Postmodernism* (2nd edn.). London: Sage.

Genter, Dedre & Brian Bowdle 2005: The career of metaphor. *Psychological Review* 112(1): 193–216.

Georgakopoulou, Alexandra & Maria Spanaki (eds.) 2001: *A Reader in Greek Sociolinguistics: Studies in Modern Greek Language, Culture and Communication*. Oxford/Bern: Peter Lang.

Giddens, Anthony 1991: *Modernity and Self-identity: Self and Society in the Late Modern Age*. Cambridge: Polity Press.

Goffman, Ervin 1990 [1959]: *The Presentation of Self in Everyday Life*. London: Penguin.

Goodwin, Marjorie Harness 2006: *The Hidden Life of Girls: Games of Stance, Status and Exclusion*. Oxford: Blackwell.

Holton, David, Peter Mackridge & Irene Philippaki-Warburton 1997: *Greek: A Comprehensive Grammar of the Modern Language*. London: Routledge.

Iordanidou, Anna & Janis Androutsopoulos 2001: Youth slang in Modern Greek. In Alexandra Georgakopoulou & Maria Spanaki (eds.), *A Reader in Greek Sociolinguistics: Studies in Modern Greek Language, Culture and Communication*, Oxford/Bern: Peter Lang.

Irvine, Judith 2001: Style as distinctiveness: the culture and ideology of linguistic differentiation. In Penelope Eckert and John Rickford (eds.), *Style and Sociolinguistic Variation in Language*, 21–43. Cambridge: Cambridge University Press.

Kailoglou, E. 2010: Style and sociolinguistic variation in Athens, PhD Dissertation. Department of Language & Linguistics, University of Essex.

Karakousis, Antonis 2006: *Meteori Hora: Apo tin koinonia tis anagkis stin koinonia tis epithymias, 1975–2005 [A country in a limbo: From the society of need to the society of desire, 1975–2005]*. Athens: Estia.

Keith, William & Christian Lundberg 2008: *The Essential Guide to Rhetoric*. Boston/New York: Bedofrd/St. Martin's.

Kövecses, Zoltán 2010a: Metaphorical Creativity in Discourse. *Insights* 3(2): 1–14.

Kövecses, Zoltán 2010b: *Metaphor: A Practical Introduction*. New York: Oxford University Press.

Lakoff George & Mark Johnson 1980: *Metaphors We Live By*. Chicago: Chicago University Press.

Lakoff George 1992: The Contemporary Theory of Metaphor. In Andrew Ortony (ed.), *Metaphor and Thought* (2nd edition), 202–251. Cambridge: Cambridge University Press.

Lave, Jean & Etienne Wenger 1991: *Situated Learning: Legitimate Peripheral Participation*. Cambridge: Cambridge University Press.

Mackridge, Peter 1987: *The Modern Greek Language: A Descriptive Analysis of Standard Modern Greek*. Oxford: Oxford University Press.

Mackridge, Peter 2009: *Language and National Identity in Greece: 1766–1976*. Oxford: Oxford University Press.

Mencken, Henry Louis 1936: *American Language*. New York: Alfred Knopf.

Muggleton, David 1997: The post-subculturalist. In Steve Redhead, Derek Wynne & Justinne O'Connor (eds), *The Club-cultures Reader: Readings in Popular Cultural Studies*. Oxford: Blackwell.

Pennycook, Alastair 2010: *Language as a Local Practice*. London: Routledge.

Pragglejaz Group 2007: MIP: A method for identifying metaphoricaly used words in discourse. *Metaphor and Symbol* 22 (1): 1–39.

Redhead, Steve 1990: *The End of the Century Party: Youth and Pop towards 2000*. Manchester: Manchester University Press.

Semino, Elena 2008: *Metaphor in Discourse*. Cambridge: Cambridge University Press.

Shannon, Benny 1992: From fixedness and selection to differentiation and creation. *Poetics Today* 13(4): 659–685.

Spark, Muriel 1960: The Ballad of Peckham Rye. London: Macmillan.

Swann, Joan 2006: The art of everyday. In Janet Maybin & Joan Swan (eds.), *The Art of English: Everyday Creativity*, 3–28. Basingstoke: Palgrave Macmillan.

Thornton, Sarah 1996: *Club Cultures: Music, Media and Subcultural Capital*. Connecticut: Wesleyan University Press.

Wenger, Etienne 1998: *Communities of Practice*. New York: Cambridge University Press.

Whitman, Walt [1885]: *Slang in America: The Collected Writings of Walt Whitman*. Edited by Floyd Stovall. New York: New York University Press.

Widdicombe, Sue & Robin Wooffitt 1995: *The Language of Youth Subcultures: Social Identity in Action*. Hemel Hempstead: Harvester Wheatsheaf.

Barbara Johnstone

"100 % Authentic Pittsburgh": Sociolinguistic authenticity and the linguistics of particularity[1]

1 Introduction

Variationist sociolinguists have traditionally chosen as their object of study the most unselfconscious, "vernacular" speech in relatively closed, homogeneous communities like traditional working-class neighborhoods, with their dense, multiplex social networks, and in the relatively self-contained symbolic econo- mies of schools. This has allowed us to explore social correlates of variation and processes of change in communities where these things appear least muddied by outside influences, and doing so has given us a solid foundation for understand- ing general patterns of variation and change. However, any claim about the best site for research is liable to be read as a claim about the best speakers or ways of speaking. For example, William Labov's (1972, 2001) claim that unselfconscious, everyday "vernacular" speech, relatively untainted by the presence of outsiders, provides the clearest evidence of the systematicity of variation and change has often been implicitly taken as a claim about what the best data is and who the most "authentic" speakers are. Other influential variationists, such as James and Leslie Milroy (Milroy 1987; Milroy & Milroy 1992) and Penelope Eckert (2000) have also been read (or mis-read) as suggesting that the kind of communities they have studied provide the best, most unsullied evidence of the mechanisms of variation and change.

However, as Bucholtz (2003), Coupland (2007: 25–26), and others have pointed out, what counts as an authentic linguistic variety or an authentic

1 I am grateful to Véronique Lacoste, Jakob Leimgruber, and Thiemo Breyer, who not only edited this book but also organized the workshop that gave rise to it. I would not have written this paper without their invitation to think and talk about sociolinguistic authenticity with an inspiring group of colleagues. The invitation would not have been issued without the support of the Frei- burg Institute for Advanced Study (FRIAS), and in particular Peter Auer of the School of Litera- ture and Linguistics there. Thanks to everyone involved. As always, I also thank the members of the Pittsburgh Social Meaning in Language group for helping me work though most of the ideas in this chapter.

speaker depends on who is counting and why. As Coupland puts it, "authenticity is not so much a condition of a research design; it is a social meaning" (Coupland 2007: 26). Many sociolinguists are now shifting our focus to situations in which authenticity seems a great deal more problematic than it did in classic variationist work: situations in which different groups of speakers may have access to very different sets of sociolinguistic resources and ways of evaluating such resources, situations in which talk is mediated or performed, situations in which social networks are looser and more changeable, situations in which the issue of what it means to say something one way or another is more complex.

The fact that we no longer take the existence of sociolinguistic authenticity for granted does not mean, however, that the idea is no longer relevant. The people we study may think of some variants and some speakers as more authentic than others, and these judgments can be consequential, as people choose or avoid particular variants, emulate or fail to emulate particular speakers, and argue about what varieties are really like. In this chapter I explore the meaning of sociolinguistic authenticity in a community where the concept of authenticity is often in play and often linked with how people talk. My analytical method is a kind of discourse analysis (by which I mean close, systematic interpretation of texts and records of talk) which is linked, at every step, with ethnography (by which I mean rigorous, long-term exploration of human systems of meaning, acting, and being). Rather than looking at a representative subset of a large set of data (such as a set of tokens extracted from a set of sociolinguistic interviews, a set of newspaper articles, a set of contributions to online chats, or a set of narratives), here I look at a single instance of a single thing. I work outward from this particular text to the sources of creativity and constraint that make it possible and shape its form and meaning. The question with which I begin is both very broad and very particular: "Why is this text the way it is and no other way?" My text is the following:

100 % Authentic Pittsburgh 100 %
The people of this great city are considered to be the nicest, warmest, and friendliest in the world. Native or visitor, when you leave this place the generosity and hospitality of its inhabitants leaves you longing to return. Here, they love their sports teams so much that the fans are said to bleed "black n' gold". Never ones to pass up a party, it's not uncommon to find almost anyone out on the "tahn" enjoying a few "irons" to "worsh" down their pierogies, chipped ham sandwiches, or kolbassi.

To paraphrase it, the text is a description of "authentic" Pittsburghers that alludes to personal characteristics (friendliness, generosity, warmth), pastimes (sports and celebrations), and food and drink (beer, pierogies, kolbassi, and chipped ham sandwiches). By means of respelling, it also makes some claims about how authentic Pittsburghers talk (*town* is spelled <tahn>, *and* <'n>, and

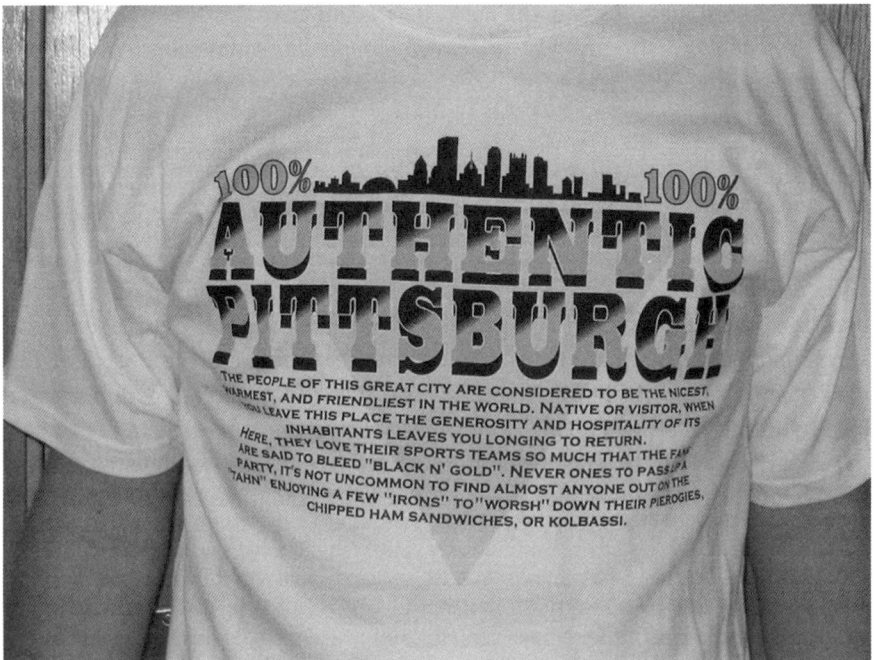

Figure 1: "Authentic Pittsburgh" T-shirt (Photograph by B. Johnstone)

wash <worsh>). Like any written text, the words are not only a linguistic artifact but also a visual one. The text appears on the front of a t-shirt (Figure 1).

The t-shirt is white; the lettering is black and a saturated yellow color; the lettering is in two different fonts, one serif ("100 %", "authentic Pittsburgh") and one sans serif (the rest of the text), all in capital letters. There is a silhouette of a city skyline above the words and in between the two iterations of "100 %" and an inverted pyramid shape in a lighter yellow under the text.

Like any cultural artifact, this one is "interactional" in the sense that it exists only because someone or some people produced it and it has meaning only in the eye of its creators and consumers. The creators of the shirt had a purpose as they designed it and circulated it, and its physical and linguistic characteristics probably have something to do with that. The t-shirt's meaning is partly shaped by the interaction between its creators and consumers. Like any text, the text on this shirt is intertextual, bearing traces of prior texts and practices surrounding texts. And, like any other artifact, the t-shirt is an artifact of some world, some set of material, historical, and ideological circumstances. The text appears on a cotton t-shirt; the shirt cost less than ten U.S. dollars; it was for sale in Pittsburgh, a post-industrial city in the northeastern United States where people think that they speak a distinctive way and where people like to talk about language, I bought it around 2009, and so on.

This chapter contributes to our understanding of sociolinguistic authenticity in several ways. From a theoretical perspective, this case study reminds us that sociolinguistic authenticity is linked with authenticity in other practices. Speaking in a particular way can only seem authentic (or not) in the context of living, being, and acting in ways that seem authentic. Ideas about sociolinguistic authenticity sometimes circulate via material artifacts, produced under particular historical and material circumstances and embedded in particular sets of social practices. In the set of ideas that surrounds "Pittsburghese", sociolinguistic authenticity is linked to place and social practices associated with place and locality. Thinking systematically about what this text is silent about, and to whom it is silent, highlights how what counts as authentic can differ even within a fairly homogeneous community, because ideas about authenticity are circulated via practices to which not everyone has access or in which not everyone chooses to participate.

Methodologically, discourse analysis of the sort I use here highlights how what Silverstein and others have called "text-metricality", or the juxtaposition of different items in parallel structures, operates in the creation of meaning. It is hard to talk about what the text on the shirt "means", or how it links authenticity with its attributes, without looking at what is juxtaposed with what. Words are juxtaposed with other words in the time span of unfolding conversation or reading, but texts are also juxtaposed with other texts over longer spans of time. Intertextual relations such as generic relations also shape the meaning of a text.

2 The linguistics of particularity: Moving from etic to emic

Arriving at an account of why this text is the way it is and no other way requires systematically interrogating the text in context, looking at it from multiple perspectives. This is a way of working associated with Alton L. Becker (Becker 1995). In much of his work, Becker started with one text – a Burmese proverb (Becker, 1984a), for example, or a sentence in classical Malay (Becker 1979) or Old Javanese (Becker 1982). Becker called this approach "the new philology" or "the linguistics of particularity" (Becker 1984b). He attributed the idea to his Ph.D. advisor, the linguist Kenneth Pike, but he also found resonances in the work of cyberneticist Gregory Bateson, critical theorist Paul Ricoeur, language philosopher Ludwig Wittgenstein, and American transcendentalist Ralph Waldo Emerson, among others. The approach is rooted in the idea that "particularity involves both the observer and the text: both are in history" (Becker 1988). Becker suggests that particular texts take the particular shapes they do for at least these reasons:

- Texts are adapted to the structural conventions of the language or languages they draw on, and they reshape these conventions.
- Texts evoke prior language and reshape the possibilities for future language.
- Texts evoke and reshape interpersonal relations.
- Texts adapt to their media and reshape the possibilities of their media.
- Texts reflect and reshape the worlds they are in and the worlds they are about, worlds that are made of things and ideas about things.
- Texts are loud about some things and silent about others; they evoke and reshape conventions about the sayable and the unsayable.

One way to move from outside of a text to inside it, then, is to interrogate what is happening along each of these axes of possibility and constraint. What we uncover along one axis will overlap and interlace with what we find along all the others. At each step, the analyst is forced to do what is necessary to move from an etic, outsider's perspective to an emic, insider's perspective. The analyst's interpretive framework thus changes as the analysis proceeds, or, as Becker puts it, "the change is not just an increasing awareness of regular patterns *in* the language, but a change in what Pike calls the observer" (Becker 1995: 72).

These six observations about discourse constitute a heuristic for exploring, in a systematic way, what is potentially interesting and important about a text or a set of texts. A *heuristic* is a set of discovery procedures for systematic application or a set of topics for systematic consideration. Unlike the procedures in a set of instructions, the procedures of a heuristic do not need to be followed in any particular order, and there is no fixed way of following them. A heuristic is not a mechanical set of steps, and there is no guarantee that using it will result in a single definitive explanation. A good heuristic draws on multiple theories rather than just one. Becker's heuristic forces us to think, for example, about how discourse is shaped by ideologies that circulate power in society, but it also forces us to think about how discourse is shaped by people's memories of previous discourse, along with other sources of creativity and constraint. It is a way to ground discourse analysis in discourse, rather than starting with a pre-chosen theory and using texts to test or illustrate the theory.

2.1 Texts are adapted to the structural conventions of the language or languages they draw on, and they reshape these conventions

I begin by exploring how the text on the shirt evokes, reinforces, and creates linguistic categories. One way to approach this is to look at what is juxtaposed with what in the text, since, as Roman Jakobson showed, juxtaposition on the real-time syntagmatic axis of actual utterances both evokes and creates semantic links on the remembered paradigmatic axis of possibilities (Jakobson 1960, 1968). Juxtapositions are often created by parallelism, either in the strict sense of repeated syntactic patterns with some different lexical matter, or in the looser sense of syntagmatic co-occurrence.

The principal structural parts of the t-shirt text are the picture, the headline, and the several-sentence passage underneath the headline. The juxtaposition of these things suggests that they be taken as related: the skyline is to be read as the skyline of Pittsburgh and the headline is to be read as the headline for the following sentences. Picture, headline, and text are also juxtaposed with the colors black and yellow. The juxtaposition on the shirt of the two colors and the expression "BLACK 'N GOLD" suggests that the yellow color should be called "gold".

Further, there are a number of lists in the text. The attributes nice, warm, and friendly are listed in the first sentence: "The people of this great city are considered to be the nicest, warmest, and friendliest in the world". Semantically, the list suggests that people who are nice are warm and friendly, people who are friendly are warm and nice, and people who are warm are nice and friendly. Many of these juxtapositions are so familiar to some of us that the words *nice, warm*, and *friendly* have come to seem almost synonymous. "Native" and "visitor" are also juxtaposed in the text: "Native or visitor, when you leave this place ...". In general, syntagmatic juxtaposition is an invitation to pragmatic implicature. It announces that the juxtaposed items are related and invites us to work out the relationship. The juxtaposition of "native" and "visitor" works via a different kind of figuration than does the juxtaposition of "nicest", "warmest", and "friendliest": antonymy rather than synonymy. Natives are not visitors and visitors are not natives. Readers are also invited to imagine the relationship between "generosity" and "hospitality": "the generosity and hospitality of its inhabitants". We might respond to this invitation by imagining generosity and hospitality as synonyms, or we might see the relationship as synecdochic, with hospitality as a subset of generosity.

Another set of parallel items consists of characteristics and actions that are syntactically predicated of Pittsburghers: Pittsburghers "are considered to be the nicest, warmest, and friendliest people in the world, "are generous and hospitable, "love their sports teams", are "not ones to pass up a party", "go out on the tahn, " and enjoy "irons", pierogies, chipped ham sandwiches, and kolbassi. The fact that all of these things are in parallel syntactic slots invites us to think of them as related. Loving your sports teams means not passing up parties, going out on the town means drinking beer and eating pierogies and kolbassi, and so on.

The fact that the words represented as "n', " "tahn", " irons", and "worsh" in the list of attribute of Pittsburghers are all in quotation marks suggests that these are all things that Pittsburghers say. Among these are three words that have been respelled in nonstandard ways: *and* is spelled <'N>, *town* is spelled <TAHN>, and *wash* is spelled <WORSH>. This invites us to imagine that it is not, or not only, the meanings of these words that are distinctive, but also the way the words sound.

2.2 Texts evoke prior language and reshape the possibilities for future language

This t-shirt borrows and re-uses the conventional Title-Body format common to many written texts. The title is larger and centered. It is followed by the body of the text in a smaller type size and sometimes (as on the "Authentic Pittsburgh" shirt) a different font. This arrangement invites people familiar with what titles are and how they relate to text-bodies to imagine that the text on the shirt is "about" the title in some way – an elaboration, an explanation, a narrative suggested by the title. We might also note that the title is in a Roman, serif font that we are used to seeing in "serious" contexts such as newspapers, while the text is in a more "playful" sans-serif font.

People who interact with and via this shirt must know by whom and why such shirts can be worn. As Miller (2002) points out in a study of t-shirts produced by fans of the rock band Phish, there is a tradition in the U.S. and elsewhere of playful t-shirts, often featuring borrowed and recontextualized images. Such shirts are purchased and worn because of their "badging" function (Glass 2008; Kelly 2003; Symes 1987). People who see Pittsburghese shirts for sale tend, in other words, to know how to consume them, both in the sense of how to interpret them and in the sense of who might wear them and in what contexts.

Representations of Pittsburgh speech on t-shirts are also highly intertextual with one another and with representations of Pittsburgh speech in other media, such as online lists and a well-known folk dictionary (McCool 1982). A comparison of one t-shirt from the late 1990s with the McCool folk dictionary makes this clear. Of the 32 words on the shirt, 26 were also in the folk dictionary, and 20 of these were spelled the same way on the shirt as in the book. When asked where they get their ideas, t-shirt vendors sometimes refer to "lists on the internet". This degree of intertextuality is made possible in large part by the fact that

Pittsburghese shirts are bought and sold in a grass-roots, often literally person-on-the-street market which is not quite legitimate, if not quite illegitimate. Trade marking is rare and designers and vendors are unlikely to sue one another for copying their ideas, word lists, or designs. Ideas for the shirts' visual design are also borrowed and re-used. Black and gold are the colors of the city's sports teams and the city shield and flag; they are almost compulsory for any item alluding to local identity. Further, images of the downtown cityscape have been featured on Pittsburghese shirts since they were first produced (Johnstone 2009).

2.3 Texts adapt to their media and reshape the possibilities of their media

The medium for this message is a cotton t-shirt. In order for this message to circulate, producing and selling shirts like this must be economically feasible. The availability of wholesale t-shirts and sweatshirts at low cost, together with inexpensive reproduction technology that is available locally, makes the shirts relatively disposable, so people are willing to purchase them without much fore-thought. According to the website of Berda CompuGraphix, a t-shirt wholesaler and printer located near Pittsburgh (Berda CompuGraphix, n.d.), a white, 100 % cotton, heavyweight or 50/50 % cotton/poly blend t-shirt, including one-color printing in one location, wholesaled at the time this shirt was for sale for $3.29 per shirt if 500 shirts were purchased. Selling such a shirt for as little as $5.00 represented a 34 % markup. Gold shirts with black printing were $5.29 per shirt for 500 shirts; these often sold for $8.00, which represents a similar markup. Dealers' overhead costs are low, since the shirts can be produced nearby and are often sold on the street. In sum, it makes economic sense both to sell shirts with Pittsburghese on them and to buy them. In particular, it makes sense to start which white t-shirts, which are cheaper, and to limit the number of colors used in the printing process, as has been done with the "Authentic Pittsburgh" shirt.

Since we are not (yet) able to embed sound or video in a cheap cotton shirt, the linguistic medium here is writing. This means that if speech is to be represented, it has to be represented in writing, not in the form of oral performance. The representation of speech in writing is necessarily partial, and, as Dennis Preston and others have pointed out, always ideological (Jaffe 2000; Preston 1985). All of the respellings on this shirt reflect the idea that it is possible to use English orthography to write phonetically. This presupposes, of course, that English orthography is not normally phonetic. Further, if the respellings are phonetic, then, the idea is, anyone who can read English should be able to sound them out. The spelling of *and* as <n'> (or one of its variants) is highly conventionalized and likely to be interpretable by almost anyone who is likely to see the shirt. It should be noted, however, that there are people who do not know the rules of this language game. Many Americans are taught in elementary school reading lessons based on "phonics" that standard English orthography is already essentially phonetic and that each English word has a single correct spelling, most of which are the most logical possibilities. For them, the idea that there could be two valid spellings for the same word, one "correct" and one more phonetic, might be foreign. (I interviewed a group of 12- and 13-year-old working-class children who did not know how to interpret the re-spelled words on a Pittsburghese postcard).

The other two respelled words on the shirt, *tahn* and *worsh*, are difficult to make sense of unless one already knows how Pittsburghers are said to pronounce the words they represent. We are led to wonder, then, who is actually being positioned as the audience for this message.

2.4 Texts evoke and reshape interpersonal relations

Interpersonal relations are created, affirmed, and reshaped through interactions involving a shirt like this. For one thing, the shirt reflects and creates interpersonal relations between the text-producer and the text-consumer. The shirt looks at first glance as if it should not require local knowledge to interpret. In fact, it shares some generic features with informational, instructional discourse. Like discourse meant to inform, the text on the shirt is high in epistemic certainty (the verbs are all in the simple present tense) and low in hedging modality ("almost" in "almost anyone" is the only hedge). The perspective is that of an outside observer ("they" love "their" sports teams) who makes the kinds of appeals to unspecified sources of epistemic authority that we are used to seeing in expert discourse (Pittsburghers "are considered" to be nice; sports fans "are said" to bleed black and gold).

But in fact readers cannot really understand the text unless they already know what "black and gold" refers to, what "chipped ham" is, how "tahn" is supposed to be pronounced, what an "iron" is, and so on. The text positions people who do not know these things as outsiders, people who do as insiders. So it serves the "badging" function attributed to t-shirts like this in two ways: by being about Pittsburghers and by being fully interpretable only by Pittsburghers.

Interpersonal relations can also be evoked and reshaped with the shirt as instrument. Pittsburghers tend not to actually wear shirts like this but rather to buy them for friends and relatives elsewhere, people who will understand them and find them funny and who can use them to distinguish themselves from other people where they live and bond with fellow ex-Pittsburghers. Interpersonal relations are evoked in the text itself, too, though the qualities and activities attributed to Pittsburghers: they are nice, warm, friendly, generous, hospitable, sports-loving, party-loving, like to drink inexpensive beer (an "iron" is an "Iron City", a local brand of beer). They eat pierogies and kolbassi, which are traditional foods with Eastern European origins, and chipped ham, a kind of locally-produced sandwich meat. And they speak with non-standard accents. All of these are things that, to people in the know, can index an unpretentious style of interaction with roots in the immigrant-heritage working class.

2.5 Texts reflect and reshape the worlds they are in and the worlds they are about, worlds that are made of things and ideas about things

What has happened, locally and in popular culture at large, to enable Pittsburgh speech to add value to a shirt? Arjun Appadurai's (1986) description of the "commodity situation" is a useful heuristic for exploring the conditions and processes that have led to the viability of Pittsburghese shirts. According to Appadurai, the "commodity situation in the social life of any 'thing' [can] be defined as the situation in which its exchangeability (past, present, or future) for some other thing is its socially relevant feature" (Appadurai 1986: 13). In order to enter into a commodity situation, a "thing" (in our case, the imagined dialect people call "Pittsburghese") must, historically, be in a "commodity phase", it must be a potential "commodity candidate", and it must be in a viable "commodity context" (Appadurai 1986: 13–15).

One of the many intersecting sets of ideas that make local speech a potential commodity in Pittsburgh is the ideology about language, place, and tradition that underlies what Regina Bendix (1988) calls "folklorism". This is the idea, which originates in 19th-century Romanticism and continues to circulate today, that old, vernacular practices and artifacts are the most authentic. According to the ideology of folklorism, "authentic" folk ways are untainted, desirable in a way that newer practices are not, even if newer ways of doing things are more practical. Ideas like these lead people to want to preserve old objects and old practices even if – or even to show that – they do not use such objects or do things that way themselves. In Pittsburgh, being able to cite the older form of a local word can be a useful way of claiming expertise about local speech (Johnstone 2007).

According to the ideology of folklorism, cultural authenticity is also linked with connectedness to place. This is because older social practices last longer in isolated places, where it is less likely that new practices will be imported. People and practices that have never moved, or that have generations of rootedness in a particular geographic area, are, according to this set of ideas, better and more authentic than others. When this ideological scheme is in play, Appalachian folk songs collected in remote valleys trump contemporary or even Classical forms, and non-standard regional accents trump national varieties. In Pittsburgh, the display of local speech is sometimes part and parcel of the display of other elements of local cultural heritage, like steelworkers' hard hats, plaques and signs commemorating local people and historical moments, buildings where memorable events occurred, and the like. The Pittsburgh historical museum has at times had a small informational poster about Pittsburgh speech on display, and a documentary film (Sebak 2001) and accompanying museum exhibit on the theme of "Pittsburgh A to Z" both featured the pronoun *yinz* ('you, pl.'; a form of *you ones*) to fill the slot for Y. Knowing the meanings of local linguistic forms is sometimes explicitly linked with Pittsburgh authenticity, as on the shirt we are examining here.

When and how did local speech in Pittsburgh acquire the potential for commodification? What set of ideas about local speech had to be in place before people could begin to think of it as having economic value in this way? Answering this question requires taking a historical perspective on the indexical meanings of Pittsburgh linguistic forms (Johnstone, Andrus & Danielson 2006). Until the middle of the 20th century, local forms were correlated with demographic facts about their users, but although dialectologists had begun to notice some of these correlations, Pittsburghers had not. Because there was no metapragmatic activity calling attention to the correlations, the forms had no indexical meaning (Silverstein 1993). Only when alternative forms began to be heard did some Pittsburgh forms become hearable, by contrast with the alternatives.

It should be noted that the set of forms that have become hearable in Pittsburgh includes many forms that are not heard only in Pittsburgh and does not include some forms that are heard in Pittsburgh. With the exception of the monophthongization of /aw/, usually represented on t-shirts as <AH> in words like "dahntahn", all occur elsewhere in western and central Pennsylvania, along the Ohio River valley, or in Appalachia. In other words, the set of forms associated with "Pittsburghese" in the local imagination is not the same as the set of forms a linguist, operating with a different set of assumptions about language, class, and place, would identify with Pittsburgh speech. Once they became hearable, features of local-sounding speech were first linked ideologically with working-class identity, incorrectness, and/or lack of education. Gradually, however, the set of features enregistered as "Pittsburghese" and the indexical meaning of using them have started to shift, so that now many people hear a slightly different subset of features of local speech as expressing local identity and some can use these features to project localness.

Pittsburgh speech entered a commodity phase only when local forms were socially meaningful in this way, that is, when they were no longer linked exclusively with class or correctness but also (or, for some people, instead) with local identity. It is at this stage that a Pittsburgh word or phrase can come to evoke local pride or nostalgia, even among people who do not identify themselves as working-class or as speakers of a non-standard variety. While the earlier (and, for some people, still exclusively) more stigmatized meanings of local forms still resonate, so that a t-shirt with Pittsburghese on it may still call to mind working-class pride and disregard for correctness, this link is now indirect, mediated by the association of local forms with authentic localness.

As we have shown in more detail elsewhere (Johnstone et al. 2006; Johnstone 2013) these changes have been enabled by social and geographical mobility. When Pittsburgh women began to get jobs as secretaries and receptionists, they came into contact with other social classes and their ways of talking and had to learn to vary their speech in order to sound more correct and careful, or, alternatively, more like their peers. When Pittsburghers began to travel, in the military and on holiday, they came into contact with people from other places who sounded different and noticed that the Pittsburghers sounded different to them, and they began to connect local speech with place and identity. Mobility has thus been perhaps the crucial factor in putting Pittsburgh speech into a commodity phase.

2.6 Texts are loud about some things and silent about others; they evoke and reshape conventions about the sayable and the unsayable

But this shirt does not evoke the whole story of Pittsburghese. For one thing, it includes only three of the many phonological features, words, and phrases that have become associated with Pittsburghese. The features represented on the shirt – "'n" for *and*, "tahn" for *town*, "worsh" for *wash* – are among the most common, but the feature that is used the most often to evoke Pittsburghese, namely the use of *yinz* as a second-person plural pronoun, is absent. The text on the shirt also fails to reflect the ways in which Pittsburghese can be heard as *in*authentic. It did not require a sociolinguist to alert some Pittsburghers that the Pittsburghese they see on t-shirts is a partial, commodified, media-driven version of "the actual speech of the Pittsburgher", as one of my consultants put it. And "the actual speech of the Pittsburgher" is not always celebrated. For many Pittsburghers, sounding like a Pittsburgher is a liability, particularly if one does not have any choice in the matter. There are speech therapists who help people lose their Pittsburgh accents.

More generally, the text on the shirt does not reflect the fact that there are many circulating ideas about what Pittsburgh is and means. For example, the shirt links Pittsburghese with maleness and with ethnicity (for at least some consumers), but is silent about what Pittsburgh means to women; it links Pittsburghese with nativeness (you can be a "native" or a "visitor") but is silent about people who are not either native or visiting, such as long-term residents who are from elsewhere.

3 Discussion

This analysis has illustrated how sociolinguistic authenticity is always linked with authenticity in other practices. Speaking Pittsburghese is semiotically linked, on artifacts like this, with a lifestyle, a way of being and acting *vis à vis* others. What we are studying when we study Pittsburghese is not just a set of words, pronunciations, and bits of grammar, but what Asif Agha would call a "register". Registers are "cultural models of action that link diverse behavioral signs to enactable effects, including images of persona, interpersonal relationship, and type of conduct" (Agha 2006: 145). Among the "diverse behavioral signs" that are linked with Pittsburghese are words like "pierogies", "chipped ham", and "irons", pronunciations like "tahn" and "worsh", activities like partying, eating kolbassi and drinking beer, watching sports and wearing "black and gold" t-shirts. Pittsburghese both evokes and creates the "characterological figure" of the Yinzer, the local term for a stereotypically local person. A characterological figure is an "image of personhood that is performable through a semiotic display or enactment" (Agha 2006: 177). The Yinzer can be performed through the semiotic display of Pittsburghese or the enactment of a stereotypical Pittsburgh lifestyle – instructions for which are provided on the "Authentic Pittsburgh" shirt.

Thinking about the media of this message, and how the message may reshape its media, highlights how ideas about sociolinguistic authenticity sometimes circulate via material artifacts, produced under particular historical and material circumstances, and thinking about how texts and interpersonal relations shape one another reminds us that artifacts like t-shirts are embedded in particular sets of social practices – the practices of wearing t-shirts, buying funny gifts for relatives, shopping in the Strip District, where such shirts are for sale, and so on. The social practices that co-occur with and are evoked by an artifact contribute to its meaning.

Looking at the material and ideological world that is evoked by and created in this text, we are reminded that sociolinguistic authenticity is, in Pittsburgh and elsewhere, linked to place. The ideology that underlies this linkage is a heritage of the Romantic movement of the 19th century and the return to regionalism in the aftermath of the First World War (Johnstone 2010). Thinking systematically about what this text is silent about, and to whom it is silent, highlights the fact that what counts as authentic can differ even within a fairly homogeneous community, because ideas about authenticity are circulated via practices to which not everyone has access or in which not everyone chooses to participate. For example, some Pittsburghers have no reason to pay much attention to artifacts like this shirt, because they are not participants in the set of ideas and behaviors that the shirts are embedded in. African-American Pittsburghers, for example, are for the most part uninterested in Pittsburghese, thinking of it as the way white people talk. Some Pittsburghers do not go to places where t-shirts like this are sold. Some Pittsburghers do, but have no reason to buy the shirts.

Taking an analytical approach informed by the linguistics of particularity, as I have done in this chapter, also requires us to look closely at the language of the text and ask how the text is shaped by the resources of language and in turn helps shape these resources. Doing this helps us see that the juxtaposition of different items in parallel structures is a key way in which meaning is signaled. Words are juxtaposed with other words in the time span of unfolding conversation or reading, but texts are also juxtaposed with other texts over longer spans of time.

References

Agha, Asif 2006: *Language and Social Relations*. New York: Cambridge University Press.

Appadurai, Arjun 1986 : Introduction: Commodities and the politics of value. In Arjun Appadurai (ed.), *The Social Life of Things: Commodities in Cultural Perspective,* 3–63. Cambridge: Cambridge University Press.

Becker, Alton L. 1979: The figure a sentence makes: An interpretation of a classical Malay sentence. In Talmy Givon (ed.), *Syntax and Semantics, Vol. 12: Discourse and Syntax,* 243–259. New York: Academic.

Becker, Alton L. 1982: Binding wild words: cohesion in Old Javanese prose. In H. Kridalaksana & A. Moeliono (eds.), *Pelangi Bahasa: A Collection of Essays for J. W. M. Verhaar, S. J.,* 19–35. Jakarta: Bhratara Press.

Becker, Alton L. 1984a: Biography of a sentence: a Burmese proverb. In Edward M. Bruner & Stuart Plattner (eds.), *Text, Play, and Story: The Construction and Reconstruction of Self and Society*, Proceedings of the American Ethnological Society, 135–155. Washington DC: The American Ethnological Society.

Becker, Alton L. 1984b: The linguistics of particularity: interpreting superordination in a Javanese text. In C. Brugman, M. Macaulay, A. Dahlstrom, M. Emanatian, B. Moonwomon & C. O'Connor (eds.), *Proceedings of the Berkeley Linguistics Society, Tenth Annual Meeting,* 425–436. Berkeley, CA: Berkeley Linguistics Society.

Becker, Alton L. 1988: Language in particular: A lecture. In Deborah Tannen (ed.), *Linguistics in Context: Connecting Observation and Understanding*, 17–35. Norwood, NJ: Ablex.

Becker, Alton L. 1995: *Beyond Translation: Essays Toward a Modern Philology*. Ann Arbor, MI: University of Michigan Press.

Bendix, Regina 1988: Folklorism: The challenge of a concept. *International Folklore Review 6:* 5–15.

Berda CompuGraphix n.d.: Berda CompuGraphix. Retrieved November 29, 2008, from http://www.berda.com/

Bucholtz, Mary 2003: Sociolinguistic nostalgia and the authentication of identity. *Journal of Sociolinguistics* 7: 398–416.

Coupland, Nikolas 2007: *Style: Language Variation and Identity*. Cambridge: Cambridge University Press.

Eckert, Penelope 2000: *Linguistic Variation as Social Practice*. Oxford: Blackwell.

Glass, Aaron 2008: Crests on cotton: "Souvenir" t-Shirts and the materiality of remembrance among the Kwakwaka'wakw of British Columbia. *Museum Anthropology* 31: 1–18.

Jaffe, Alexandra 2000: Non-standard orthography and nonstandard speech. *Journal of Sociolinguistics* 4(4): 497–634.

Jakobson, Roman 1960: Concluding statement: Linguistics and poetics. In Thomas Sebeok (ed.), *Style in Language*, 350–377. Cambridge, MA: MIT Press.

Jakobson, Roman 1968: Poetry of grammar and grammar of poetry. *Lingua* 21: 597–609.

Johnstone, Barbara 2007: Linking identity and dialect through stancetaking. In Robert Englebretson (ed.), *Stancetaking in Discourse: Subjectivity in Interaction,* 49–68. Amsterdam/Philadelphia: John Benjamins.

Johnstone, Barbara 2009: Pittsburghese shirts: Commodification and the enregisterment of an urban dialect. *American Speech* 84(2): 157–175.

Johnstone, Barbara 2010: Language and geographical space. In Peter Auer & Jürgen E. Schmidt (eds.), *Language and Space: An International Handbook of Linguistic Variation* (Vol. 1: Theories and methods), 1–18. Berlin/New York: De Gruyter.

Johnstone, Barbara 2013: *Speaking Pittsburghese: The Story of a Dialect*. Oxford/New York: Oxford University Press.

Johnstone, Barbara, Jennifer Andrus & Andrew E. Danielson 2006: Mobility, indexicality, and the enregisterment of "Pittsburghese." *Journal of English Linguistics* 34(2): 77–104.

Kelly, Marjorie 2003: Projecting an image and expressing identity: T-shirts in Hawaii. *Fashion Theory* 7: 191–212.

Labov, William 1972: *Sociolinguistic Patterns*. Philadelphia: University of Pennsylvania Press.

Labov, William 2001: *Principles of Linguistic Change: Social Factors*. Malden, MA/Oxford, UK: Blackwell.

McCool, Sam 1982: *Sam McCool's New Pittsburghese: How to Speak Like a Pittsburgher*. Pittsburgh, PA: Hayford Press.

Miller, Sylvia Jean 2002: Phish phan pholklore: Identity and community through commodities in the Phish parking lot scene. *Midwestern Folklore* 28: 42–60.

Milroy, Lesley 1987: *Language and Social Networks*. Oxford: Basil Blackwell.

Milroy, Lesley & James Milroy 1992: Social network and social class: Toward an integrated sociolinguistic model. *Language in Society* 21(1): 1–26.

Preston, Dennis R. 1985: The Li'l Abner syndrome: Written representations of speech. *American Speech* 60: 328–337.

Sebak, Rick 2001: *Pittsburgh A to Z*. Documentary, WQED Public Television, QED Communications.

Silverstein, Michael 1993: Metapragmatic discourse and metapragmatic function. In John A. Lucy (ed.), *Reflexive Language*, 33–58). Cambridge: Cambridge University Press.

Symes, Colin 1987: Keeping abreast with the times: Towards an iconography of T-shirts. *Studies in Popular Culture* 12: 87–100.

Britta Schneider

'Oh boy, ¿hablas español?' –
Salsa and the multiple value of authenticity in late capitalism

> ... surprisingly enough, authenticity persists. (Coupland 2003: 427)

1 Introduction

In times of globalization, speaking a language does not ensure that a speaker has ethnic ties to the language in question. In public discourse, however, this is still hardly recognized. This leads to expressions of awe with regard to, for example, football players who look 'African' but speak Bavarian or politicians who have 'foreign-sounding' names but use local regional dialects. Linguists and socio-linguists also struggle to get a precise understanding of language use and the role and functions of authenticity if language use and ethnicity are not congru-ent (see, however, studies like Rampton 1995); and it is a commonplace that, so far, sociolinguistics has invested too heavily with 'the authentic speaker' (see e.g. Coupland 2003: 418; Rampton 2000: 6).

Examining language ideologies in non-ethnic cultural practices, this article focuses on the complex functions of linguistic authenticity in higher order index-ical meanings of language (Silverstein 2003). The discussion is based on empiri-cal research in Australian Communities of Practice constituted by Salsa dancing, where the non-native use of Spanish features prominently. The indexical meaning of this language choice, at first sight does not seem to be based on authenticity; rather, it might be understood as an instance of 'pseudo-authenticity' (Coupland 2003: 417). As will be discussed, however, the example confirms that "to rule out 'the authentic speaker', absolutely and in principle, would deny sociolinguistics access to a productive theoretical interface." (Coupland 2003: 418). Yet, today, 'authentic speakers' may come in surprisingly diverse fashions.

2 Transnational indexicalities, linguistic authenticity and *Language*

Language form has indexical meanings (see e.g. Eckert 2008; Johnstone & Kiesling 2008; Silverstein 2003 and others), and indexing 'authentic' uses of language overall has important social values. Performing 'the real thing', to be a 'native' speaker of a language, to be able to apply and interpret fine-grained distinctions between variables accurately and to thereby show belonging to those who have 'really' understood what's going on – all these are possible dimensions of constructions of authenticity with regard to language use. In sociolinguistics, authenticity has often been tacitly constructed as based on territory or class, where certain forms of speech are understood as indexical of ethnic or class membership. More contemporary work on language variation has emphasized the notion of *style* (see e.g. Auer 2007; Coupland 2007; Rickford & Eckert 2001). This not only brings forward the shifting and contingent nature of language variation but also considers linguistic variables to be indexing and performing more subtle social categorisations than large demographic values (place, class, gender), without losing sight of the relevance of these larger categories. Eckert's seminal study on *Jocks* and *Burnouts*, for example, demonstrates how linguistic distinctions are employed to construct styles that relate to very local categories, which are, at the same time, linked to larger cultural and demographic patterns (Eckert 1989).

The local situation is thus related to and embedded in larger cultural and social structures, which allow the speaker, in a process of *bricolage* (Eckert 2008: 456), to construct styles on the basis of categories that have been discursively constructed and made available through processes of *enregisterment* (Agha 2003: 231) on a broader level. It is thus no accident that, in Eckert's study, the non-conformist group of pupils chooses the colour black as one of its means to index their non-conformity, and not, for example, rose pink. Such choices can also be observed with regard to language and, in this sense, linguistic variation "constitutes an indexical system that embeds ideology in language and that is in turn part and parcel of the construction of ideology." (Eckert 2008: 454). While such processes of the local development of indexicalities are extremely complex in themselves, global "flows" (Pennycook 2007: Ch.7) of discourses, images and languages have brought about even further complexity. Meanings are not tied to space but can be mobile; the indexical systems from far-away places can affect local linguistic economies and enter into their constructions of ideology. Thus, through transnational media, travel, migration and intercultural contact (on transnationalism, see Glick Schiller, Basch & Szanton Blanc 1997), indexical systems of social meaning from potentially any place in the world become available to potentially anyone anywhere (for a broader discussion of the sociolinguistics of globalization, see e.g. Blommaert 2010). This potentially leads to new (or formerly invisible) regimes of language ideology. Obviously, in these, constructions of authenticity are not easy to grasp.

With regard to the study of language, a particular point of interest is the very powerful discursive constructs of *language*. The discursive construction of language as separate systemic entity – as Spanish, English, Swahili – has been discussed as constituted in and through colonial and national discourse and as a modernist category with a continuing strong social force (see e.g. Blommaert 2003: 608; Errington 2008; Johnstone 2008: 43–44; Makoni & Pennycook 2007; Muehlmann & Duchêne 2007: 105; Schneider 2014: 18–23). *Languages* index territorial and political entities and, in this sense, function as metonyms for larger, geographically locatable speech communities. The discursive construct of language, as signifying national or ethnic groups, thus has an intricate relationship to the study of authenticity, as linguistic authenticity – with the exception of artificial languages like Esperanto – is historically interwoven with ethnicity and national discourse (see also Coupland 2003: 419–421). It is therefore interesting to observe that, due to linguistic/indexical resources becoming globally available, non-ethnic affiliations with languages have become possible.

In the following, I introduce an empirical study that examines the indexical meanings of a language that is locally associated with an 'other' culture. Usage of the language of a cultural 'other' might easily be dismissed as unauthentic and "[w]e value authenticity and we tend to be critical of pseudo-authenticity" (Coupland 2003: 417). So, if people start to identify with a non-native language, this, on the one hand, questions language ideologies of nativeness; on the other hand, it opens the way to study anew the role of authenticity as expressed in language. Crucial questions that arise in this context are: What are the functions of 'non-authentic' uses of language? Which discourses are employed in order to make 'non-authentic' uses of languages meaningful and where do they come from?

The context in which this is studied is Communities of Practice (CofP) based on Salsa music and dance. Salsa has become an urban cultural practice, found all over the world (see below). In a lot of Salsa communities, the ability to speak (any variety of) Spanish is important in constructing membership to the community, irrespective of the 'native' language of the dancers. In the context that I will introduce – a Salsa Community of Practice in Sydney, Australia – most dancers have no 'native' background in Spanish, and the local/ national language English remains the medium of communication. Spanish nevertheless has important functions in constructing a genuine approach to the cultural practice of Salsa dancing. Although this intrinsically questions approaches to language that assume the *a priori* existence of 'authentic' uses of language, it is crucial to observe that constructions of authenticity remain central in the analysis of empirical data.

In the following, I firstly give background information on the cultural practice of Salsa dancing and briefly present the methodological approach with which language ideologies of Salsa dancers have been studied. Secondly, I introduce empirical data that displays local ideologies of language and linguistic authenticity. Afterwards, I discuss the results and bring them in relation to contemporary sociological theory that illuminates the 'pseudo-authentic' behaviour of Salsa dancers. Finally, I comment on the possible consequences of the results for sociolinguistic theory and method in an age of transnationalism.

3 Transnational language ideology: The case of Sydney Cuban *Salsa*

3.1 Historical and ethnographic insights into a global urban phenomenon

Within the last two decades, Salsa has become a truly global phenomenon. Salsa parties and dance schools can be found from Caracas to New York, from Sydney to Frankfurt, from Athens to Bangkok, from Kinshasa to Tokyo (see e.g. Aparicio 1998; Hosokawa 2002; Papadopulos 2003; Schneider 2009; Waxer 2002 and the sheer endless number of web resources on the topic). Yet, already the historical roots of Salsa are transnational and hybrid. The music style has emerged in a transnational space between countries of the Caribbean and New York, and "even in its 'birthplaces', Salsa has always been deterritorialised: the history of Salsa involves such intricate transnational connections that it is difficult to pinpoint its 'original' location." (Pietrobruno 2006: 20). Next to Afro-Cuban dance and music, European influences and North American Jazz music are its constitutive elements. While it was as an expression of ethnic pride in the beginning of the 1970s, within a pan-Latin political movement in the US (Pietrobruno 2006: 50), the commercialized version of Salsa that has become dominant after the 1990s is now much more popular. *Salsa rómantica*, as it is called, is usually taken to be the 'authentic' form of Salsa in non-Latin contexts. The political history of Salsa is mostly unknown, and newer, Latin American-derived styles that fuse Salsa with, for example, Hip Hop, are refused as 'unauthentic'. Thus, in many Western contexts, Salsa seems to satisfy the desire of a mainstream population to engage in an 'other' lifestyle, where Salsa is constructed as a monolithic, authentic and traditional activity.

In local Salsa communities all over the world, dance is the central activity on the basis of which the respective communities are constituted. Dance brings along the music, whose lyrics are virtually always in Spanish. Despite the difficulty to define Salsa's origin, the language and also the rhythms of Salsa connect to a transnational 'Latin' identity, which is many times constructed as monolithic as is Salsa culture (Aparicio & Jáquez 2003; Pietrobruno 2006: 17). It is important to note that the values and meanings attached to Salsa dancing and to the Spanish language can differ in the respective re-locations (Robertson 1998). There are a number of different dance styles, such as Cuban Style, Puerto Rican, New York or L.A. Style Salsa. These styles and the ideological meanings they carry differ from context to context and not all of the styles are danced in each city. There seems to be tendency that styles that have been developed in the US – New York and L.A. Style – represent the 'cleaner', more professional types of the dance. Interestingly, differing stances towards the language Spanish are constructed locally but in alignment with the ideological connotations that each style brings about (see below for more).

Generally, the language used as medium of communication in Salsa contexts changes in relation to the national environment. Yet, it can be assumed that wherever Salsa occurs, Spanish comes along. Although the respective dominant language will be present where people learn, listen or dance to Salsa, empirical observation in Germany and Australia has shown that in many Salsa CofPs, a lot of people are not only interested in dance and music but also in the culture and language that they perceive to be the origin of Salsa (see e.g. Papadopulos 2003; Schneider 2010; on observations in Japan, see also Hosokawa 2002). There are many enthusiastic learners of Spanish, and although Latin American varieties of Spanish are more popular, linguistic variety is not an issue and Castilian Spanish is also accepted (which links to the construction of 'Latin' culture and Salsa as monolithic). Many non-native Spanish-speaking Salsa dancers, to a certain extent, identify with the language, without this enthusiasm stemming from either their ethnic heritage or instrumental considerations.

Adding to that, there are also native Spanish speakers who are visible, active and also central members in many of the multiethnic CofPs. Yet, their presence should not be mistaken to necessarily be an expression of their cultural heritage. Native Spanish speakers are not Salsa dancers by birth, and in many Latin American countries, Salsa has only become popular after its success in the US and Europe. Furthermore, in the countries in which Salsa is part of the local heritage, it is often strongly associated with working-class culture. Thus, many Salsa dancers with a Latin American background have only started to learn one of the styles of Salsa once they have left their country of origin. Non-Latin Salsa dancers nevertheless often assume people from Latin America to be the 'authentic' conveyors of Salsa dance and performing an 'authentic' Latin identity therefore sometimes implies a certain degree of self-'othering'. The construction of ethnic identity of an individual, in these cases, is not necessarily the "result of his or her geographic location or national identity but [is rather a consequence of] how the dance is acquired and maintained" (Pietrobruno 2006: 2). Taken together, all these aspects make the study of the Salsa phenomenon highly illuminating for studying linguistic and cultural contact zones (Pratt 1987: 60).

Methodologically, the study on which the discussion is based takes Communities of Practice as a starting point. These are here useful units of analysis as the circular reproduction of essentialist categories such as citizenship, country of origin or 'native language' can be avoided, while contemporary theories of cultural practice and of linguistic identity are taken into account (see e.g. Holmes & Meyerhoff 1999). The assumption that language ideology is primarily determined by large demographic categories (nation, class, gender) is in this way sidestepped.

The study introduced does not analyze actual language use but draws data mainly from ethnographic observation and from interview data with members of the community. Interviewing methods include ethnographic and expert interviews (Gobo 2008: Ch.3; Pfadenhauer 2005), 16 of which have been conducted. The interviews have as topics the culture and the local history of Salsa and the role of language in the community. They have the aim to study the indexical meanings of particular language uses, in other words, the language ideologies that are constructed and performed in the community (and also in the interviews). In order to understand these meanings, the cultural and discursive background of the ideologies of language form part of the research focus. Obviously, the method is no substitution for the study of conversational data but gives insight into discursive constructs and not into language use. As high levels of reflexivity on language choice are found, the methodological choice is here appropriate and further links to the observation that there is a "need for a bottom-up phenomenological approach to indexicality to supplement the more top-down approaches that have been dominant to date." (Johnstone & Kiesling 2008: 25). To ask users why they use a particular language and to link this to the broader ideological and cultural context through ethnographic observation is thus meant to avoid the pitfall of studying indexical meanings that are assumed by the researcher but not relevant to informants.

3.2 Ideologies of language and authenticity in Sydney Cuban Style Salsa

The Community of Practice that I introduce dances Cuban Style Salsa, and, as the name suggests, this style stems from Cuba, although it is referred to as *Casino* in Cuban contexts (Pietrobruno 2006: 2). The community is constituted through the existence of a dance school that is located in central Sydney. The school's environment is rather shabby, relatively cheap and inhabited by students, artists and the like. The building of the school is an old warehouse. Inside, it is decorated with the school's logo – a red star – and a flag with the image of Che Guevara. The school's owner, an Australian of Anglo descent, consciously hires dance teachers and other staff of Latin descent. The majority of dance pupils and people who come to dance venues and parties are from an Australian 'mainstream' ('white', presumably Anglo) background, and only very few of the lay dancers stem from Latin America. These mostly have come to Australia as international students. Generally, the educational background of most dancers is high and many have a university degree or are university students.

Authenticity in the CofP links to constructs of ethnicity but also to other forms of being 'authentic'. Above all, it is noticeable that the non-native use of Spanish and the performance of Salsa in Australia deconstruct ideologies of ethnic authenticity in actual practice. However, concepts that present behaviour as 'real' and 'truly' from Latin America are highly important in the community. Ethnic authenticity of Latin American music, dance and people are celebrated. Interestingly, it is also important in the construction of non-commercialist positions and in local boundary marking, as will be discussed later. Furthermore, there are contradictory lines of argumentation, particularly with reference to the role of 'authentic' Latin people in the CofP.

Overall, the fact that the concept of ethnic authenticity is important in the community, not only with reference to language, can be inferred from various observations and interview quotes. So, for example, although Salsa does not only stem from Cuba and is characterized by its hybrid character, Salsa dancers of this CofP generally assume that it is important to travel to Cuba to get in touch with the 'real' feel of Salsa, an idea that is presented in the following quote:

(1)   If you want to learn the body movement,
     the way they feel, the happiness,
     the enjoying of the music,
     you <u>have</u> to go to Cuba. (M 23[1])

Several dance teachers of the dance school stem from Cuba, which is meant to ensure that Salsa can be learned in a Cuban way. Although Cuba, due to its relative political isolation, has a very particular history in relation to dance culture and has not been a main actor in the global (commercial) distribution of Salsa

---

1 Giving only the first letters of the names of the informants serves to ensure their anonymity; numbers indicate the minute of the interview recording.

(Pietrobruno 2006: 66), Cuba is here presented as the essential place for someone who is to acquire the intricate body moves of this style. This is not explained by, for example, the techniques employed by Cubans. It is rather assumed that only people who have made experiences with the emotions of Cuban dancers can learn these moves. The relationship between these feelings and the body moves remains unclear; yet, the argument may be interpreted as the claim that only contact with authentic Cuban cultural practices will somehow lead to the ability to 'really' learn to dance Salsa. Contact and experience with an 'other' culture is constructed as essential and the actual existence of a common 'authentic' culture of Cubans thus remains unquestioned. Cubans are the authentic dancers of Salsa for this informant and it is "the way they feel" which one needs to have contact with. Due to the vagueness of the notion of 'feelings', cultural essentialism is enforced; it is not possible to falsify the statement.

As Cuban culture is, on the one hand, constructed as essential itself and, on the other hand, as essential for becoming a 'real' Salsa dancer, it does not come as a surprise that the language spoken in Cuba is also seen as a central element in the local culture of the Community of Practice. Ethnographic observation shows that, although English is the medium of communication, Spanish is heard often, especially in the dance school, where the receptionist is a native Spanish-speaker and where all dance teachers are able to speak Spanish. Additionally, within dance lessons, dance moves are referred to with Spanish names. When I speak to the dance school owner and tell her about other communities of Salsa that I have had contact with in which no Spanish is spoken, she replies:

(2) S: Oh God, oh no, <u>everybody</u> speaks Spanish /here.
    B: /Oh, real/ly?
    S: /Not everybody but (.) almost. (S 7)

People regularly boast about their linguistic abilities, and it seems that these give access to an 'inner circle' of the community. This is also shown by the language use in the interviews themselves, where, for example, the ability to speak Spanish and to pronounce Spanish according to native standards constructs the interviewee as 'expert' and as able to switch smoothly between different codes. This ability gives access to the 'insiders' of the CofP:

(3) The other day,
    I was speaking to one of them. [a Latin American employee]
    And then the other girl was discovering that.
    And came and said
    'Oh boy, ¿hablas español? <u>Sí</u>, yo tam<u>bién</u>.'
    ['Oh boy, do you speak Spanish? Yes, I do too']
    And I'm like

'Yóu do tóo?'
And we all spoke in Spanish. (S 8)

The above quote demonstrates that "[d]ifferent ways of saying things are intended to signal different ways of being, which includes different potential things to say." (Eckert 2008: 456). Expert knowledge in Spanish in this context indexes membership to the local community of Spanish-speakers within the Community of Practice. Yet, it is, at the same time, indexical of membership to a transnational community of Spanish-speaking Salsa dancers (which becomes more obvious in quote 4). It does not, however, express membership to the ethnic community of native Spanish-speakers. Spanish, for 'white' Salsa dancers gives access to an 'other' culture and in this way produces a local identity that has transnational ties.

Furthermore, the identity produced does not only index access to an 'other' culture, it is also based on particular associations that are made between people who speak Spanish and personal traits that are attributed to them. In the following quote, this becomes very explicit:

(4)   And you know,
        the first thing that I do when I come to another country
        is to find a Salsa club
        because I know that I meet people there
        and I know that I meet like-minded people, (0,5)
        uhm (.) people who speak Spanish
        and people who are ópen (.) and fun
        and it's like a point of contact. (G 6)

People who are able to speak Spanish – irrespective if native or not, 'authentic' or 'inauthentic' speakers – are presented as "open and fun". It is illuminating to note that "variables index demographic categories not directly but indirectly (Silverstein 1985), through their association with qualities and stances that enter into the construction of categories." (Eckert 2008: 455). It has to be assumed that the discourse that produces Spanish-speakers as having these particular qualities is connected to folkloristic stereotypes on Latin people (which are also a topic in Hill 2001). This discourse comes into being in a transnational context, where nations and cultures attribute each other with specific traditions and qualities. It is interesting to note that stereotypical qualities of Hispanic people are seen as a very positive trait that people want to adapt by learning the accompanying language. It does not matter whether or not people are native speakers, what matters are the qualities that are indexed by speaking Spanish, which can be appropriated by those who make the effort to learn the language. Positive qualities associated with the Spanish language are furthermore enforced through a local cultural pattern that is based on the presence of different communities of Salsa in Sydney that engage in different Salsa styles.

In Sydney, the most visible and dominant Salsa community does not dance Cuban Style but L.A. Style Salsa. In this other local community, only English is spoken and it has a more competitive approach to dancing. Discourses of competition are here linked to a commercial discourse, in which Salsa is understood as a way to accumulate material wealth, at least on the sides of dance school owners, teachers and music producers (see e.g. Schneider 2010). A dichotomous construction of L.A. versus Cuban Style Salsa is, first of all, a local historical development within Sydney, where L.A. Style has come to Sydney later than Cuban Style and then, due to cooperation with commercial sponsoring partners, turned into the biggest local Salsa CofP. L.A. Style dancers tend to see L.A. Style as the endpoint of a cultural evolution and accordingly consider Latin American ways of dancing Salsa as 'under-developed' (see also Schneider 2014). Although boundary marking between L.A. and Cuban Style is thus a local construction, the ideological associations that are linked to the two styles are an effect of longer histories and ideologies from a broader level. L.A. Style has been developed in the US and has many elements from European derived dance, while Cuban Style celebrates the African-derived elements of Salsa (Pietrobruno 2006: 34). It is therefore not an accident (but see the links to these ideological histories) that Cuban Style is by some considered 'less developed' and by others as more 'authentic', while L.A. Style is seen as either 'advanced' or as 'plastic' (in reference to a famous early Salsa song by Colón and Blades, *La chica de plástica*). And, to quote Eckert again, this shows that, while "styles and stylistic moves can be quite local, ultimately they connect the linguistic sign systematically to the political economy." (Eckert 2008: 456).

In this context, speaking Spanish in order to differentiate from L.A. Style dancers thus instrumentalizes linguistic authenticity as to construct an anti-commercialist stance. Interestingly, L.A. Style Salsa dancers are also referred to as 'tourists' and the style and the CofP are often described as in the following quote:

(5) It is so showy, L.A. Style, it's really funny.
     They don't speak Spanish,
     they only do the silly stuff.
     They haven't been to Cuba. (2)
     Not, nothing against it.
     (laughs)
     But teachers, they all learn Cuban Style. (S 22)

For the construction of identity in Sydney Cuban Salsa, local boundary marking towards L.A. Style is very important, as in the eyes of Sydney's Cuban Style dancers, L.A. Style is considered the 'capitalist', unauthentic version of Salsa. It is sometimes also called '*McDonalds Salsa*'. Dancing Cuban Style Salsa and being able to speak Spanish is therefore related to an indexical field that implies an ideological and political stance against commercialist culture. Access to ethnic authenticity thus constructs a type of authenticity that does not express being authentic in a cultural/ ethnic way but means that one is 'authentic' in not having given way to capitalist ideology.

Yet, as has been discussed elsewhere, contemporary neoliberal culture renders a truly non-commercial position almost impossible, as there is no 'outside' of capitalism (Hardt and Negri 2002). Cuban Style Salsa is, of course, also part of market logics and, in order to exist, the Cuban Style dance school also has to sell what is constructed as Cuban culture. The unavoidable influence of capitalist market structures on the local Salsa context can be inferred from the fact that the acquisition of Spanish is symbolically relevant in performing class identity in Australia. Transnational mobility, indexed by bilingualism, has become a class marker all over the world and bilingualism as a class marker might have an even stronger weight in the Australian context. Here, second language learning has a relatively marginal status in public schooling as "Australia's school students spent the least time on second languages of students in all OECD countries" (Lindsey 2008). Although Australia is famous for its inclusive and diverse language poli-cies on immigrant languages – here referred to as *community language* (see e.g. Clyne 1991) – the way of teaching language in Australian public schools is often criticized as mediocre, and "[i]n fact, half the children in compulsory education in Australia are not being taught a language other than English (LOTE) in a main-stream school" (Clyne et al. 2007). Accordingly, monolingualism with English is not exceptional in Australia. Having learned to speak a second language (in con-trast to having grown up with a second language) thus has rather elitist connota-tions, as it usually means that a person has either attended an expensive private school, has learned the language at university, or has travelled to another country to learn the language. As, due to discourses of globalization, the potential to be transnationally mobile has gained relevance, also in local or national economies (as can be inferred e.g. from national publications like Lindsey 2008), language learning, particularly of dominant and globally distributed languages, functions as an indexical marker of class. In the following quote, this is also embedded into a lifestyle discourse, in considering bilingualism as 'cool':

(6)   People are actually waking up to the fact
      that it's actually quite cool to speak a second language.
      Because it's, as Australians,
      we travel a lot to other countries,

just like the Germans or Scandinavians.
So you've got to travel.
After uni and before you buy a house,
you have to travel
and it's very eye opening.
You understand the value of other cultures, you know,
it's also the cool factor. (JL 2–3)

Australians, in the quote above, are presented as people who generally attend university, then travel around the world and afterwards buy houses. Obviously, 'the cool factor' of learning another language, is here relevant in constructing a form of national class identity. For this social cohort of Australians, social mobility, taking place on the national scale, is obviously interlinked with the transnational scale. Geographic mobility, implying economic mobility, is constitutive of this type of identity. Non-native speakers of Spanish appropriate the 'other' world language, and this is done by those who can afford a lifestyle that includes travel, culture, time and money to spend in dance studios and language classes.

Although local discourses of anti-capitalism, national discourses of class and transnational discourses of cultural stereotyping assign 'Spanish' authenticity a positive value, contradictory attitudes on the value of ethnic authenticity are present. Ethnically 'authentic' Latin Americans are not necessarily allocated a leading role in the CofP and it seems that it is in particular the Australian discourse of multiculturalism that brings about certain discursive discontinuities. In the tradition of Australia as a country of immigration, national discourses on ethnical inclusion are vital. Australian identity is therefore not officially constructed as based on a common ethnic descent but on a diversity of cultures (see e.g. Australian Government 2011). Furthermore, becoming Australian, for an outsider, is generally dependent on the degree of education or on financial capital and on the state of health (see e.g. www.immi.gov.au/immigration/, but note that humanitarian refugees are excluded from these policies). Being able to care for oneself is here constructed as crucial. Interestingly, the informant in the quote below speaks about the fact that Salsa dancers should not be evaluated on grounds of their ethnic background but in terms of performance and ability, which reflects official Australian discourses of belonging:

(7) Oh, look (.)
    I think for us (2)
    this is about moving on the dance floor. (2)
    I know some Latin, I've met some Latin people, they're <u>ok</u>.
    They are not that <u>hót</u> (1)
    But I've met some non-Latin people,
    it's a whole lot of dancers, they're <u>so</u> good.
    So that's the thing with Australia,

it's about, like (1)
at the end of the day,
what's a true Australian, you know,
well (2) it's how you <u>live</u> your life,
your values, that's what makes you Australian,
it's not,
'Ok, I'm born in Dubbo and I use *Vegemite*[2], you know,
ah (2)
(both laugh)
It's about who you are, I think that's what it is about. (JL 26)

Ideologies of the intrinsic value of ethnic authenticity are here openly rejected and the opportunities given by inclusive attitudes that enable anyone who has the willingness and ability to take part are considered more important and also as particularly Australian. Ethnic authenticity, in this understanding, is here actually understood as an excluding construction.

Complex and conflicting positions with regard to ethnic authenticity also impact on interethnic competition between Latin and non-Latin Salsa performers. Although the Cuban Style community is very proud of its connections with the 'real' stuff of culture and language, conflicts are reported on in contact with Latin American people. The Australian discourse of ethnic inclusion is here employed as an argument to counter ideologies of ethnic essentialism. In one instance, the owner of the dance school talks about a situation in which a Latin woman complains that, in a Salsa concert, it was her (the Anglo dance school owner) who performed as singer, although she is not a Latina. The dance school owner, who partly constructs her identity and the image of her school on the connection to 'authentic' Latin culture, accuses this Latin woman of engaging in a form of racism:

(8) I don't know what it was
     but it was kind of racist,
     Australia is such a multicultural society,
     I think I can (work?) in my country, <u>too.</u> (S 27)

It is remarkable that, as in the quote above, the claim that it is racist to exclude people on the basis of descent is directly related to the Australian discourses of ethnic inclusion. Even in an environment in which cultural difference is actually celebrated, the contradictory value of authenticity is obvious. Although ethnic authenticity is adhered to when it comes to producing a culturally 'other'

---

2 A yeast spread for bread (like *Marmite*) with a high symbolic value in indexing 'Australianess'.

place and although Latin people are employed in the school to attract customers, ethnic authenticity is rejected when it results in the exclusion of non-Latin
('white' Australian) people. In fact, this is an indication of power hierarchies as
the Anglo-Australian population remains dominant in Australia and seems to be
able to instrumentalize different and conflicting discourses in their own interest.

All in all, the discussion of these interview quotes shows that, where culture
is globalized, authenticity is not 'inherited', which requires new methodological
perspectives on the phenomenon:

> If individuals cannot securely inherit authenticity from the social circumstances of their
> birth and socialisation, how can they achieve it? We have to look much more at 'authenticity
> in performance' – how people can do complex self-identification work that ends up being
> authenticating for them and possibly for audiences. (Coupland 2003: 428)

Many times, in these authenticating moves, ethnic authenticity has a central role.
Yet, depending on the discourse that is employed, authenticity has different functions. The contradictions emerging with reference to authentic culture are based
on the simultaneous presence and contradictory interrelatedness of two different
effects of authenticity: access to authentic 'otherness' enables (some) to construct
class identity and an anti-commercial stance, while it can exclude people on the
basis of ethnic descent. In the case of Sydney Cuban Salsa, categorising people
in terms of their ethnicity is seen as a negative tradition of the past. Yet, the existence of ethnic authenticity is necessary to index transnational mobility – and
using the 'ethnic' language is a central means to construct this.

In the following discussion, I will summarize the results of these empirical
observations and link them to the questions posed above – what are the functions
of 'non-authentic' uses of language and to which discourses do they link?

3.3 What's the use of authenticity in a transnational community?

Above all, the usage of Spanish in the Cuban Style Salsa Community of Practice
does not symbolize ethnicity but is an indexical means to produce access to an
authentic 'other' culture. In a nutshell, there are three different interrelated levels
where the notion of authenticity becomes relevant:
- political stances
- personal/emotional qualities
- class identity

As has been introduced, Spanish in the Cuban Style community has left-wing/
anti-commercial implications. These are partly constructed by a boundary con-

struction with regard to L.A. Style Salsa, which is seen as the 'artificial' and capitalist version of Salsa – *McDonalds Salsa*. The local history of this discourse is linked to concepts that are historically older and have a wider distribution. L.A. Style Salsa is more aligned with European 'high' culture (see Pietrobruno 2006: Ch.1) than Cuban Style, which openly rejoices in Salsa's African ('authentic'!) elements. This, ultimately, links Salsa to political ideology on a global level, in particular, to the opposition between capitalist USA and communist Cuba. In this post-Cold War setting, references to ethnic authenticity are used to index distance from the capitalist exploitation of culture. The result is a non-ethnic form of authenticity, in which the withdrawal from market logics is crucial. Certain practices are understood as unsalable and not to sell culture in this sense indexes to remain 'true' to oneself – to be 'authentic'. Interestingly, not being monolingual with English is a means to construct this position, at least in the context of the Cuban Style community.

The desire to index certain emotional qualities (openness – fun) is closely interwoven with this form of authenticity. We could call this 'personal' authenticity. It is based on cultural stereotypes on Latin Americans, which are associated with the practice of dancing Salsa and also with the Spanish language. People who are interested in the 'real' thing and who not only learn dance steps to compete and perform (as L.A. Style dancers are accused of), also learn Spanish and in this way are able to acquire the positive personal qualities that Latin Americans are seen to have. Similar to the construction of anti-commercial authenticity, this construction of personal authenticity is the result of the complex interplay of local and transnational discourses. We are here reminded of Silverstein's discussion of higher orders of indexicality (Silverstein 2003), which illuminates how macro-social frames enter micro-social contexts through various layers of indexicality (it should be noted, though, that in a transnational context, orders of indexicality might be related differently to geographical space than in more traditional contexts and that *first, second* and *third* orders do not necessarily evolve from territorial locality).

Central to these observations is that these two forms of authenticity – anti-commercialist and being a 'fun' person – tacitly presuppose that different ethnic/linguistic groups exist, in other words, that ethnic authenticity exists. The tacit reproduction of ethnically authentic 'otherness' constructs the 'other' as relatively static and tends to overgeneralize (which is linked to the observation that it does not matter which variety of Spanish is spoken; on 'erasures' see also Irvine and Gal 2000). A relatively simplistic and essentialist idea of cultural authenticity is here implied. It has to be noted that the role of ethnic authenticity in the production of different forms of 'genuine' identity and practice is very particular in the Salsa context and not a feature of music styles in general. A similar role may be found in some other types of music, and it may be present in particular local contexts, but there are many genres of music in which authenticity is constructed by other means. Techno music and House music, usually not displaying a lot of singing, for example, have different ways of signalling authenticity, which is also true for Hip Hop music. In order to grasp the indexical meanings of language use in different music styles, ethnographic observation of the local production and consumption of music is required, but it can be maintained that Salsa has a rather intense relationship to constructions of *ethnic* authenticity. The worldwide success of Salsa might therefore be understood as a desire to reproduce cultural essentialisms in an age of globalization (for a related argument, see e.g. Grillo 2003).

Next to the instrumentalization of access to ethnic 'otherness' for producing political stances and personal qualities, it is the construction of class identity that is central in understanding why Salsa dancers want to learn Spanish. On the one hand, this has to do with national Australian discourses, in which language learning is indexical of membership to a particular fraction of society (university students, travellers, house owners). Beyond these national discourses, access to authentic ethnic 'otherness' simultaneously indexes access to the transnational realm. Forming (upper-middle) class identity through access to a transnational, meta-cultural level can be described as 'cosmopolitan' identity. Constructions of cosmopolitan identity are not particular to Australia but can be found globally. Cultural anthropologist Ulf Hannerz developed theoretical perspectives on this transnational phenomenon during the 1990s (see e.g. Hannerz 1990, 1996) and his concept proves to be particularly useful for understanding Salsa dancers' strive for Spanish. According to Hannerz, it is the engagement with a cultural 'other' that gives access to a privileged position in national and transnational contexts alike and the identity produced through this engagement is what he calls 'cosmopolitan'. Obviously, the advance of such forms of identity is based on increased flows of globalization. There are several effects of the construction of cosmopolitan identity. One is the cosmopolitan's relationship to his or her culture of origin. Through knowledge and expertise in a different culture the cosmopolitan can "choose to disengage" (Hannerz 1996: 104) from the native culture. This results in a privileged position towards non-cosmopolitan identities, which typically construct the given culture as 'normal'. In contrast, through the acquisition of non-native cultural practices, including languages, the cosmopolitan can acquire meta-cultural knowledge, culturally de-contextualized knowledge. At the same time, the cosmopolitan never has the intention to 'go native': "The cosmopolitan may embrace the alien culture, but he [sic] does not become committed to it. All the time he knows where the exit is." (Hannerz 1996: 104). In Hannerz' framework, the cosmopolitan is differentiated from people who have non-voluntary access to another culture. He explicitly excludes labour migrants from his concept of the cosmopolitan and claims that in order to be cosmopolitan, the engagement with other cultures has to be intentional and not based on need (Hannerz 1996: 105–106). While this has been criticized for its elitist connotations and the downgrading of meta-cultural knowledge of more underprivileged parts of society (Römhild 2007), Hannerz' concept is useful for understanding the value of access to linguistic and cultural otherness in the Salsa context. The contradictions in relation to ethnic authenticity that emerge in the discourses of Salsa informants (see 3.2.) are partly explainable through the privileged position that the cosmopolitan creates through accessing but not committing to Latin culture.

The construction of a 'meta'-perspective on culture has the consequence of relativizing constructions of ethnic authenticity, as people can develop a kind of 'on/off' relationship with culture and it is the reflexive distance to cultural norms that defines the cosmopolitan view. And yet, at the same time, in the discourses observed in the Salsa context, a cosmopolitan position depends on the existence of 'traditional' ethnic authenticity. It is access to 'real' Spanish-speakers that is central for becoming cosmopolitan in the case of Cuban Salsa. This reproduction of essentialist concepts of culture is involved in the maintenance of power differentials. While it is relatively easy for the dominant majority to construct an 'on/off' relationship with Latin culture, this is harder for Latin Americans. Although they can redefine their ethnic heritage as cosmopolitan to a certain degree, they are regarded as 'authentic' (and therefore more traditional) people. Thus, the inter-ethnic conflicts described in 3.2. are an effect of power differentials between different groups, which affect the extent to which people are mobile with regard to their culture of origin. Latin Americans are accused of 'racism' if they demand employment on the basis of ethnic descent, while they are employed elsewhere for exactly this reason (it is in this context interesting to note that virtually all Salsa teachers from Cuba have been trained in European classical dance, not Salsa, but are almost never hired as ballet teachers). It is easier for the dominant majority to perform a cosmopolitan persona and to switch between identities, whereas the minority is supposed to remain 'ethnic'. Obviously, different discourses on ethnicity meet and it is this encounter of different – local, national, transnational – discourses that explains the struggles with authenticity. Fields of indexicality get into contact, render indexical orders very complex and thus different constructions of authenticity interact and sometimes contradict each other.

So, returning to the questions posed at the beginning, it can be seen that authenticity is contested but indeed it is a central concept and by no means irrelevant. It is the interplay of different discourses that meet in local contexts that makes constructions of authenticity very complex. The multiple layering of simultaneously existing meanings thus has to be a matter of concern in order to "find ways to acknowledge that fixed categories are also mobilised as an aspect of hybridity" (Otsuji & Pennycook 2010: 244). People use essentialisms – but they do so in ways that are beneficial to their own purposes. The same person may behave differently in different contexts, with different underlying motives and on grounds of different discourses (an observation that is also central in the research agenda of scholars concerned with style, see e.g. Coupland 2007; Rickford & Eckert 2001).

Speaking a language is here not the result of 'natural' acquisition in the family, it is neither required by national educational regimes. It becomes a conscious choice of which people are reflexively aware, and functions as a tool in accumulating symbolic capital (Bourdieu 1979), primarily through the development of meta-perspectives on culture. The actual idea of cultural practices as forms of (symbolic, cultural, material) capital has the effect of 'unaware', unreflexive – authentic – linguistic identity becoming a legacy of a more traditional past (of First Modern Society see below and see Beck et al. 2003). Reflexive language choice creates "second-level authenticities" and here, "[p]erformers often 'earn' degrees of authenticity precisely through their disavowal of first-order authenticities. Indeed it is an interesting speculation that, in late modernity, authenticity needs to be earned discursively rather than automatically credited" (Coupland 2007: 184). This can be understood as an effect of late capitalism (Heller & Duchêne 2012), where linguistic competence becomes a form of capital in selling 'human resources' on a global job market.

Further, ethnic authenticity seems to gain multiple functions in this context. According to contemporary sociological theory, the functional multiplication of categories of modernity is a general tendency of late modern society. As it may help to get authenticity off the modernist hook, I will briefly introduce this theoretical perspective on modernist categories in late modernity in the following.

4 Linguistic authenticity and reflexive modernity

Cultural symbols traditionally related to ethnic or national spaces (like *languages*) can become a complex means to index several social boundaries at the same time. To speak Spanish, in Sydney Cuban Salsa, creates a local boundary to L.A. Style Salsa, and at the same time links to national boundaries of class, where second language learning is indexical of high levels of education. Simultaneously, political discourses and the construction of class identity with transnational ties are relevant in the symbolic meanings of being able to speak Spanish.

It is not one social boundary that is marked by this language choice but several social boundaries at the same time, and these are in part interlinked.

Modernist categories – including as languages or ethnic groups – remain vital and do not dissolve. Ethnic and linguistic authenticity therefore does not become irrelevant. Yet, such categories can take up multiple functions and thus construct multiplex and sometimes contradictory boundaries. This is a central tenet of sociological theories on so-called *reflexive* modernity (Beck et al. 2003). These argue that modernity has modernized itself as globalisation, the dissolution of the welfare state, changed gender roles, flexible employment forms and the ecological crisis are an outcome of modernity but have put into question the old certainties of what they call *first* modern society (for more detail, see Beck et al. 2003; Beck et al. 1994). Thus, "modern structures are progressively losing their naturalness and their categoriality" (Coupland 2003: 425). One effect of the contested nature of modern categories is that people are more likely to gain reflexive knowledge of social boundaries as being constructed. These boundaries do not become irrelevant (as some strands of postmodernism might argue) but are used to construct higher-level categories, where authenticities are instrumentalized to develop new positions. And therefore "we will have to model the processes which recreate authenticity as a second-order phenomenon, as a relativised phenomenon, generated more locally" (Coupland 2003: 427).

A heightened awareness – a more reflexive stance – also has effects on linguistic boundaries, which then not only serve to mark cultural or inner-cultural class boundaries but can link to diverse political, cultural and economic boundaries in social formations from very small to very large, from very local to very global. It additionally has to be noted that power differentials on a global level can be constructed on the basis of constructions of authenticity. One example for this is if, as in the case of Cuban Salsa, it is only *some* people who are supposed to stay ethnically and linguistically 'real' (the 'others'), while the dominant majority instrumentalizes the 'others' otherness' to construct lifestyle and class identity. Minority cultures continue to be regarded as *first modern* (they have 'a culture') and dominant groups are associated with *reflexively modern* positions (they know about culture but are not limited by it). As reflexivity and recognition of the constructed nature of social boundaries is seen as cultural advancement, today's way of being 'authentic' is often based on the disavowal of traditional or *first modern* authenticities – even if these are instrumentalized to construct new 'authentic' positions. Not being ethnically authentic indicates access to meta-levels and is therefore required to become authentic in a reflexively modern world.

5 Consequences of multiple authenticities for sociolinguistics

I finally want to comment on what reflexively modern authenticity might mean for sociolinguistic theory and method. First of all, speakers can no longer be assumed to be a reflection of broad demographic categories but behave more strategically (Coupland 2003: 426) and display conscious choices in positioning themselves in a social world in which local, national and transnational cultures and discourses interact. The heightened reflexivity of speakers can lead to unexpected uses of varieties that can index various social boundaries at the same time. In this context, the methodological focus of sociolinguistics should be on the production of authenticity in stylistic performance (for an overview of different approaches to style, see Rickford & Eckert 2001: 1–6). Only if we understand authenticity to be produced locally, in performance, where meanings can also be employed in contradictory and multiple fashions can we get access to the potential meanings of language use and do not tacitly reproduce modernist categories as given.

Secondly, the link between the social and the linguistic has to be understood as very complex and multi-dimensional. Languages can index membership to groups – but they don't have to. Languages can also be used to construct identity positions that relate to political, social and economic discourses from different geographical scales. In this context, the transnational mobility of signs, discourses and ideologies has to be taken into account and recognized as interlinked with national and local scales. Research into local language ideologies is crucial to understand the effects of discursive interactions and to develop more general ideas on the social relevance and function of language boundaries. Where categories are seen as flexible and constructed, this may even have effects on the category of language itself.

Lastly, we have to be aware that traditional forms of ethnic authenticity continue to have analytical relevance and tacitly recreate power differentials that are responsible for reconstructing first modern global social hierarchies.

Appendix: Transcription Conventions

(.)	pause of less than a second
(1.5)	approximate length of pause in seconds
(text?)	speech hard to discern, analyst's guess
text	stressed, louder
téxt	rising intonation
/	overlapping

* I want to express gratitude to the editors of this book for having invited me to a truly inspiring conference and for giving me the chance to publish in this book. I also want to thank Miguel Souza for valuable comments on an earlier version of the article.

References

Agha, Asif 2003: The social life of cultural value. *Language and Communication* 23: 231–273.

Aparicio, Frances R. 1998: *Listening to Salsa: Gender, Latin Popular Music, and Puerto Rican Cultures*. Hanover, N.H.: Wesleyan University Press.

Aparicio, Frances R. & Cándida Jáquez (eds.) 2003: *Musical Migrations. Transnationalism and Cultural Hybridity in Latin/o America*. Basingstoke: Palgrave Macmillan.

Auer, Peter (ed.) 2007: *Style and Social Identities. Alternative Approaches to Linguistic Heterogeneity*. Berlin/New York: Mouton de Gruyter.

Australian Government 2011: *The People of Australia. Australia's Multicultural Policy*. Canberra: Commonwealth of Australia. http://www.immi.gov.au/media/publications/multicultural/pdf_doc/people-of-australia-multicultural-policy-booklet.pdf

Beck, Ulrich, Wolfgang Bonss & Christoph Lau 2003: The theory of reflexive modernization. Problematic hypotheses and research programme. *Theory, Culture & Society* 20: 1–33.

Beck, Ulrich, Anthony Giddens & Scott Lash 1994: *Reflexive Modernization. Politics, Tradition and Aesthetics in the Modern Social Order*. Cambridge: Polity Press.

Blommaert, Jan 2003: Commentary: A sociolinguistics of globalization. *Journal of Sociolinguistics* 7: 607–623.

Blommaert, Jan 2010: *The Sociolinguistics of Globalization*. Cambridge: Cambridge University Press.

Bourdieu, Pierre 1979: *Die feinen Unterschiede. Kritik der gesellschaftlichen Urteilskraft*. Frankfurt a. M.: Suhrkamp.

Clyne, Michael 1991: *Community Languages. The Australian Experience*. Cambridge: Cambridge University Press.

Clyne, Michael , Anne Pauwels & Roland Sussex 2007: The state of languages education in Australia. *Curriculum Leadership* http://cmslive.curriculum.edu.au/leader/the_state_of_languages_education_in_australia,19754.html

Coupland, Nikolas 2003: Sociolinguistic authenticities. *Journal of Sociolinguistics* 7: 417–431.

Coupland, Nikolas 2007: *Style. Language Variation and Identity*. Cambridge: Cambridge University Press.

Eckert, Penelope 1989: *Jocks and Burnouts: Social Categories and Identity in the High School*. New York: Teachers College Press.

Eckert, Penelope 2008: Variation and the indexical field. *Journal of Sociolinguistics* 12: 453–476.

Errington, Joseph 2008: *Linguistics in a Colonial World. A Story of Language, Meaning and Power*. Malden, MA.: Blackwell.

Glick Schiller, Nina, Linda Basch & Cristina Szanton Blanc 1997: From immigrant to transmigrant: Theorizing transnational migration. In Ludger Pries (ed.), *Transnationale Migration*, 121–140. Baden Baden: Nomos.

Gobo, Giampietro 2008: *Doing Ethnography*. London: Sage.

Grillo, Ralph D. 2003: Cultural essentialism and cultural anxiety. *Anthropological Theory* 3: 157–173.

Hannerz, Ulf 1990: Cosmopolitans and locals in world culture. *Theory, Culture & Society* 7: 237–251.

Hannerz, Ulf 1996: Cosmopolitans and locals in world culture. In Ulf Hannerz, *Transnational Connections. Culture, People, Places*, 102–111. London: Routledge.

Hardt, Michael & Antonio Negri 2002: *Empire. Die neue Weltordnung*. Frankfurt a. M.: Campus.

Heller, Monica & Alexandre Duchêne 2012: Pride and profit: Changing discourses of language, capital and nation-state. In Monica Heller and Alexandre Duchêne (eds.), *Language and Late Capitalism. Pride and Profit*, 1–20. New York: Routledge.

Hill, Jane H. 2001: Language, race and white public space. In Alessandro Duranti (ed.), *Linguistic Anthropology. A Reader*, 450–464. Oxford: Blackwell.

Holmes, Janet & Miriam Meyerhoff 1999: The Community of Practice: Theories and methodologies in language and gender research. *Language in Society* 28: 173–183.

Hosokawa, Shuhei 2002: Salsa no tiene fronteras: Orquesta de la luz and the globalization of popular music. In: Lise Waxer (ed.), *Situating Salsa. Global Markets and Local Meanings in Latin Popular Music*, 289–312. New York: Routledge.

Irvine, Judith T. & Susan Gal 2000: Language ideology and linguistic differentiation. In Paul V. Kroskrity (ed.), *Regimes of Language. Ideologies, Polities and Identities*, 35–83. Santa Fe, NM: School of American Research Press.

Johnstone, Barbara 2008: *Discourse Analysis*. Oxford: Blackwell.

Johnstone, Barbara & Scott F. Kiesling 2008: Indexicality and experience: Exploring the meanings of /aw/-monophthongization in Pittsburgh. *Journal of Sociolinguistics* 12: 5–33.

Lindsey, Tom 2008: *Australia 2020 Summit. Australia's Future in the World*. Canberra: Commonwealth of Australia. http://www.australia2020.gov.au/topics/future.cfm

Makoni, Sinfree & Alastair Pennycook 2007: Disinventing and reconstituting languages. In Sinfree Makoni and Alastair Pennycook (eds.), *Disinventing and Reconstituting Languages*, 1–41. Clevedon: Multilingual Matters.

Muehlmann, Shaylih & Alexandre Duchêne 2007: Beyond the nation-state: International agencies as new sites of discourses on bilingualism. In Monica Heller (ed.), *Bilingualism: A Social Approach*, 96–110. Basingstoke: Palgrave Macmillan.

Otsuji, Emi & Alastair Pennycook 2010: Metrolingualism: Fixity, fluidity and language in flux. *International Journal of Multilingualism* 7: 240–254.

Papadopulos, Maria 2003: Salsa no tiene frontera. Eine Szene ohne Grenzen? In Sven Bergmann and Regina Römhild (eds.), *Global Heimat: Ethnographische Recherchen im transnationalen Frankfurt*, 75–104. Frankfurt a. M.: Notizen.

Pennycook, Alastair 2007: *Global Englishes and Transcultural Flows*. London: Routledge.

Pfadenhauer, Michaela 2005: Das Experteninterview – Ein Gespräch zwischen Experte und Quasi-Experte. In Alexander Bognerr, Beate Littig and Wolfgang Menz (eds.), *Das Experteninterview. Theorie, Methode, Anwendung*, 113–130. Wiesbaden: VS Verlag für Sozialwissenschaften.

Pietrobruno, Sheenagh 2006: *Salsa and its Transnational Moves*. Lanham, MD: Lexington Books.

Pratt, Mary Louise 1987: Linguistic utopias. In Nigel Fabb, Derek Attridge, Alan Durant and Colin MacCabe (eds.), *The Linguistics of Writing*, 48–66. Manchester: Manchester University Press.

Rampton, Ben 1995: *Crossing: Language and Ethnicity among Adolescents*. London: Longman.

Rampton, Ben 2000: Speech Community. *Working Papers in Urban Language & Literacies* 15.
Rickford, John R. & Penelope Eckert 2001: Introduction. In Penelope Eckert and John R. Rickford (eds.), *Style and Sociolinguistic Variation*, 1–8. Cambridge: Cambridge University Press.
Robertson, Robert 1998: Glokalisierung: Homogenität und Heterogenität in Raum und Zeit. In Ulrich Beck (ed.), *Perspektiven der Weltgesellschaft*, 192–220. Frankfurt a. M.: Suhrkamp.
Römhild, Regina 2007: Alte Träume, neue Praktiken: Migration und Kosmopolitismus an den Grenzen Europas. In Transit Migration Forschungsgruppe (eds.), *Turbulente Ränder. Neue Perspektiven auf Migration an den Grenzen Europas*, 211–228. Bielefeld: Transcript.
Schneider, Britta 2009: ¿Hablemos el mismo idioma? Salsa, multilingualism and national monolingual ideology. In Patrick Stevenson and Jenny Carl (eds.), *Language, Discourse and Identity in Central Europe*, 203–223. Basingstoke: Palgrave.
Schneider, Britta 2010: Multilingual cosmopolitanism and monolingual commodification. Language ideologies in transnational Salsa communities. *Language in Society* 39: 647–668.
Schneider, Britta 2014: *Salsa, Language and Transnationalism*. Bristol: Multilingual Matters.
Silverstein, Michael 1985: Language and the culture of gender: At the intersection of structure, usage and ideology. In Elizabeth Mertz and Richard Parmentier (eds.), *Semiotic Mediation: Sociocultural and Psychological Perspectives*, 219–259. New York: Academic Press.
Silverstein, Michael 2003: Indexical order and the dialectics of sociolinguistic life. *Language and Communication* 23: 193–229.
Waxer, Lise 2002: Situating Salsa: Latin music at the crossroads. In Lise Waxer (ed.), *Situating Salsa. Global Markets and Local Meanings in Latin Popular Music*, 3–22. New York: Routledge.

Monica Heller
The commodification of authenticity

1 From the nation-state to the globalized new economy

In recent years, sociolinguists have noticed a shift in how we think about authentic identities, or authentic linguistic and cultural performances. We can trace much of the discursive assemblage on authenticity to Romantic ideas about human relationships to nature, locating the essence of who we are as individuals or groups outside of ourselves (Williams 1973). Romantic versions of nationalism locate authenticity in naturalized ideas of the nation, and place it in the role of primary principle of social organization. It is thus central to serve our ideas about citizenship, and indeed, personhood (Hobsbawm 1990; Bauman & Briggs 2003). Put differently, we accord rights of participation in social activities to those we count as authentic members of the nation, and judge moral worth on the same basis.

In this vision of citizenship, authenticity is, if not absolutely freely available to everyone, at least claimable (albeit with more or less difficulty). It is therefore not supposed to be marketized, that is, it is not supposed to be a commodity one can exchange for money. This has, however, in some ways long been the case (for example, since the early days of tourism); nonetheless, the major shift noted in the past decade or so has been a much greater move of authenticity from the realm of the political to the realm of the economic.

In this paper, I will use the lens of Bourdieu's ideas about linguistic legitimacy (Bourdieu 1977), as a way to operationalize who and what counts as authentic, and how that shifts as authenticity is commodified. Bourdieu (1977: 650) argues that participation in social activity is regulated through judgements of linguistic legitimacy, in all its dimensions:

> (W)e can state the characteristics which legitimate discourse must fulfil, the tacit presuppositions of its efficacy: it is uttered by a legitimate speaker, i.e. by the appropriate person, as opposed to the impostor (...); it is uttered in a legitimate situation, i.e. on the appropriate market (...) and addressed to legitimate receivers; it is formulated in the legitimate phonological and syntactic forms (...) except when transgressing these norms is part of the legitimate definition of the legitimate producer.

He points us to the importance of understanding the conditions of the (symbolic and material) market as the major source of value of linguistic forms and practices, of constraints on the circulation of resources (and hence on people's access to them), as well as, further, on the ability of differentially-positioned social actors to define what counts as the rules of the game, through exercising control over the production and distribution of those resources. As Bourdieu reminds us, political economic conditions are not evenly distributed, and hence people do not have equal access to resources or to the ability to define their value. What we are examining here is a shift in market conditions, from industrial to globalized tertiary (late) capitalism, and its effect on what constitutes linguistic legitimacy.

I will focus on what this shift has looked like for one example of a category particularly invested in Romantic nationalism: linguistic minority movements. These movements emerged at moments of state formation (for example, 19th century nation-states, post-WWI, 1960s decolonization) as a contestation of the legitimacy of centralizing states seeking to erase differences. Using the same principles of nation-state formation as the centralizing states whose legitimacy they contested (historical continuity, territorial occupation, linguistic and cultural homogeneity), groups in places like Corsica, Brittany, Wales and Québec argued that they had just as legitimate a claim to nation-statehood as did the larger polities to which they were supposed to belong (rather than, say, rejecting the principles altogether and arguing for a different basis for state formation). As contestatory movements, they still find themselves in the position of constantly defending and demonstrating their national authenticity, and thus provide an illuminating case for examining what happens when such authenticity is commodified.

Here I will examine the specific case of francophone Canada, where I have been following the development of discourses of the nation for some time (see Heller 2011). I will first discuss some of the reasons for increased commodification of the resources constructed by nationalism, namely authentic linguistic and cultural forms and practices, as they have unfolded in that particular space. Those specific processes will be linked to broader processes characteristic of late capitalism, showing how peripheral linguistic minorities are positioned in the globalized new economy. I will then show how the production of arts and culture, especially in tourism and popular culture, has emerged as a particularly important terrain of commodification of authenticity, as part of a search for alternative means of cultural reproduction as older political economic bases collapse. I will focus mainly on how social actors living the shift from linguistic minority activism to production of commodifiable authenticity handle the tensions between commodification and the uncommodifiable source of the value of authenticity, by separating out discursive fields into front and backstage, by extending the scope of what counts as authentic, or by ironizing authenticity. I will close by arguing that this tension calls into question the possibility for reproduction of authenticity as we have long understood it, and hence for the idea of the citizen and the nation.

2 Late capitalism and neo-liberalism in francophone Canada

As Alexandre Duchêne and I have argued elsewhere (Heller & Duchêne 2011: 8–9; see also Heller 2010), late capitalism has a set of characteristics which are particularly relevant for understanding how it is that language and identity have become more readily commodifiable than before. The key characteristics are the *saturation* of markets and the concomitant *expansion* of capital in the search for new markets and cheaper sources of goods and labour. Another strategy for increasing (or at least preserving) profits is the *addition of value* to widely-consumed goods, notably through the addition of symbolic resources, and the development of *niche markets* seeking distinction. Finally, the ability to shift quickly from one geographic zone to another, from one market niche to another, from one type of product to another (usually referred to as *flexibility*) is important to maintaining competitive edges.

All these developments heighten the role of communication generally, and language and other cultural forms and practices more specifically. As networks of production and consumption spread globally (Castells 2001; Harvey 2006), it becomes necessary to find modes of managing the process. Communication across time and space (however compressed), within shifting networks, and across increasingly diverse populations of producers and consumers, is crucial. While corporate actors often look to English or automatic translation to manage the multilingual dimension of this communicative network, it is often necessary or advantageous to function in more than one language. Language is also one dimension of the symbolic added value that can distinguish niche markets and niche goods from each other. It is here that the semiotic resources indexing authenticity created by industrial capitalist nationalism are usually brought into play.

In the Canadian context, we can look at the example of cheese. In the post-War period, cheese production became increasingly industrialized, and cheese itself took only a few forms (cheddar, swiss, maybe gouda, mozzarella for pizza, and the excitingly industrial innovation of cheddar-based cheese products like Velveeta and Cheez-Whiz). The one cheese that could possibly be claimed as unique, Oka (made by Trappist monks in Quebec), was eventually ceded to Kraft, the US-based multinational giant. Being bought out by large corporations was indeed typical of the fate of many regional producers, although some, like the Fromagerie St-Albert in eastern Ontario, survived as independents (usually as cooperatives). As the market for such cheese became saturated, as the middle class grew and travelled and learned to use food as a basis for social distinction, cheddar and swiss and gouda, and even Velveeta, became boring, and even a bit embarrassing.

At the same time, it became difficult for European cheesemakers to find a niche in a crowded market. It was Swiss, Belgian and French farmers, immigrating to Canada in the 1970s and 1980s, who introduced the idea of artisanal cheese. Quebec was the first region to adapt agricultural regulations to this concept, and to appropriate the French ideas of *terroir* and *labellisation* – essentially the idea that products are uniquely characterized by the natural conditions of production (much the same ideas we had about nation and race in the years before World War II), and that only they can be identified as being what they are; imitators cannot ride on the coattails of their success.

These products, not surprisingly, mobilize indices of Romantic nationalism to signal their status as artisanal: the wrapping is the locus of symbolic added value, with images of pastoral rural scenes, 19th century local settlers (real and fictive) and buildings, and French place and cheese names. They were collectively marketed outside of Quebec as products of Quebec, with special supermarket cases rendered visible by bright blue-and-white *fleurs de lys* (the symbol of Quebec). Such marketing, of course, required the judicious use of English and French: enough French to index authenticity, but not so much as to bewilder the consumer. In the meantime, the Fromagerie St-Albert now capitalizes on the fact that it never sold out to big agribusiness by rebranding itself as a producer of artisanal cheese (although it is still industrial cheddar, albeit from local cows), as part of a regional attempt to retool an agriculture-and-lumber economic base to one based on agro-tourism and services to the expanding urban area around nearby Ottawa, the Canadian capital.

We will hear more about this region below. It serves, however, as a first glimpse into the changing political economy of francophone Canada, and hence to an appreciation of how the commodification of French Canadian authenticity has become an issue. Indeed, industrial agriculture is no longer sustainable, and nor are the other main categories of economic activity which have been central to the construction of the category "francophone" in Canada and to the development of its linguistic nationalism.

As Lindsay Bell and I have argued (Heller & Bell 2011), it is possible to understand the category "francophone" in Canada as a labour category, that is, as part of a system of ethnolinguistic differentiation which legitimizes and masks class differences, and allows for the construction of pools of reserve labour. This process was especially important in Canada's colonial economy, devoted as it was to extraction of primary resources for consumption by the metropole (Wolf 1982).

Furs, lumber, fish, and eventually minerals have all played important roles, even today, although the pulp-and-paper industry has declined with the advent of digital media, and the nature of the mineral resources of interest has changed as well, giving way largely to oil and gas. Francophones have historically been over-represented in primary resource activities, or as industrial labour. Spatial segregation has been tied to dreams of autarky as part of élite forms of political resistance, and francophone nationalism has borrowed heavily from Romantic nationalist tropes linking the nation to the land (Morissonneau 1978).

As elsewhere in North America, that political economy has changed dramatically. In the Atlantic provinces, an important site of reserve labour, the fishing stocks have been weakened, closing fisheries once the mainstay of Acadian traditional bastions. Lumber mills, mines and factories have closed across the country, as cheaper sources are found or demand dries up. Some workers find jobs in new sites, usually much farther away, such as the mines of Latin America or the oil fields and sands of Alberta. Their income remains important for sustaining their communities of origin, as much of their work is seasonal or temporary, or they simply send money home. But those communities have also been forced to seek new modes of economic reproduction in the activities of the new economy, with an emphasis typically on communications (call centres), tourism, *terroir* and arts and culture (the last two both exportable and consumable as part of a tourist product).

At the same time, the Canadian government has realigned its cultural and linguistic policy with the neoliberal stance now typical of state regimes in late capitalism. Attempts to facilitate the global circulation of capital have led governments away from their post-War role as welfare states, and refocused them on economic development. The immediate impact on francophone Canada was a reframing of support for minority francophone language and culture. Starting in the late 1980s, the Canadian federal government redefined its funding programs, so that an elite long used to obtaining funding simply for activities aimed at the development of language and culture as a means of ensuring minority "vitality" (Landry & Allard 1989) found itself cut loose. After much negotiation (see Silva & Heller 2009), a new process emerged in the early 2000s, aimed at recasting language and culture in terms of community economic development.

Changing political economic conditions in Canada, as elsewhere, have shifted the value and meaning of linguistic and cultural forms, and call into question who gets to decide what counts as linguistic legitimacy. While in the past, legitimacy came from remaining close to the land, practicing Catholicism and speaking good French (and preferably only French, or at least French kept clearly separate from English), its commodification muddies the boundaries between French and English, sidelines religion, and requires rural producers to become part of broader networks which affect them much more directly than used to be the case, and requires urban working-class francophones to turn to the service industry as factories close (Roy 2003). Language and culture become increasingly both the process and the product of labour (Heller & Duchêne 2011), introducing a degree of reflexivity (Giddens 1990) through which authenticity is in fact hard to sustain. As we will see below, this reflexivity is expressed both through explicit discussion and questioning of the foundations of normative practices, as well as through the ironization of authenticity.

In the following section, I will examine how some of the traditional bastions of francophone Canada have turned to the commodification of authenticity through tourism, and how they have (or have not) managed some of the tensions related to that process.

3 Selling authenticity[1]

For francophone communities used to organizing around struggles for rights and recognition, the requirement to recast old values in terms of community development often came as a shock. Minimally, it caused some re-thinking and questioning about how best to move forward. While some people abandoned the struggle, or were pushed to the side because they were unable to adapt, other actors in existing institutions used the opportunity to re-orient their activities, their discourse and their modes of recruitment. I will examine two cases here which show us how the commodification of authenticity affects the framing of legitimate language and participation.

The first is the village of Chéticamp, Nova Scotia (see Moïse et al. 2006; White 2005). Situated on the coast of Cape Breton Island, on the Gulf of St. Lawrence, the village actually had long lived off a combination of fishing and servicing summer tourism. Americans frequently visited the island from the late 19th century onward, getting away from the heat of eastern seaboard cities. In the 1920s, one of them (in fact, a guest of Alexander Graham Bell) noticed the hooked rugs produced by local women since at least the 1880s. She saw in those rugs

1 The data presented here come from a series of projects funded by the Social Sciences and Humanities Research Council of Canada and the Wenner-Gren Foundation for Anthropological Research. Many colleagues and graduate students participated in different phases of the research; I will thank here those directly involved in gathering and analyzing the data I report in this chapter: Annette Boudreau, Gabriele Budach, Lise Dubois, Alexandre Duchêne, Mireille McLaughlin, Claudine Moïse, Mary Richards, Emanuel da Silva, Chantal White, Maia Yarymowich and Natalie Zur Nedden.

the possibility of marketization, organizing the women into a business whose products she placed on the American market. Chéticamp authentic goods have long been commodities, then, although the women themselves relied on American brokers to both organize them and to bring their goods to market. They were communicatively removed from their consumers.

With the collapse of the cod fishery, which was closed due to over-fishing in 1992 (it has recently slowly been reopening), and difficulties in the lobster fishery, Chéticamp, like many other such villages, faced a challenge. Building on the long tradition of servicing summer resident tourism, the town developed those activities more intensively. The men used their fishing boats to take tourists out whale-watching, while the women focussed more on direct sales of hooked rugs to visiting, albeit passing, new tourists. They were able in particular to aim at not only the established American market, but also new tourists from Québec and, in particular, France.

Two tensions arose immediately from this development. The first has to do with the product itself. Following a labour dispute with the initial American organizer, and following a movement to cooperativize widespread in Nova Scotia in the mid-20th century, the women organized their business into a cooperative. The rugs they produced largely repeated patterns developed initially for the tastes of early 20th century American consumers, nonetheless thus guaranteeing authenticity through both consistency of product and legitimacy of cooperative control. The images drew heavily from Romantic nationalist ideas about Acadie, with representations of bucolic scenes, the sea, lighthouses, and the Acadian flag (adopted in 1881). The possibility of direct access to passing tourists, as well as economic difficulties, drew more women into the production market, and with them, controversy over the images to be represented in the rugs. The older established group did not wish to deviate from established practice, while a newer, and generally younger, group sought to introduce new patterns into the repertoire. This caused a rift, and ended up with the second group excluded from the cooperative, as not sufficiently "Acadian", and setting up a rival shop elsewhere in the village. So we see already how this shift brings in new actors, with new interests, and provokes ideological struggle over who gets to decide what counts as Acadian.

The second example has to do with another space where constructing a specific form of *acadianité* occurs: in the tourist encounter. With the recent growth in tourism to francophone Canada from France, the performance of local identity becomes an interactional issue between producers and consumers. We have noted elsewhere how the circulation of identity goods from francophone Canada in France requires the linguistic presentation of the goods in question: consumers will ask sellers to talk to them in Canadian French before they turn their attention to objects to buy (Budach et al. 2007). Sellers do this whether or not they have spent any time recently in Canada, and whether or not these are forms they produce under any other circumstances than the commercial transaction. In Chéticamp, the consumers have to come to the producers, but the principle of linguistic indexing of authenticity is the same. It is not enough to buy (or sell) hooked rugs; it is necessary to tie the rugs themselves to a cultural performance, whose authenticity is signalled by specific linguistic features.

In the extract below, Anna, one of the cooperative members, recounts to a member of our research team how she does this. She points out that she explains the whole process of rug production, which helps to show how the rugs really are produced on site by these particular people, from locally-produced wool (this is not an out-sourced effort, or an artificially imported one). Within that story, she flags certain features as distinctive. She reports that she draws attention through pausing, repetition and emphasis to the phonetic variation between *nétteye* and *nettoie* (clean) and to the lexical variation between Acadian *bosses*, and European *mottons* (lumps or clumps of wool), clearly opposing the two varieties ("*mais*"– but) and situating her audience as speakers of the European one (you pl. say...), as well as reporting that at least one of them collaborated in this categorization ("ben oui" – well yes). She then reports that she explains that she uses the same word (*bosse*) for a lump of wool and a lump from an injury, whereupon her interlocutor enters the boundary-making process by providing her European equivalent (*prune* – which can also mean "plum"). Anna's brief report, then, provides a synoptic view of how Acadian producers and European consumers co-construct the hooked rugs as authentic.

> Anna: pis je leur dis souvent l'histoire que j'étais en train de filer « quand que je file si je **nétteye** pas ma laine/**nettoiE** si je **nétteye** pas bien ma laine ben il reste de la saleté pis ça fait des **bosses** »/ « mais » je dis « vous-autres vous appelez ça des **mottons** » (...) pis il y en a un qui dit/ « ben oui » j'ai dit « aussi quand je tumbe moi je me fais une **bosse** » ielle elle dit « ben moi je me fais une **prune** » (Moïse et al. 2006: 101)

> [Anna: and I often tell them the story that I was spinning "when I spin if I don't clean (Acadian) my wool/clean (European) if I don't clean (Acadian) my wool well, well there's still some dirt and it makes lumps (Acadian)"/but I say "you (pl) call that lumps (European)" (...) and then one of them says/"well yes" I said "also when I fall (Acadian) I get a lump (Acadian)" nshe she says "well, I get a lump (European)"]

While the encounter with the European francophone requires some positioning, other new audiences are more problematic. The most problematic audience is the one that speaks English, since the ideology of ethnonationalism, which produced these identity goods in the first place, requires a certain degree of homogeneity. What makes francophone goods francophone is not just that they are produced by francophone bodies, but that they are produced in French, and only French. Further, many new producers still see the activities they are now trying to commercialize as directly connected to (indeed often exactly the same as) the linguistic and cultural maintenance activities they have long been running (and which the state will no longer fund as community identity activities, but only as community economic development ones). As such, they only make sense as monolingual francophone activities. After years of activism aimed at creating spaces where francophones would be protected from English, what does it mean to have to deal with English-speaking consumers of your identity?

The following example is drawn from a recording of a meeting that took place in 2003 in a small Ontario town with a long history of activism (see Heller 2011: 128–144). Like many such towns, this one was trying to develop a cultural festival, with the distinctiveness of French and Franco-Ontarian culture as the chief drawing point. For this strategy to work, the product needed to be of interest either to people who saw it as a chance to participate in their own community, or to people who find it exotic – and who therefore are likely to be English-speakers. Further, the small size of the local francophone community made reliance on those numbers a weak basis for confidence in sufficient numbers to make the festival solvent, and the distance from major centres of francophone population farther east, as well as the availability of similar events in other communities, made it unlikely that the event would draw sufficient numbers of francophones from farther away. The organizing committee found itself having to confront the problem of dealing with anglophones.

In the following extract we see one organizing committee member, Sylvie, reporting on her conversation with one of the outside (English-speaking) bodies the committee also had to deal with over issues like permits and safety regulations. This body expressed concern about provision of information to festival participants who might not speak French, triggering a veritable soul-searching about how to maintain the authenticity of the event while catering to English-speakers.

> Sylvie: (...)/ pis elle me demandait si notre intention était d'avoir pas seulement des francophones mais aussi la communauté anglophone (...) pis il a parlé aussi des ateliers d'avoir uhmmm peut-être d'avoir des personnes qui parlent français anglais (...)
> Nina: mais à quelque part les gens viennent pour un peu d'immersion dans la culture pis la langue pis (...)
> ?: est-ce que les ateliers vont être bilingues?
> Nina: non écoute où est-ce qu'on met la ligne là? (...)
> Sylvie: non je lui ai dit que ben c'est sûr les francophones mais aussi je lui ai dit aussi qu'on veut montrer à la communauté anglophone la tradition francophone
> Mario: pis qu'on existe

[Sylvie: (...)/ and she asked me if our intention was to have not only francophones but also the anglophone community [. . .] and he also talked about the workshops to have uhmm maybe people who speak French and English (. . .)
Nina: But somewhere people come for a bit of immersion in the culture and the language and (. . .)
?: Are the workshops going to be bilingual?
Nina: No listen where are we going to draw the line there (. . .)
Sylvie: No I told her that well of course the francophones / but also I told her also that we want to show francophone tradition to the anglophone community
Mario: And that we exist]

Selling linguistic authenticity turns out to be complicated. It calls into question the stance of the producer, and his or her subjectivity: am I a producer or transmitter of an authentic good, am I an embodiment of that commodity? How much control do I retain over this process, given the conditions of the market? It also calls into question how to resolve the conundrum of selling monolingualism multilingually. The festival organizers ended up agreeing to put up some bilingual signage, and assuming that the bilingualism of volunteers would allow for backstage management of communications with anglophones (cast in this discussion as a matter of "politeness").

At other events, such as large historical pageants, organizers began after a few years to include a welcome to "our visitors who speak English", assuring them that they would so enjoy the music and the visual effects that not speaking French would not affect their appreciation of the experience. In these ways, it became possible to protect the francophone integrity of the event, while recognizing the participation of anglophones, cast as "other" in the same way Anna cast her European clients. At the same time, the projected presence of all these others (Canadian and American anglophones, European – and indeed Québécois – francophones) serves primarily to reinforce a Romantic nationalist view of identity, rooting authenticity in fixed rural villages with unified distinctive linguistic and cultural practices. We can understand this as a kind of neo-colonialism, insofar as it occurs within a discursive regime in which the dominant groups (Europeans and Anglophones) reproduce symbolic domination through exoticizing alterity of the colonial subject. In the next section, we will consider a different dimension of colonialism with discursive consequences: the relationship of francophones to North American indigeneity.

4 Reinventing authenticity

As the new market conditions opened the discursive construction of *la francité canadienne* to a wider network, other perspectives needed to be taken into account. We have briefly touched on the role of European francophones and Canadian and American Anglophones (although much more could be said about the effect of their colonial gaze). Here we will explore how commodification has forced francophones to re-examine one of their strongest claims to political (national) legitimacy and hence to (eventually commodifiable) authenticity: indigeneity.

As discussed earlier, claims to authenticity are linked to Romantic views of the nation as natural, with a core, or essence, located outside of history; this is the central foundation of ideas about indigeneity (Wolf 1982). In Canada, francophone claims to legitimacy and recognition (see Mario's comment above on the importance of the festival showing anglophones that "we exist") depend on locating francophones as present on Canadian soil before anglophones, and linked more strongly and enduringly to that soil. It depends also, as we have seen, on linking francophones to nature and rurality.

Both of these have been recently contested. I will first discuss the indigenous claims to priority which threaten those of francophones, and the ways in which francophones react to them by incorporating indigeneity into francophone identity narratives. I will then turn to new claims by urban francophones to new, cosmopolitan modes of constructing Frenchness.

From the perspective of First Nations peoples (also known as aboriginal or indigenous peoples), francophones can be cast as colonial European settlers, indeed must be in order for indigeneity to make sense. This is of course threatening to francophone claims, especially as indigenous rights movements have gained ground, and attracted sympathy across the world – and certainly among the most important consumers of commodified Frenchness.

One result has been the appropriation of indigeneity by francophones. I first saw movement in this direction in the late 1990s, in the village where the festival eventually was developed. A number of community members began to avail themselves of the bureaucratic system set up by the state to recognize not only First Nations (Inuit and Indian) status, but also that of the Métis – the descendants of unions between francophones and indigenous peoples. As several of them told me, in their youth any link with indigenous peoples was considered shameful, but now they were learning to reclaim a lost heritage. Some individuals, then, recast themselves entirely as Métis, while others opted for simultaneous affiliation as a francophone and as a Métis. About five years later, in the second year of the festival, the nearby indigenous community was invited to open the activities, and provincial Métis were invited to formally participate in the crafts sale; both First Nations and Métis flags flew alongside the Franco-Ontarian and Canadian ones, as we can see in the images presented.

Figure 1

Figure 2

Figure 3

We saw similar forms of inclusion in events across the country, including ones on a bigger scale. Major francophone musical events now regularly include Métis and French-speaking indigenous artists, for example, with figures such as the folk-country-rock singer Florent Vollant and the hip-hop artist Samian (both from Quebec) frequently appearing around the country. Many festivals and theatrical representations begin with multiple re-enactments of the first encounter of the French and local indigenous groups, and a narrativization of that encounter which insists on its mutuality and its melding. The image below is taken from the website of l'Écho d'un Peuple (Echo of a People), one of the many historical pageants which emerged in the 2000s; in this case, regional élites in eastern Ontario built on a political and educational infrastructure to develop a commodifiable narrative in the form of summer theatre. As the audience saw the French arrive on the shores of Canada, to be greeted with open arms by the indigenous people on the shore, the voice-over explained that these first encounters produced mixed populations, and that, in the end "Nous sommes tous des Métis" (we are all Métis).

Figure 4

Finally, on a more traditional political level, we find established francophone lobbying groups seeking out alliances with their Métis and indigenous counterparts. For example, in the mid 2000s, l'Assemblée fransaskoise, the organization representing the francophones of the province of Saskatchewan, developed a strategy of making alliances with other minority groups in the province, opening discussions first with the Métis. Informal discussions were followed by a public round table, which was filmed and distributed with the goal of promoting further discussion.

In all these ways, we see francophone responses to indigenous counterclaims to authenticity, in the form of a realignment which includes indigeneity within the borders of the francophone community, and no longer outside them. In this sense, commodified performances serve as a particularly potent discursive space for a redefinition of what it means to be francophone in ways which serve to shore up the legitimacy of francophone political claims and the value of authenticity of its commodifiable identity.

At the same time, the urban centres are re-positioning themselves. Cities have long attracted francophones as domestic and industrial labour, as well as small business owners and employees and professional, political and religious elites; nonetheless, they were cast as dangerous places for francophones, who would risk assimilation there (Heller 2005). Those urban populations, however, have grown and consolidated as sites of discursive production, as francophones develop important urban institutions (all levels of education, including universities; media; culture; health) which attract local francophones as well as immigrants for both training and employment. They thus produce people who live their Frenchness differently, and are claiming the right to redefine *la francité* in urban ways (see McLaughlin 2009).

One clear example is the emergence in 2003 of a website called *Acadieurbaine.net*, whose title explicitly evokes an urban, as opposed to the unmarked rural, way of understanding Acadie. The choice of the extension .net (as opposed to say .org), is consistent with the claim that Acadie is a network, more than it is a rooted location in space. Another is the emergence in Montréal of multilingual rap, performed largely by children of immigrants, and which explicitly contents the racial and linguistic uniformity of dominant visions of Québécois (LeBlanc et al. 2007; Sarkar & Winer 2006). Cities have become the site of debates about diversity and mobility as defining facts about francophone life, and about the value of urban (and often mixed) vernaculars.

Both the processes we have seen here (appropriation of indigeneity by francophones and claims by previously excluded urban groups to racial and linguistic diversification of francophone identity, as well as to urban cosmopolitanism and middle-class mobility) extend and diversify the definition of authenticity. They respond to changing conditions by trying to adapt. They do not call into question the importance of that authenticity, however; the stakes are high and the emotional investment profound.

5 Ironizing authenticity

While at one end of the spectrum we see efforts to save francophone authenticity, we simultaneously see efforts to create some distance from that discursive position. Some of these, of course, involve complete abandonment, but these seem largely to be confined to those who take up instead the indigenous cause (McLaughlin 2009: 232–237). Others involve efforts at commodifying an authenticity wrapped in humour and irony. These efforts all emerge in popular culture, once again showing how commodification opens up opportunities for debates about the nature of Frenchness, on new grounds. Interestingly, they emerge more often in minority areas (such as Acadie or Ontario) than they do in Quebec, where there is a greater investment in modern state-territorial nationalism. While Quebec has certainly profited from the consolidation of a francophone cultural product circuit, minority francophones add value by virtue of their niche quality and their rarity, and have even more to gain from globalized cultural consumption than do Québécois. In addition, Quebec remains the centre of francophone cultural production in Canada, providing the market and the credentializing needed to launch careers. It is not surprising that it might be the outsiders to this market (who nonetheless rely on it), who produce ironizing stances the most often.

Figure 5

The one that has attracted most attention is the comic strip Acadieman (Perrot 2010; Comeau & King 2011; Heller 2011). Acadieman is the creation of Dano LeBlanc, who says he created this anti-superhero out of anger at the francophone élite's insistence on imposing "good" French and devaluing the vernaculars most Acadians actually speak (LeBlanc, personal communication). Like many modern-day Acadians, Acadieman does not fish, he works at a call centre (note the brand name on the computer: Hell). The Acadian flag on his t-shirt has a skull-and-crossbones in the place of the Star of the Sea (symbol of the Virgin Mary, patron saint of Acadie). Finally, Acadieman speaks *chiac*, the mixed French-English vernacular Leblanc wants to defend.

Acadieman, however, travels less well than actual musicians; he is harder to take on the road. Better examples might be groups like the Acadian rappers *Radio Radio*, who use humour and *chiac* on a regular basis. Here is what they said about it in an on-line interview in 2011:

> Sur le premier degré, je pense c'est l'humour. Mais au deuxième degré c'est des choses un peu plus sérieuses, si tu vraiment penses... prends Jacuzzi. Jacuzzi c'est peut-être la chanson le plus connu au Canada. Le monde dit « ah, c'est le fun le jacuzzi » mais au deuxième niveau, « il y a de place en masse dans mon jacuzzi » il y a de place en masse dans mon territoire, dans mon pays, chez nous, ma maison. Tout le monde est invité. On juge pas. Si tu es blanc, noir, chinois, arabe, on s'en fout. Vous êtes bienvenue. Viens fêter avec nous. Alors, c'est comme ça qu'on utilise l'humour pour traiter des choses sérieuses.

> [On one level, I think it is humour. But on another level, it's about things that are a little more serious if you really think about it. Take Jacuzzi. Jacuzzi is our most well known song in Canada. People say "ah, Jacuzzi is so much fun" but on the next level "there is lots of room in my Jacuzzi" there is lots of room in my territory, my country, my home, my house. Everyone is invited. We don't judge. If you are black, white, Chinese, Arab, we don't care. You are welcome. Come party with us. So, that is how we are able to use humour to get at more serious things]
> CitaZone (http://www.citazine.fr/article/radio-radio-interview) April 28, 2011

As a final example, I provide below an extract from an interview in the Montréal weekly cultural newspaper *Voir* with Damien Robitaille, a singer-songwriter from Ontario. The writer's questions are informed by dominant ideologies of francophone identity, for example, that someone from rural Ontario should be wearing a lumberjack shirt and love the country. Most importantly, given his roots in English-speaking Ontario, with an English-speaking mother to boot, one assumes that being francophone would be really difficult, but that his choice to sing in French must reveal his attraction for expressive possibilities unavailable in English. Robitaille sends up each one of these expectations, causing the writer to be unsure of how to interpret him.

> (...)
> Il est sérieux. Peut-être pas. Bienvenue dans la tête de Damien Robitaille. Damien Robitaille: mi-vingtaine, shape de loup-garou en poids comme en poils; auteur-compositeur-interprète de campagne, il pourrait venir de la Louisiane, mais vient de (l') Ontario; on l'imagine en chemise carreautée et il nous arrive en chemise hawaïenne.

(…)
Qui est-ce que tu admires le plus?
"Dans le temps, j'admirais mon grand-père et son tracteur. J'aimais ça au boutte, les tracteurs! J'voulais en conduire un! Mais plus asteure. Pas en ville."
(…)
Damien Robitaille, quand il vous parle, cherche le mot juste en bégayant un autre mot. Son rythme est saccadé, éparpillé. On met ça sur le dos de son franglais et on pardonne tout à un gars qui l'aurait eu plus facile dans la langue de Johnny Cash. Papa franco, maman anglo, village où le français en arrache, vous voyez le genre.
(…)
Damien, qu'est-ce que la langue française te permet de chanter que tu ne peux pas chanter en anglais?
"En français, mettons, je parle d'un chien. En anglais, ben, je dis dog."
(David Thibodeau, *Voir*, October 20, 2005)

[(…)
He's serious. Or maybe not. Welcome inside the head of Damien Robitaille. Damien Robitaille; mid-twenties, shape of a werewolf in pounds and in body hair; an singer-songwriter from the country, he could come from Louisiana, but he comes from (. . .) Ontario; one imagines him in a lumberjack shirt and he shows up in a Hawaiian one.
(…)
Whom do you admire the most?
"I used to admire my grandfather and his tractor. I loved them to bits, tractors! I wanted to drive one! But not anymore. Not in town."
(…)
When Damien Robitaille talks to you, he searches for the right word by stuttering another word. His rhythm is choppy, diffuse. One explains that by virtue of his Frenglish, and you forgive a guy whose life would have been easier in the language of Johnny Cash. Daddy a Franco, Mummy an Anglo, a village where French has to really try hard, you get the picture.
(…)
Damien, what does the French language allow you to sing that you can't sing in English?
"In French, let's say, I'll talk about a *chien* (dog). In English, well, I say dog."]

Rather than situate himself as a failed or lame francophone who has to work harder than usual to construct his legitimacy, Robitaille insists on the banality of his bilingualism and of his rural-urban rooted-cosmopolitan existence. In this way, he distances himself from the accepted frames of interpretation of what it means to be francophone. At the same time, of course, his career depends on francophone institutions set up to nurture young talent – so he walks a fine line.

Indeed, ironizing authenticity can be understood as calling dominant discourses into question, but it doesn't fully undermine their legitimacy. It certainly does not offer any alternatives. It is, however, a meaningful response to the gap created by commodification between conditions of discursive production and discursive legitimacy, and in that sense it is not surprising that it appears exactly where commodification happens most obviously. It also provides a window into the subjectivity of francophone identity under the conditions of late capitalism, showing us how hard it is to maintain the notion of national belonging as a primary means of defining personhood. Robitaille and the members of Radio Radio are probably unlikely to respond seriously to questions about what language they dream in, or to touch their hearts when speaking of Frenchness. They still understand those questions, though, because they still frame our imaginations.

6 Francophone citizenship and commodified authenticity

In this paper, I have described some of the ways in which the conditions of late capitalism have increased the terrain and the means for the commodification of authenticity. We have seen some of the forms it takes, particularly in the production of cultural and linguistic goods or goods with cultural and linguistic added value, putting performance in the centre of the discursive space of national identity.

I have mainly focussed here though on the ways in which the commodification of authenticity disrupts formerly hegemonic discursive production, forcing an extension and a reflexivity (expressed through explicit discussion and through irony) which make it difficult to conduct business as usual. Both greater inclusiveness and reflexivity, especially the funny kind, have their value, on and off the commodities market. (Of course, reflexivity wouldn't even be funny unless it got into some uncomfortable place.)

They certainly disrupt taken for granted ways of deciding who is and who is not one of us. By doing that, they open doors to a reassessment of francophone citizenship, creating the possibility that different kinds of people might perhaps enjoy its benefits, as well accepting its limitations. That very possibility then creates questions about how to perform Frenchness. Finally, it raises questions about what it feels like to be francophone, or rather, what it is supposed to feel like, and why.

Barth (1969) famously said that what matters in ethnicity (and I would argue this can be extended to any social category) is not the "cultural stuff" (his term) within the boundary, but the process of boundary-making itself. When it becomes difficult to be a member of a particular group for some reason connected to the political economic basis of social reproduction, individuals can choose to become something else (or at least try to, it is usually a really hard thing to accomplish), the group can decide to become something else, or the group can decide to try being itself differently.

My data on francophone Canada shows, I believe, people trying to do being francophone differently. At the same time, there are some underlying doubts about the sense of ethnolinguistic categorization in contemporary life. Commodification affords us a window into ongoing change, allowing us to link up individual subjectivity, interactional processes, and the conditions of the symbolic market.

References

Barth, Fredrik (ed.) 1969: *Ethnic Groups and Boundaries*. Boston: Little, Brown.

Bauman, Richard & Charles Briggs 2003: *Voices of Modernity: Language Ideologies and the Politics of Inequality*. Cambridge: Cambridge University Press.

Bourdieu, Pierre 1977: The economics of linguistic exchanges. *Social Science Information* 116(6): 645–668.

Budach, Gabrielle, Claudine Moïse, Alexandre Duchêne & Mary Richards 2007: Bison, feuille d'érable et fleur de lys au Canada: les stéréotypes existent-ils toujours? In Henri Boyer (ed.), *Stéréotypage, stéréotypes, fonctionnements ordinaires et mises en scène*, 29–45. Paris: l'Harmattan.

Castells, Manuel 2001: *The Information Age: Economy, Society and Culture*. Oxford: Blackwell.

Comeau, Philip & Ruth King 2011: Media representation of minority French: Valorization, identity and the Acadieman phenomenon. *Canadian Journal of Linguistics* 56(2): 179–202.

Giddens, Anthony 1990: *The Consequences of Modernity*. Berkeley, CA: University of California Press.

Harvey, David: 2006: *The Limits of Capital*. New York: Verso.

Heller, Monica 2005: Une approche sociolinguistique à l'urbanité. *Revue de l'Université de Moncton* 36(1): 321–346.

Heller, Monica 2010: The commodification of language. *Annual Review of Anthropology* 39: 101–148.

Heller, Monica 2011: *Paths to Post-nationalism: A Critical Ethnography of Language and Identity*. Oxford: Oxford University Press.

Heller, Monica & Lindsay Bell 2011: Frontiers and Frenchness: pride and profit in the production of Canada. In Alexandre Duchêne and Monica Heller (eds.), *Language in Late Capitalism: Pride and Profit*, 161–182. London: Routledge.

Heller, Monica & Alexandre Duchêne 2011: Pride and profit: changing discourses of languages, nation and state. In Alexandre Duchêne and Monica Heller (eds.), *Language in Late Capitalism: Pride and Profit*, 1–21. London: Routledge.

Hobsbawm, Eric 1990: *Nations and Nationalism since 1760*. Cambridge: Cambridge University Press.

Landry, Rodrigue & Réal Allard 1989: Vitalité linguistique et diglossie. *Revue québécoise de linguistique théorique et appliquée* 8(2): 73–101.

LeBlanc, Marie-Nathalie, Alexandrine Boudreault-Fournier & Gabriella Djerrahian 2007: Les jeunes et la marginalisation à Montréal: la culture hip=hop francophone et les enjeux de l'intégration. *Diversité urbaine* 7(1): 9–30.

McLaughlin, Mireille 2009: L'Acadie post-nationale: producing Franco-Canadian identity in the global economy. Ph.D. thesis, Ontario Institute for Studies in Education, University of Toronto.

Moïse, Claudine, Mireille McLaughlin, Sylvie Roy & Chantal White 2006: Le tourisme patrimonial: la commercialisation de l'identité franco-canadienne et ses enjeux langagiers. *Langage et société* 118: 85–108.

Morissonneau, Christian 1978: *La Terre promise: le mythe du nord québécois*. Montréal: HMH Hurtubise.

Perrot, Marie-Ève 2010: Acadieman et l'"Académie chiac". In Michael Abecassis and Gudrun Ledegen (eds.), *Les voix des Français*, vol. 2, 59–70. Bern: Peter Lang.

Roy, Sylvie 2003: Bilingualism and standardization in a Canadian call center: challenges for a linguistic minority community. In Robert Bayley and Sandra Schecter (eds.), *Language Socialization in Multilingual Societies,* 269–287. Clevedon, UK: Multilingual Matters.

Sarkar, Mela & Lise Winer 2006: Multilingual code-switching in Quebec rap: poetry, pragmatics and performativity. *International Journal of Multilingualism* 3(3): 173–192.

Silva, Emanuel da & Monica Heller 2009: From protector to producer: the role of the state in the discursive shift from minority rights to economic development. *Language Policy* 8(2): 95–116.

White, Chantal 2005.: L'affirmation ou la négation de la différence: pratiques et représentations linguistiques de francophones de Chéticamp dans le contexte du tourisme patrimonial. M.A. thesis, Département d'études françaises, Université de Moncton.

Williams, Raymond 1973: *The Country and the City*. London: Chatto and Windus.

Wolf , Eric 1982: *Europe and the People without History*. Berkeley, CA: University of California Press.

Section 2:
Indexing authenticity in delocalised settings

Michael Silverstein

The race from place: Dialect eradication vs. the linguistic "authenticity" of *terroir*

On 19 November 2010, an article in the *New York Times* by reporter Sam Roberts sympathetically described the almost Sisyphean task of native speakers of *Newyorquais* to achieve that point at the stratificational top and center of their language community's sociolinguistic imaginary, the dialect-less voice "from nowhere" in the register sometimes labeled "General American." It became an instant flashpoint in online publication, stimulating over 600 comments before such responses were editorially terminated. This naturally effervescent stream of ethno-metalinguistic reflexivity, richer, in its way, than any sociolinguistic interview, reveals what we might term the post-"dialectal" (Gumperz) status of "dialect" in American English – cf. "Pittsburghese" (Johnstone, Kiesling, et al.). Indeed, "accent" has become a naturalized – if not natural – fact about an ineffable inner identity, a fact of human *terroir*, as it were (compare upscale menus with their Israeli couscous, Wisconsin farm-raised organic veal, Florida oranges, genuine Idaho potatoes, etc., let alone *appellation* and DOCG wines), that people seem to cherish and hold on to as much when contemplating its suppression or eradication as when celebrating its properly contextualized performance.

1 Dateline: Noo Yawk, Noo Yawk

"The rain in Spain stays mainly on the plain. In Hertford, Hereford, and Hampshire, hurricanes hardly ever happen." No New Yorker of a certain age can forget how Lerner & Loewe's musical *My Fair Lady* – which ran on Broadway for over six years beginning in 1956 – drove home the point about a person's verbal pronunciation as an index of his or her position in a stratified society. Based on George Bernard Shaw's *Pygmalion*, its plot develops from a bet by phonetics Professor Henry Higgins (aka Henry Sweet [1845–1912]) that the uneducated Cockney flower seller, Eliza Doolittle, can be passed off as an aristocrat (if, as it turns out, of suspected Hungarian origin!), solely on the basis of transforming her pronunciation of English from Cockney to what is termed in Great Britain, "Received Pronunciation," the London-centered standard register of the privileged and educated that used to be heard on BBC and equivalently well-spoken venues. Of course, for New Yorkers of the time this had – and still has – a particularly poignant interest, because no matter the musical's plot had been transposed, following Shaw, from Ovid's statue coming to life to the context of class relations in Edwardian England, the cultural sense in America – including New York – is that speaking identifiably local New York dialect – *Newyorquais*, we might more fashion-ably call it – is indeed like speaking Cockney in Britain. That is to say, "tawkin' Noo Yawk" indicates not just an urban, but inevitably as well a non-privileged class identity. The long-running Broadway musical, soon followed by a 1964 film version, could only have increased a kind of subliminal anxiety in its New York audience. New Yorkers would understand the allegory that compounded their already long-standing insecurities that the sociolinguist William Labov had been systematically revealing in his dissertation work (published in 1966) on the Lower East Side of Manhattan, especially in the upwardly mobile "lower middle class."

So, for example, as my humorous spelling above indicated, lack of a notice-able syllable-coda [r]-pronunciation in words that are spelled with an <r> in standard orthography is one of the most salient and stereotypical characteristics of New York dialect (as also of Boston, Richmond, Charleston and a few other coastal conurbations along the Atlantic and Gulf of Mexico, together with their inland surround).

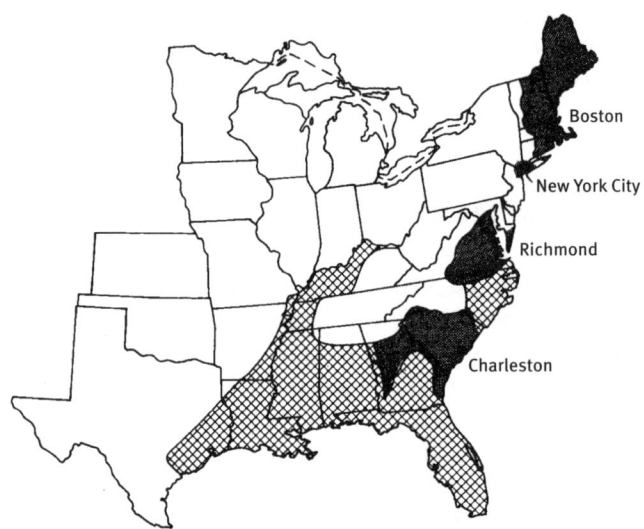

Figure 1: Geographical distribution of absence of syllable-coda [r] in American English. (Reproduced from Nancy F. Conklin & Margaret A. Lourie, *A Host of Tongues: Language Commu-nities in the United States*, p. 78, Fig. 11. New York: The Free Press, 1983.)

At one point it was a pronunciation widely accorded a certain prestige, matching that of fashionable speech in r-less Britain. But now Americans not only notice, they have a clear metalinguistic sense of the "incorrectness" of r-lessness in relation to the imagination of a standard register, and a sense that lack of syllable-coda r causes all kinds of ambiguities of pronunciation to arise in what one is trying to say. (Note how particularly this sense is driven by indexical factors associated with standardization, since we have no trouble with homonymy in general, illustrated by many complete homophones like led the past of lead, and lead- the heavy metal.) We can compute what Labov termed a speaker's "r-index" from a sample of that speaker's talk under various speaking conditions, which is a direct function of how many of the "possible" or "target" r's are actually pronounced where they could occur for the words pronounced were the subject speaking standard American English guided by orthography and its norms of spelling pronunciation.

(r)-index = **f** (% r pronunciations after vowels)
Examples: wire, soared, glared
           (...R) : (...∅)
'*standard*'-*like* : *form rhymes with*
      WIRE : W[H]Y A...
   SOARED : SAWED
   GLARED : GLAD

Figure 2a: Measuring syllable-coda r-fulness

If you say consistent [wɑⁱɹ], [sɒˑɹd], [glæɹd] for the words spelled wire, soared, glared whenever these words occur in speech, you have the maximally high r-index. If you consistently say [ˈwɑyə], [sɒːd], [glæˑd], your r-index is zero.

So note how the anxiety about actually speaking r-less *Newyourquais* manifested in relation to the class-stratification of the New York City population studied.

These actual data curves from Labov's early 1960s research are separated according to the r-indexes distinctive to the several socioeconomic class fractions he recognized for his subject population on Manhattan's Lower East Side. The measurements were taken from comparable samples of usage done under, on the left, ordinary social conversation, and on the right reading two words that contrast in spelling, like soared and sawed, where the graphically distinct visual cues – "r here!" vs. "no-r here!" – hit one in the face with their contrast-suggesting salience as a phonological minimal pair. The most important thing to see is that everybody slopes upward in the percent of post-vocalic r they pronounce, but those at the bottom of the socioeconomic class stratification, termed the "lower working class" by Labov, and those at the top, the "upper middle class" in this instance, have the flattest slopes, while those just below the top – what Labov identifies as the "lower middle class" in his sample – not only have the steepest slope of change, but once confronted with the contextual task of reading aloud

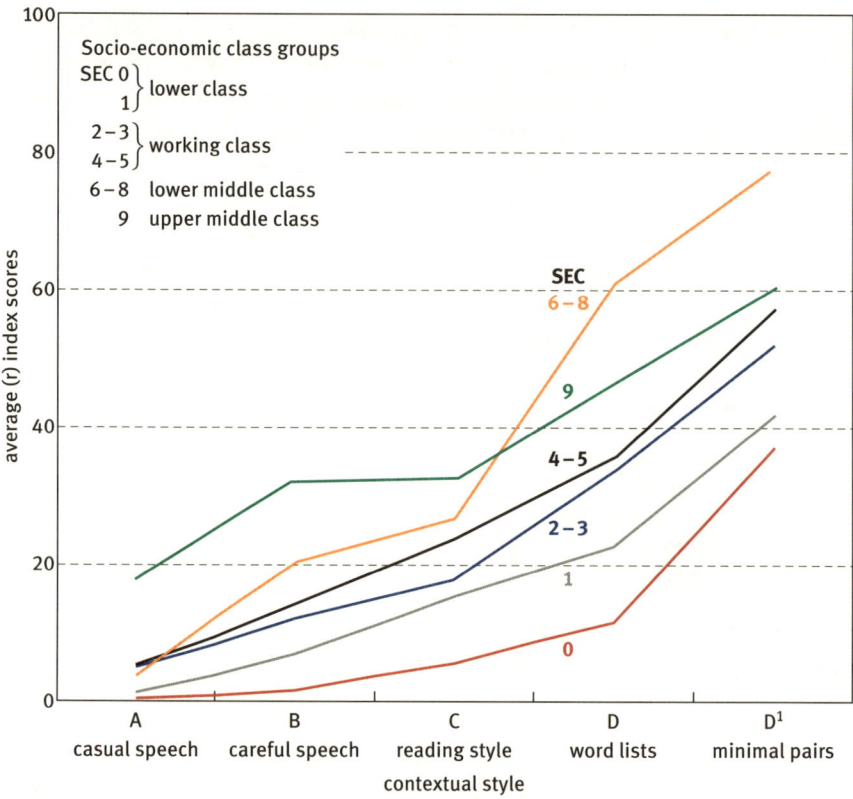

Figure 2b: NYC syllable-coda [r] by socio-economic class, as a function of speaking task (W. Labov). (Adapted from William Labov, "The study of language in its social context," p. 196, Fig 3. In: Joshua A. Fishman (ed.), *Advances in the Sociology of Language*, vol. 1. The Hague: Mouton, 1971.)

(speech condition C on the graph) shoot past the upper middle class speakers in their taking care to use a kind of reading or spelling pronunciation.

The results were comparable in shape and direction for a number of features that people identify as the characteristics of New York City pronunciation, where it is, in particular, the upwardly mobile upper working class/lower middle class who reveal the greatest anxieties about use of standard register – both in themselves and in others. Labov termed them the "linguistically insecure", in fact, those who apparently feel they are living with an articulatory deficiency, a verbal scar, or a self-stigmatizing behavioral quirk they at least secretly wish they could change – and which, indeed, they do change with alacrity when faced with such tasks as reading aloud.

Actualizing the standard register of the language community is frequently thought of as speaking "the language" (rather than merely speaking "a dialect" with a noticeable "accent").[1] In people's folk model of their language community,

---

1 Given the long history of the association of standardization, in Euro-American and, thence, in more recent post-colonial contexts, with inscriptional techniques of writing and printing, Bloomfield (1927) spoke of folk concepts of "language" and "dialect," i.e. standard and non-standard registers, in folk terms of "literate" and "illiterate" speech. Standardization has long been a class-focused project of political economic centrality to modern mass social formations, and was embraced by governments among the techniques of forging the modernist nation-state by projecting a language community (as standardized) into a polity, thereby creating fringe or marginal members and excluding those who resisted membership or had divided loyalties. See Silverstein 1985, 1996 [1987], 1996, 1998, 2000, 2010 and references cited there on language community, speech community, the cultural politics of standardization, etc.

Our seeing standardization as a mode of 'enregisterment' with consequences for norms within a language community builds on the Reid (1956)—McIntosh—Halliday (1964) precedent in the use of the term 'register'. The term alludes to the pipe-organ, where different registers provide distinct timbral envelopes for what is otherwise precisely the same melodic sequence of pitch-over-time. For language, the idea is that there is a mode of folk-consciousness (an ethno-metap-ragmatics) of "superposed" (Gumperz) indexical variability that posits the existence of distinct, indexically contrastive ways of saying what counts as "the same thing," i.e. communicating the same denotational content over intervals of text-precipitating discourse that differ as to their appropriateness to and effectiveness in conceptualized contexts of use. These contexts may be defined along any of the usual sociolinguistic dimensions describing who communicates with what forms to whom about whom/what, where and under what institutional conditions.

Language users evaluate discourse with intuitive metrics of coherence of enregistered features of form co-occurring across such stretches, generally focusing on highly salient 'register shibboleths' that reveal a basic register setting around which cluster the compatibility or lack of compatibility of other aspects of usage. In European languages, indexes of "honorification" have been saliently enregistered around second-person personal deictic usage, form of terms of address, and certain formulae for mands, but many other indexically loaded variants within pragmatic paradigms concurrently operate at many different planes of language so long they compatibly co-occur with the more salient shibboleths. In languages like Japanese, Javanese, Tibetan, etc., honorification is enregistered around the density of special lexical items, usage of which constitutes a performance of deference-to-addressee and/or deference-to-referent. The number of such indexically special lexical items within contrastive paradigms of indexical value differs as a function of the particular area of denotation one is communicating about in-and-by the use of a member of that set – many Javanese sets, for example, have only two members; second-person deixis seems to include at least five contrastive forms – so such registers are gradient affairs, the co-occurrence of some shibboleths of which have, rising to consciousness and explicit normativity, as well conventionally led to ethno-metapragmatic names (see Errington 1988; Silverstein 1979, 2003). "Standard" registers, too, are gradient in nature, denoting, within sloppy margins of performance, the coherent co-occurrence of a sufficient number of prescriptive 'standard'-shibboleths and the non-occurrence of the preponderance of proscribed 'non-standard' ones within the cultural order of institutionalized standardization. Registers, it

their sociolinguistic ethno-metapragmatics, as it were, using standard register is generally thought to indicate nothing of one's actual demographic profile or biography; it is the neutral top-and-center of a kind of conical folk-model of variation that ranges down and around the standard, a register of usage thus ideologically associated with speaking in "the voice from nowhere," that is, from no recognizable demographic position. So such people most fiercely in the grip of such standard anxiety become, of course, the perfect market for those selling verbal-cosmetic goods and services, the verbal equivalent of cosmetic surgery proffered for a fee.

2 Standard and "dialects" in North America

In respect of the emergence of its now continent-wide nation-state linguistic standard, in fact, the sociolinguistic landscape of North American English is rather remarkable. It has been the case in much of modern Europe that in a nation-state – think of France or even of Great Britain/England – the varieties considered to be within the "standard" of linguistic usage are formally close to the language of the middle- to upper-middle-class of the financial and cultural capital city: in France, Paris, of course; in Great Britain, London. There are, to be sure, interesting historical circumstances for some of the European standards when considered from the point of view of the political economy of culture during their respective period of standardization, involving competing regionalism sometimes only very lately – if at all – resolved in favor of one or another polity anchored in a place. Thus, within the Spanish state, standardized Catalan has become the distinctive ethnolinguistic expression of Barcelona and surround as a distinctive regional polity, Catalonia, as opposed to "Castilian," that is, Spanish, the distinct state language standardized in respect of Madrid.[2] Switzerland's major languages of state comprise the heteroch-

---

should be noted, have all the properties of languages as structures immanent in denotational discourse; since registers are, however, indexically particular to context, whether in positive or negative stipulation, the set-theoretic union of the elements of all registers in a community, sociolinguistically viewed, thus constitutes the inclusive envelope of the community's 'language'.
2 See the several works of Kathryn Woolard, e.g. 1989, 2003, 2008, on the sectorized and stratified nature of Catalan-Spanish bilingualism in and around Barcelona. To be sure, all during the Franco years in Spain, Catalan had been officially derided as nothing but divergent and therefore bad non-standard Spanish, notwithstanding its distinctiveness structurally and historically within Iberian and southern Gallo-Romance; its resurgence when implemented as a political emblem of Catalan ethno-linguistic separatism in contemporary institutional contexts has been nothing short of amazing. Still, as Frekko (2009) has noted, given the long history of suppression

thonous standards of French and German, emanating from across its borders. Italy's literary as well as commercial and industrial north – Tuscany, Emilia-Romagna, Lombardia – have been much more influential than Rome and Lazio in standard- izing Italian. In this late-formed (1870) state, to this day continuing local orienta- tions of identity remain strong; the erstwhile Vatican-controlled city of Rome was declared the then recently unified monarchy's political capital only in 1871.

Looking at North America, we must as well note distinctive historical circum- stances in the four-hundred-year-long westward continental expansion of the settler states of Canada and the United States.

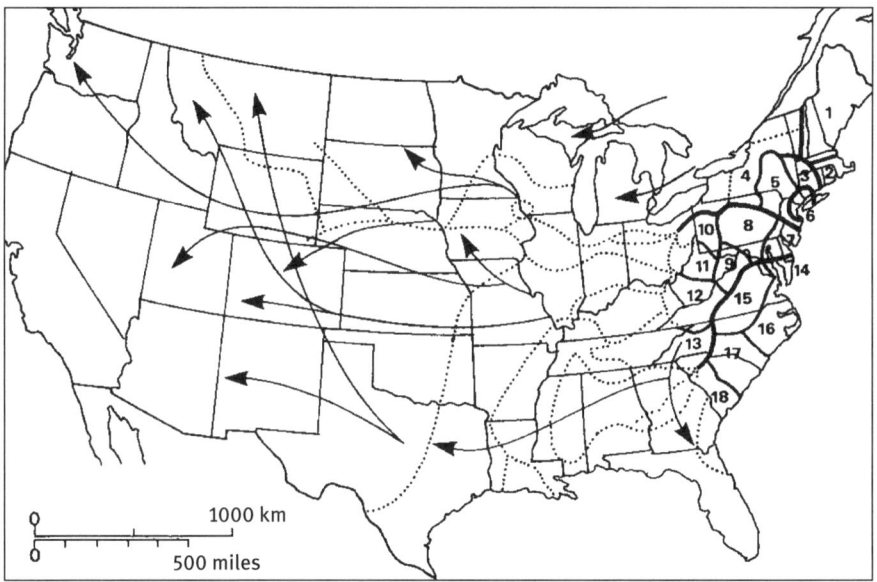

Figure 3: Paths of migrational spread of North American English-speaking populations . (Reproduced from Walt Wolfram, "Varieties of American English," p. 50, Fig. 3.3. In: Charles A. Ferguson & Shirley Brice Heath (eds.), *Language in the USA*. New York: Cambridge University Press, 1981.)

Indeed, the original colonial transplantation of English (as well as of French, Dutch, Spanish, and Swedish, to note competing colonizations) to the Atlantic coast set the initial conditions for repeated westward migration of settlers descen-

---

and the relatively class-associated and institutionally constrained standardization of Catalan, there are interesting problems of its serving across the range of contexts with the same indexical subtlety of enregisterment as does Spanish.

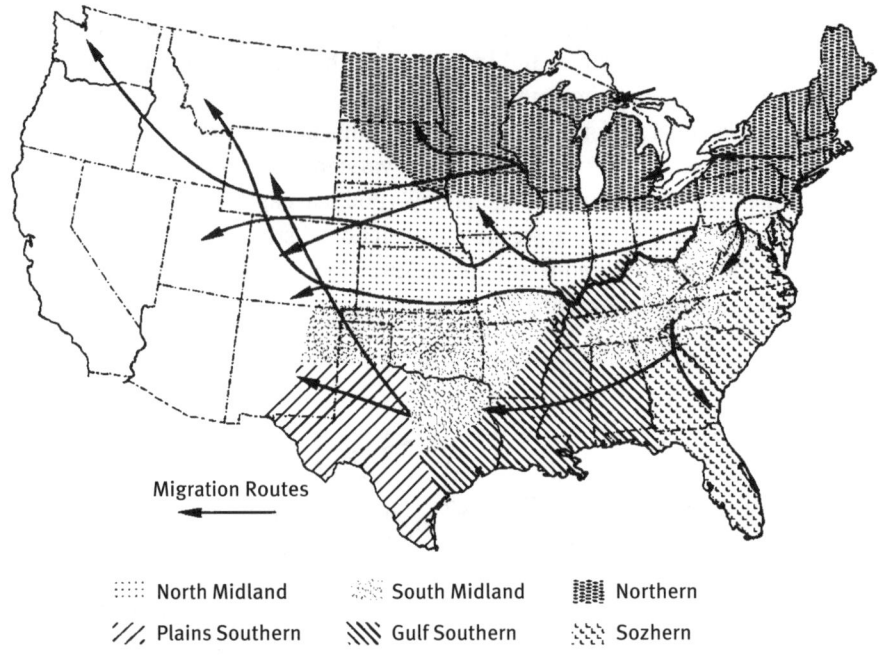

Migration Routes

◄———

| ::::: North Midland | ⠿ South Midland | ⦀⦀ Northern |
| ⁄⁄ Plains Southern | ⧵⧵⧵ Gulf Southern | ⣿ Sozhern |

Figure 4: Dialect regions of North American English .
(Reproduced from Nancy F. Conklin & Margaret A. Lourie, *A Host of Tongues: Language Communities in the United States*, p. 89, Fig. 15. New York: The Free Press, 1983.)

dants as well as for vast immigrations from many linguistically different regions of Europe. When one looks at the maps of American English dialect regions compiled on the basis of inter-war period dialectological sampling of phonological and lexical isoglosses, it is striking how closely the axes of these regions follow the stages of westward migration of English-speakers.

In several regions where there was dense and continued direct immigration of non-English-speaking people, such as the Germans and Scandinavians of the central and northern Plains states, or where populations of non-English-speaking people were incorporated through annexation, such as French and Cajun speakers in southern Louisiana, or Spanish-speakers of "California Alta" and the Southwest, distinctive regional features of American English have resulted overlaid on the general trend.

Perhaps because of the extraordinary land mass of the United States and Canada, both which have undergone gradual, cumulative processes of Atlantic-to-Pacific settlement by mostly inland English speakers' step-wise, generally westward, radiating migrations, the dialectological map of North American English, the dominant national-level language, has a recognizable topology.

There are numerous small regions on the Atlantic coast, each generally organized around an urban center or cluster of close-by urban centers, old and relatively stable regions of settlement oriented as well in a topology of coast and
hinterland. As one looks west of the original Atlantic colonies, the dialectological regions encompass more capacious land-mass, bespeaking perhaps lesser
urban/rural clines of population density, the lateness and perhaps rapidity, due
to changing means of transport, of the processes of settlement, and the nature of
the communicative infrastructures as these regions distinctively formed.

In addition to these factors of gradual trans-continentalization of American English, it is also important to observe the historical patterns of urbanization and then sub- and ex-urbanization in the distribution of people. The 1790
census counted 5.1 % of the U. S. population as urban, residing in cities of 2,500
or more; 94.9 % were rural. (The only three cities of greater than 15,000 people
were Boston, New York, and Philadelphia, by the way.) By 1920, 51.2 % of the population counted was urban. The figures rise to 75.2 % in the 1990 census, and over
80.7 % by the 2010 census. The rates of urbanization of the erstwhile rural south,
southwest, and west in the U.S., indeed, of the growth, outside the northeast, of
conurbations in the hundreds of thousands and even millions, is a rapid post-WW
II phenomenon that is a function of shifting commerce and industry from the
industrial northeast and midwest – now termed "the Rustbelt" – where, to be
sure, the urban population centers had earlier been located, certainly at the time,
beginning in 1928, that American dialectologists organized and undertook the
Linguistic Atlas project in the image of those earlier undertaken in Europe.

Thus, it is important to observe that contemporary Americans' consciousness
of "accent" and its distribution, that is, their ethno-metapragmatics of dialectal
differentiation, emerges against the backdrop of these complex historical trends.
Major urban centers, landmark conurbations that anchor their suburbs and the
exurban fringe, are nodes of life-course mobility for the most socio-economically
and socio-culturally privileged, the speakers who most manifest and live in the
institutional universe of standard on its continent-wide scale. Hence, among the
resident upper middle class segments of language users, urban centers in the
contemporary period have less regionally recognizable linguistic distinctiveness
and more connectivity than formerly, whatever the case for those of other segments of the local population, whose phonologico-phonetic patterns may indeed
be "local" to the standard-sensitive and thus inevitably ascribed some negative
indexical value.[3]

---

3 This is a distinct phenomenon from the kind of due westward connection across cities of the
northeast and midwest revealed in the "Northern Cities Vowel Shift" explored in some detail in

So, whatever we might expect from the European cases, and especially given the history of North American demography, New York City's historically local urban dialect is not, as might otherwise be expected, the basis of the national standard – what, since Krapp (1925: 1.35), some have termed "General American," the kind of pronunciation cultivated on broadcast media, for example. While, to be sure, as Mair (2006: 176) notes, during the 1920s and 1930s, "[n]on-rhotic accents were much more common in radio broadcasts...than they are now" – one need only think of such New York-based or -identified broadcast luminaries as H. V. Kaltenborn (1878–1965) or Gabriel Heatter (1890–1972) whose distinctively local pronunciations can be heard on various websites – the older prestige pattern of the city was definitively in decline by the 1940s, even if President Roosevelt (1882–1945) had used a patrician variant of it to such effect in his nationally broadcast "Fireside Chats" between 1933 and 1944.[4]

Buffalo, Cleveland, Detroit, Chicago, etc., by variationists under William Labov's (1994: 177–201) lead. These systematic push-pull chains in the vocalic phonologico-phonetic space are, as expected, innovations locatable in the upper-working-to-lower-middle socio-economic (and white ethnic) segments of the relevant populations within the cities. Similarly, the countervailing "Southern Vowel Shift" characterizing a dialectally distinct transformation, is a predominantly rural-to-urban phenomenon not characteristic of the privileged classes of southeastern cities. (A good summary is found in Wolfram & Schlling-Estes 2006: 140–159.)

4 In a remarkable and wide-ranging study arguing for the effectiveness of linguistic ideology in this matter, Thomas P. Bonfiglio (2002) traces the widespread institutionalization of an anti-immigrant, and specifically anti-semitic discourse directed against Jews of the Eastern European immigrations (and other upwardly mobile, racially marked ethnics) emblematized by the immigrant-rich populations in New York City (and, to a certain extent, Chicago). For example, in the 1920s elite cultural organizations such as the Ivy League universities, all clustered in the northeast, discovered the perils to their "brand," as we now say, of having too many of such people around. One might note that such reactive racialism to protect and further "Old American" values complemented the anti-immigrant nativism of a vast swath of U. S. politicians inclined to exclusionary laws and the views of those eugenicists and other racists bemoaning the "passing of the great race" (Madison Grant's best-selling jeremiad about Nordic peoples of 1916). University administrators promoted a scheme to "nationalize" and "democratize" the student bodies of these institutions by restricting admission of Jews and promoting admission of "well rounded" young Christian men from rural hinterlands, with Nordic virtues, seeking the very populations of the regions of the United States where "General American" was spoken, not ethnically marked urban varieties. Such "General American" phonic virtues, in fact, were part of what made this targeted group of students attractive, as against the vices of talking like a second-generation New Yorker or Chicagoan or – gasp! – like an African American. (Somehow, the r-lessness of Boston Brahmins, Virginia gentlemen, and others from upper-class Atlantic coastal backgrounds was not perceived in the same way as the speech habits of New Yorkers of immigrant background. Of course, as we must always remember, given how conventional indexicality operates, that linguistic ideology is never *only* about language, frequently *not at all* about language!) See now

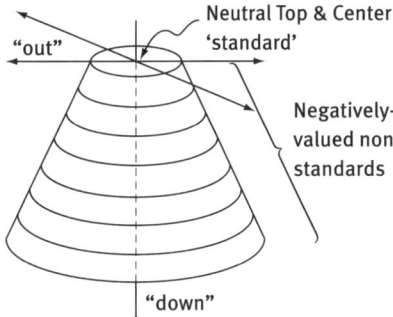

Figure 5: Ethno-metapragmatic conical model of sociolinguistic variation under standardization

So, given the institutionalization of a stratified conical ethno-metapragmatic model of neutral, top-and-center "General American" from nowhere, relegating speech indexing local identity, especially New York City identity, to the always down-and-outer position, linguistically anxious folks in and around New York City who speak the local dialect are all potential Eliza and Elias Doolittles, waiting for their Henry Higgins to transform them and thereby enhance their ability to "self-express for success."

3 Twenty-five years plus of fleeing "Noo Yawk"

So I thought it was "*déjà voo* all over again," to quote Yankees baseball legend Yogi Berra, when I encountered a *New York Times* article on the topic published on November 19th 2010. Here the reporter, Sam Roberts, sympathetically described the almost Sisyphean task of native speakers of *Newyorquais* to achieve that point at the stratificational top and center of their language community's sociolinguistic imaginary, the dialect-less voice "from nowhere" they imagine the standard to be. Each of the article's case studies reveals an upwardly mobile, ethnically identifiable someone – a lawyer, an actor – who has become a paying client of a speech therapist so as metaphorically to be cured of an oral-aural dysfunction, "tawkin' Noo Yawk."

The image is, to be sure, by no means new. William E. Geist, then a *Times* reporter, wrote a wonderful article that tracks virtually the same story in 1984 (almost 27 years earlier!), an article that formed part of my multi-year collection

---

also Winfield 2007. Again, Bonfiglio elaborately traces the parallel and conforming ideological input to the creation of "Broadcast Standard" for the radio networks starting in the late 1920s (2002: 161–180), which, he argues, was also no happenstance in focusing on "General American."

about the ideology of standardization in American English during those Reagan go-go years of dressing – and addressing – for success. My paper on the topic, "Monoglot Standard in America" of 1987 has even been reprinted a couple of times. Mr. Geist, indeed, described a *Zeitgeist* of those years of a political economy of what I term "greed revival," New York City "becoming more upscale," in the words of one of his characters. I used Mr. Geist's article as well in a paper (1999) on what I termed "linguistic NIMBYism,"[5] about people who distance themselves from the ethnolinguistic reference group in which they are positioned as marginal, rather than central members by virtue of wishing to escape from the group's speech-based identifiability. Such linguistic NIMBYs may certainly take a certain pleasure in the reference-group -lect, and may very well want the group's ways of speaking to continue, only not in their back yard – that is, associated with them! Indeed, those people who become the clients of speech therapists with a view to class ascendancy and de-ethnicization are swept up into the conical structure of the sociolinguistic stratification down-and-around standard struggling to climb higher and toward the axial apex: I love my demographically revealing "dialect," to be sure, but let those others speak it in their own back yards – not me!

So Mr. Roberts's article as such is not news, but there are very revealing differences of emphasis in the two accounts, that reflect the 27-year social history of change in-and-around New York City, and the changing cultural foci of language-consciousness, our American "culture of language" as I've termed it. Mr. Geist's 1984 article is centered in mid-town East-Side Manhattan in relation to the boroughs and non-upper-class suburbs: those he terms "the afflicted," from Brooklyn ("of course"), Queens, The Bronx, Staten Island, Long[g] Island, and northern New Jersey, "com[ing] in droves" for corrective therapy.

Note how the geography on the horizontal plane figures the inward (as well as upward) trajectory through a socioeconomically stratified sociolinguistic space down-and-around standard register in the expected way. ("Saturday Night Fever," a famous 1977 film with John Travolta as the male lead, had his Italian ethnic working-class character, too, travel from then down-market Brooklyn to mid-town to acquire his patina of choreographic grace and sexy bzazz.)

At the same time, in Ronald Reagan's America, displaying such marked or unbleached ethnicity of immigrant origin was still almost uniformly the inverse of socioeconomic class status. The large numbers of visible cosmopolitan socioeconomic elites that transnational cultural and business enterprises have

---

5 The acronym is based on the phrase "Not in my back yard!" typically focused upon a governmental body's plans to locate a garbage dump or a recovering drug addict halfway house or equivalent next door to one's residential real estate.

Figure 6a: Boroughs of New York surrounding the borough of Manhattan

Figure 6b

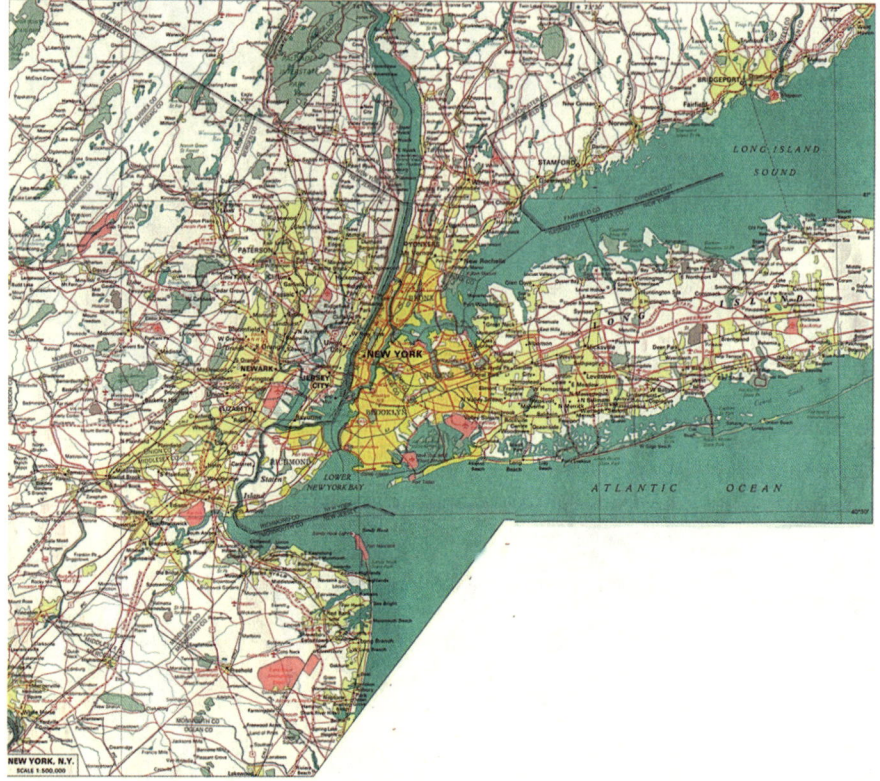

Figure 6c: The immediate New York metropolitan region

brought to American cities had not, in 1984, yet transformed the corresponding ethno-national communities in America, some being of very long standing as non-elite ethnic enclaves.[6] The class ascendancy via higher education paid for by the post-WW II G.I. Bill for veterans, and other such mechanisms of mobility, was only a generation old at that time. So Mr. Geist's 1984 "afflicted" are named Howard Belasco, identifiably Jewish to any *Times* reader, from the Bronx, John

---

6 One might note such facts as the transformation of the "Chinese-American" ethnic communities from Cantonese-based to Mandarin-based, as post-Maoist China has become a positive, pride-conferring locus of diasporic self-identification and flow of people and cultural value. Or the transformation of South Asian-American ethnic communities by the influx of cosmopolitan global technical and business elites to North America. Ditto for Latin Americans of various nationalities. The older inverse relationship presumed to hold between displays of ethnicity in public and class standing has been decidedly complicated and transformed.

Figure 7: Patrick Mullin, left, started weekly speech therapy sessions 11 years ago and still goes about once a month. His therapist, Sam Chwat, is considered the dean of his profession. (©*New York Times* [Redux Pictures]; reprinted by license.)

Girollomo, identifiably Puerto Rican, from East Harlem, and Elizabeth Alpert, identifiably Jewish, from Flatbush in Brooklyn. "It's so easy to slip back when you're with family and friends," poor Ms. Alpert notes. Indeed the whole story – which early on references Eliza Doolittle, the flower-girl of Shaw's *Pygmalion* and Lerner & Lowe's *My Fair Lady* – is really about the accent eradication industry as a kind of popular if cosmetic deracination for the class- and ethnicity-marked. The speech therapists, it suggests, capitalize on people's anxieties of self-presentation at the down-and-out periphery of the sociolinguistic space of standardization, but perhaps "accent eradication" ironically compounds the very anxieties of those who now do well in Manhattan corporate offices and pick-up bars, but are aliens among their relatives, for whose more intimate and comforting approbation for their upwardly mobile success they yearn.

Mr. Roberts's story in almost-2011 post-modernity builds from the same basic situation. Here, the characters are Andrew Ramos (Latino from Passaic, New Jersey), Patrick Mullin (Irish), Alan Steinfeld (Jewish, from Brooklyn) and Lauren LoGiudice (Italian from Howard Beach, though she is "a young actress who is 'tall and Anglican-looking'"). To be sure, these people are still traveling to the center of Manhattan to work on eliminating their accents. (As a linguistically trained reader, one is almost tickled to note that the "dean of speech therapists", who founded his accent eradication practice the very year Mr. Geist wrote his article, is named Sam Chwat, pronounced like the technical name for '[ə]', though poor Mr Chwat died early in 2011, on the 3rd of March. A *New York Times* obituary on the 8th quotes his very savvy sociolinguistic credo: "[Your] accent [is] charming as long as you're part of the power structure that has the accent of the ruling class").

Mr. Roberts repeats the same ideologically pregnant speculation as did Mr. Geist, to the effect, in Geist's words, that the New York City accents result from "the mixture of immigrant dialects" – note, not languages! – that gave "the philological flavor of this polyglot city." Mr. Roberts enumerates: "The New York accent is a distinctive amalgam of Irish, German, Yiddish and Italian – now infused with black and Hispanic dialects and a Caribbean lilt." All this is far from correct, but, as sociocultural data it is important to take note of: these writers emphasize the non-mentionability of socioeconomic or social class as such, deflecting attention, as it were, onto ethnicity and the geography of the boroughs, Manhattan, the (if you pardon) world trade center itself the first and centralized one among them. Inward and upward with de-ethnicization, then, we might note, thinking of the conical model of sociolinguistic stratification.

The other expectable themes are here in Mr. Roberts's article as well. Ms. LoGiudice, the Anglican-looking actress who had just landed a role in a film, voices the linguistic NIMBY's continuing anxiety of deracination: "I felt if I lost my accent I'd lose part of who I was. Almost no one thinks I'm from Queens anymore." But the sociolinguistic space in which such work on pronunciation goes on in 2010 is not merely a locally up-scaling and de-ethnicizing class structure; it is "globalization" itself seen to be a driving force. "The accent was rarely an asset," Mr. Roberts reports, citing such scholars as E. H. Babbitt in 1896 as well as William Labov in 1966, "but" – he emphasizes – it "has become more of a handicap in an era of globalization, when people and jobs are more mobile and a more generic identity can be seen as an advantage".

So here we have the key rationalizing trope for why Messrs. Ramos, Mullin, Steinfeld and Ms. LoGiudice are engaged in the pursuit of "General American." It is the dichotomy of 'global' vs. 'local', expansive vs. restricted, in the anxious cultural consciousness of the bourgeoisie now attuned to geo-political mobility; these are professionally oriented segments of the class-stratified population working in particular sectors of endeavor where corporatized and in particular trans-regionally and even trans-nationally corporatized value reigns. Mr. Ramos, a television reporter at WPIX-TV, felt himself being mocked for clinging to his northern New Jersey accent as an "endearing characteristic integral to his [local] identity," but "if you ever want to work outside New York, it may put you in a box". Mr. Steinfeld, also a broadcaster, "hosts a New Age program on local access cable television channels in New York that is also streamed over the Internet, and he fears his accent prevents him from appealing to a wider audience". Mr. Mullin, "a tax and criminal lawyer who practices in Manhattan and New Jersey, said he grew tired of going to legal training seminars in which fellow lawyers complained about not understanding him. 'I didn't want to be boxed in regionally,' he said. 'I wanted to be a clear communicator. My accent got in the way'". Even Ms. LoGiudice was awakened to her fiercely indexed localness when she attended Wesleyan University, an almost-Ivy in Middletown Connecticut: "I grew up with people who could be the cast of 'Jersey Shore'," she realized, feeling that her speech pigeonholed her, though now she will be seen in a film as "an international model".

"Boxed in regionally" – losing "wider audiences" – "put you in a box" – being "pigeonholed" rather than "international" in image: the here vs. every- or any-where trope of mobility is unmistakable in these people's imagination of the indexical power of speaking with vs. without regional accent. A new trope for how language fits into social stratification.

4 Readers react: Two cents worth and then some

Published online on the morning of the 19th of November (though it did not see print, p.A20, until the edition of the 21st), by 11:16 AM the first reader's comment was posted. And the commentary quickly gushed forth, resulting in 640 posts by 9:26 AM on the 22nd, when the commentary was closed. Here, as one can imagine, is a treasure-trove of spontaneous, reflexive reactions to a sociolinguistic phenomenon by an active, though lay commentariat. The postings on the *Times* website after Mr. Roberts's article appeared claim – with, so far in my systematic tabulations, one exception – no linguistic expertise. The postings are in vernacular style, highly personal voice, filled with first-person stories of experiences with New York City – or equivalently devalued – dialect either as speaker or hearer, and dealing not so much with the reportorial voice of the article and its factual correctness, as with the doings and attitudes of the characters in the article, Ms. LoGiudice, Mr. Ramos et al., and Mr. Chwat and the other speech therapists, in relation to the writers' own experience of "accent." With few exceptions, the writers of these posts have pointed opinions about the specific phenomenon reported, about New York City and environs as a sphere of the social life of language, and about the larger field of linguistic variation in American – and wider – English usage. Here are the kinds of comments we find:

249.
S. Sharpe
Austin, TX
November 19th, 2010
2:01 pm
While I understand that heavy accents can hold people back because of negative stereotypes or work requirements, this article makes me sad. As a longtime resident of Texas who was born in NYC, I am proud of the little bit of New York that comes out when I say "coffee" and "water." I love hearing regional accents and it would be a loss to our culture if they vanished.
Recommend Recommended by 4 Readers

Figure 8: Comment #249: A loss to our culture

Reader # 249 from Austin, Texas laments the sociolinguistic reality of stratification around the standard, counterposing the beloved "regional accents" and him-or herself feeling fulfilled by the minor self-revelations of New York City origin in-and-by saying "['kʰɒʷfɪy]" and "['wɔ˞ɾə]" in this expatriate context. The loss of such pronunciations is a "loss to our [national] culture".

134.
KZ
New York
November 19th, 2010
12:16 pm
For heaven's sake. A real New York accent is charming, a reminder that we have region differences. It's also becoming a rarity, as everyone's accent merges into some kind of standard speech. When is the last time that you heard a really terrific Southern drawl from anyone under 50? What is not appealing is the affected, gravel-throaty, up-talking speech of a huge segment of the under-35 college-educated set. If only that were a detriment to being hired...
Recommend Recommended by 23 Readers

Figure 9: Comment #134: Charming regional accents

Reader # 134, a peeved New Yorker, is opposed to seeking a standard verbal self-presentation, as you can see, something that he or she associates with younger people of the "college-educated set" – note the appeal to cultural class – losing their sense of place, being rendered "affected, gravel-throaty, [and] up-talking [in] speech," i.e. having pretensions. Longing to hear, as well, "a really terrific Southern drawl" from the educated young, there is a palpable nostalgia here for the genuineness of being rooted in place.

42.
Mackenzie
Greenville, NC
November 19th, 2010
11:44 am
As a southerner I feel the people's pain. Often maligned and frequently imitated, the southern accent has a similar reaction. I read a study that followed nonclinical observers who had been briefly educated in the IQ system. A southern accent droped your IQ 20pts in the study. Most of my southern friends who are professionals have a "professional accent" (still slow and sweet, but less notic[e]able and more grammatically correct) and a "home accent" (laying it on thick). Seems silly, but these things do effect [sic] your future and your career.
Recommend Recommended by 19 Readers

Figure 10: Comment #42: A Southerner's lament and bi-registral usage

North Carolina Reader # 42 realizes the practicalities involved in accent therapy, for "things do [a]ffect your future and your career", if one sounds stupid by talking one's local dialect; and therefore "[a]s a southerner I feel the people's pain". (Remember Bill Clinton?) But as # 42 notes, the practical solution to deracination is to become what we term "bi-registral", controlling a more- and a less-standard, that is, a less and more decidedly regional way of talking to move between the two universes.

149.
Tom Renda
Washington
November 19th, 2010
12:31 pm
DON'T DO IT!

I moved away from New York in 1976. Lost my accent by 1980.

It's SO comforting for me to hear a New Yorker in full blown Brooklynese.

Treasure who you are, New York!
Recommend Recommended by 26 Readers

Figure 11: Comment #149: Treasure who you are

Here's a Washington, D.C. cheerleader in Reader # 149: "Treasure who you are, New York!" Mr. Tom Renda, once a New Yorker, shouts – we hope in pure r-less-ness! He is comforted just by hearing someone speak in local accent. And note the emphasis on that accent indicating "who you are", that is, something essential about what we might term "Newyorkness", insofar we can project a quality of being.

163.
Mike
Brooklyn, NY
November 19th, 2010
12:40 pm
The N.Y. accent is about the most unattractive thing I've ever heard and I've been all over the planet. Long Island (which is 100 times worse than NYC) should have a program in it's [sic] school system that teaches the students to loose the accent ("Losing your accent 101"). It's brash, coarse and I liken it to rubbing a metal cheese grater against one[']s face.
Recommend Recommended by 4 Readers

Figure 12: Comment #163: Long Island accent grates

Even Brooklyn-based – though clearly not Brooklyn-born! – reader # 163, Mike, who finds the accent "the most unattractive thing [he's] ever heard", reveals in his tirade that he is thinking geographically. In fact, he reproduces the conical model from his Brooklyn locus within the city limits. He asserts that the "brash, coarse" accent of those immediately to the east beyond the city limits, in the socio-economically upwardly aspiring lower middle class and densely ethnic Nassau County suburbs on Long Island, is a hundred times worse – can you imagine! – "liken[ing] it to rubbing a metal cheese grater against one's face". This shows the overdetermined contemptuousness of one who is sensitive to minute differences, I guess, but who operates in microcosm entirely in a geographically conceptualized system of accent just like that of those who **love** the very fact of local accent on a national scale.

I think you can see how personally engaged these folks are, how articulately precise in their views, pro or con. Many of the commenters register their views with exemplifying shibboleths, words like [tʰɒʷk] ("tawk") for standard ta<u>lk</u>; they recall in personal anecdotes where and when dialect differences became the cruxes – or cruces – of their own identity-work, indexing their demographics, whether with positive or negative outcome. The most important thing to understand here is that there is a cultural geography of "accent" that is part of the linguistic consciousness of these writers; a spontaneously offered scheme of language differentiation that is part of these people's ethno-geography of North America. Important to note is that there are three kinds of geographical schematizations with reference to which people's views are articulated.

5 The ethno-geographical frames of "accent"

One is the view of North America as a network of cities and their surrounding conurbations: Boston – New York – Chicago – Houston – Minneapolis, are, for example, urban landmarks in the way people think about dialect. Indeed, in keeping with a major finding linking standardization to urban class privilege, as noted above, there is a cultural geography that sees these landmark cities and their subtended regional surrounds – suburbs and exurbs – as the key identifiers to which dialect variation points, so that northern New Jersey and Nassau and Suffolk County suburbs of New York City are included within its nodal reach. (Think of people from an exurb of an American city telling people in Europe or Asia that they are from that city, for example; it is the landmark of cultural consciousness with which they identify – and wish to be identifiable).

Of course, the changing political economy of commerce and residence in American cities, particularly the largest and most globally connected, is relevant here. As class and other language-relevant stratification comes to mirror the conical diagram of sociolinguistic variability down-and-around the top-and-center standard, people increasingly see the local "dialect" or "accent" or "patois" as coming from the peripheries of urban cores, downtowns that are increasingly service-industry – not manufacturing or retailing – focused and more and more the sites of elite residence by service-industry sector upper and upper-middle classes in renovated architecture no longer in commercial use. (European cities have long had this model under post-WW II rebuilding, their *Lumpenproletariat* and ethnically marked immigrant populations out – as well as down – in the *banlieus* of Paris, Berlin, London, etc.) New York City English is called "Brooklynese" or "Long Island patois," consistent with the ethno-geography of the two newspaper articles themselves.

At the same time, many writers note that the New York City accent is dying, since it is so rarely encountered in Manhattan, but requires one to travel to such outlier places as Howard Beach (at the extreme southwest periphery of the borough of Queens), from which Ms. LoGiudice, if you will recall, hails.[7] The point caught here is that in the class stratification of standardization in such socioeconomically renovating conurbations, urban cores are more and more populated by standard-speaking and even foreign cosmopolitan elites of tremendous job and residential mobility, who move from city to city in the course of their labor life cycle and find congenial others in just the same condition wherever they go.

So the "decline" of New York and equivalent dialect usage is noted again and again, though, other than to presume it is because therapists are succeeding, our writers seem to think of this disappearance as like the decline of endangered species in the natural landscape. Hence, one has to travel to the outer urban reaches still to find it, where somehow its habitat has not been destroyed, a kind of temporality-laden ethno-theory of relic areas not yet penetrated by modernity's standardization, perhaps. Some of these dialect features have become lovingly invested emblems of local urban identity, stereotypes – register shibboleths rather than shibboleths of dialect – that have entered into the brisk commerce of reflexive museologization of culture, labels for the *appellation*: in our posted material, for example, we find the dominant spelling of "New Yawk" (and even sometimes "Noo Yawk") and especially a rendering of "fuhgeddaboudit!" ['forget about it'] as such reflexive emblems of landmark locale.

---

7 Howard Beach, a working class and lower middle class enclave relatively densely populated with Italian-American ethnics, has been the scene of repeated attacks on African American men whom happenstance caused to be in the neighborhood at night, a notorious such attack in late 1986 evolving into a national cause célèbre and an indelible stereotype about the area.

A second scheme among our comment-writers is regional. That is, people imagine a continuous landmass with a more or less agreed-upon perimeter, such as "New England" or "The South" (meaning the southeastern United States). In these materials "The South" is the most salient such regionalization, conforming with Preston's experiments (1999) in so-called "perceptual dialectology", though some writers signing on from Texas differentiate East Texas from the more general – perhaps Yankee – concept of undifferentiated "southern" speech. The next most salient regionalization is what one writer terms, with ironic double-voicing, the "flyover" region of somewhat indefinite inclusiveness termed "The Midwest". It sometimes seems to stretch from wherever the outskirts of New York City lie – perhaps 15 miles west of the George Washington Bridge – clear to California, so variously is it invoked. There is a marvelously iconic quality to the way people conceptualize so-called Midwestern accent: like the topography itself, it seems almost always to be characterized as "flat". Perhaps, factually, it is the Northern Cities Vowel Shift (see n. 3 and refs. there) that translates into this adjective. But perhaps the term is metaphorically taken in the sense of a quality space in which noticeable features do not stand out – note, standing up vs. lying flat – and hence the non-noticeability of Midwestern speech is its "flatness", or its noticeability as non-notable "General [=Broadcast] American". Flatness is boring sameness, then, whether one likes and encourages it, or no. But there is a differentiation in the comments between those advocating for the virtues of uniform standard and those bemoaning the lack of interest of "flat" Flyoverlandese.

This second ethno-geographical schema oozes over into the third one found in these materials, the geo-political partonomy or partitioning of America into states. A few states, ones with high regional salience as well, are endowed by writers with a distinctive dialect, such as Texas or occasionally a state in the "Midwest," like Ohio or Minnesota.

Interestingly, California as so named seems to have a dual status, as both a region and a state in these web posts. Its dialect or accent is sometimes equated to "General American", a couple of times to "Valley Girl," rather than to a set of distinctively Western dialect regions. Most importantly, as the place salient to most Americans as the Pacific coastal opposite to New York's cultural anchoring of the Atlantic East Coast, it seems to figure in numerous anecdotes of people's poking fun at the way New York City people speak, particularly when plopped down by relocation among native, or at least relatively more native, Californians. (There is a grain of demographic historical truth to this, especially the several reminiscences by older writers recalling when they were transplanted as children to California. When I was a child in the 1950s, I estimate that on my Brooklyn block alone five or six households with then young school-age children relocated to southern California in the Los Angeles region. Recall that the aerospace industry was booming in 1950s California, becoming the politico-economic powerhouse within the military-industrial complex that backed Ronald Reagan in his state-wide and national political career, with payback on the investment via that fabulous Department of Defense boondoggle, Mr. Reagan's "Star Wars" initiative of the mid-1980s. Note the tie-in to the other booming southern California industry, film and television).

6 Themes and imaginaries

In studying these materials, which are so rich as data that I have hardly yet exhausted them, I tabulated a partition of themes in a systematic serial sample of 200 Posts, examining numbers 1–50; 151–200; 301–350; and 451–500, with gaps of 100 posts between each two samples; thus ca. 31 %. I extracted from each reader comment what we might term its principal theme, and as further posts in the corpus seemed to repeat the same theme, I entered these instances in numerical order within the emerging thematic category, along with the notable phrasing of the theme, if any, in the writer's own words slightly edited to fit in the space of the table.

Complex posts sometimes do hit more than one theme, and when I complete the re-tabulation of the whole 640 item corpus, I will use the themes already discovered in the sample of 200 and score each post for as many of these themes as it manifests. So for example Mackenzie from Greenville, North Carolina, our writer # 42, posts about the maligning not only of New York speech but also of Southern U. S. speech.

42.
Mackenzie
Greenville, NC
November 19th, 2010
11:44 am
As a southerner I feel the people's pain. Often maligned and frequently imitated, the southern accent has a similar reaction. I read a study that followed nonclinical observers who had been briefly educated in the IQ system. A southern accent droped your IQ 20pts in the study. Most of my southern friends who are professionals have a "professional accent"(still slow and sweet, but less notic[e]able and more grammatically correct) and a "home accent" (laying it on thick). Seems silly, but these things do effect [sic] your future and your career.
Recommend Recommended by 19 Readers

Figure 13: Comment #42: A Southerner's lament and bi-registral usage

This is its main point, though at the end there are two further thoughts: one, on the strategy of using contextually appropriate register that has been hit upon by "professionals" in the South, i.e. upper middle class speakers of Southern, able to use both a less and more standard degree of speech register; and second, no. 42 expresses sympathy with those anxious about their accent, observing that though it "seems silly ... these things do [a]ffect your future and your career". With some fringe themes represented by one or a few writers, the coherence of the themes is what most impresses me. Note the table of themes in rank order of frequency.

Frequency	Theme-as-Captioned	Range [1–500]
31	Pride in greatness of New York City/New Yorkers and hence of its/their accent	100–500
28	Against creeping homogenization of language	11–494
23	Pitiable/silly self-loathing the phenomenon illustrates	2–492
21	Non-New Yorkers' mockery of New York City accent	3 – 487
13	There is social realism reflected by the phenomenon of accent reduction	47–498
13	One's accent persists and only sometimes shifts	46–482
13	Southern accent – also devalued	8–486
7	Justifiable low valuation of NYC accent	17–461
6	Approving or noting bi- or multi-dialectism inflected by context	14 463
6	Correction of or addition to the cited dialect facts in article	319–469
5	Plurilingualism and use of a Standard "International" English	176–464
4	What is and is not actually "New Yorkese"	40,182,324,332
3	Ethical culpability of speech therapists	180,318.347
3	Identifiable pronunciation "accent" vs. bad grammar	33,306,337
3	Approval of accent-reduction because it assuages feelings of social stigma	22,175,456
3	Justifiable low valuation of a non-NYC accent	9,26,341
3	Decline of genuine/real NYC accents by generation & over time	1,6,172
2	Boston accent – also devalued	38,43
2	Philadelphia accent – also devalued	41,178
1	One can just say 'No' to accent!	157
1	Gender differences noted in NYC dialect use	19
1	New York City ex-pats' mutual recognition by dialect	15
1	Canadian accent – also devalued	349
1	Chicago accent – also devalued	496
1	This phenomenon reveals the decline and fall of U.S.A.	154
1	New York City accent as conversation piece at parties	308
1	Understanding people with foreign accents	346

Figure 14: Rank-order of themes in partitioned 200-comment sample [197 published comments]

The most common theme in the 200-sample is what I've termed "Pride in greatness of New York City/New Yorkers and hence of its/their accent", with a frequency of nearly 16 %. Next in frequency, at 14.2 %, is "Against creeping homogenization of language" – not only in respect of New York City's linguistic distinctness but in respect of all -lectal diversity. And so on. If we look at the top four categories, totaling 103 or more than half the thematic instances, they all bespeak a pro-New York City, anti-homogenization point of view, though one that, all the while recognizing the dislike of local dialect by some of those people from elsewhere, are very much opposed to resorting to therapies for accent eradication such as are described in the article. In short, people tend to be pro-local-accent in general and hence pro-local-New York City accent in particular. Indeed, when one adds the thematic categories noting that other local accents, too, such as southeastern U.S., or the accents of cities such as Boston, Philadelphia, and Chicago, are as well subject to mockery, it is clear that the overwhelming sentiment is indignantly and encouragingly pro-local – all in the face of people's sense of an homogenization of language that they generally seem to deplore.

In terms of cultural value, dialect, or accent has moved from being mere 'dialect', a first-order indicator (index) of the geographical place of one's mother-tongue origin, to being a "second-order" (Silverstein 2003) cultural self-positioning of one's voice or stance as a kind of American in alignment with – or taking one's distance from – the particular cultural values of a locale ascribed to people of that place.[8] Pronunciations and other such – as we say – "shibboleths" of the place are the emblematic markers of identity, almost inescapable, as they come out when one is not suppressing them, numerous writers of comments note. Like provenance of the prestige foodstuffs as seen on restaurant menus appealing to a certain segment of society, like *"appellation d'origine contrôlée"* of one's wine, identifiable geographically connected accent, too, has become a positive emblem of a sense of placèdness, and therefore of one's place in society. The writers in the *Times* seem to exemplify this emerging cultural value.

In this connection, it is interesting to consider another, cross-cutting 20 % sample of web-posts I performed on every fifth item (thus 5, 10, 15, 20, …), totaling 128, as shown in Figure 15.

Almost uniformly everyone who could be identified as a speaker of New York City dialect positively supports it, even those people who claim to have lost it to one or another extent when transported to another environment. It is an

---

8 See Johnstone et al. (2006) on the historical movement of "Pittsburghese" across the cline of cultural indexicalities, as also Remlinger (2009) in a special issue she has edited of *American Speech* devoted to such processes of 'enregisterment'.

	Positive Attitude		Negative Attitude	
Location of Post	Speaker of NYC	Not-speaker of NYC	Speaker of NYC	Not-speaker of NYC
NYC and environs	32 [27 %]	4	2	4
Non-NYC place	25 [21 %]	22 [18 %]	8	22 [18 %]

Positive Attitude n = 83/119 [70 %]
Negative Attitude n = 36/119 [30 %]
Figure 15: Attitudinal correlates in a cross-cutting 20 % sample of comments

ideologically naturalized – if not natural – fact about inner identity (compare your Israeli couscous, Wisconsin farm-raised organic veal, Florida grapefruits, genuine Idaho potatoes, sparkling pinot noir called "champagne" only when from Champagne, etc.). "Accent," then, is a fact about one's identity that people seem to cherish and hold on to as much by violation as by performance. The tabulation is interesting, in that a very small number, 4 (or 3 %) in each category, of non-dialect speakers who are resident in New York City either are positively inclined or negatively inclined toward it, while twice that number, 8 (6 %) of former New York residents – most of whom claim to have somewhat mitigated their accents – reasonably enough express a negative attitude toward their former mode of speech. Much more significant is the fact that self-reported speakers of New York City accent/dialect are overwhelmingly positive about it 57 or 48 % of the total, whether they live currently in the area or have moved away, and that even non-speakers not in the area are equally split on positive or negative attitudes at 22 each or 18 % of the respondents. Thus, overall, 70 % of respondents tabulated are positive, no matter whether speakers or non-speakers, residents or former residents or non-residents, while only 30 % are negative.

In fact, the overwhelming positive attitude is not merely, or specifically, focused on New York City as such. It is a combination of the kind of city-focal chauvinism that many writers point out, as discussed above, with the notion that locale-indexing language is essential to the cultural diversity of the society, standardizing tendencies notwithstanding and in contra-indication thereto. It is, in short, the celebration of region as a superposed or second-order indexical fact about language, one that easily becomes part of a repertoire of modes of linguistic self-presentation one turns on and off as a function of context, another recurrent theme, as noted above, in many of the posted comments.

Finally, what I found fascinating is that of the 200 thematically classified posts, only 12 of them (6 %) actually directly reference at least one other comment. One would think that commentary is supposed to mirror discussion; but this is more like individuals emoting in relation to the article itself. Only one comment sparked a unique **four** responses – all angry. The comment that sparked four responses was number 20, by a Texan.

20.

John

Big Texas

November 19th, 2010

11:33 am

I find it amusing how all you people here find this sad. Well, guess what folks? You arrogant New England liberals have been making fun of Texan accent for centuries now. You mock how we speak with our drawl, our unique words, our culture .... and now you complain that people will not tolerate you??? Our Texan accent is associated with stupidity and ignorance. Heck, many of you call our accent 'broken English.'

Well, guess what? Ya'll be getting a taste of your own medicine!

Recommend Recommended by 25 Readers

Figure 16: Comment #20, from John in Texas

Both New York City people – remember the famous *New Yorker* magazine map of the world by Saul Steinberg? – and New Englanders rose up, as only "New England liberals" can do, to protest John's "stupidity and ignorance" – presumably confirming what they thought in the first place. Ah fig'r poor guy couldn't win with th' arrogant folks!

References

Babbitt, Eugene Howard. 1896: The English Pronunciation of the Lower Classes in New York and Vicinity. *Dialect Notes* 1: 457–464

Bloomfield, Leonard 1927: Literate and Illiterate Speech. *American Speech* 2: 432–439.

Bonfiglio, Thomas Paul 2002: *Race and the Rise of Standard American*. Berlin/New York: Mouton de Gruyter.

Errington, J. Joseph 1988: *Structure and Style in Javanese*. Philadelphia: University of Pennsylvania Press.

Fox, Margalit 2011: "Sam Chwat, Dialect Tutor for Film Stars, Dies at 57." *New York Times*, digital edition 8 March. http://www.nytimes.com/2011/03/08/nyregion/08chwat.html?_r=1&hpw. Accessed and archived 8 March 2011.[A version of this article appeared in print on March 8, 2011, on page A20 of the New York edition.]

Frekko, Susan K. 2009: "Normal" in Catalonia: Standard Language, Enregisterment, and the Imagination of a National Public. *Language in Society* 38: 71–93.

Geist, William E. 1984: "Accent's on Cleaning Up The Language." *Chicago Tribune*, 17 October 1984, Section 7, Styles, p. 3. [reprinted from *New York Times* news service].

Halliday, Michael, Angus McIntosh & Peter Strevens 1964: *The Linguistic Sciences and Language Teaching*. London: Longmans.

Johnstone, Barbara et al. 2006: Mobility, Indexicality, and the Enregisterment of Pittsburghese. *Journal of English Linguistics* 34: 77–104.

Krapp, George Philip 1925: *The English Language in America*. New York: The Century Co. for the Modern Language Association of America.

Labov, William 1966: *The Social Stratification of English in New York City*. Washington, D.C.: Center for Applied Linguistics.

Labov, William 1994: *Principles of Linguistic Change*. Vol. 1. *Internal Factors*. Oxford: Blackwell.

Mair, Christian 2006: *Twentieth-Century English: History, Variation, and Standardization*. Cambridge: Cambridge University Press.

Preston, Dennis Richard 1999: *Handbook of Perceptual Dialectology*. Amsterdam/Philadelphia: John Benjamins.

Reid, T[homas] B[ertram] W[allace] 1956: Linguistics, Structuralism and Philology. *Archivum Linguisticum* 8(1): 28–37.

Remlinger, Kathryn A. 2009: *American Speech* 84 (2).

Roberts, Sam. 2010. "Unlearning to Tawk Like a New Yorker". *New York Times*, digital edition 19 November. http://www.nytimes.com/2010/11/21/nyregion/21accent.html?_r=2&ref=gen eral&src=me&pagewanted=all. Accessed and archived on 21 November 2010. A version of this article appeared in print on November 21, 2010, on page MB1 of the New York edition.]

Silverstein, Michael 1979: "Language Structure and Linguistic Ideology.". In P. Clyne et al. (eds.), *The Elements: A Parasession on Linguistic Units and Levels*, April 20–21, 1979, 193–247. Chicago: Chicago Linguistic Society.

Silverstein, Michael 1985: Language and the Culture of Gender: At the Intersection of Structure, Usage, and Ideology. In E. Mertz & R. J. Parmentier (eds.), *Semiotic Mediation: Sociocultural and Psychological Perspectives*, 219–259. Orlando, FL: Academic Press.

Silverstein, Michael 1996 [1987]: Monoglot "Standard" in America: Standardization and Metaphors of Linguistic Hegemony. In D. Brenneis & R. H. S. Macaulay (eds.), *The Matrix of Language: Contemporary Linguistic Anthropology*, 284–306. Boulder, CO: Westview Press, 1996. [Reprint of: Working Papers and Proceedings of the Center for Psychosocial Studies, no. 13. Chicago: Center for Psychosocial Studies.]

Silverstein, Michael 1996: Encountering Language and Languages of Encounter in North American Ethnohistory. *Journal of Linguistic Anthropology* 6: 126–144.

Silverstein, Michael 1998: Contemporary Transformations of Local Linguistic Communities. *Annual Review of Anthropology* 27: 401–426.

Silverstein, Michael 1999: NIMBY Goes Linguistic: Conflicted 'Voicings' from the Culture of Local Language Communities. *Proceedings of the Chicago Linguistic Society 35*, part 2: Papers from the Panels, 101–123. Chicago: Chicago Linguistic Society.

Silverstein, Michael 2000: Whorfianism and the Linguistic Imagination of Nationality. In P. Kroskrity (ed.), *Regimes of Language: Ideologies, Polities, Identities*, 85–138. Santa Fe, NM: School of American Research Press.

Silverstein, Michael 2003: Indexical Order and the Dialectics of Sociolinguistic Life. *Language and Communication* 23(3–4): 193–229. [Special issue: Words and Beyond: Linguistic and Semiotic Studies of the Sociocultural Order, ed. P. Manning.]

Silverstein, Michael 2010: "Society, Polity, and Language Community: An Enlightenment Trinity in Anthropological Perspective." *Journal of Language and Politics* 9(3): 339–363.

Winfield, Ann Gibson 2007: *Eugenics and Education in America: Institutionalized Racism and the Implications of History, Ideology, and Memory*. New York: Peter Lang.

Wolfram, Walt & Natalie Schilling-Estes.2006: *American English: Dialects and Variation*. 2nd Ed. Oxford: Blackwell.

Woolard, Kathryn A. 1989: *Double Talk: Bilingualism and the Politics of Ethnicity in Catalonia*. Stanford: Stanford University Press.

Woolard, Kathryn A. 2003: "'We Don't Speak Catalan Because We Are Marginalized'; Ethnic and Class Connotations of Language in Barcelona." In R.K. Blot (ed.), *Language and Social Identity*, 85–103. Westport, CT: Praeger.

Woolard, Kathryn A. 2008: "Language and Identity Choice in Catalonia: The Interplay of Contrasting Ideologies of Linguistic Authority." In Kirsten Süselbeck, Ulrike Mühlschlegel and Peter Masson (eds.), *Lengua, nación e identidad. La regulación del plurilingüismo en España y América Latina*, 303–323. Frankfurt a. M.: Vervuert / Madrid: Iberoamericana.

Graham M. Jones
Reported Speech as an authentication tactic in computer-mediated communication[1]

A recent editorial in the *Christian Science Monitor* (2012) reports that, during a commencement address at Boston University, Google's executive chairman Eric Schmidt exhorted graduates to spend at least an hour a day offline. "Take your eyes off that screen and look into the eyes of the person you love," he said. "Have a conversation, a real conversation." *Monitor* editors savored the paradox of "the man who helped turn the Internet into a must-search obsession" advocating the benefits of "real" rather than virtual conversation. Following Schmidt's lead, they portrayed a conversation's *realness* as hinging on qualities intrinsic to the communicative affordances of face-to-face interaction. Members of "the first fully connected generation the world has ever known," they fretted, "may not learn enough social skills to function in the nonvirtual world. They might think they really should speak in 140 characters. They begin to 'like' someone without really knowing how to like them in person … What families should be doing is having more sit-down meals together. Those are the times when kids pick up the nuances of conversation, or how the smiles, glances, smirks, and other body language are part of human interaction."

Schmidt's remarks and the editorial that amplified them reflect widely held ideologies of language (Woolard & Schieffelin 1994) and media (Gershon 2010a) associating "real conversation" with face-to-face co-presence and qualities of affective depth and expressive nuance supposedly lost in the forms of computer-mediated communication (CMC) ascendant among young people today. There may well be social and psychological dangers associated with increased dependence on CMC (Turkle 2011). Unfortunately, metadiscourses about CMC often take the form of moral panics (Herring 2008; Jones & Schieffelin 2009a; Squires 2010; Thurlow 2006, 2007) that systematically exaggerate the verbal deviance of stereotypical language variants and the social deviance of stereotypical users – mostly young people who are already members of a "delegitimized age group …

1 I thank Thiemo Breyer, Véronique Lacoste and Jakob Leimgruber for organizing the stimulating conference from which this chapter emerged, and for their editorial feedback. I am also very grateful to Lauren Hall-Lew, Amy Johnson, and Bambi B. Schieffelin for generous and perceptive comments on various drafts.

commonly viewed as sloppy, rebellious and irresponsible" (Eckert 2005: 93).[2] Whether or not heavy involvement in online interaction comes at the expense of the middle class American idyll of dinner-table heart-to-hearts (*pace* Ochs and Taylor 1996!), does it deprive young people of essential forms of communicative competence such as the ability to "pick up" the paralinguistic cues *Monitor* editors posit as the marrow of "real" conversation?

In this chapter I provide some evidence that it does not, at least not necessarily and not uniformly. Focusing primarily on Instant Messenger (IM) conversations between college-aged speakers of American English collected from 2003 to 2007 (and using a variety of software programs), I examine how evolving practices of reporting speech and thought make this mediated channel more talk-like, while apparently also expanding a multimodal conception of talk from face-to-face and telephone conversation to CMC. Approaching reported discourse as a sociolinguistically significant stylistic phenomenon, I show how the use of a reporting format associated with orality in the written context of IM shapes relationships of *intermediality*, "configurations which have to do with a crossing of borders between media" and *transmediality*, "the appearance of a certain motif, aesthetic, or discourse across a variety of different media" (Rajewsky 2005: 46). While these notions have some currency in literary and cultural studies, to my knowledge they have not been widely addressed within linguistic anthropology, which leads me to experiment with their usefulness for research on language in multimodal communication ecologies. In the context of this study, reported speech offers a particularly provocative vantage for considering relationships of intermediality and transmediality since speakers are found to quote utterances *between* media with whose particular capacities and constrains they creatively contend.

1 Phatic authentication

In sociolinguistics, considerations of authenticity generally revolve around speech variety, speaker identity, and the relationship between them – be it context-defined or context-defining (Bucholtz 2003; Coupland 2003; Eckert 2003a). In this chapter, I consider an alternate, but not unrelated, locus of authenticity: the communicative channel. Authoritative discourses in the U.S. and elsewhere reflect a widespread cultural consensus that digital communications technolo-

---

2 Moral panics about CMC also reprise alarmist metadiscourses about forms of mediated communication that now seem banal to most Americans, such as the telephone (Kearney 2005).

gies impede authentic communication (and the associated development of communicative competence), which is conceptualized on the paradigm of face-to-face talk. Taking a step back from metacommunicative framings of face-to-face talk as quintessentially authentic, I examine the metalinguistic categories and metapragmatic cues emergent in naturalistic conversations, both face-to-face and computer-mediated, occurring among young (college-age) male and female speakers of American English. Proceeding inductively, I identify stylistic attributes that these speakers appear to associate with "talk" as an interactional genre, and then show how they developed strategies for enacting some of these features in the mediated channel of IM. I argue that, in so doing, they render this form of dyadic typewritten communication stylistically and expressively commensurable with spoken interactional channels.

I am inspired by the way Bucholtz and Hall (2005: 601) "call attention not to authenticity as an inherent essence, but to authentication as a social process played out in discourse." Elsewhere, Bucholtz (2003: 408) elaborates: "It is the tactic of authentication that produces authenticity as its effect. Thus sociolinguists should speak not of authenticity but more accurately of authenticity effects, achieved through the authenticating practices of those who use everyday language. This perspective does not deny the cultural force of authenticity as an ideology, but emphasizes that authenticity is always achieved rather than given in social life, although this achievement is often rendered invisible." I take this performative approach to authenticity as an emergent property and apply it *mutatis mutandis* to communicative channels that are also construed and experienced along a continuum of authenticity and artificiality (on the latter, more shortly). In settings where talk is multimodal and unfolds across a variety of channels coexisting diacritically in a complex media ecology, what tactics/practices of authentication develop around producing authenticity effects associated with the selection and use of particular channels?

I am aware of the felicitous polysemy of the term "authentication" in this question: as features of natural language may authenticate the quality of talk between users of CMC, features of machine language simultaneously (and generally outside of speakers' immediate awareness) authenticate the interface between the devices they use. The dual pertinence of authentication tactics here reflects not only the experiential and structural vulnerabilities of mediated channels, but also the fundamental element of risk and uncertainty in all communication (see Peters 1999). Recent trends in computer security suggest increased overlap between the authentication tactics used by speakers and machines, as we witness the development of biometric measures that verify speaker identity based on "behavioral characteristics such as typing rhythm, gait and voice" (Cobb 2011: 17). According to a new DARPA research initiative, future security measures may even focus on "how the user crafts written language in an e-mail or document" (Sengupta 2011), extending the reach of biometrics to *individual style* (Johnstone 2009).

I draw on Jakobson's (1985) schematization of the speech event to foreground the functional specificity of the tactics of authentication I describe below. Bucholtz and Hall associate authentication primarily with considerations of speaker identity (Jakobson's "expressive" function) and code variety (Jakobson's "metalingual" function). Building on Jakobson's notion of the "phatic function," which emphasizes the medium of communication and "checks whether the channel works" (1985: 152), I propose we might identify a dimension of *phatic authentication* that mobilizes metacommunicative and metapragmatic features to validate the legitimacy and efficaciousness of a particular channel in respect to interaction-relevant criteria and desiderata. I argue that meaning emerges in the co-constitutive relationship of message and medium, with language choices and the formal properties of entextualized utterances conveying attitudes toward the medium of transmission that may, in turn, complement or complicate the message.

Phatic authentication relates to central concerns to recent linguistic anthropological research on mediated communication. A growing body of work explores the locally specific cultural, ideological, and linguistic mediations involved in the authenticity effects associated with particular communications media – from audio recording (Eisenlohr 2010, 2011) to stenography (Inoue 2011) and literacy (Schieffelin 2000). Focusing on a North American setting in which college-aged communicative partners can simultaneously or sequentially address each other using a variety of channels (face-to-face, text messaging, Instant Messaging, social networking sites, telephone, letters, etc.), Gershon (2010b) explores subjective (and not always consensual) clines of authenticity and intimacy involved in media choice and media switching. The "iconization" (Irvine and Gal 2000) of features associated with particular modes of communication and their users has been found to inform tactics of authenticating idealized speaker personae – in the case of letter writing (Ahearn 2001) or text messaging (McIntosh 2010), for example. Studies like these shape my approach to phatic authentication as a situated micro-process enmeshed in a broader skein of macro-level relationships.

2 Cross-channel polyphony

In this section, I compare conversational data collected from comparable samples of American teenagers and young adults (ages 18–22) communicating across two principal channels – face-to-face and IM – between 2003 and 2007. In a recent article, Bambi Schieffelin and I presented the results of a synchronic and diachronic analysis of the data collected in 2003 and 2006 (Jones and Schieffelin 2009b). For an overview of the corpus used in this study, and to which I subsequently refer, see table 1.

	Total Speakers	Total Conversations	Total Words
2003 face-to-face	40	14	28,891
2003 IM	45	66	26,881
2006 face-to-face	43	19	56,968
2006 IM	52	66	56,254

Table 1: Corpus of face-to-face and IM conversations between college-age (18–22) Americans in 2003 and 2006 analyzed here

In succeeding sections, I draw upon these findings to qualitatively analyze comparable data collected in 2007.

We found that from 2003 onward this sample population refers to typewritten IM using the metalanguage of *talk*. In other words, the metalinguistic verbs used in reference to IMing do not differ significantly from those used in reference to face-to-face conversation, as with "yell" and "talk" in Example 1 and "speak" in Example 2:

Example 1 (2003 IM)

```
1    e0303   (12:47:11 AM): i need to go to bed
2    e0303   (12:47:16 AM): before i start yelling at you
3    e0303   (12:47:45 AM): thanks for talking to
```

Example 2 (2006 IM)

```
1    wandawoman  (10:00:59 PM): you should have seen when I
2                IMed Anna back last night, for some reason I could
3                not speak English
```

A number of scholars have commented on innate and aspirational similitudes between IM and spoken talk (Blum 2005; Baron 2004; Childs & Mallinson 2006; Lewis & Fabos 2005; Squires 2012). We can reasonably assume that the speakers' classification of IM as "talk" in the above examples reflects the interactional dynamics of a communicative channel that is dyadic and synchronous, allowing for a turn-taking architecture that closely resembles that of spoken interaction, whether face-to-face or over the phone.

In both 2003 and 2006, speakers in our sample made widespread use of reported speech in face-to-face talk, particularly when telling affectively and morally charged stories. Overwhelmingly, they used quotative *be+like* to construct both reported speech and thought, as in the following spoken example:

Example 3 (2006 Face-to-Face)

```
1   Louise:  I was walking past this guy who was waiting
2            for the elevator and he was talking and he was like
3            "so what are you into like whips and chains and
4            stuff?" And I was like "why are you having this
5            conversation in public?"
```

Here, Louise, in telling a story to her friends, uses *be+like* to enquote both an utterance she putatively overheard ("he was like 'so what are you into like whips and chains and stuff?'") and an internal thought, something she privately said to herself ("I was like 'why are you having this conversation in public?'").

Quotative *like* has been widely documented in most varieties of English worldwide, as a form closely associated with the speech of adolescents and young adults (e.g., Buchstaller & D'Arcy 2009; Tagliamonte & Hudson 1999). In discourse, it can present both speech and thought as directly quoted utterances, blurring the boundaries between what was actually said and what was merely thought (Romaine & Lange 1991). It can also enquote nonlexicalized noises and gestures (Fox & Robles 2010), giving speakers tremendous histrionic license to demonstrate rather than describe (Clark and Gerrig 1990) the comportment of themselves and others. The mimetic and impersonative quality of quotative *like* serves to add vividness and build listener involvement (Buchstaller 2003); Levey (2003: 28) argues that "discourse *like* not only appeals to hearers to interpret an utterance as a less than literal rendering ... it also invites the collaboration of the hearer in the negotiation of meaning," thereby creating interactional solidarity. In terms of its pragmatic specificity, quotative *like* also seems closely associated with encoding dimensions of attitude, stance, or demeanor (Ferrara & Bell 1995; Jones & Schieffelin 2009b), privileging the animator's subjective "take" on the situation over verbatim fidelity.

According to Buchstaller and Van Alphen (2012: xi), innovations linguistically and sociolinguistically similar to quotative *like* "have been reported in a wealth of languages across the world, including Dutch, Hebrew and Japanese ... but also German, Swedish, Russian, Greek, Norwegian, Icelandic, Portuguese, Spanish, Italian, and many others." More broadly, Streeck (2002: 595) notes that "the mimetic mode of narrative representation" so closely associated with these forms "has gained new popularity in the U.S. and other societies, a mode of reporting experiences and events that favors reenactments, however stylized as brief, over descriptions." The reasons for this trend are difficult to ascertain, although its close association cross-culturally with teenage speakers and their storytelling activities suggests it may have to do with the advent of adolescence itself as "a product of industrial society, its history closely tied to the development of universal institutionalized secondary education" and "to the constraints (and opportunities) that these conditions place on the age group" (Eckert 2003b: 112).

The pervasiveness of "constructed dialogues" (Tannen 1986) involving quotative *like* – and sometimes also quotative *all* (Bucholtz and Hall 2005: 592–593; Rickford et al. 2007; Waksler 2001) – in our face-to-face conversational data from 2003 to 2006 led us to identify this feature as the hallmark of a "style" (Eckert and Rickford 2001) of informal talk between young peers. We termed this style *polyphony*, following Bakhtin (Jones & Schieffelin 2009b: 99).[3] The polyphonic style uses novel demonstrative quotatives to dramatically act out situations in which similarities and differences of identity, taste, affiliation, and membership become clear through exchanges of words. Thus, in the previous example, Louise constructs a dialogue that dramatizes two competing notions of verbal propriety – that of someone who talks about kinky sex in public, and her own.

Surprisingly, while speakers in both 2003 and 2006 consistently referred to IM as a kind of *talk*, the 2003 IMs showed virtually no evidence of polyphonic style. However, the 2006 IMs much more closely resembled the face-to-face talk from both 2003 and 2006 in terms of the prominence of polyphonic dialogues constructed with quotative *be+like*. Table 2 summarizes our statistical findings.

	Total Quotatives	Be+Like % Quotatives	Be+Like % Speakers
2003 face-to-face	248	75 %	80 %
2003 IM	35	6 %	2 %
2006 face-to-face	468	67 %	84 %
2006 IM	175	50 %	31 %

Table 2: Quotative *like* as a percentage of total quotatives and percentage of speakers using quotative *like*

In face-to-face interaction, quotative *like* appears relatively stable over this three-year interval when viewed both as a percentage of total quotative tokens and in

---

3 Günther (1999) fruitfully applies the Bakhtinian notion of polyphony to the analysis of constructed dialogues in German, focusing on prosodic considerations rather than sociolinguistic variation.

terms of the percentage of speakers who employ it. During the same period, these same proportions increase dramatically for IM, as Figure 1 and Figure 2 vividly illustrate.

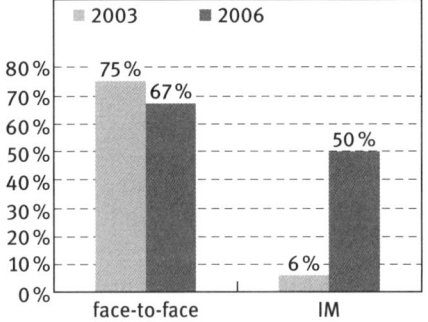

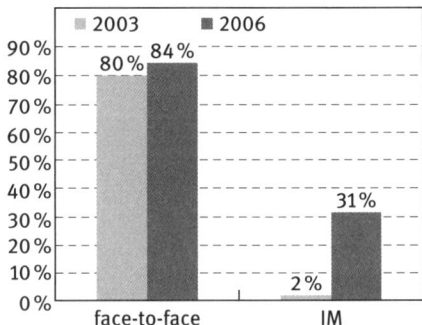

Figure 1: Quotative like as a percentage of total quotatives

Figure 2: Percentage of speakers using quotative *like*

I propose that approaching quotative *like* as an index of phatic authenticity is one way to account for these changes. From a sociolinguistic standpoint, it has already been analyzed as an index of membership in trendy, youthful categories of speakers (Buchstaller 2006; Dailey-O'Cain 2000; Tagliamonte & D'Arcy 2007). What I am arguing is that, insofar as quotative *like* is heavily implicated in the polyphonic style characteristic of face-to-face talk among members of this cohort, its increasing presence in IM can be seen as a tactic of phatic authentication, aligning this typewritten channel more closely with spoken analogues. But given the apparent value of this feature, why wouldn't its use in IM co-occur simultaneously with the embrace of that medium as a form of talk?

3 Mediational barriers

Richard Bauman (2010: 255) uses the term "mediational barriers" to describe the social, institutional, technological, and linguistic challenges users new to a particular communications medium must contend with in order to domesticate it. While 2003 and 2006 study participants categorized IM as talk, I hypothesize that there were ideological and formal mediational barriers that they were still working to overcome to align IM and face-to-face talk stylistically. One of those barriers may involve ideologies of register. While IM conversations in our corpus are informal and intimate, written language has tended to be more closely associated with formal, academic or professional, registers than speech. This may account for some subtle resistance to the use of quotative *like*, which indexes informal, oral, and peer-focused talk—and can be associated with a speaker sounding uneducated (Buchstaller 2006; Dailey-O'Cain 2000; Eckert 2005; Tagliamonte & D'Arcy 2007). Finding quotative *like* present in Canadian English IM collected from a sample similar to our own between 2004 and 2006 but statistically underrepresented in respect to face-to-face talk leads Tagliamonte and Denis (2008: 19) to conclude that IM is more "conservative" than speech in this respect.

A second mediational barrier to the extensive use of polyphonic style in IM might have to do with epistemic stance. Quotative *be+like* and *all* apply the format of direct reported speech to demonstrative performances that aren't strictly limited to what has been literally said, opening the door to other kinds of representational equivalencies. Buchstaller and Van Alphen (2012: xv) associate this with a function of epistemic hedging, such that the construction's "comparative/similative semantics" allows speakers to "acknowledge and even highlight the approximative value of the quotation and thereby shield themselves from potential criticism regarding the inexact nature of the reproduction."[4]

I hypothesize that higher standards of epistemic commitment in writing than speech may have created an ideological mediational barrier for a form of constructed dialogue involving a citational format marked as epistemically hedged. While this line of argument is somewhat speculative, note how the following example demonstrates the epistemic latitude speakers take (and recognize each other to take) with quotative *like*, here instantiated in an IM setting:

Example 4 (IM 2007)

1	Hachoo	(3:48:20 PM): Tina's going all "why can't a boy
2		and girl just be friends??!!!"
3	Hachoo	(3:48:30 PM): and I'm like.. well you really –
4		aren't- helping that impression
5	Wendy111	(3:48:30 PM): XD
6	Hachoo	(3:48:30 PM): so grow the hell up
7	Wendy12	(3:48:33 PM): did you tell her that?
8	Hachoo	(3:48:39 PM): no XD
9	Hachoo	(3:48:39 PM): I wasn't in a drama mood
10	Wendy111	(3:48:39 PM): XD

---

4 Without denying that quotative *like* may indeed have this epistemic hedging function, I would simply add that in many situations it may indicate increased exactitude in representational detail, particularly detail of a paralinguistic nature, rather than inexactitude.

In this extraordinary strip of talk, Hachoo represents a previous conversation between herself and an absent third party, Tina, who espoused a position that Hachoo deemed fatuous. In the first utterance, Hachoo reports: "Tina's going all 'why can't a boy and girl just be friends??!!!'" And in her next two utterances (lines 3–4, 6) gives what appears to be her response: "and I'm like.. well you really – aren't- helping that impression [...] so grow the hell up." This would be a sharply confrontational thing to say, and Wendy12 initiates repair, asking if Hachoo did, in fact say it (line 7). It turns out that she did not (line 8). Quotative *like* allows her to encode her stance (what she may have been *saying to herself*) as a spoken turn, as hypothetical talk in a dialogue that she in part constructs for dramatic effect. Note that Wendy111 responds to this information with a smiling/laughing emoticon ("XD" in line 10)[5] suggesting that this conflation of speech and thought was not a particularly grave matter.

The potentially restrictive expressive affordances of typewritten interaction may constitute a third mediational barrier: the presentation of mimetic, dramatized enactments (often gestures and noises) as directly reported utterances so closely associated with quotative *like* and *all* may be intrinsically difficult to realize in a typewritten medium. Speakers in our sample did not overtly acknowledge these difficulties. However, they did allude to the difficulty of conveying contextualization cues (Gumperz 1982: 131) in the absence of paralinguistic features, as in the following exchange:

Example 5 (2006 IM)

1	hardwired6	(9:23:39 PM): compliments wont work via
2		AIM
3	hardwired6	(9:23:55 PM): it all comes through as sarcasm
4	babeeDoll12	(9:23:56 PM): hahah i suppose you are right

Here, one speaker complains (lines 1–3) that compliments sound like sarcasm in AIM (i.e., AOL Instant Messenger). The difficulties of encoding affect, tone, or footing in typewritten IM to which these speakers allude is reminiscent of the editorial criticisms of CMC I cited in the opening section ("how the smiles, glances, smirks, and other body language are part of human interaction").

Examples like this serve as a reminder that authenticity often coexists in a delicate balance with artificiality. This leads Bucholtz and Hall (2005: 601) to pair

---

5 This emoticon also appears to function as a recurring coherence device produced by both interlocutors throughout this strip of talk.

the notion of authentication with a contrary process, *denaturalization*. If authentication "focuses on the ways in which identities are discursively verified," they write, then denaturalization concerns "how assumptions regarding the seamlessness of identity can be subverted." Transposing this notion to considerations of channel, we might characterize the way speakers in the above example call attention to ways IM is "crafted, fragmented, problematic, or false" (Bucholtz & Hall 2005: 602) *vis-à-vis* spoken channels of communication as a form of *phatic denaturalization*.

The expressive restrictions of a written channel would seem inherently inimical to the demonstrative, mimetic emphasis of this novel quotative paradigm. Along these lines, Clark and Gerrig (1990: 782–783) argue: "Written English is limited in what it can depict. Through its orthographic conventions, it can represent such things as sentences, words, phonetic segments, and some temporal and intonational information, but not tone of voice, voice pitch, nasality, many speech defects, singing, or gestures. Nor can it depict wolf whistles, belches, head nods, or faces." The following examples suggest otherwise.

By 2006, IMs were replete with creative solutions to presenting iconic representations of tone of voice—and demeanor more generally—through the format of reported speech, and even to enquoting nonverbal demonstrations such as gestures or nonlexicalized noises. I'll present a few examples from 2007 that exhibit the range of creativity associated with the typewritten entextualization of these kinds of enquoted utterances. In this example, Sandie is describing her roommates' reaction to a stray cat they have found.

Example 6 (IM 2007)

> 1   Sandie: theyre all "she loves us <333333333 we must keep
> 2   her now <3333333333333"

Within the citational frame established with the quotative *be+all* (which pragmatically functions analogously to *be+like* here), she uses a heart emoticon (a less-than sign with the Arabic numeral 3) to indicate her roommates' affective stance. The repetition of the numeral 3 is an iconic intensification, highlighting the tone of adoration in the roommates' speech and their adoring stance towards the stray. It is notable that these emoticons occur *within* the enquoted utterance (as signaled by quotation marks), indicating that they are intended to constitute part of the imitative demonstration, not part of the animator's description of it.

In the next example, Wendy12 narrates a story about an objectionable third party who commends her for cheering at a relatively non-serious sporting event (lines 1–2). Drawing on conventionalized paralinguistic resources of typewritten

CMC to evoke qualitative dimensions of the face-to-face speech she reports, she uses capitalization to convey gushing enthusiasm ("and she was like, 'OMG R U A CHEERLEADER!'"). Insofar as she is depicting a grating or pitiable persona, her use of standardized IM initialisms (Crystal 2008: 41) such as "OMG" and logograms (Crystal 2008: 37) such as "R U" may index the undesirable qualities (particularly of teenage girls) with which these forms are so often associated (Jones & Schieffelin 2009b).

Example 7 (IM 2007)

```
1    Wendy12  (7:51:50 PM): ...once i cheered on my team
2             during dodgeball!
3    Wendy12  (7:51:59 PM): and she was like, "OMG R U A
4             CHEERLEADER! CHEERLEADER WENDY
5             YAY"
6    Wendy12  (7:52:03 PM): and it was like, "...; ;"
7    Pippar   (7:52:11 PM): ...yeah
```

In line 4, Wendy12 reports her response using *be+like* to enquote a demonstrative facial expression, using a version of a conventional Asian emoticon denoting sadness ("; ;"), which Katsuno and Yano (2002: 227) gloss as "crying (eyes with tears)." The preceding ellipsis may be a prosodical marking of an interactional pause (as one might expect in a performed enactment) or it may represent a stream of tears, amplifying Wendy12's profoundly negative reaction to being lauded as a "cheerleader" in this context.

This skillfully constructed dialogue is rich in social detail. Arguably, the juxtaposition of an interlocutor's cloying effusion with her own ironic, nonverbal reaction, emphasizes Wendy12's detachment from the situation and iconically conveys a comportmental difference between two speakers. Insofar as she is presenting a contrast between another speaker's obliviousness and her own worldliness, this Anglo-American adolescent's use of an Asian emoticon here may be a marker of desirable personal attributes. Her interlocutor seconds her assessment (line 7), indicating an achievement of intersubjectivity. What's important for my argument is that the enquoted object in line 6 is obviously not a spoken turn, but rather an iconic representation of how Wendy12 felt at the time. It offers a striking example of the transposition of mimetic enactment into typewritten IM through the creative manipulation of channel-specific verbal resources and entextualization conventions—an example that in turn reflects specialized forms of communicative competence and attentiveness to the social meaning of language.

In both of the above examples of typewritten reports of face-to-face interactions, speakers use punctuation and other graphic features to iconically represent paralinguistic elements of spoken interaction within a demonstrative, mimetic quotative frame. If authenticity is connected to constituting intersubjectivity in these exchanges, it seems that the care speakers take to encode affectively rich detail adds additional elements of expressivity and "audience design" (Bell 2001) that make utterances and interactions appear more sincere, engaged, and personal. In part, examples like these reflect a process of remediation (Gershon 2010a: 287–288), whereby ideologies associated with a typewritten channel of synchronous, dyadic communication converge with the ideologies of face-to-face talk (cf. Rajewsky 2005). At the same time, and perhaps more significantly, they also indicate a transmedial process of the consolidation of a polyphonic style across channels.

4 Reprojective authentication

In the previous section, I made the argument that the incorporation of quotative *like*, understood to stylistically index "talk" as a genre, can been seen as an authentication practice in the mediated setting of IM. In this section I want to ask a slightly different question about the object of quotes presented with this citational format. Establishing a relationship between reported and reporting frame of reference, and between the speech of author and animator, reported discourse has an inherently intertextual dimension (Bauman 2004). Examples in the previous section introduce an additional component of intermediality, whereby discourse from one medium is represented in another. The instances I consider of speakers representing face-to-face interaction in IM illustrate the expressive ingenuity involved in domesticating this medium as a form of talk. In this section, I focus on the "recontextualization" (Bauman & Briggs 1990: 73–74) of material originating in mediated (as opposed to face-to-face) channels into the reporting context of IM using quotative *like* as a citational device. If the previous section asks what quotation using *be* + *like* might convey about the *target* medium into which the quoted object is recontextualized, this section asks – more speculatively – what quotation using *be* + *like* might convey about the *source* medium from which the quoted object is decontextualized.

Elsewhere, I have described how polyphonic talk takes the form of metacommunicative gossip focusing on other people's verbal behaviors involving the use of communications media (Jones, Schieffelin, and Smith 2011). Here I want to examine a few instances in which metacommunicative gossip employs quotative *like* to enquote, for instance, IM discourse (Example 8) or email discourse (Example 9) – both in the target channel of IM:

Example 8 (IM 2006)

1	ItsTom76	(11:43:58 PM): cause i stayed over (even tho i
2		requested an air mattress lol) and he just imed me
3		like "omg sorry i havent called you ive been so busy
4		this weekend with my family" and im just like...oh
5		its fine lol

Example 9 (IM 2007)

1	Wendy12	(3:47:19 PM): so jacob exploded at elena nad
2		wrote her an angry email
3		[...]
4	Wendy12	(3:47:27 PM): he's like, "she's lazy and never
5		helps us usually"

As a provisional – and strictly qualitative – interpretation, I propose that the use of quotative *like* to enquote objects originating in CMC not only adds vividness to the quotation as an impersonative enactment, but also confers added dimensionality upon the originating channels (here, IM and email) themselves. These examples could be seen as reflecting a media ideology according to which the reported interactions are held to be sufficiently rich to serve as the basis for dramatic reenactment, such that the selection of the object of quotation following *like* constructions itself serves an in index of phatic authenticity reprojected onto the originating channel.

I want to explore this dynamic of *reprojective authentication* in respect to one final example, this time concerning the source channel of text messaging. The following example is an IM exchange between two young female friends, Titi2 and Rubbadubdub. Titi2 recounts a previous conversation with a third party, William, that began with a brief face-to-face encounter and subsequently continued via text message. The conversation with William troubled Titi2, and she represents a sequence of interactional turns as evidence of a social transgression.

Example 10 (IM 2007)

1	Titi2:	uhm well we ran into eachother briefly when I was
2		coming into 3n and he was walking out
3	Titi2:	so it was just like HEY hey!
4	Titi2:	type thing
5	Titi2:	he texts
6	Rubbadubdub:	yeah
7		[...]
8	Titi2:	how are you, blah blah

9	Titi2:	eventually I stopped replying. dunno why
10	Titi2:	so he txts again and was like "uh well it was nice
11		talking to you"
12	Titi2:	and I was like sorry I was eating I got distracted
13	Titi2:	to which I got:
14	Titi2:	oh damn I deleted it
15	Titi2:	something like
16	Titi2:	oh I don't know where I'd get the idea that you were
17		ignoring me

Titi2 reports that when she got distracted from the conversation with William and stopped responding to his texts (line 9), he responded tartly (lines 10–11). In her report, he refers to their exchange of text messages as talk ("uh well it was nice talking to you"). With the proliferation of cellphones making text messaging a ubiquitous part of everyday life for many in this age-group (Lenhart 2010), by 2007 texting too comes under the metalinguistic umbrella of "talk"—a pattern reflected in other conversations that I do not analyze here.

There are several instances of direct reported speech in this strip of talk that employ quotative *like*. In line 3, Titi2 artfully depicts the face-to-face conversation that initiated her interaction with William as a minimal adjacency pair ("so it was just like HEY hey!"). Titi2's "he texts" (line 5) appears to enquote the utterance "how are you, blah blah" (line 8).[6] At this point, Titi2 continues her story using quotative *like*. In line 10, she reports: "so he txts again and was like 'uh well it was nice talking to you'." Given the context, it is clear that William's remark is meant (at least in Titi2's rendition of it) to sarcastically reproach her for leaving an open channel without initiating a closing sequence (he also thereby denaturalizes their interaction). The discourse markers "uh well" appear to play an important role in constituting his sarcastic tone (and hence accusatory stance). In the following line, Titi2 reports her response to William, providing an account for her disattention: "and I was like sorry I was eating I got distracted."

The point of this strip of metacommunicative gossip is to construct a negative assessment of William as someone who took unreasonable offence to what Titi2 frames as contextually understandable disattention to his inopportune stream of messages. A critical piece of evidence in the story is a particularly irksome, hence "storyable" (Sacks 1984: 417), text message from William. In line 13, Titi2 uses "I got" to frame what she expects will be a verbatim report of the message. Unfor-

---

6 Alternately, "he texts" (line 5) could be read as a description of William's communicative act, in which case the direct reported speech in line 8 is introduced with a zero quotative, a form Tagliamonte and Denis (2008: 19) find surprisingly common in IM.

tunately, when she consults her cell phone to furnish an exact quote, she finds that she has deleted the evidence (line 14)! This shift in quotative framing devices reflects a pattern I have documented elsewhere (Jones & Schieffelin 2009b: 97–99), in which quotative *like* as a form that dramatizes the story and highlights the emergence of contrastive attitudes in conversation maintains salient diacritical relationships with other forms that signal the importance of attending to precisely what was said.

Where forms vary, choices have meaning. Titi2's shift in line 13 demonstrates that she is not using quotative *like* unreflectively, but rather purposely, to achieve intentional discursive effects. One of those effects may be the modulation of epistemic stance (line 15), but I would like to argue that her quotative usage is also a tactic of phatic authentication. In employing the same quotative format to directly report face-to-face and text messaged utterances originating in the same multimodal interaction, she enacts an understanding of talk as a transmedial genre, which is reinforced by the application of the metalanguage of talk to texting. In addition, the use of a quotative format pragmatically associated with mimetic impersonations of contrastive speaker roles hints at the experiential intensity of these mediated interactions, which may not have the same interactional parameters as face-to-face conversation (Titi2 can disattend her partner at any time), but do seem to carry considerable communicative nuance (such as sarcasm) and social significance enough to warrant intensive subsequent scrutiny.

Constructing these intermedial quotes may require some work of translating between mediums and medialects. Titi2 does not call attention to the origin of the utterances she quotes by stylizing enquoted objects with features iconic of text messaging such as abbreviations or acronyms. At the same time, one may note that the enquoted utterances in Examples 8–10 do not exhibit the same degree of paralinguistic and typographical embellishment as those analyzed in the previous section (Examples 6–7), where the originating channel was face-to-face speech. A more systematic comparison of the objects of quotations might provide additional perspective on thresholds between literacy and orality: if the prototype of a quoted utterance was originally entextualized in a typewritten form, do speakers give themselves less license in introducing paralinguistic features? If so, is this because within the participant framework of text-based talk the range of paralinguistic features available for consideration is somewhat restricted, or because there is a different regime of evidentiality associated with reporting typewritten communication? Such questions could certainly provide a basis for future research.

5 Conclusion

Building upon the apparent complementarity between a new quotative paradigm and a polyphonic style in young Americans' talk, I have framed the gradual
spread of quotative *like* and *all* into typewritten IM as an index of phatic authenticity, which serves to reinforce the metalinguistic framing of this form of CMC as
talk. I have traced the creativity and agency involved in entextualizing spoken
quotatives intermedially, and suggested that the form of these intermedial entex-
tualizations reflects a larger transmedial shift towards an expansively multimodal
conception of talk, incorporating CMC alongside face-to-face and telephonic conversation. The quotation of utterances (and interactions) originating in channels
of CMC such as IM, email, and text messaging using quotative *like* may enhance
this process by reprojectively highlighting the expressivity of original entextualization formats.

A more exhaustive version of this argument would emphasize the special
considerations of authenticity attendant upon reported speech as a form of
"reflexive language" (Lucy 1993). Insofar as it putatively represents a previous
utterance (or otherwise enquotable state of affairs), reported speech inevitably
involves considerations of *referential authenticity*. As Holt (2009: 195) writes,
"reported speech purports to be a replaying of a prior utterance … [Direct reported
speech], in particular is considered to be an authentic reproduction of a prior
locution." When speakers report the speech of themselves and others (or treat
other qualities as enquotable), they are making implicit claims about authenticity of representation, although there may be culturally and contextually different
criteria of what counts for an "authentic" quote. Given these considerations, the
intermedial entextualization of enquoted utterances inevitably raises questions
about the representational adequacy of the target medium and, perhaps, medi-
alect. What interests me particularly in the examples I have analyzed here is the
role of quotative *like* in both promoting added expressivity in CMC (as animating
target medium) and conferring added expressivity upon CMC (as authorial source
medium).

Simmel (1950: 52) describes *sociability* in conversation as "the *art* of conversation that has its own artistic laws." The data that I have presented here should
be seen as evidence of problem-solving activities, in which members of a loosely
defined speech community creatively elaborate verbal devices and communicative practices associated with extending and enriching a kind of artful sociability
they value. In order to achieve certain desirable characteristics in conversation,
speakers engage in linguistic innovation, while continuing to depend upon consensus and convention as a basis of intersubjectivity. Further research might
reveal that the practices of intermediality and transmediality I describe here are

themselves part of a broader "indexical order" (Silverstein 2003) that semiotically marks these speakers as members of a sociolinguistically and/or culturally distinctive group. At the very least, the present analysis demonstrates the communicative competence and social acuity of a generation of speakers often depicted as wanting in precisely these two areas.

References

Ahearn, Laura M. 2001: *Invitations to Love: Literacy, Love Letters, & Social Change in Nepal*. Ann Arbor: University of Michigan Press.

Baron, Naomi S. 2004: See you online: Gender issues in college student use of Instant Messaging. *Journal of Language and Social Psychology* 23(4): 397–423.

Bauman, Richard 2004: *A World of Others' Words*. Malden, MA: Blackwell.

Bauman, Richard 2010: "It's not a telescope, it's a telephone": Encounters with the telephone on early commercial sound recordings. In Sally Johnson and Tommaso M. Milani (eds.), *Language Ideologies and Media Discourse: Texts, Practices, Politics*, 252–273. New York: Continuum.

Bauman, Richard & Charles L. Briggs 1990: Poetics and performances as critical perspectives on language and social life. *Annual Review of Anthropology* 19: 59–88.

Bell, Allan 2001: Back in style: Reworking audience design. In Penelope Eckert and John R. Rickford (eds.), *Style and Sociolinguistic Variation*, 139–169. New York: Cambridge University Press.

Blum, Susan 2005: Buzzing and writing the day away instant messaging. *Anthropology News*, February, 29–30.

Bucholtz, Mary 2003: Sociolinguistic nostalgia and the authentication of identity. *Journal of Sociolinguistics* 7(3): 398–416.

Bucholtz, Mary and Kira Hall 2005: Identity and interaction: A sociocultural linguistic approach. *Discourse Studies* 7(4–5): 585–614.

Buchstaller, Isabelle 2003: The co-occurrence of quotatives with mimetic performances. *Edinburgh Working Papers in Applied Linguistics* 12: 1–8.

Buchstaller, Isabelle 2006: Social stereotypes, personality traits and regional perception displaced: Attitudes towards the 'new' quotatives in the U.K. *Journal of Sociolinguistics* 10(3): 362–381.

Buchstaller, Isabelle & Alexandra D'Arcy 2009: Localized globalization: A multi-local, multi-variate investigation of *be like*. *Journal of Sociolinguistics* 13(3): 291–331.

Buchstaller, Isabelle & Ingrid Van Alphen 2012: Introductory remarks on new and old quotatives. In Isabelle Buchstaller and Ingrid Van Alphen (eds.), *Quotatives: Cross-Linguistic and Cross-Disciplinary Perspectives*, xi–xxx. Philadelphia: John Benjamins.

Childs, Becky & Christine Mallinson 2006: The significance of lexical items in the construction of ethnolinguistic identity: A case study of adolescent spoken and online language. *American Speech* 81 (1): 3–30.

Christian Science Monitor 2012: Message from Google chief: Have a heart – turn off this screen. May 24.

Clark, Herb & Richard Gerrig 1990: Quotations as demonstrations. *Language* 66 (4): 764–805.

Cobb, Michael 2011: Biometrics for the rest of us. *Information Week*, November 21: 17.

Coupland, Nikolas 2003: Sociolinguistic authenticities. *Journal of Sociolinguistics* 7(3): 417–431.

Crystal, David 2008: *txtng: the gr8 db8*. New York: Oxford University Press.

Dailey-O'Cain 2000: The sociolinguistic distribution of attitudes toward focuser *like* and quotative *like*. *Journal of Sociolinguistics* 4(1): 60–80.

Eckert, Penelope 2003a: Sociolinguistics and authenticity: An elephant in the room. *Journal of Sociolinguistics* 7(3): 392–431.

Eckert, Penelope 2003b: Language and adolescent peer groups. *Journal of Language and Social Psychology* 22(1): 112–118.

Eckert, Penelope 2005: Stylistic practice and the adolescent social order. In Angie Williams and Crispin Thurlow (eds.), *Talking Adolescence: Perspectives on Communication in the Teenage Years*, 93–110. New York: Peter Lang.

Eckert, Penelope & John R. Rickford (eds.) 2001: *Style and Sociolinguistic Variation*. New York: Cambridge University Press.

Eisenlohr, Patrick 2010: Materialities of entextualization: The domestication of sound reproduction in Mauritian Muslim devotional practices. *Journal of Linguistic Anthropology* 20(2): 413–433.

Eisenlohr, Patrick 2011: Media authenticity and authority in Mauritius: On the mediality of language in religion. *Language & Communication* 31(3): 266–273.

Ferrara, Kathleen & Barbara Bell 1995: Sociolinguistic variation and discourse function of constructed dialogue introducers: The case of *be + like*. *American Speech* 70(3): 265–290.

Fox, Barbara A. & Jessica Robles 2010: It's like *mmm*: Enactments with it's like. *Discourse Studies* 12(6): 715–738.

Gershon, Ilana 2010a: Media ideologies: An introduction. *Journal of Linguistic Anthropology* 20(2): 283–293.

Gershon Ilana 2010b: Breaking up is hard to do: Media switching and media ideologies. *Journal of Linguistic Anthropology* 20(2): 389–405.

Gumperz, John 1982: *Discourse Strategies*. New York: Cambridge University Press.

Günther, Susanne 1999: Polyphony and the 'layering of voices' in reported dialogues: An analysis of the use of prosodic devices in everyday speech. *Journal of Pragmatics* 31: 685–708.

Herring, Susan 2008: Questioning the generational divide: Technological exoticism and adult constructions of online youth identity." In David Buckingham (ed.), *Youth, Identity, and Digital Media*, 71–92. Cambridge, MA: MIT University Press.

Holt, Elizabeth 2009: Reported speech. In Sigurd D'hondt, Jan-Ola Östman and Jef Verschueren (eds.), *The Pragmatics of Interaction*, 190–205. Philadelphia: John Benjamins.

Inoue, Miyako 2011: Stenography and ventriloquism in late nineteenth century Japan. *Language & Communication* 31(3): 181–190.

Irvine, Judith T. & Susan Gal 2000: Language ideology and linguistic differentiation. In Paul Kroskrity (ed.), *Regimes of Language*, 35–83. Santa Fe, NM: School of American Research Press.

Jakobson, Roman 1985: Closing statement: Linguistics and poetics. In Robert E. Innis (ed.), *Semiotics: An Introductory Anthology*, 147–175. Bloomington: Indiana University Press. First published Cambridge, MA: MIT Press [1960].

Johnstone, Barbara 2009: Stance, style, and the linguistic individual. In Alexandra Jaffe (ed.), *Sociolinguistic Perspectives on Stance*, 29–52. New York: Oxford University Press.

Jones, Graham M. & Bambi B. Schieffelin 2009a: Talking text and talking back: My BFF Jill from boob-tube to YouTube. *Journal of Computer Mediated Communication* 14(4): 1150–1179.

Jones, Graham M. & Bambi B. Schieffelin 2009b: Enquoting voices, accomplishing talk: Uses of *be + like* in Instant Messaging. *Language & Communication* 29(1): 77–113.

Jones, Graham M., Bambi B. Schieffelin & Rachel E. Smith 2011: When friends who talk together stalk together: Online gossip as metacommunication. In Crispin Thurlow and Kristine Mrozeck (eds.), *Digital Discourse: Language in the New Media*, 26–47. New York: Oxford University Press.

Katsuno, Hirofumi & Christine R. Yano 2002: Face to face: On-line subjectivity in contemporary Japan. *Asian Studies Review* 26(2): 205–232.

Kearney, Mary Celeste 2005: Birds on the wire: Troping teenage girlhood through telephony in mid-twentieth century US media culture. *Cultural Studies* 19(5): 568–601.

Lenhart, Amanda 2010: Teens, cell phones and texting: Text messaging becomes centerpiece communication. http://pewresearch.org/pubs/1572/teens-cell-phones-text-messages

Levey, Stephen 2003: He's like 'do it now!' and I'm like 'no!'. *English Today* 19(1), 24–32.

Lewis, Cynthia & Bettina Fabos 2005: Instant Messaging, literacies, and social identities. *Reading Research Quarterly* 40(4): 470–501.

Lucy, John 1993: Reflexive language and the human disciplines. In John Lucy (ed.), *Reflexive Language: Reported Speech and Metapragmatics*, 9–32. New York: Cambridge University Press.

McIntosh, Janet 2010: Mobile phones and Mipoho's prophecy: The powers and dangers of flying language. *American Ethnologist* 37(2): 337–353.

Ochs, Elinor & Carolyn Taylor 1996: "The Father Knows Best" dynamic in family dinner narratives. In Kira Hall (ed.), *Gender Articulated: Language and the Socially Constructed Self*, 97–212. New York: Routledge.

Peters, John Durham 1999: *Speaking into the Air: A History of the Idea of Communication*. Chicago: University of Chicago Press.

Rajewsky, Irina O. 2005: Intermediality, intertextuality, and remediation: A literary perspective on intermediality. *Intermédialités* 6: 43–64.

Rickford, John R., Thomas Wasow, Arnold Zwicky & Isabelle Buchstaller 2007: Intensive and quotative *all*: Something old, something new. *American Speech* 82(1): 3–31.

Romaine, Suzanne & Deborah Lange 1991: The use of *like* as a marker of reported speech and thought: A case of grammaticalization in progress. *American Speech* 66(3), 227–279.

Sacks, Harvey 1984: On doing 'bring ordinary'. In J. Maxwell Atkinson and John Heritage (eds.), *Structures of Social Action: Studies in Conversation Analysis*, 50–69. New York: Cambridge University Press.

Schieffelin, Bambi B. 2000: Introducing Kaluli literacy: A chronology of influences. In Paul Kroskrity (ed.), *Regimes of Language*, 293–327. Santa Fe, NM: School of American Research.

Sengupta, Somini 2011: Technology could make passwords a thing of the past. *Boston Globe*, December 24.

Silverstein, Michael 2003: Indexical order and the dialectics of sociolinguistic life. *Language & Communication* 23(3): 193–229.

Simmel, Georg 1950: *The Sociology of Georg Simmel*. New York: Free Press.

Squires, Lauren 2010: Enregistering internet language. *Language in Society* 39: 457–492.

Squires, Lauren 2012: Whos punctuating what? Sociolinguistic variation in instant messaging. In Alexandra Jaffe, Jannis Androutsopoulos, Mark Sebba and Sally Johnson (eds.),

Orthography as Social Action: Scripts, Spelling, Identity and Power, 289–324. Boston/Berlin: Mouton de Gruyter.

Streeck, Jürgen 2002: Grammars, words, and embodied meanings: On the evolution and uses of so and like. *Journal of Communication* 52(3): 581–596.

Tagliamonte, Sali A. & Alexandra D'Arcy 2007: Frequency and variation in the community grammar: Tracking a new change through the generations. *Language Variation and Change* 19(2), 199–217.

Tagliamonte, Sali A. & Derek Denis 2008: Linguistic ruin? LOL! Instant Messaging and teen language. *American Speech* 83(1): 3–34.

Tagliamonte, Sali & Rachel Hudson 1999: Be *like* et al. beyond America: The quotative system in British and Canadian youth. *Journal of Sociolinguistics* 3(2): 147–172.

Tannen, Deborah 1986: Introducing constructed dialogue in Greek and American conversational and literary narrative. In Florian Coulmas (ed.), *Direct and Indirect Speech*, 311–332. Berlin/New York: Mouton de Gruyter.

Thurlow, Crispin 2006: From statistical panic to moral panic: The metadiscursive construction and popular exaggeration of new media language in the print media. *Journal of Computer Mediated Communication* 11: 667–701.

Thurlow, Crispin 2007: Fabricating youth: New-media discourse and the technologization of young people. In Sally Johnson and Astrid Ensslin (eds.), *Language in the Media: Representations, Identities, Ideologies*, 213–233. London: Continuum.

Turkle, Sherry 2011: *Alone Together: Why We Expect More from Technology and Less from Each Other*. New York: Basic Books.

Waksler, Rachelle 2001: A new *all* in conversation. *American Speech* 76(2): 128–138.

Woolard, Kathryn A. & Bambi B. Schieffelin 1994: Language ideology. *Annual Review of Anthropology* 23: 55–82.

Andrea Moll
Authenticity in dialect performance?

A case study of "Cyber-Jamaican"

1 Introduction: Sociolinguistic authenticity in the 21st century

Sociolinguistic studies in the Labovian tradition have concentrated on the language produced by members of closely-knit vernacular speech communities inhabiting well-defined and delimited/delimitable geographical spaces. In addition, their exclusive focus has been on the spontaneous, unmonitored speech recorded in sociolinguistic interviews as the most reliable source of authentic language use. The simultaneous absence of theoretical works on sociolinguistic authenticity, however, suggests that this academic practice has not been sustained by a well-defined concept of authenticity. Attending to this research gap, "third wave" sociolinguists (cf. Eckert 2000) have recently challenged the following tacit assumptions about authenticity that have, indeed, guided "first wave" sociolinguistic studies in the Labovian tradition from the 1960s onwards and continue to impact on current research. Interestingly, aspects of performativity assume an important role in this context:

The first assumption concerns the traditional equation of authenticity with non-reflexive language. In particular, "third wave" sociolinguists have questioned the spontaneous nature of speech obtained via sociolinguistic interviews, which instead appear to offer speakers a stage for the artful performance of language:

> Sociolinguistics has often treated its own empirical research settings as if they were platforms for speakers to produce 'everyday speech behaviour' rather than stages for performance. The classical sociolinguistic interview is a case in point, where devices used to trigger 'casual speech' [...] might be better described as stage-building for narrative performance. (Coupland 2007: 185)

Furthermore, it seems that the straight division between performance on the one hand and patterns of everyday communication on the other hand as postulated by the Labovian approach is, indeed, hard to sustain from a linguistic perspective: Not only is it incompatible with Coupland's (2007: 28) idea of the increasing performativity of everyday speech, but it also contradicts Schilling-Estes' (1998) findings on the linguistic similarities of both registers: "[...] performance speech may display quite regular patterning, rather than the irregularity traditionally associated with a shift toward an exaggeratedly vernacular version of one's dialect" (Schilling-Estes 1998: 54).

Second, the concept of authenticity propagated by the Labovian approach appears to be void of social considerations, given that "[...] there is *no* significant presumption of authentic membership in Labovian research on speech communities, because membership is not conceived in *any* social or psycho-social sense other than demographic (Coupland 2010: 102)." The resulting semi-automatic selection of authentic informants and data according to pre-defined, context-independent criteria is rejected by "third wave" sociolinguists. Instead of considering authenticity as an inherent quality of individual speakers, "third wave" researchers focus on authentication as the outcome of discursive negotiation:

> [...] rather than presupposing the authentic as an object to be discovered, [authentication] instead makes the notion of authenticity available for analysis as the outcome of the linguistic practices of social actors and the metalinguistic practices of sociolinguistics. (Bucholtz 2003: 398–399)

When we concentrate on discursive authentication as part of "[...] a set of intersubjective 'tactics', through which people can make claims about their own or others' statuses as authentic or inauthentic members of social groups" (Coupland 2010: 105), it is, however, once again interesting to note that performance assumes a pivotal role in the process of social meaning-making:

> Performance matters – it cannot be dismissed as mere aesthetic embellishment layered upon some independently constituted social reality. [...] performance is a consequential, efficacious mode of linguistic practice, a potent means of creating, negotiating, and displaying social meaning and value in the communicative accomplishment of social life. (Bauman 2000: 4)

In addition to these more general arguments about the authenticity of performance, the traditional research focus on authentic speech as produced by members of closely-knit vernacular speech communities is apparently out of tune with ongoing processes of deterritorialisation and the recontextualisation of languages and linguistic resources as a consequence of social and linguistic globalisation:

> We now see that the mobility of people also involves the mobility of linguistic and sociolinguistic resources, that 'sedentary' or 'territorialized' patterns of language use are complemented by 'translocal' or 'deterritorialized' forms of language use, and that the combination of both often accounts for unexpected sociolinguistic effects. (Blommaert 2010: 4–5)

Notable consequences of language contact in the era of globalisation include, for example, the emergence of "post-native varieties" (Patrick 2004) in diaspora communities as well as the phenomenon of "truncated repertoires" (Blommaert 2010). Although both terms arguably emphasise the limited linguistic competence of speakers, related concepts such as "crossing" (cf. Rampton 1995) and "sociolinguistic styling" (cf. Coupland 2007) by contrast help to put the focus on speakers as agents who regularly draw on linguistic resources for purposes of identity management. In this context, it is interesting to note that Bucholtz (2003: 398) considers "[...] the sociolinguistic investment in authenticity as an implicit theory of identity", arguing that both are the result of metalinguistic practices, including performance.

While "third wave" approaches thus offer useful tools for the study of recent sociolinguistic phenomena in "real" space, Georgakopoulou (2006) draws attention to the fact that their emergence also responds to the methodological challenges encountered by linguists working on computer-mediated communication (henceforth CMC):

> This internal shake up [of sociolinguistics as a discipline] has partly had to do with social and cultural phenomena that, if subtly embedded into ordinary everyday life, certainly seem to be emblematic of CMC contexts: the de-localization of interactions, the formation of communities across time and space, the performativity, transience and ephemerality of identities, the networking and interdependence of communities, the mobility and transposition of peoples, languages, and micro-cultures, the unprecedented flow of information and exchange among different groups that transcend the local and the national, the individuals' heightened processes of reflexivity on their communication. Many of these phenomena tend to be described and dealt with within a theorizing of globalization that is by no means a stranger to sociolinguistics [...]. (2006: 548)

Following these observations, "third wave" sociolinguistics, indeed, appears to be the only viable research method in the context of this paper on language use in an online discussion forum frequented by Jamaicans in the diaspora: Instead of the traditional sociolinguistic concept of speech community as a closely-knit vernacular community anchored in a well-defined geographical location, we are dealing with a deterritorialised "community of practice" (henceforth CofP) (cf. Eckert 2000) whose members can be observed to reflexively exploit their linguistic repertoires in order to style and perform their virtual in-group identity as "Cyber-Jamaicans". According to Mair (2011), such uses of Jamaican Creole (henceforth JC) in CMC can be considered as part and parcel of Blommaert's (2010) (socio)linguistic globalisation and thus call for a new concept of authenticity in 21st century sociolinguistics:

> JC is no longer the 'local' language that it used to be in earlier stages of its development, firmly rooted in its community of speakers and largely confined to use in face-to-face interaction. Today, JC is among the vernaculars which are regularly heard on the media, have gone on the move and become globally available linguistic resources. One thing which the CCJ [Corpus of Cyber-Jamaican] shows beyond doubt is that JC on the web is used by real people in authentic communication. (Mair 2011: 226)

In order to examine the interplay between competing concepts of sociolinguistic authenticity in connection with the use of JC on the web, this paper is split up into the following sections: Section 2 presents the "Corpus of Cyber-Jamaican" (henceforth CCJ), which will serve as a database for the ensuing analyses, and introduces Mair's (2011) tripartite classification of sociolinguistic styling in the CCJ. Following a quantitative-variationist approach, section 3 concentrates on the stylistic differences between JC in the discussion forum and its use in face-to-face communication. In particular, special attention will be paid to the "anti-formal" (cf. Allsopp 1996) use of basilectal progressive forms on the one hand and the sociolinguistic styling of the digraph <aw> as an orthographic resource on the other hand. While sections 2 and 3 thus adopt the perspective of the linguistically-informed academic, sections 4 and 5 by contrast focus on language users' concepts of authenticity. In this context, both forum-external and –internal perspectives are taken into account as the evaluation of "Cyber-Jamaican" by native and near-native speakers of JC (section 4) is compared to forum members' strategies of authentication (section 5). While discourse analysis is used as a method to investigate the negotiation of authenticity and identity by forum contributors as in-group members, out-group members' assessment of "Cyber-Jamaican" is based on the results of an online questionnaire. This mix of quantitative and qualitative analyses is well in accordance with the impetus of "third wave" studies on sociolinguistic style to arrive at results via the triangulation of various research methods:

> [...] style analysis can be very usefully informed by earlier variationist surveys, where the quantitative distribution of sociolinguistic variables gives us a generalised appreciation of which speech variants are symbolically active, and in what general ways. [...] Attitude surveys are a different sort of resource again. [...] They can fill our understanding of general ideological beliefs about language variation. So multiple research methods can be combined in the analysis of sociolinguistic style, even though the main challenge is to build local analysis of styling *in situ*, and this will probably involve qualitative rather than quantitative analysis [...]. (Coupland 2007: 27)

2 Jamaican Creole on the web: The "Corpus of Cyber-Jamaican"

The compilation of the "Corpus of Cyber-Jamaican" (henceforth CCJ) forms part of a larger web corpus project on the use of non-standard varieties in CMC, which is led by Christian Mair (English Department) and Stefan Pfänder (Department of Romance Languages) at the University of Freiburg (cf. Mair and Heyd, this volume). As illustrated in Table 1, the CCJ is a large-scale corpus that features more than 17.0 million tokens in the form of discussion forum posts downloaded from the website www.jamaicans.com:

Languages	JC/ Jamaican English
Date of download	21.10.08
# Thematic categories	35 (all)
# Websites	32.149
Size of download in GB	2,6
Time period covered	2000–2008
# Forum users	2.141
# Forum Posts	252.480
# Tokens	17.042.382
# Tokens/post	67,5

Table 1: Overview of data downloaded from www.jamaicans.com

According to the results of long-term observation prior to the actual download of the data in 2008, there are at least three reasons why this specific discussion forum particularly lends itself as a data source to the investigation of JC in CMC: First of all, the earliest forum contributions date back to the year 2000, which allows for a diachronic arrangement of the data between 2000 and 2008 and a resulting time depth of eight to nine years. Second, the forum consists of thirty-five diverse thematic subcategories and thus enables the researchers to additionally investigate correlations between topic and language choice.

What is, however, most important in the context of this paper is the fact that forum members' use of JC shows interesting stylistic differences to more traditional oral and written varieties of JC. From a sociolinguistic point of view, this styling of JC can be interpreted as an exploitation of linguistic resources for the purposes of virtual identity management - at least if we take into account that sociolinguistic identity and authenticity are particularly precarious concepts in "cultural diasporas [as] groups maintaining a sense of cultural belonging, physically distant from their 'homelands'" (Coupland 2007: 122).

According to the information provided in their individual user profiles, the majority of forum contributors were, indeed, living in such "cultural diasporas" at the time of the data download. As indicated by the size of the red circles in Figure 1, web users were especially located on the North American continent followed by the United Kingdom, while only few of them actually claimed to be residents of Jamaica.[1] Although the empirical validity of such personal background information would surely have to be handled with care in other research contexts, this study is exclusively interested in the discursive interaction between web personae in cyber-space, an approach which is also preferable in terms of ethical considerations.

To protect users' privacy, screen names have been substituted by a numeral code, so that only researchers should be able to draw any connections between particular posts and their author. Despite this precaution, the download, long-term storage and publication of web-based corpora of CMC surely remains a serious issue of debate that ranks high on the agenda of recent conferences and publications focussing on the legal aspects of compiling web corpora: In a paper on German copyright law and the long-term storage of digital media, Euler et al. (2011) warn that the current legal situation could lead to some kind of "digital amnesia of the cultural memory", and they thus argue in favour of an amendment to the German Copyright Act that allows for the automatic collection called "web harvesting" as well as the long-term storage, handling and replication of digital documents at least for institutions such as archives and libraries. Until legal issues in connection with the study of web corpora of CMC will be definitely resolved, access to the CCJ is therefore limited to researchers at the English Department of the University of Freiburg and registered research partners only. The citation of post content for purposes of qualitative research in this work is in accordance with § 51 of the German Copyright Act, since citations were directly taken from the online discussion forum.

While detailed studies on North American varieties of JC yet remain a largely untouched item on the agenda of future sociolinguistic research,[2] work on varieties of JC in the United Kingdom since the 1980s (cf. Sebba 1993, Sutcliffe 1982,

---

1 Note that Figure 1 only illustrates the residence of 1,318 of a total of 2,141 users registered to the discussion forum. This is due to the fact that the remaining forum members either did not provide any geographical background information or resorted to fictional places.
2 Apart from Winer and Jack's (1997) study on New York City, current research focuses on JC in Toronto, including, for example, a collaborative research project conducted by Laura Baxter and Jacqueline Peters, both graduate students at York University. At present, Hinrichs' (2011) study on Jamaicans in Toronto is the only publication available for the Canadian context.

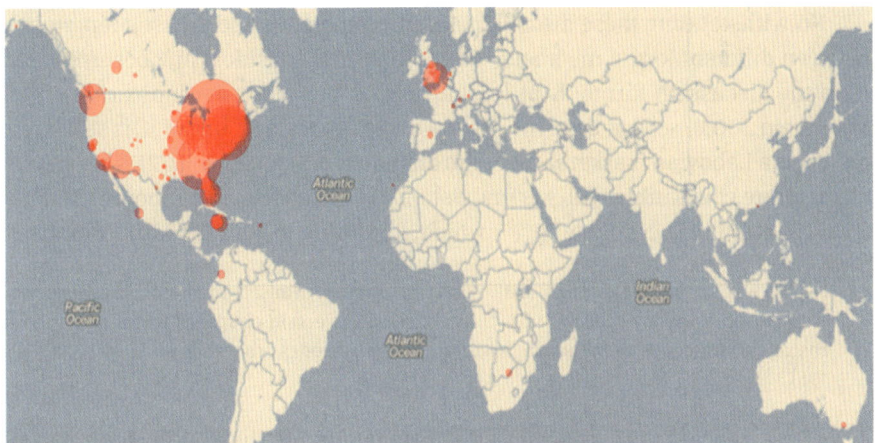

Figure 1: Geographical residence of forum users at the time of data download

Hewitt 1986, Edwards 1986 as well as Kerswill et al. 2008) shows that linguistic transplantation has entailed an important shift to a more self-reflexive and styled or even stylised use of JC:

> However, the status of the Creole is changed profoundly – from an unselfconsciously used majority *language* linked to standard English in a complex linguistic continuum to a politically charged additional – and optional – communicative **code** whose chief function is to enable blacks to "perform" their ethnicity and negotiate community boundaries when necessary or desirable. (Mair 2003a: 232)

As far as the sociolinguistic styling of JC in the CCJ is concerned, Mair (2011) distinguishes between three different categories, which cover the range from spontaneous and assumedly non-reflexive usage to elements of unconscious stylisation to the overt performance of JC:

a) passages which read as if spontaneously produced spoken JC was transferred on the screen
b) passages [...] in which a presumably unconscious element of stylization is evident, and
c) passages which are consciously crafted with rhetorical skill. (Mair 2011: 226)

In this context, we surely need to take into account that the stylistic repertoires of forum users are not only the product of individual linguistic choices, but also depend on their varying linguistic proficiencies in JC, which is more often an additional communicative code than a mother tongue. This is especially true for Mair's (2011: 226) category of "spontaneously produced spoken JC on the screen", which arguably presupposes a near-native competence.

Notwithstanding these discrepancies in competence and stylistic repertoires between different forum members,[3] Mair (2011: 227) considers any occurrence of JC in the discussion forum as at least a case of "second-order indexicality" (cf. Silverstein 2003), so that even the assumedly least strategic use of JC is still interpreted as a Labovian marker rather than an indicator (cf. Labov 1972). This view is furthermore compatible with his understanding of Le Page and Tabouret-Keller's (1985) concept of "acts of identity", which, according to Mair (2003b), comprises

> [...] the whole range of communicative practices, from routinised and automatic choices of variables in everyday speech to the fully conscious selection of speech forms as part of a rhetorical strategy or even the playful appropriation of codes other than one's own. (2003b: 196).

Before we proceed to language users' evaluations of these different "acts of identity", it is, however, useful to start the discussion on sociolinguistic authenticity by highlighting some of the stylistic peculiarities of "Cyber-Jamaican" as perceived by linguists. Not only will this analysis yield important background information for the discussion of language users' perspectives on authenticity in sections 4 and 5, but it may also draw attention to ongoing processes of linguistic grassroots conventionalisation in the discussion forum as a virtual CofP with its own emerging (socio)linguistic norms.

3 Styling 'Cyber-Jamaican': Toward a digital ethnolinguistic repertoire

Due to users' variable proficiency in JC, "Cyber-Jamaican" in the discussion forum cannot be adequately described as a stable ethnolect. To account for inter- and intraspeaker variation on the one hand and the selectivity of non-standard orthographic and JC morphosyntactic features on the other hand, a linguistic "repertoire approach" as suggested by Benor (2010), indeed, seems much more adequate:

> Intra-group variation does not pose a problem for the ethnolinguistic repertoire approach. Rather than characterizing ethnic group members as speakers or non-speakers of their group's ethnolect, researchers can see them as making selective use of an ethnically distinctive repertoire, along with resources from other sources, as they construct their identities within a diverse ethnic landscape. (2010: 165)

---

3 See Moll (2013) for a detailed discussion of individual 'repertoire portraits' that illustrate style-shifting in the CCJ according to different communicative contexts.

In accordance with Hinrichs and Farquharson's (2011) suggestions, this study thus applies Benor's (2010) concept to the field of CMC and conceptualises "Cyber-Jamaican" as a digital "ethnolinguistic repertoire":

> It may also be helpful to incorporate the idea of an "ethnolinguistic repertoire" into our thinking about creole community grammars. A better understanding of the way that the grammars of different varieties in the same sociolinguistic system are linked becomes more pressing as new domains of creole literacy continue to emerge, e.g. in computer-mediated communication. (Hinrichs & Farquharson 2011: 6–7)

In the following, detailed quantitative analyses will concentrate on two specific linguistic variables that forum members regularly draw on as part of a shared pool of sociolinguistic resources: While basilectal progressive forms of the grammatical formula "a + infinitive of the verb" undoubtedly score high on the list of well-known shibboleths of JC, respelling with the digraph <aw> is particularly interesting from the perspective of sociolinguistic styling due to its extensive "indexical field" (cf. Eckert 2008). Apart from drawing attention to the stylistic distinctiveness of "Cyber-Jamaican", the main purpose of the following analyses is, however, to inform the folk-linguistic and discourse-analytic research on sociolinguistic authenticity as presented in sections 4 and 5 respectively. As already pointed out in section 1, this procedure is in accordance with the method mix propagated by "third wave" sociolinguistics in so far as

> [...] a quantitative approach can provide a detailed and contextualized background against which a qualitative analysis may be carried out. This approach not only assists in terms of embedding the qualitative results, but also facilitates the process of selecting the relevant data required for a qualitative analysis. (Siebenhaar 2008: 11)

3.1 The anti-formal use of JC basilectal resources: The present progressive

In contrast to wide-spread assumptions about the pseudo-orality of CMC, a comparison of the forum data with JC as used in face-to-face communication shows considerable linguistic and sociolinguistic differences between these two modes of communication: While the use of linguistic resources in the oral medium patterns along the principles of the so called "creole continuum" (cf. DeCamp 1971; Rickford 1987), "Cyber-Jamaican" in the CCJ does not abide by any rules of implicational scaling. More often than not, forum members' contributions appear to be characterised by a juxtaposition of acrolect and basilect, yielding a mix of grammatical forms that is unprecedented in traditional descriptions of JC: In the following post, basilectal elements include, for instance, negation with *no* (unit

a) and *never* (unit b), past tense with *did + infinitive* (unit c), a serial verb construction (unit d) as well as a progressive with *a + infinitive* (unit e).

Example 1: User [3194][4]; Forum category: "Parenting and Family Matters"; 2007
Topic: "Di devil move eena mi house ovanite in di form of"

(a) *mi like people children yes, but mi naw kip dem more dan so...*
[I like people's children, sure, but I am not going to mind (i.e. babysit) them and make it a habit.[5]]

(b) *but dis one even pick up mi crystal lion dem whe mi collek an mi neva seh prips... she play wid dem an not a wud leave mi lips...*
[but this one even picked up my crystal lions that I collect and I didn't say a word... she played with them and not a word left my lips...]

(c) *an memba seh is mi did put out a man wid him dawta who did mess wid mi yaad basket of fruits*
[and remember that it was me who put a man and his daughter out (door) who messed with my yaad basket of fruits.]

(d) *she soo quiet mi juss get up go look...*
[She was so quiet I just got up and looked...]

(e) *all mi see is har face turn to me a grin wid di few teets dem she ha...*
[All I saw is her face turned towards me, grinning with the few teeth that she has...]

However, a look at the plural forms in this post quickly reveals that the resulting style cannot be classified as an example of purely basilectal writing: Although the noun phrase "mi crystal lion dem" 'my crystal lions' (unit b) is totally in accordance with the rules of JC analytic plural formation, inflectional plurals such as "lips" (unit b) and "fruits" (unit c) are definitely the product of acrolectal, that is Standard English (henceforth StE), grammar. What is even more, the plural "di few teets dem" 'the few teeth' (unit e) shows double plural marking with the inflectional suffix {-s} and the analytic particle *dem*, with the basilectal form thus assuming the function of a stylistic asset used to top up the Jamaican flavour of this post.

The same phenomenon can be observed in the following contribution written by User [3556], which includes double plural marking in the noun phrase "the boys dem" 'the boys' (unit c):

---

4 Note that in order to preserve forum users' privacy, screen names are substituted by a numeral code only known to the research team currently working with the forum data included in the CCJ.
5 In this context, I would like to thank Joseph T. Farquharson for his help with transliterations from JC to StE.

Example 2: User [3556]; Forum category: "Parenting and Family Matters"; 2006
Topic: "Re: small dogs that not yappy yappy"

(a) *chrismus come and mi still noh get the dawg.*
[Christmas comes and I still didn't get the dog...]
(b) *bwoy me trying hard fi be a dawg person but it just not happening*
[Boy, I am trying hard to be a dog person but it is just not happening.]
(c) *mi contemplating a likkle kitten...but me know seh is not dat the boys dem want...*
[I am contemplating a little kitten... but I know that it's not what the boys want.]

Notwithstanding this stylistic similarity with the preceding example by User [3194], the post by User [3556] is, however, rather exceptional when compared to other forum members' use of JC resources, since it primarily features mesolectal forms. This includes, for example, the progressives "me trying" 'I am trying' and "it just not happening" 'it is just not happening" in unit (b) as well as "mi contemplating" 'I am contemplating' in unit (c). The exceptionality of this style is illustrated by the following thorough quantitative analysis of third person singular feminine progressive forms in the CCJ: As Table 2 demonstrates, there is an almost dichotomous use of acrolectal forms on the one hand and basilectal realisations on the other hand, with both alternatives reaching almost equivalent frequencies of about 40 % each in 2008[6].

	ACROLECT		MESOLECT		BASILECT	
	# tokens	per cent	# tokens	per cent	# tokens	per cent
2001	1	14.3 %	1	14.3 %	5	71.4 %
2002	21	27.6 %	7	9.2 %	48	63.2 %
2003	102	69.4 %	9	6.1 %	36	24.5 %
2004	135	76.3 %	8	4.5 %	34	19.2 %
2005	73	59.3 %	8	6.5 %	42	34.1 %
2006	101	48.1 %	31	14.8 %	78	37.1 %
2007	414	46.5 %	119	13.4 %	357	40.1 %
2008	380	39.7 %	174	18.2 %	402	42.1 %
Σ	1,227		357		1,002	

Table 2: Percentages of realisational variants of the progressive (3rd person sing./fem.)[7]

---

6 Note that the following results are based on Mair (2011: 220–221), but specify his observations in terms of diachronic development as well as the number of alternative orthographic variants included in the counts.
7 Concordances of acrolectal realisations include the orthographic variants "she/shi is *in(g)", "she's/shi's *in(g), "shes/shis *in(g)" and "she s/shi s *in(g)". For the mesolect, the forms "she/

The error bars[8] in Figure 2 indicate that these quantitative results are valid despite a considerable variation in the absolute frequencies of tokens per year due to annually changing numbers of contributors and posts.

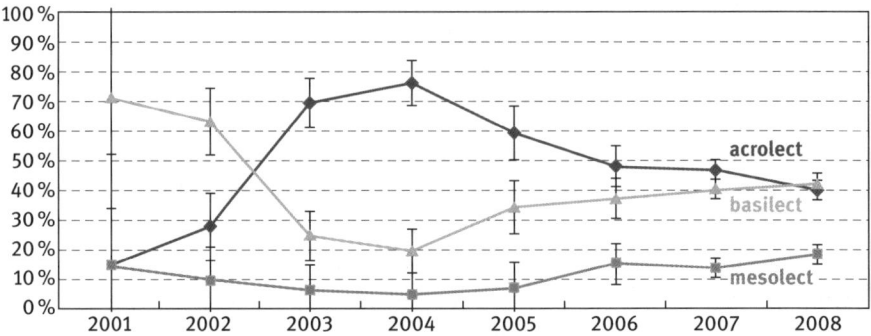

Figure 2: Realisational variants of the progressive (3rd person singular feminine)

As the use of the JC mesolect is considered as typical of informal conversation, the over-representation of basilectal forms in "Cyber-Jamaican" can be classified as an example of "anti-formal" usage, by means of which forum users aim at a "wilful closing of social distance" (cf. Allsopp 1996). This interpretation is well in accordance with the absence of a classical socio-hierarchical structure in the forum as an online CofP, where the use of JC basilectal resources as part of "Cyber-Jamaican" as a "digital ethnolinguistic repertoire" is no longer associated with low social class status, but has come to index "Jamaicaness" as a lifestyle. Regarding the study of sociolinguistic style, this ties in well with Coupland's (2007) observation that

> [l]ifestyle [...] is often said to be supplanting social structure (e.g. class) as an organising principle of late-modern living [reference deleted]. Studying social meaning through sociolinguistic styling gives us a way of understanding social identities and social relationships with sufficient flexibility and dynamism to capture some of the qualities of late-modern social life. (Coupland 2007: 30)

---

shi *in(g)" were taken into account, while basilectal forms include "she/shi a + infinitive" as well as the variants "she/shi ah + infinitive".

8 The error of the measurements is the statistical error, which is calculated in percentages like $\sigma = \pm 100 * N^{-1/2}$, where s represents the error and N the total number of concordances obtained for a particular search.

Selectivity and overshoot of specific linguistic features, including JC shibboleths such as the basilectal progressive forms, are furthermore a characteristic of linguistic performance as described by Bell and Gibson (2011). Interestingly, the authors consider these phenomena to be "[...] more likely when a performer is targeting a variety which they do not use in their daily life" (Bell & Gibson 2011: 567) as can in fact be assumed for many of the forum members living in the diaspora. The majority of posts can therefore be classified as "passages [...] in which a presumably unconscious element of stylization is evident" (Mair 2011: 226), given that the extensive use of highly salient basilectal resources appears to be an effect of forum users' limited linguistic competence in JC. Interestingly, this observation is also confirmed by User's [3556] explicit self-classification as a native speaker of JC, which helps to explain her exceptionally frequent use of mesolectal resources. Notwithstanding possible stylistic differences in conversational contexts such as those quoted in examples 1 and 2, all forum writers unanimously employ basilectal resources to index "Jamaicaness" in "passages which are consciously crafted with rhetorical skill" (Mair 2011: 226). The resulting "staged performances" (Bell and Gibson 2011: 558) are in fact extremely interesting in the context of this study on sociolinguistic authenticity, since they discursively establish the link between language use and sociolinguistic identity by illustrating how forms and meanings are related. This process of "enregisterment" (Agha 2003, 2005) and its importance for the authentication of "Cyber-Jamaican" in the discussion forum will be discussed in more detail in section 5.

3.2 Orthographic practices in 'Cyber-Jamaican': Respelling with <aw>

While the use of specific phonetic features forms part of the well-known system of implicational scaling established for the "creole continuum" (cf. DeCamp 1971; Rickford 1987), Hinrichs (2004) argues that it is, indeed, impossible to find similar correspondences for the use of orthographic resources in CMC:

> In sum, my data shows that the position on the creole continuum of a stretch of text has no systematic relation to the writer's choice of a StE or a deviant spelling. Consequently, the degree of standardness of spelling cannot be used as a factor in determining the place of any particular e-mail message on the creole continuum. The e-mail messages represent the reality of a continuum in speech, but all levels of linguistic analysis are simply not available to writers who want to indicate style shifts. In spoken language, phonological choices can indicate greater or lesser basilectality. The lack of this expressive device in writing is not compensated for by orthography. (Hinrichs 2004: 94)

However, the regular co-occurrence of non-standard orthography with basilectal JC clearly indicates that specific cases of "regiolectal spelling" (cf. Androutsopoulos 2000) and "eye dialect" are part of "Cyber-Jamaican" as a digital "ethnolinguistic repertoire". In this context, respelling with the digraph <aw> is particularly interesting from a stylistic point of view as its "indexical field" (Eckert 2008) comprises a large variety of potential pragmatic meanings. While the subsequent description aims at a comprehensive description of this respelling strategy in the CCJ, it is, however, important to be clear about the general difference between such a linguistically informed analysis on the one hand and the perspective of language users on the other hand, whose orthographic choices may or may not be motivated by the factors described in this section.

Although the CCJ also contains idiosyncratic spellings such as, for example, <avitawr> 'avitar' or <awkastrayshun> 'orchestration', the vast majority of tokens (18,233 out of 21,009 hits in total) are, in fact, orthographic variants of the thirty-one lemmata presented in Table 3, each of which features at least 100 tokens.

In addition, a quantitative comparison with their respective StE counterparts reveals that non-standard spelling variants with <aw> are not only employed by many forum users for a variety of lexical items, but in fact witness a sharp increase in frequency from 2003 onwards, reaching an average frequency of 9.9 % of all standard and non-standard tokens in 2008. It should be noted that in order to facilitate the comparison of non-standard and standard orthography, the analysis in Figure 3 has been limited to those lexical items listed in Table 3 that have a one-to-one lexical correspondence in StE. Apart from the old-fashioned StE expression <mawga> 'mauger', which is unlikely to occur in CMC, this excludes JC items such as the negator <naw>, the noun <fawt> as well as the emphatic particle <yaw>. In addition, the prepositions <awn> 'on' and <awf> 'off' had to be discarded as their non-standard spelling variants only occur as part of a prepositional verb, so that a thorough analysis would require extensive manual editing processes to weed out irrelevant examples among the concordances obtained for StE <on> and <off>. Despite these reservations, Figure 3 still accounts for 66.6 % (13,996 tokens) of all non-standard respellings with <aw> in the CCJ:

As indicated in the rightmost column of Table 3, respelling with <aw> variably corresponds to the General American vowels /ɑ/ or /ɔ/. While the result is an eye dialectal variant in the case of <Gawd> 'God', <cawse> '(be)cause' and <dawg> 'dog', respellings such as <Lawd> 'Lord' and <mawnin(g)> 'morning' visually help to represent a non-rhotic pronunciation that contrasts with the phonetic principles of General American. However, these orthographic variants can be classified as instances of eye dialect from the perspective of non-rhotic varieties, including, for example, Standard British English as well as African American Vernacular English (henceforth AAVE). From an academically-informed point of

Lexical item	Major respelling variant	# of tokens	Corresponding vowel in General American
'Lord'	\<lawd>	2,549	/ɔ/
'(be)cause'	\<caw>, \<caws>	2,052	/ɔ/
'not'	\<naw>[9]	1,590	/ɑ/
'morning'	\<mawn>	1,303	/ɔ/
'start'	\<stawt>	1,119	/ɑ/
'gone'	\<gawn>	921	/ɔ/
'off'	\<awf>	846	/ɔ/
'part'	\<pawt>	705	/ɑ/
'on'	\<awn>	699	/ɔ/
'yard'	\<yawd>	681	/ɑ/
'dog'	\<dawg>	569	/ɔ/
	\<fawt>[10]	512	/ɑ/
'call'	\<cawl>	452	/ɔ/
'daughter'	\<dawta>	422	/ɔ/
'talk'	\<tawk>	402	/ɔ/
'born'	\<bawn>	299	/ɔ/
'short'	\<shawt>	295	/ɔ/
'God'	\<Gawd>	287	/ɔ/
'alright'	\<awrite>	413	/ɔ/
'party'	\<pawty>	242	/ɑ/
'all'	\<awl>	254	/ɔ/
'hard'	\<hawd>	247	/ɑ/
	\<yaw>[11]	207	/ɑ/
'father'	\<fawda>	194	/ɑ/
'corn'	\<cawn>	171	/ɔ/
'heart'	\<hawt>	168	/ɔ/
'darling'	\<dawlin>/\<dawling>	142	/ɑ/
'ask'	\<awks>/\<hawks>	126	/ɑ/
'mauger'	\<mawga>	126	/ɑ/ ~ /ɔ/
'corner'	\<cawna>	118	/ɔ/
'after'	\<awfta>	122	/ɑ/
Σ		18,233	

Table 3: Major respellings with the digraph \<aw>

---

9 According to Cassidy and Le Page (2002: 314, 317), \<naw> is an alternative spelling of \<naa> 'not', which is followed by a verb in the progressive tense. However, the CCJ also contains several tokens of \<naw> that do not precede a verb. In these cases, \<naw> is arguably better translated as 'no'.

10 According to the "Urban Dictionary", \<fawt> is often used as a combination of 'fucking' and 'hawt', meaning something like 'really attractive' in internet slang. However, it is also said to be an orthographic variant of 'fart' used in Black English, an explanation which seems to fit better in the contexts where it occurs in the CCJ.

11 *Yah* is a Jamaican emphatic concluding particle that also often occurs in the phrase *ya-so*, where it can roughly be translated as an accentuated variant of *here* (Cassidy & Le Page 2002: 483ff).

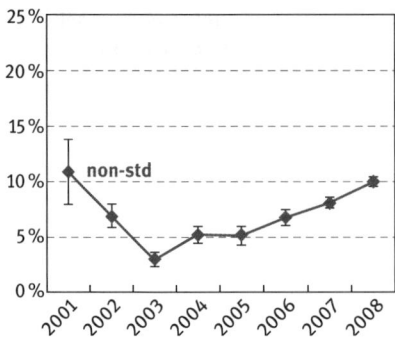

Figure 3: Annual frequencies of non-standard spellings with <aw>

view, the variants <Lawd> 'Lord' and <dawg> 'dog' are additionally associated with long-standing writing practices in AAVE and hip hop culture respectively. In the general absence of distinct allusions to African American culture on the level of discourse, we should, however, be careful to rashly interpret forum users' orthographic choices as an "act of identity" signalling such cultural affiliation.

The stylistic potential of respelling with the digraph <aw> is also evident if we take JC phonology as a starting point: As the vowel /ɔ/ is not part of the phoneme inventory of JC, all of the lexical items listed in Table 3 are, in fact, pronounced with the vowel /aː/ (cf. Cassidy & Le Page 2002: l). This obviously contrasts with non-standard spelling variants with the digraph <aw>, which visually suggest a pronunciation with /ɔ/ according to the phoneme-grapheme correspondences of StE.

What is even more, forum writers also choose non-standard spelling with <aw> in words such as, for example, <yawd> 'yard' and <pawty> 'party'. Although they consequently seem to adopt a common spelling for words pronounced with the vowel /aː/ in JC, they simultaneously achieve to establish a visual contrast with the norms of both StE and JC. One possible explanation of this phenomenon is forum members' more or less conscious use of a hyper-correct register called "speaky spoky":

> Speaky-spoky involves the substitution of the vowel /ɔ/, which does not exist for most mesolectal JC speakers as a distinct phoneme [...], into low-vowel environments, including many which do not have a rounded vowel in standard dialects. It also involves insertion of /h/, which is normally absent in JC, before non-emphatic vowel-initial lexical items, again including ones that lack it in English. Both phones are recognized by Jamaicans as belonging to standard metropolitan varieties. (Patrick 1999: 277)

While, this interpretation, however, once again depends on the existence of further indicators on the level of discourse, it is rather uncontroversial to assume that forum writers are primarily aware of the visual contrast between non-standard spelling variants and their StE counterpart as part of the "indexical field" (cf. Eckert 2008) of orthographic resources. Referring to the respelling of *Lord* as <lawd> in the poems of the famous Jamaican artist Louise Bennett, Hinrichs (2004) accordingly argues that orthography "[...] suggests some unspecified difference in pronunciation between JC *laad* and StE *lord*, even if the /a:/ sound is not represented directly" (2004: 89). As a consequence, the use of <aw> as part of an orthographic "anti-standard" (cf. Halliday 1975, Romaine 2005) can arguably be considered as the lowest common denominator of individual respelling in the discussion forum.

Irrespective of its actual meaning in the CCJ, the multiple contexts in which <aw> is used as a non-standard respelling strategy all around the globe have surely contributed to its saliency as a stylistic resource adopted by forum members as part of their digital "ethnolinguistic repertoire". From a "third wave" perspective, this phenomenon is arguably best explained by combining Blommaert's (2010) concept of a "sociolinguistics of globalisation" with Meyerhoff and Niedzielski's (2003) idea of "a broadening of the vernacular base" in order to account for the more or less strategic use of linguistic resources in the CCJ as outlined in Mair's (2011: 226) classification. Most importantly, however, both approaches equally account for the spread and local recontextualisation of linguistic features across varieties and CofPs, which Pennycook (2007: 103) lists as a possible strategy for the authentication of language and culture.

4 Authenticity from a folk linguistic perspective

Section 3 has focused on the stylistic particularities of "Cyber-Jamaican" in the discussion forum by concentrating on the quantitative use of linguistic resources as part of a digital "ethnolinguistic repertoire" indexing "Jamaicaness". The analysis has demonstrated that, from a linguist's perspective, forum members' choice of the basilectal progressive appears to be first and foremost distinct in terms of its over-representation as a marker of "anti-formal" usage (cf. Allsopp 1996), which contrasts with the mesolect as a characteristic of informal face-to-face conversation. In the case of respelling with <aw>, the results show that stylistic considerations by far outweigh writers' motivation to orthographically imitate JC pronunciation on the screen.

While both case studies thus illustrate the challenge that "Cyber-Jamaican" poses to "first wave" concepts of authenticity as linked to spontaneously produced language, they are by no means conducive to examining the criteria that actual language users might apply when assessing the authenticity of anyone speakers' or writers' linguistic output. Empirical evidence from a folk linguistic perspective is, however, clearly warranted if we want to investigate the mechanisms of authentication as a socially negotiable concept.

Focussing on the evaluation of "Cyber-Jamaican" from a forum-external perspective, I therefore conducted an online survey by using the tools provided on the website www.surveymonkey.com (cf. Appendix for a detailed version). The questionnaire was available online between April and December 2011 and targeted native and near-native speakers of JC, whom "first wave" sociolinguists would accept as "authentic" speakers of the language. In total, fifty-five responses were obtained. According to their personal details, the great majority of informants (forty-eight participants) were registered as students to the University of the West Indies in Kingston, Jamaica (henceforth UWI), forty of whom had never left their home country for a longer period of time. The remaining seven participants were between thirty-nine and seventy years old, and five of them had lived abroad for an extended period of at least ten years. Based on age differences as well as their international experience, survey participants could be classified into the following four categories:

a) UWI students; 18 – 35 years; no time abroad: 40 participants
b) UWI students; 18 – 35 years; spent time abroad: 8 participants
c) Older participants; no time abroad: 2 participants
d) Older participants; 39 – 70 years; spent time abroad: 5 participants

The survey results indicate that all but one of the informants regularly used CMC, including email, discussion forums, chats and social network services such as facebook, in order to communicate with their family and friends. Taking their age and affiliation with tertiary education into account, groups a) and b) furthermore match the informants that Hinrichs (2006) selected for the compilation of his e-mail corpus as part of COJEC (Corpus of Jamaican E-mail and other CMC). In contrast to the predominance of basilectal resources in the CCJ, Deuber and Hinrichs, however, remark that "[...] the primary unmarked code of the texts [in COJEC] is English, but there is pervasive code-switching into mesolectal JamC [...] with occasional forays into the basilect" (2007: 28). In addition, respelling with the digraph <aw> is not mentioned as a characteristic of JC writing in COJEC, which suggests that we might, indeed, be dealing with the emergence of a forum-internal orthographic convention.

In order to investigate whether survey participants based their evaluations of the authenticity of "Cyber-Jamaican" on similarities and/or dissimilarities with their own assumedly more mesolectal style of JC writing in CMC, the questionnaire featured five posts that show different stylistic uses of JC resources in the forum. Since a comprehensive discussion of all survey results is unfortunately beyond the scope of this paper, the following analysis will, however, be limited to the evaluation of those examples that clearly illustrate forum members' use of the basilectal progressive and respelling with <aw>.

The post quoted below was taken from the forum contributions of User [3290] and demonstrates the extensive use of basilectal resources (marked in bold) that has been identified as characteristic of "Cyber-Jamaican" as a digital "ethnolinguistic repertoire".

Example 3: User [3290]; Forum category: "Technology"; 2006
Topic: "Re: How do I get my cell phone unlocked

(a) ***mi nah guh ask mi*** phone company ***fi*** unlock ***mi*** phone cause too much people ***a ask dem*** and ***a get sheg*.**.
[I am not going to ask my phone company to unlock my phone because too many people are asking them and are getting screwed.]

(b) and ***mi*** know ***seh*** if mi reach ***dung deh*** and it ***nuh*** unlock when ***mi*** reach back ***a farrin*** dem ***gwine carry mi guh madhouse*** after mi bun ***dung*** the phone company
[and I know that if I arrive in Jamaica and it doesn't unlock, when I go back abroad they are going to carry me to the madhouse after I have burnt down the phone company.]

(c) I dont see ***wah the big deal fi*** dem unlock it.
[I don't see why it is a big deal for them to unlock it.]

Apart from the consistent use of the JC pronoun *mi* and the particle *fi*, important basilectal features in the example post include two progressive forms in unit (a), analytic negation with *no* in units (a) and (b), a serial verb construction in unit (b) as well as the grammatical future expressed by the formula "a go + infinitive" in unit (a).

Similar to the discussion of example (1), units (a) and (b), however, do not represent a purely basilectal style as the repeated co-occurrence of the StE article *the* defies any categorisation along the lines of the implicational scaling postulated for the JC continuum. In addition, the intricate sentence structure in unit (b), which consists of a whole complex of subclauses, challenges the idea of a pseudo-oral character of CMC as assumed by "first wave" sociolinguistic approaches (cf. Crystal 2001). As a consequence, unit (b) may be classified as an instantiation of Koch and Oesterreicher's (1985) concept of "language of distance" rather than as an example of "language of proximity" associated with online production in informal conversation. Moreover, unit (c) contrasts with the stylistic baseline of units (a) and (b) in so far as it consists of a main clause in StE and a subordinate clause characterised by copula deletion, a characteristic feature of the JC mesolect.

From the perspective of non-standard orthography, the passage is, however, rather inconspicuous as it does not contain any innovative cases of eye dialect,

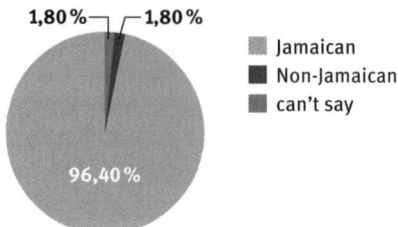

1,80% 1,80%

■ Jamaican
■ Non-Jamaican
■ can't say

96,40%

Figure 4: Survey results for user [3290]

but limits itself to the use of more or less conventionalised orthographic variants such as, for example, the respellings <farrin> 'foreign' and <guh> 'go'. The result is an orthographic style that does by no means adhere to the phonemic writing system developed by Cassidy (1961). Rather, it "[...] is characterized by a high degree of adherence to StE orthography, because it is the standard to which the Jamaican school system socializes pupils and with which Jamaicans are most familiar" (Hinrichs 2004: 91). Taking the high amount of inter- and intraspeaker variability into account, Cooper (2000: 95) refers to this style as "chaka-chaka" spelling, a JC term which can be translated into StE as 'disorderly' or 'irregular' (Cassidy & Le Page 2002: 97).

In spite of these obvious stylistic discrepancies between "Cyber-Jamaican" in example 3 and the informal use of mesolectal resources found in face-to-face communication, Figure 4 shows that survey participants almost unanimously rated the post as being the product of a "Jamaican" writer. Indeed, one informant even identified the passage as emblematic of young Jamaicans' use of JC in CMC, including the use of "chaka-chaka" spelling: "This is the social network language that Jamaicans on a daily basis use; the spelling and use of mix standard and dialect is similar to what me and my friends use" (UWI student, 23 years).

A similar self-assessment can be gained from looking at the answers to question number ten in the survey (cf. Appendix), where nineteen out of forty-three informants who reported to use CMC on a regularly basis explicitly referred to the post written by User [3290] to illustrate their own writing style in JC:

UWI student, 26 years, Computer Science and Electronics
Number 5 and the context within which it would be used is during a time of anger. Eg. Cable acting up when I should be watching an NBA game. Yow [Company name here], mi nah ramp wid unnuh innuh. Mek di game start and the cable nuh come back on and see if mi nuh walk come up deh and tell unnuh supp'n. [...].

What makes this answer particularly interesting is the fact that the informant associates the use of basilectal resources with the expression of anger, an argument also advanced by another 19-year-old UWI student when asked to explain his evaluation of the post by User [3290] as "Jamaican": "Because of its violent and somewhat terrifying tone something that jamaicans are known for". Interestingly, this finding confirms Ochs's (1993) observation that rather than indexing social identity categories directly, linguistic features are more commonly associated with stance-taking in interaction:

> The choice of linguistic structure themselves is treated as *arbitrary* [by many sociolinguists] – that is, social identity is often considered to be signaled through arbitrary phonological, morphosyntactic, lexical, or discursive structures. When researchers focus exclusively on social identity in this way, they do not see *other* social meanings, *other* social contexts – such as social acts and stances – that those same linguistic structures encode, and they do not see that, far from arbitrary, these linguistic structures are linked to social identities *rationally*, because of systematic cultural expectations linking certain acts and stances encoded by these linguistic structures to certain identities. (1993: 296–297)

For many survey participants, this link between language, stance and identity was most obvious in User [3290]'s choice of the JC expression "get sheg" ('get messed up'; cf. Urban Dictionary), which a 34-year-old UWI student identified as a "dead give away" of "Jamaicaness". Listing individual lexical items generally also scored high as a strategy employed by informants when explaining their evaluation of example posts. This is in accordance with

> [s]tudies of speaker awareness of language features [which] indicate that speakers demonstrate greater awareness of linguistic features that are referential, such as content lexical items, than of those that are non-referential, such as vowel variants uttered in isolation. (Schilling-Estes 1998: 64)

Referring to the post by User [3290], this list particularly included the following lexical items: *get sheg, madhouse, fi, mi, nuh/nah, guh, dung, deh, farrin* and *gwine*. In addition, students repeatedly referred to the typical use of grammatical shibboleths, including the basilectal progressive forms investigated in section 3.1:

UWI student, 29 years, Linguistics
The words choices, the syntax and the phonology all correspond to the typical Jamaican language. For example, "mi nah go ask" (mi naa go aks), "a get sheg", "when mi reach back a farrin" (wen mi riich bak a farin). "Sheg is a very common and unique word for Jamaicans, and is used in the correct manner, meaning "to get screwed". I see the use of locative "a" before the word "farrin" (farin), which is also typical of Jamaican syntax. There is also the use of the progressive marker 'a' before 'get' putting the verb in it's (sic!) progressive tense.

The next example post that is of particular interest in the context of this study on sociolinguistic authenticity was written by User [3563], and it features, inter alia, respellings with <aw>:

Example 4: User [3563]; "Style and Fashion"; 2006
Topic: "Chrismuss pawty frackz"

(a) *Enny ideas fi a formal but scandalous pawty frack fi di Chissmuss pawty dis year?*
[Any ideas for a formal but sexy party dress for the Christmas party this year?]
(b) *Nuff successful menz widd nuff financial coverage potential agguh be dere an mi want tuh leave mi print. Tanks.*
[A lot of successful men with a lot of financial coverage potential are going to be there and I want to make an impression. Thanks.]

Far from being limited to respelling *party* as <pawty> in unit (a), non-standard orthographic practices are used throughout this post and range from non-conspicuous phonetic spelling as in <di> 'the' to more idiosyncratic variants such as, for example, the noun <Chissmuss> 'Christmas' or the basilectal future marker <agguh> 'a go'. What also sets this post aside from the previous one is its repeated use of the inflectional suffix {-s}, yielding the StE plural form <ideas> as well as the non-standard plural <menz> '*mens'. The following quotes illustrate that both grammar and orthography are, in fact, regularly referred to by survey participants as indicators of "non-Jamaicaness". In particular, respelling with <aw> is explicitly dissociated from JC pronunciation and classified as "atypically Jamaican":

UWI student, 34 years, Linguistics, 3 years abroad
pluralization with the suffix '-s' on ideas, pawty – sound more like an attempt to represent in writing a cockney English pronunciation, the Jamaican attempt would more be like 'paati' to get the long vowel sound. where's the rhotic sound in 'chissmuss'?. The redundant pluralization of men is suspect. The future construction 'agguh be dere' sounds very non – jamaican to me.

UWI student, 28 years, Linguistics
The spelling is atypically Jamaican (e.g. "enny", "pawty", "agguh"). The use of "menz" and "chissmus" are ungrammatical ("menz" should be "man dem", and there should be an "r" in "chissmus"). Lastly, "financial coverage potential" seems a bit verbose, but I guess anything's possible.

Overall, the example post by User [3563] consequently received a very negative evaluation and was in fact rated as the most "non-Jamaican" style represented in the questionnaire as a whole:

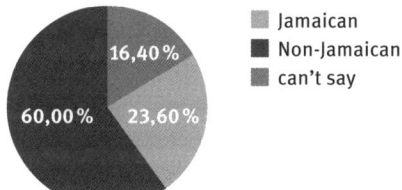

Figure 5: Survey results for user [3563]; example "Style and Fashion"; 2006

As with the previous example post, participants' comments were, however, not limited to forum writers' use of specific linguistic resources, but mingled with reactions to stance: While the expression of anger as a form of emotional involvement in the post of User [3290] was perceived by many as "authentically" Jamaican, informants by contrast strongly objected to the use of elaborate but supposedly unidiomatic vocabulary such as the adjective "scandalous" or the expression "financial coverage potential" in the post by User [3563]. Most importantly, these lexical choices seemed to clash with their notions of JC as an informal code primarily characterised by simplicity:

UWI student, 34 years, Geology, 1 year abroad
the use of the word "scandalous" jamaicans (sic!) would say sexy or skimpy; "successful menz... financial coverage" rich man ore money man would be used in Jamaican; [...] The use of words such as scandalous and financial coverage and potential is not language that would normally be used if they are using the vernacular."

UWI student, 21 years, History, 1 year abroad
i can tell a bit from the language and some pronunciation based on the spelling. also the words used are a bit complex for patwa which tends to lean more on the simple side.

5 Authentication in high performance

Stance-taking is without doubt also one of the most central aspects of the authentication of "Cyber-Jamaican" in the discussion forum as it regularly acts as a mediating factor between the use of linguistic resources on the one hand and forum members' sociolinguistic identity as "Jamaicans" on the other hand. This process of "enregisterment" by which "[...] distinct forms of speech come to be socially recognized (or enregistered) as indexical of speaker attributes by a population of language users" (Agha 2005: 38) is, however, nowhere more emblematic than in "staged performance" (Bell and Gibson 2011), which offers important insights into language users' metalinguistic awareness:

> The *form* of the performance is more likely to be scrutinized than in routine communicative practice, and the metalinguistic and poetic functions of language come to the fore. There is heightened reflexivity – social stereotypes can be explicitly put on display, offering a space for critical reflection on self and society. (Bell & Gibson 2011: 558)

In the following, I would like to discuss this discursive negotiation of sociolinguistic identity and authenticity by focussing on two types of "staged performance" that center on some sort of "translation" between GA and JC. In particular, these examples of "staged performance" do not only demonstrate the process of "enregisterment" via stance-taking, but they also serve to illustrate forum users' ludic approach to language in general. As in the previous sections, special attention will be paid to the occurrence of basilectal progressive forms and respelling with <aw> (both marked in bold) as part of the digital "ethnolinguistic repertoire" of "Cyber-Jamaican".

The first communicative practice I am concerned with is referred to as "Patois Contest" and largely consists of "translating" a pre-defined passage in StE into JC. Due to its competitive character, the resulting "translations" are particularly interesting as they can be interpreted as ideal examples of "Cyber-Jamaican" from the perspective of forum users:

Example 5: "Best of Jamaicans.com"; 2005
Topic: "Patois Contest – Good Friday Activity"

> User [3273]:
> *Ok, someone post a passage in the Queen's English. (No more than 2 paragraphs) each contestant translate it to patois. Then we'll vote [...] and decide who chat di wussis pan di boad each contestant can once and cannot edit. once you edit, you are disqualified. i can't post the passage cause mi waan play to so who coming up wid di passage?*
> [Ok, someone posts a passage in the Queen's English. (No more than 2 paragraphs) each contestant translates it to patois. Then we'll vote [...] and decide who speaks the worst on this board. Each contestant can (write) once and cannot edit. Once you edit, you are disqualified. I can't post the passage because I want to play too so who is coming up with the passage?]
> [...]

User [3573]:

[...] Jerk is a hot, spicy uniquely Jamaican seasoning which has been developed over centuries. Traditional jerking is a method of cooking highly spiced meat outdoors, slowly over a pimento wood fire. As this method is difficult to recreate at home, Mr Smith has developed his very own renowned line of Jerk seasonings to capture this unforgettable flavor. Jerk cooking is fast becoming more and more popular worldwide.

[...]

User [3273]:

*Bwoy **mi a tell** yu! Jerk peppa eenuh???Di seasonin weh dem rub up pan it yu know seh a ongle yaad alone yu can find dat deh! An a nuh yessideh dem come up wid it needa! Yu know seh granny cook it outta door nuh choo? An a soh fi har madda dweet to so yu know seh wi stick to di evil wah wi know. An plus, soh long as di meat season good good, yu jus put it ova likkle pimento wood fiya an yu know seh a you dat! But yu si choo yu cyaaan do dem sinting deh inna di yaad? Smitty nuh do a ting more dan mek him owna seasonin fi set up di meat right! An chuss mi when mi tell yu seh di sinting tayse like di real ting. When yu done, yu nuh stop lick off yu finga dem. An guess wah? Anyweh inna Massa Gad werl weh yu go, yu boun fi fine **smaddy a cook** jerk.*

[Boy, I am telling you! Jerk pepper, you know??? The seasoning that they rub on it you know that you can only find it in Jamaica! And they didn't come up with it yesterday either! You know that granny cooked it outdoors, not true? And so did her mother, so you know that we stick to the evil that we know. Plus as long as the meat seasoning is very good, you just put it over a little pimento word fire and you're set. But because you can't do that sort of thing in the yard, Smitty just made his own seasoning to set up the meat right! And trust me when I tell you that it tastes like the real thing. When you finish, you don't stop licking your fingers. And guess what? Anywhere in God's world you go, you are bound to find someone cooking jerk.]

User [3179]:

*[...] Yuh si jerk, is a strickly Jamaican spice weh tek wi centuries fi develop it to perfeckshan seen. Now di tradishanal way fi jerk, is wan weh di meat tek it time cook ova a pimentah wood fiyah seen. Now dis is a ting weh **hawd** fi chry do a yuh yaad. Missa Sumit come up wid a kine a Jerk season weh do justis to jerk in a way weh yuh can dweet a yuh yaad an wance yuh chry ee yuh **naw** goh figget it it so nice. Chroo dat now jerk cookin is a ting weh get papulah all rung di worl.*

[You see, jerk is a strictly Jamaican spice (and) it took us centuries to develop it to perfection, right. Now, the traditional way to (cook) jerk is one where the meat cooks slowly over a pimento wood fire, right. Now this is a thing that is hard to try at home. Mr. Smith came up with a kind of Jerk seasoning that does justice to jerk in a way that you can do it at home and once you try it you won't forget it as it is so nice. Because of that, cooking jerk is now a thing that is getting popular all around the world.]

While the first example translation by User [3273] includes the extensive use of JC lexical items as well as grammatical shibboleths such as the basilectal progressive, the second version is especially noteworthy for the massive amount of both innovative and conventionalised non-standard spelling variants employed by User [3179]. The two forum members thus do not only select quite different linguistic resources from the digital "ethnolinguistic repertoire", but they more generally appear to apply different strategies of sociolinguistic stylisation. Still, both approaches clearly represent instances of Mair's (2011: 226) category of "passages which are consciously crafted with rhetorical skill". Even more importantly, User [3273] and User [3179] can be seen as using "feature dropping" (cf. Johnstone and Baumgardt 2004), the strategic use of linguistic resources associated with a particular linguistic variety, as an effective device to demonstrate their linguistic expertise of "Cyber-Jamaican". Similar to Johnstone and Baumgardt's (2004) findings on the use of "Pittsburghese" on the web, forum writers thus claim "[...] the right to evaluate local speech by displaying their knowledge of it – thus reinforcing beliefs about what ['Cyber-Jamaican'] is and suggesting new norms" (Johnstone and Baumgardt 2004: 115).

Apart from feature dropping, the discursive authentication of forum members' sociolinguistic identity as "Jamaicans" is also effectuated by linking the use of "Cyber-Jamaican" to personal experience. Indeed, a comparison between the StE original and its JC counterparts quickly reveals that writers engaged in the "Patois Contest" are not necessarily aiming at a precise translation. In particular, User [3273] embellishes the text by adding anecdotal details and replacing descriptions by images. This includes, for example, references to her grandmother and mother as the sources of "authentic" jerk cooking as well as the translation of "unforgettable flavour" into "yu nuh stop lick off yu finga dem" (*You don't stop licking your fingers*).

In addition, both User [3273] and User [3179] transform the StE text as an example of Koch and Oesterreicher's concept of "language of distance" into JC as the "language of proximity" by manipulating the interpersonal level of the text. This is mainly achieved through their consistent use of the personal pronoun *you* and the regular occurrence of confirmation-seeking tags, including <eenuh> 'you know' and <nuh choo> 'isn't it' in the version produced by User [3273] and <seen> 'right', which is employed twice by User [3179]. As a consequence of these "translation" practices, the StE text clearly emerges as neutral, distant and maybe even stilted, while the Jamaican version gives the reader the impression of being engaged in an informal face-to-face conversation with a friend.

Interestingly, these strategies of authentication via stance-taking thus seem to echo survey participants' notions of "authentic" JC as a primarily informal code of communication that signals emotional involvement (cf. section 4).

A similar effect of "othering" StE as the cultural and linguistic antipode of "Jamaicaness" can be observed in a type of "staged performance" referred to as "US vs. Jamaica", which repeatedly occurs in the forum category "Best of Jamaicans.com" in 2002, 2003 and 2008. The following examples illustrate both the extensive use of 'feature dropping' as well as the playful spirit of this activity:

Example 6: "Best of Jamaicans.com"; 2002, 2003, 2008
Topic: "US vs. Jamaica"

(a) US: Go 1/2 mile south on West Main St, then go 2 miles heading north on East Main St; then go 5 miles on the East Beltway.
*JA: go dung di road til yu si Missa Chin Patty Shop and tek di turn pon di **cawna**; go all di way so til you see di big Milo sign (yu caan miss dat) and den just go straight til you reach. Oh, if yu reach one dead-end just go back up wey yu dis a come from and look fi di big Milo sign …*
yu caan miss dat!
[Go down the road until you see Mr. Chin's Patty Shop and take the turn at the corner; go all the way until you see the big Milo sign (you can't miss it) and then just go straight until you arrive. Oh if you arrive at a dead end, just go back where you were coming from and look for the big Milo sign …. You can't miss it!]

(b) US: Little Robert is dyslexic and has a spatial perception problem.
JA: si miss Ivy likkle washbelly lang mout big hed heeediat bway deh.
[Look at Miss Ivy's youngest son, long mouth, big head idiot boy.]

(c) US: Sir, please don't trow (sic!) my luggages like that.
JA: Aye buff teet bwoy, tap fling up-fling up mi bag dem suh man.
[Hey you boy with the protruding teeth, stop flinging my bags like that.]

(d) US: Perspiration odour
JA: Him smell green.
[He/she smells green.]

(e) US: my daughter has bad acne.
JA: me seh me likkle lass gyal face bumpy bumpy like a soursop.
[I say my youngest daughter's face is bumpy like a soursop.]

(f) US: you look very pensive are you ok.
JA: dem a how fi yuh face fayva when donkey siddung unda cool shade so.
[Why does your face resemble a donkey's one sitting in the cool shade?]

(g) US: Hors d'heurves (sic!)
*JA: Ah wah dis likkle sinting **you a gi** me?*
[What is this small something you are giving me?]

As with the "translations" in the "Patois Contest", personalisation also plays a central role for the 'authentication' of 'Cyber-Jamaican' in the street direction in example (a): The StE version operates with street names and abstract distances measured in miles, whereas its JC "translation" orients to landmarks such as shops and advertisement signs and includes a personal address to the interlocutor, thus once again giving the impression of direct informal conversation.

In the remaining examples, the use of JC is closely connected to a "bald-on-record" style of language (cf. Brown and Levinson 1987) that gets directly to the point and thus starkly contrasts with the corresponding over-formal version in StE, which appears to "beat around the bush" to avoid any face-threatening act. While the StE original is characterised by the use of French, technical and/or very formal vocabulary, endowing the text with an air of sophistication or scientific respectability, the plain words used in the JC version by comparison result in a breach of politeness. This is, for instance, obvious in example (c), where the highly formal address "Sir" is replaced by the insulting epithet "buff teet bwoy". However, it is by this contrastive use of half funny, half repellent imagery that the StE passage is exposed as pretentious and stilted, whereas the JC version emerges as unfiltered by considerations of politeness, but consequently also more "authentic". Finally, one could argue that the "translation" practices in the "US vs. Jamaica" threads can be interpreted as a "discourse of diaspora" in that they offer forum members, the majority of whom were living in the North American diaspora at the time of corpus compilation (cf. Figure 2 in section 2), an opportunity to voice their understanding of cultural differences and to authenticate their own idea of the Jamaican way of life. While all of these interpretations co-exist as part of the "indexical field" (cf. Eckert 2008) of "Cyber-Jamaican" in the "US vs. Jamaica" thread, Johnstone (2011) argues that it largely depends on the acculturation of the audience which of the various layers of indexicality is being activated in instances of "staged performance".

As illustrated for the concepts of informality and emotional involvement, the following comment demonstrates that there are once again striking parallels between strategies of authentication employed by forum members and survey participants' association of authenticity with a particular stance:

UWI student, 32 years
[...] I used creole in informal settings, it used to bring off an expression in a certain way. It used (sic!) to identity, that you are speaking to one of your own. **Creole is fun, it makes you laugh**. (my emphasis)

Tracing the ethnographic origins of this link between the use of JC and a jocular stance, it is furthermore interesting to note that "scandalizing practices", including the breaching of politeness, are widely recognized as part of both African American and West Indian culture:

> [t]his highly aggressive joking domain is known by a number of names in the United States, such as *rapping* or *signifying*, whereas in the West Indians it is called *giving rag*, *making mock* and *giving fatigue*. [...] Joking is in this way related to the entire tradition of scandal performances and the various practices of clowning or playing the fool. These scandalizing practices are equally widespread and important in African and Afro-American communities. (Abrahams 1983: 57)

As a consequence, forum members' "bald on record" style in connection with their "anti-formal use" of JC resources in "staged performance" can thus be linked to Abraham's (1983) concept of West Indian "broad talk" as a form of cultural authentication.

6 Conclusion

Investigating the use of "Cyber-Jamaican" in a large-scale corpus of online forum data, this paper has focussed on aspects of sociolinguistic authenticity in connection with dialect performance in CMC. In particular, it has been argued that a "third wave" sociolinguistic approach, which concentrates on authentication as the product of discursive negotiation, is more adequate than the traditional "first wave" approach to account for the recontextualisation of JC as a sociolinguistically globalised resource that forum members draw on for purposes of virtual identity management. From a methodological point of view, this adoption of a "third wave" approach has warranted a method mix between quantitative and qualitative analyses in order to examine the authenticity of "Cyber-Jamaican" both from a linguistic and from a folk linguistic perspective.

Focussing on a linguistic perspective, the quantitative-variationist analyses in section 3 have concentrated on the stylistic peculiarities of "Cyber-Jamaican" as a digital "ethnolinguistic repertoire". In particular, section 3.1 has demonstrated an over-use of basilectal progressive forms in the data, which contrasts with the predominance of mesolectal variants in face-to-face conversation. This phenomenon can be interpreted both as the outcome of an "anti-formal" use of JC as a stylistic resource as well as an effect of diasporic forum members' often limited linguistic competence in JC. On the level of orthography, non-standard spelling with the digraph <aw> has been identified as a regularly employed respelling strategy that occurs with a large variety of lexical items. While its notable increase in frequency over the years (cf. section 3.2) can be interpreted as a sign of ongoing 'grassroots' conventionalisation, its widespread cultural distribution as a stylistic resource helps to explain writers' familiarity with <aw> as a respelling strategy and is likely to have fuelled its adoption by forum members in the first place. Despite its vast "indexical field", the analysis of forum data, however, shows that its quality as an orthographic "act of identity" primarily resides in its "anti-standard" opposition to the norms of StE spelling.

The survey results presented in section 4, however, clearly demonstrate that these linguistic discrepancies between JC in the discussion forum and in face-to-face conversation do not necessarily entail native speakers' rejection of "Cyber-Jamaican" as inauthentic. From a folk linguistic perspective, they thus challenge "first wave" categorical ideas about spontaneous speech as the only source of authentic language use. Indeed, the example posts show informants' positive reactions to the performative over-use of basilectal resources, including progressive forms, which were readily recognized as indicators of "Jamaicaness". Respelling with <aw>, by contrast, was repeatedly mentioned as inauthentic, since the example post illustrating this feature was rated as "non-Jamaican" by the majority of informants. However, informants' evaluations of the example posts were only partly based on the occurrence or non-occurrence of specific linguistic resources, given that "Jamaicaness" appears to be essentially linked with stance: In this context, informality and emotional involvement as characteristics of "language of proximity" were identified as "Jamaican", whereas the use of formal language and vocabulary was interpreted as an indicator of "non-Jamaicaness".

Interestingly, forum members appear to create a similar indexical link between "Jamaicaness" and stance as an authenticating device employed in "staged performance": In the "translation" practices presented in section 5, a stilted and over-formal English original is juxtaposed with a funny, informal JC version that draws on personal address and the West Indian practice of "broad talk" to emotionally involve its reader. Since "feature dropping" is, indeed, a constitutive part of these cultural "translations", "staged performance" can surely be considered as a prime site for the "enregisterment" of "Cyber-Jamaican" via stance as a mediating factor. This may well include the incorporation of new resources and forum-specific practices such as, for example, respelling with <aw>, a widespread orthographic phenomenon in the corpus data that survey participants appear to be unfamiliar with.

References

Abrahams, Roger D. 1983: *The Man-of-Words in the West Indies. Performance and the Emergence of Creole Culture*. Baltimore: John Hopkins.

Agha, Asif 2003: The Social Life of a Cultural Value. *Language and Communication* 23: 231–273.

Agha, Asif 2005: Voice, Footing, Enregisterment. *Journal of Linguistic Anthropology* 15(1): 38–59.

Allsopp, Richard 1996: *Dictionary of Caribbean English Usage: with a French and Spanish Supplement*. Oxford: Oxford University Press.

Bauman, Richard2000: Language, Identity, Performance. *Pragmatics* 10(1): 1–5.

Bell, Alan & Andy Gibson 2011: Staging Language: An Introduction to the Sociolinguistics of Performance. *Journal of Sociolinguistics* 15(5): 555–572.

Benor, Sara Bunin 2010: Ethnolinguistic Repertoire: Shifting the Analytic Focus in Language and Ethnicity. *Journal of Sociolinguistics* 14(2): 159–183.

Blommaert, Jan 2010: *The Sociolinguistics of Globalization*. Cambridge: Cambridge University Press.

Brown, Penelope & Stephen C. Levinson 1987: *Politeness: Some universals in language use*. Cambridge: Cambridge University Press.

Bucholtz, Mary 2003: Sociolinguistic Nostalgia and the Authentication of Identity. *Journal of Sociolinguistics* 7(3): 398–416.

Cassidy, Frederic G. 1961: *Jamaica Talk: Three Hundred Years of the English Language in Jamaica*. London: MacMillan.

Cassidy, Frederic G. & Robert B. Le Page (eds.) 2002: *Dictionary of Jamaican English*. Second edition. Mona: University of the West Indies Press.

Cooper, Carolyn 2000: (W)uman Tong(ue): Writing a Bilingual Newspaper Column in 'Post-Colonial' Jamaica. *2000 Conference Presentations: 13th Biennial Conference of the Society for Caribbean Linguistics*, 91–96. Jamaica: Mona.

Coupland, Nikolas 2007: *Style: language variation and identity*. New York: Cambridge University Press.

Coupland, Nikolas 2010: The Authentic Speaker and the Speech Community. In Carmen Llamas and Dominic Watts (eds.), *Language and Identities*, 99–112. Edinburgh: Edinburgh University Press.

Crystal, David 2001: *Language and the Internet*. Cambridge: Cambridge University Press.

DeCamp, D. 1971: Toward a generative analysis of a post-creole speech continuum. In D. Hymes (ed), *Pidginization and Creolization of Languages*. Cambridge: Cambridge University Press.

Deuber, Dagmar & Lars Hinrichs 2007: Dynamics of Orthographic Standardization in Jamaican Creole and Nigerian Pidgin. *World Englishes* 26(1): 22–47.

Eckert, Penelope 2000: *Linguistic Variation as Social Practice: The linguistic construction of identity in Belten High*. Oxford: Blackwell.

Eckert, Penelope 2008: Variation and the Indexical Field. *Journal of Sociolinguistics* 12(4): 453–476.

Edwards, Viv 1986: *Language in a Black Community*. Clevedon: Multilingual Matters.

Euler, Ellen, Eric Steinhauer & Christina Bankhardt 2011: "Digitale Langzeitarchivierung als Thema für den 3. Korb zum Urheberrechtsgesetz. Urheberrechtliche Probleme der digitalen Langzeitarchivierung." *Bibliotheksdienst* 45(3–4): 322–328. Web. 4 April 2012 http://files.d-nb.de/nestor/berichte/nestor-Stellungnahme_AG-Recht.pdf.

Georgakopoulou, Alexandra 2006: Postscript: Computer-mediated Communication in Sociolinguistics. *Journal of Sociolinguistics* 10(4): 548–557.

Halliday, Michael A. K. 1975: Anti-Languages. *American Anthropologist* 78(3): 570–584.

Hewitt, Roger 1986: *White talk black talk: Inter-racial Friendship and Communication amongst Adolescents*. Cambridge: Cambridge University Press.

Hinrichs, Lars 2004: Emerging Orthographic Conventions in Written Creole: Computer-Mediated Communication in Jamaica. *Arbeiten aus Anglistik und Amerikanistik* 29(1): 81–109.

Hinrichs, Lars 2006: *Codeswitching on the web: English and Jamaican Creole in e-mail communication*. Amsterdam: Benjamins.

Hinrichs, Lars 2011: The Sociolinguistics of Diaspora: Language in the Jamaican Canadian Community. In J. Ryan Sullivant (ed.), *Texas Linguistics Forum* 54, 1–22. Austin: University of Texas.

Hinrichs, Lars & Joseph T. Farquharson 2011: Introduction. In: Lars Hinrichs and Joseph T. Farquharson (eds.), *Variation in the Caribbean: From Creole Continua to Individual Agency*, 1–9. Amsterdam: Benjamins.

Johnstone, Barbara 2011: Dialect Enregisterment in Peformance. *Journal of Sociolinguistics*. 15(5): 657–679.

Johnstone, Barbara & Dan Baumgardt2004: 'Pittsburghese' Online: Vernacular Norming in Conversation. *American Speech* 79(2): 115–145.

Koch, Peter & Wulf Oesterreicher 1985: Sprache der Nähe - Sprache der Distanz: Mündlichkeit und Schriftlichkeit im Spannungsfeld von Sprachtheorie und Sprachgebrauch. *Romanistisches Jahrbuch* 36: 15–43.

Kerswill, Paul, Eivind Torgersen & Sue Fox 2008: 'Reversing 'Drift': Innovation and Diffusion in the London Diphthong System. *Language Variation and Change* 20(3): 451–491.

Labov, William 1972: *Sociolinguistic Patterns*. Philadelphia: University of Pennsylvania Press.

Le Page, Robert B. & Andrée Tabouret-Keller 1985: *Acts of Identity. Creole-Based Approaches to Language and Ethnicity*. Cambridge: Cambridge University Press.

Mair, Christian 2003a: Language, Code, and Symbol: The Changing Roles of Jamaican Creole in Diaspora Communities. *Arbeiten aus Anglistik und Amerikanistik* 28(2): 231–248.

Mair, Christian 2003b: Acts of Identity – Interaction-based Sociolinguistics and Cultural Studies: An Introduction. *Arbeiten aus Anglistik und Amerikanistik* 28(2): 195–199.

Mair, Christian 2011: Corpora and the New Englishes: Using the 'Corpus of Cyber-Jamaican' to Explore Research Perspectives for the Future. In Fanny Meunier, Sylvie De Cock, Gaëtanelle Gilquin and Magali Paquot (eds.), *In honour of Sylviane Granger*, 209–236. Amsterdam: Benjamins.

Meyerhoff, Miriam & Nancy Niedzielski 2003: The Globalisation of Vernacular Variation. *Journal of Sociolinguistics* 7(4): 534–555.

Moll, Andrea 2013: Jamaican Creole Goes Web: A Case Study of Style Shifting in CMC. In Emanuele Miola (ed.), *Languages Go Web. Standard and non-standard languages on the Internet*, 107–128. Alessandria: Edizioni dell'Orso.

Ochs, Elinor 1993: Constructing social identity: A language socialization perspective. *Research on Language and Social Interaction* 26(3): 287–306.

Patrick, Peter L. 1999: *Urban Jamaican Creole: Variation in the Mesolect*. Amsterdam: Benjamins.

Patrick, Peter L. 2004: British Creole: Phonology. In Edgar Schneider (ed.), *A Handbook of Varieties of English. Volume 1: Phonology*, 23–246. Berlin/New York : Mouton de Gruyter.

Pennycook, Alastair 2007: *Global Englishes and Transcultural Flows*. London: Routledge.

Rampton, Ben 1995: *Crossing: Language and Ethnicity among Adolescents*. London: Longman.

Rickford, J.R. 1987: *Dimensions of a Creole Continuum*. Stanford: Stanford University Press.

Romaine, Suzanne 2005: Orthographic Practices in the Standardization of Pidgins and Creoles: Pidgin in Hawai'i as Anti-Language and Anti-Standard. *Journal of Pidgin and Creole Languages* 20(1): 101–140.

Schilling-Estes, Natalie 1998: Investigating 'Self-Conscious' Speech: The Performance of Register in Ocracoke English. *Language in Society* 27: 53–83.

Sebba, Mark 1993: *London Jamaican: Language Systems in Interaction*. London: Longman.

Siebenhaar, Beat 2008: Quantitative Approaches to Linguistic Variation in IRC – Implications for Qualitative Research. *Language@Internet* 5(4): 1–4. Web. 4 April 2011 <http://www.languageatinternet.org/articles/2008/1615/siebenhaar.pdf>.

Silverstein, Michael 2003: Indexical Order and the Dialectics of Sociolinguistic Life. *Language and communication* 23: 193–229.

Sutcliffe, David 1982: *British Black English*. Oxford: Blackwell. Urban Dictionary. "Fawt". *Urban Dictionary*. Web. 25 October 2011 <http://www.urbandictionary.com/define.php?term=fawt>.

Urban Dictionary. "Get sheg". *Urban Dictionary*. Web. 5 July 2012 <http://www.urbandictionary.
    com/define.php?term=sheg>.
Winer, Lise & Lona Jack 1997: Caribbean English Creole in New York. In Ofelia García and Joshua
    A. Fishman (eds.), *The Multilingual Apple. Languages in New York City*, 301–37. Berlin/
    New York: Mouton de Gruyter.

Appendix: Online Questionnaire: Patwa on the Internet

1. **Participant Information**

    Please provide your personal details concerning your:
    – nationality?
    – gender?
    – age?
    – University?
    – Major?
    – Years spent outside Jamaica?

2. **How often do you communicate with your friends and family via email?**

    ☐ every day
    ☐ 1 × a week
    ☐ 1 × a month
    ☐ not at all

3. **How often do you communicate with your friends and family via internet discussion forums, facebook or chat rooms?**

    ☐ every day
    ☐ 1 × a week
    ☐ 1 × a month
    ☐ not at all

4. **Please read through the post below from a discussion forum and answer the following questions**

    User 1
    Enny ideas fi a formal but scandalous pawty frack fi di chissmus pawty dis year? Nuff successfull menz widd nuff financial coverage potential agguh be dere an mi want tuh leave mi print. Tanks.

    This post was written by:
    ☐ a Jamaican
    ☐ a non-Jamaican
    ☐ can't say

    Can you tell this from the LANGUAGE used? Identify what about the language in the post led you to your answer.

5. **Please read through the following post as well:**

User 2

Mi nah guh ask mi phone company fi unlock mi phone cause too much people a ask dem and a get sheg... and mi know she if mi reach dung deh and it nuh unlock when mi reach back a farrin dem gwine carry mi guh madhouse after mi bun dung the phone company.

This post was written by:
☐ a Jamaican
☐ a non-Jamaican
☐ can't say

Can you tell this from the LANGUAGE used? Identify what about the language in the post led you to your answer.

6. **What about the following post?**

User 3

Dem knew bout itt fii a while. mi read paypahs bye ecaanyamists punninn fiyah pon dat fram a lang thyme. invisible hand aff da market principle ting.

This post was written by:
☐ a Jamaican
☐ a non-Jamaican
☐ can't say

Can you tell this from the LANGUAGE used? Identify what about the language in the post led you to your answer.

7. **What do you think about the post below?**

User 4

bout ten years ago mi waling fru di eaton centa wid mi size 14 self. dis jamaican guy seh to me "hi fatty". it was dere and den mi decide seh mi haffi change habits. i had just kept getting one size bigger every year... and this is a person who people always seh mi look like wan likkle chinese ooman how mi sumall.

This post was written by:
☐ a Jamaican
☐ a non-Jamaican
☐ can't say

Can you tell this from the LANGUAGE used? Identify what about the language in the post led you to your answer.

8. **What about the next one?**

User 5

one a mi store yessiday an dem had shoes off 30 % off di original price wid addt'l 50 off dat fuss sale price... den mi tek fass so go ovah di handbags an suffice it fi seh mi ha small leather DnB wallet fi 23.50

This post was written by:
☐ a Jamaican
☐ a non-Jamaican
☐ can't say

Can you tell this from the LANGUAGE used? Identify what about the language in the post led you to your answer.

9. **Please read through the last post and answer the questions.**

User 6

Suh mi use mi honey vice agenn an sey. Zawwrite, mi handastan hiff yuh nuh waah diskuss it, but tell me watt happ'n since we lass talk-tid dawlin, mi juss want tuh seeef mi can lenn mi support in enny way. By denn mi payshence a run hout. Shi tell mi sey shi guh a har sista yaawd an immediately shi cawl har bredda dem whe mi kno an dem BIG-BIG (shi have 4) 2 livva BX, 1 live uppa Croton panni Hudson an wan live a Pelham. Di four a dem come a har sista yaad Mondey mawnin, (for shi nuh guh home since Fridey nite) an dem climb inna di sista Hesscallayde an jrive guh outta Queens. Dem tepp inna di yaawd, hawks har fi har key, an opin di doe. Har husban deppan di couch a sleep, jump outta him sleep, fryt'n suh til. Shi sey dem tell him sey if shi as much as cawl dem widd wan yeyewata inna har yeye, dem will be bokk.

This post was written by:
☐ a Jamaican
☐ a non-Jamaican
☐ can't say

Can you tell this from the LANGUAGE used? Identify what about the language in the post led you to your answer.

10. **Can you see yourself using any of these language styles when communicating via the internet? If yes, which one and in which contexts would you use it? Thank you very much for your help!**

Theresa Heyd and Christian Mair[1]

From vernacular to digital ethnolinguistic repertoire: The case of Nigerian Pidgin

1 Introduction

(1) lol I'm not that good in pigin myself. born and raised in the states but i know more pigin than my mom who was raised in nigeria.
    sometimes when i speak the little that i know she has no idea what i'm talking about. lol
    but i hardly speak pigin, it sounds horrible coming out of my mouth.
    i just write/type it on the computer[2]
    (http://www.nairaland.com/15282/how-many-you-speak-pidgin/5)

This quote is taken from a discussion thread on the topic "How many of you speak pidgin to your parents?" that was posted to the web forum www.nairaland.com in January 2010. Nairaland is one of the major online meeting places for discussions on Nigeria and all things Nigerian. While many of the participants are Nigerian locals, the forum appears to be a highly valuable resource for participants with other, diverse backgrounds, in particular first- and second-generation emigrants, other (West) Africans, spouses and friends of Nigerians, and people with a general interest in the country and its culture; the forum's welcome page describes it as the "Home Of Nigerians And Friends Of Nigeria". The spectrum of subforums and topics is broad, ranging from politics, culture and religion to health, travel and food[3]. From the sociolinguist's perspective, the amount of dis-

---

1 The authors gratefully acknowledge the support of Deutsche Forschungsgemeinschaft (DFG), which funds their work on diasporic vernaculars as part of grant MA 1652/9. Theresa Heyd additionally wishes to acknowledge academic hospitality extended by Prof. Joybrato Mukherjee, University of Gießen.
2 For all quotations from Web material, a URL is given as a reference, regardless of whether they were found on the Web or via the Nairaland corpus.
3 Note on legal and ethical issues: We recognise that most posts in our data are their authors' own intellectual creations and hence protected by German and international copyright law. By joining the forums as (admittedly passive) members, we have agreed to respect forum guidelines. The analysis of selected posts in this paper represents personal scholarly use covered by the legal doctrines of "implied license" and "fair use", which have been recognized to hold in similar cases in several German and US trials. This notwithstanding, we recognize over-arching ethical issues in our work which go beyond the merely legal. Among others, these relate to protection

cussion surrounding language and metalinguistic observation is striking – and intriguing for analysis.[4] The posting quoted above is emblematic for these metalinguistic discussions, and for our research interests in the study presented here, for a number of reasons:

- The participant includes a personal narration of her ethnic background and heritage (in this case, 2nd generation emigrant to the United States) in assessing her own language use;
- The discussion focuses on more or less specifically Nigerian language use (in this case, usage of Nigerian Pidgin as the vernacular popular among young people);
- The discussion takes into account the factor of digital mediation (in this case, the notion of using pidgin in written rather than in spoken form).

In this sense, the folk-linguistic discussions on Nairaland provide an ideal locus to study contact varieties as globalized vernaculars that are particularly used in mediated, mobile, and diasporic contexts, and whose usage is becoming increasingly important in deterritorialized contexts where the vernacular may primarily be used as a written resource.

The research presented here is part of a larger ongoing project on contact varieties in globalized communication (for a survey see Mair and Pfänder 2013). It is one of the central tenets of recent research in computer-mediated communication (CMC) that the Internet, and particularly the Web, is slowly becoming a place of more linguistic diversity. Most notably, the research presented in Danet and Herring (2007) on the multilingual Internet provides strong evidence that this is true not only on the global scale (so that the relevance of linguistic settings beyond the Anglophone Internet are becoming relevant) but also for individual languages, and particularly the Anglophone Internet itself: thus nonstandard and previously peripheral varieties are gaining in presence and visibility. Thus previous case studies have examined the digital enregisterment (Squires 2010) of originally spoken vernaculars such as Jamaican Creole (Hinrichs 2006); Ger-

---

of personal privacy, anonymization, and long-term archiving and dissemination of the data after they have been removed from the Web (see Mann & Stewart 2002: 39–64 or Crystal 2006: 200–201). As yet, no agreement has been reached on standard procedures. In our future work on the corpora, we will therefore carefully follow the relevant debates and follow the generally accepted sociolinguistic principle that research should not exploit but empower the community in which it is carried out.

4 The subforum on culture carries the specific tagline: "Nigerian languages, traditions, practices, et cetera"; however, discussions of language use are not limited to this subforum.

man-Turkish ethnolect (Androutsopoulos 2006); or Swiss German (Siebenhaar 2006).

In the project presented here, an array of corpora is used. The corpora are based on data from web forums, one of the quintessential and pervasive genres of CMC, in order to investigate the digital instantiations of globalizing vernaculars such as Nigerian Pidgin and Jamaican Creole. The Nairaland corpus in particular spans a period of three years (2005 to 2008); it contains contributions from 11,718 members which make up a total of ca. 17.3 million tokens.

Based on these data, we can investigate how a previously oral vernacular makes the transition into the written domain of CMC. How do norms for writing Nigerian Pidgin evolve? How does the spread of this digitized vernacular proceed? And centrally, how do members of an online community such as Nairaland assess the linguistic competence and authenticity of different Pidgin users? This latter question is of particular importance given the globalized nature of the community: with users hailing both from the Nigerian heartland and the suburbs of New York City, with residents of Nigeria, recent emigrants and other members with quite heterogeneous ethnic backgrounds, the issue of ethnolinguistic gate keeping becomes central. In digital communication, questions of authenticity, reliability and trustworthiness have played an important role from the earliest days due to the delocalized nature of CMC and its relative anonymity (or pseudonymity). In this sense, it is hardly surprising that the importance of 'being real' is also extended to the digital use of ethnolinguistic repertoires. As has been noted in recent discussions of such repertoires, charting the metalinguistic perceptions that surround this kind of language use is a powerful analytical tool. Thus, Benor notes that

> it is important to point out that ethnic groups do not exist a priori but are socially-constructed phenomena that come into being through the discourse of members and non-members. When describing an ethnic group's distinctive linguistic repertoire, researchers might begin by identifying ideologies surrounding the group and its boundaries in the discourse of core members, marginal members, and non-members. (Benor 2010: 170)

In the analysis provided below, we therefore place a strong emphasis on the metalinguistic beliefs and attitudes that the members of Nairaland display in their contributions; this approach provides a valuable 'point of entry' into our dataset and is then used to extend the analysis to actual patterns of usage.

While the corpus-based nature of our data allows for both quantitative and qualitative analyses of the discourse material, the findings presented here are first and foremost interpreted within the framework of recent qualitative approaches in sociocultural linguistics, which treat ethnolects as repertoires (Sharma 2011; Benor 2010) or as supervernaculars (Blommaert 2011) rather than as uniform varieties. The theoretical framework of these approaches is outlined in greater detail in section 2. Section 3 presents data from our corpus according to four related scenarios. The discussion and outlook provided in section 4 points to ways in which the notion of digital ethnolinguistic repertoire is intermeshed with indexing authenticity – the overarching topic of this volume.

2 Theoretical background: World Englishes – from localized lects to mobile linguistic resources

The study of "varieties of English around the world" (or the "New Englishes," or "World Englishes") emerged as a new sub-field at the interface of historical linguistics, dialectology, sociolinguistics and applied linguistics in the early 1980s (e.g. landmark publications such as Bailey & Görlach 1982; Trudgill & Hannah 1982; Kachru 1982), with early research very much aiming to account for the linguistic impact of colonialism in the English-speaking world. One major result of this pioneering phase of research was the recognition of the pluricentric nature of English. Moving beyond the two established and globally present reference standards of British and American English, linguists documented new standard varieties in various stages of emergence, first in former "settler" colonies such as Australia, New Zealand or Canada, where English was the dominant native language, and, subsequently also in former "exploitation" colonies such as India or Nigeria, where for the vast majority of users English was not a native but a second language. This line of research has seen its culmination in major handbooks and surveys, such as Kortmann and Schneider (2004) or Schneider (2007). As for its methodological underpinnings, research followed traditional dialectological and sociolinguistic lines, for example by not questioning the supposedly natural links between vernaculars/ dialects and local speech communities or by assuming standardization to be taking place primarily within the confines of the new post-colonial nation states.

This approach has enabled us to see important facts of the recent history and current sociolinguistic status of English in the world very clearly. We would argue, however, that at the same time it prevents us from adequately accounting for aspects of the "English-language complex" (McArthur 2003; Mesthrie & Bhatt 2008: 1–3) which are coming to the fore as the world is moving out of the immediate aftermath of colonialism and entering into a new stage of globalized interconnectedness. For example, we can ask how relevant a traditional notion of Nigerian Standard English, defined strictly along territorial lines as the English of the educated élite in Nigeria and described by listing its phonetic and lexico-grammatical features, is for a contemporary world in which millions of Nigerians live in the North American and European diaspora, while frequently commuting between Nigeria and their adopted new homes and additionally maintaining extensive transnational family networks through the use of digital communication technologies. In this situation it is little wonder that across a broad social spectrum of its population Nigeria is very open towards influences from other regions of the Anglophone world, in particular from standard and non-standard varieties of American English, which are disseminated by the global media and entertainment industries. At the same time, Nigeria itself is slowly becoming an exporter of its own linguistic resources, including Pidgin, the stigmatized local English-lexifier vernacular, through migration or the international success of segments of its music business or its "Nollywood" movie industry.

To fully account for such phenomena, the study of varieties of English around the world has much to gain from recent methodological developments in "third wave" sociolinguistics (Eckert 2005, 2008), "sociocultural linguistics" (Bucholtz & Hall 2008a, 2008b), and in particular the emerging research program of the sociolinguistics of globalization (Blommaert 2010; Coupland 2010), which Blommaert defines as the "sociolinguistics of mobile resources" (2010: 41).

For one thing, such a methodological re-positioning would help redress an implicit monolingual bias in the study of "English as a world language" by placing the emphasis on the use of English in multilingual settings and the role of English in a multilingual global language ecology (Mesthrie 2006). In a similar vein, the notion of consistent, pure and territorial "varieties of English" will lose much of its constraining power. Varieties surviving as truncated repertoires in diasporic communities, situational ethnicity expressed through optionally available and post-natively acquired communicative styles, or the use of vernaculars by speakers not historically "entitled" to them in acts of ethnic "crossing" (Rampton 1995) would not have to be regarded as inauthentic or reduced versions of some real thing, but as worth studying in their own right, for clearly all these practices are based on the creative use of linguistic resources in new settings. In a sociolinguistics of mobile resources, speech-communities can be defined more broadly, to include "communities of practice" (Wenger 1998; with a focus on sociolinguistics: Eckert 2006; Meyerhoff 2008), which are not communities through permanently sharing a local space and its language but through temporarily engaging in the pursuit of shared goals. A prime example of such a sociolinguistic community of practice is provided by the very diasporic web-forum which is at the center of the present investigation. In the Nairaland forum, Nigerian Pidgin is present as a visual/written and as a digitally mediated vernacular, less complex in some ways than its spoken analogue, more complex in others, but – and that is the most important thing – fully functional in its new domain of use.

Sociolinguistic authenticity is thus not tied to unreflected and spontaneous use of the vernacular in face-to-face interaction in a local community, but becomes a relational concept:

> Instead of glorifying authenticity or dismissing it out of hand, we can approach it in other ways. Authenticity could be a powerful concept to use within the analysis of style. Styling, for example, creates social meanings around personal authenticity and inauthenticity, when speakers parody themselves or present themselves as 'not being themselves'. [...] We can think of 'self-authentication' and 'other-authentication', but also 'de-authentication', as strategic possibilities for how we construct identities in talk. (Coupland 2007: 25)

If we replace "talk" by "CMC in forum interaction," this is an excellent description of what is going on in the data to be discussed in section 3 below. Many leading variationist sociolinguists have long been skeptical about the use of mediated language as sociolinguistic data, arguing that media language may influence informants' vocabulary but that vernacular norms in pronunciation and core morphosyntax are defined exclusively in face-to-face interaction. If we take this objection to be valid, then notions such as "media sociolinguistics" or "sociolinguistics of CMC" are indeed oxymora. However, as the media are becoming increasingly interactive and participatory, integrated into informants' life worlds, and hence more "vernacular" themselves, the objection is losing much of its force. Again, in the words of Coupland:

> The boundary between private and public life-domains is less clear than it was previously, and mass-mediated language is often based on informality and intimacy as well as on formality and distance. [...] The media are increasingly inside us and us in them. (Coupland 2007: 28)

Post-colonial currents of migration have ensured that many previously local and marginal varieties of English have now been dispersed throughout the world, providing many new opportunities for contact between languages and varieties. It is probably far easier to hear Nigerian English, or – come to that – Nigerian Pidgin, spoken in Toronto, Miami, New York or London today than it was during the days of Empire. The early 21st-century global African diaspora is extremely heterogeneous socially and extremely complex culturally and linguistically, comprising long-established communities of "Black Atlantic" slave descendants (Gilroy 1993), but also many more recent and looser diasporic networks running the full gamut from the global academic and business élites to the disfranchised underworld of asylum seekers and undocumented aliens. As Salikoko Mufwene has pointed out, this changing situation in the world requires new sociolinguistic models:

> The increasing population mobility brought about by European colonization and associated especially with today's patterns of economic globalization and war refugeeism have also produced non-hegemonic diasporas, in which languages of the politically and/or economically under-privileged have spread (far) beyond their homelands, making traditional, static geolinguistics clearly out of date. (Mufwene 2010: xi–xii)

On a related note, Coupland asserts that today, generally, "[p]eople's memberships of 'communities' are increasingly complex, more contextualized, and less well predicted by socio-structural facts" (Coupland 2003: 426). Indeed, several of the contributors to the Nairaland forum seem to fit this description quite well, such as a young woman who describes herself as follows:

(1) I am proud to be what I am. I'm Nigerian, Bahamian and British. When people ask me where I'm from, I don't say 'Nigeria', I say 'Nigeria and the Bahamas'. That is the truth. I'm not fully Nigerian so why claim to be one? When people on the internet ask me where I'm from, I say 'I'm originally from Nigeria and the Bahamas but I'm currently living in Belgium'. Again, it's the truth.
(http://www.nairaland.com/3386/you-proud-nigerian/6)

In the course of her life, this user has developed sociolinguistic resources which are rather different to the regulation Nigerian repertoire, i.e. at least one ethnic/native language, plus varying degrees of competence in Nigerian English, Pidgin and, commonly, other indigenous language(s). To judge from the user's posts to the forum, in addition to input from various Englishes, there is also French and Dutch. It is tempting to regard her as an exceptional individual who is irrelevant to a sociolinguistic analysis of community norms because of an exceptional life story. However, we think that it is probably more appropriate to consider her as a member of an increasingly important sociolinguistic avant-garde.

The specific analytical concept which we wish to develop for our present analysis of vernacularized web-forum data is the "digital ethnolinguistic repertoire". Although the default language of forum communication is (Standard) English, our data exhibit high degrees of stylistic variability involving features from several standard and non-standard Englishes, such as Nigerian English, British or American English, Nigerian Pidgin or African American Vernacular English. Nigerian Pidgin, in particular, is involved in various types of code-switching and code-mixing, as are – to a lesser extent – Nigeria's major indigenous languages, and occasionally even German, Dutch or French (as major languages of some of the destinations of the emigrants). In the analysis of our data, the classical reference descriptions of the relevant "varieties" (Gut 2004 and Alo & Mesthrie 2004 for Nigerian English; Faraclas 1996 for Nigerian Pidgin) provide useful orientation. However, in our view it is not a productive approach to measure practices on the web against the yard-stick of such reference descriptions. On the one hand, there is an inevitable mimetic deficit whenever vernaculars are reduced to writing, and there is an inevitable truncation of speaker competence when vernaculars are used by second- and third-generation Nigerian emigrants who have only limited input in the diaspora. On the other hand, in some respects the digital vernaculars are actually richer than the ones spoken on the ground, because writers may exploit visual resources (e.g. expressive spellings) or explore new modes of contact and combination among varieties and languages for which the new medium provides opportunities.

Rich and varied though it presents itself, "Cyber-Nigerian" is thus not a "variety", or an ethnic dialect of a more general "Netspeak" (itself a notion which hardly survives closer scrutiny). Rather, we argue, it should be seen as similar to the ethnic "style repertoire" described for Asians in Britain by Sharma (2011) or to the "ethnolinguistic repertoire" described for orthodox Jews in the United States by Benor (2010). In her introduction, Benor defines her notion of the "ethnolinguistic repertoire" by demarcating it against an older notion of "ethnic variety" or "ethnic dialect":

> Ethnolinguistic repertoire [...] is defined as a fluid set of linguistic resources that members of an ethnic group may use variably as they index their ethnic identities. In this paper, I describe the ethnolinguistic repertoire approach and show how it solves five theoretical problems with the notion of 'ethnic language variety' as a bounded entity.
> – Intra-group variation.
> – Intra-speaker variation.
> – Out-group use.
> – Delineating the ethnic group.
> – Delineating 'ethnolect'. (Benor 2010: 160)

As the analyses in section 3 will make clear, the five "problems" mentioned address our most important concerns in the analysis of the forum data, too. We assume that adapting the notion of "ethnolinguistic repertoire" to the analysis of CMC is easy and appropriate. Trivially, "digital ethnolinguistic repertoires" are special because they lack the phonetic dimension. But as we shall see, this truncation is partly compensated for by the visual semiotic potential of expressive orthography or CMC-specific iconography. There is also a massive truncation of real-life ethnolinguistic repertoires in CMC at the macro-level. With around 500 languages in use in face-to-face interaction, Nigeria is an intensely multilingual society. However, of these 500 languages, only English, Pidgin, Yoruba, Igbo and Hausa regularly make it into the Nairaland forum. Other indigenous languages seem to be excluded for lack of a suitable script or because of insufficient demographic weight. On the side of gains, on the other hand, we expect that linguistic resources will be freed up for new uses in CMC, if only because language is an even more important means of self-authenticating and indexing ethnicity in the fluid and ill-defined space of the digital forum than in face-to-face interaction on the ground.

3 Nigerian Pidgin as a digital ethnolinguistic repertoire: Four scenarios

The following examples constitute a case study on Nigerian Pidgin (also abbreviated as NigP below) on its trajectory from a local vernacular to a deterritorialized, and diasporic linguistic resource serving as a central component in a digital ethnolinguistic repertoire. The data, organized in four different scenarios, show how far Nigerian Pidgin has come from a purely spoken vernacular localized in Nigeria to a globalized repertoire that is employed by speakers in a variety of ethnic backgrounds and geolocational settings; and how the digital domain is an active and central factor in this process. In this context, it becomes particularly apparent why a repertoires approach is helpful here: as will be shown, the linguistic features that are perceived as distinctive for Nigerian Pidgin are used and discussed by members of the online community in a very diverse way that varies according to situation. In other words, we are seeing users of a repertoire of features – not members of a uniform speech community.

The four scenarios for the spread of Nigerian Pidgin as a digital vernacular are labeled as follows:
1. The web as a **stage**: Vernacular mixing and appropriation
2. The web as a **classroom**: Cataloguing and teaching pidgin
3. The web as a linguistic **resource**: Pidgin and Netspeak features
4. The web as an **infrastructure**: Nigerian Pidgin in digital interfaces

Scenarios 1 through 3 are based solely on the data from the Nairaland corpus; the final point provides an outlook to other websites and digital environments. While this is certainly not an exhaustive list, these four aspects do seem emblematic of the practices surrounding the use of Nigerian Pidgin that our data reveal.

The examples that are subsumed under these four headers may be quite heterogeneous; yet it can be argued that taken together, they are evidence of two underlying trajectories. Thus Nigerian Pidgin on the web appears to be marked by (a) increasing mediatization and (b) increasing commodification. By mediatization, we understand here the increasing integration of NigP features into digital discourse, and even increasing structural bundling with the medium. This becomes particularly evident in scenarios 3 and 4, where we examine the evolution of a NigP-based 'netspeak', and the use of NigP in digital interfaces. Commodification is understood here in the sense of Heller (2003), in that Nigerian Pidgin is on a trajectory from a vernacular (a stigmatized one, in fact), to social capital, to an asset that can be marketed and, ultimately, monetized. This kind of development has been demonstrated for varieties with a certain pop-cultural appeal such as AAVE or Jamaican Creole (Mair 2003, 2011) – a kind of prestige that NigP, until recently, did not hold. But with the emergence of a Nollywood movie scene, and the rise and increasing popularity of musicians that associate with Nigeria, this may be changing; thus our data can be seen as evidence of early-stage commodification of NigP.

3.1 The web as a stage: Vernacular mixing and appropriation

For many participants on Nairaland, the forum serves as a virtual stage where one's own vernacular skills can be explored and performed. Due to the heterogeneous makeup of the community, this often involves crossing and mixing of different repertoires. In addition, the forum is also a place for the metalinguistic discussion of these vernacular skills. As a result, we find many personal narratives of belonging, where users reflect on their own ethnic and ethnolinguistic identity. A forum such as Nairaland is a particularly insightful platform for these phenomena, because it makes evident the delocalized nature of the vernacular, and at the same time provides a virtual space where its features can be explored and performed by members; these factors may be reinforcing each other.

This dynamic is very tangible in the many metalinguistic discussion threads on Nairaland, for example concerning the "Terrible state of the English language in Nigeria." This long thread contains almost 600 contributions, most of them made in late August/early September 2007, and was opened with the following posting:

(2) Have you ever wondered about the falling standard of the English Langauge in Nigeria. In schools, TV, churches and even on radio standards have fallen beyond redemption. There seems to be the Nigerian version of the mall English. How would non-Nigerians understand us? Is the "Niglenglish" evolving?
Shay?
Abi?
Leave me jare!
O sha mo?
As in you know sha?
(http://www.nairaland.com/nigeria/topic-75696.0.html)

Strikingly, the contributor uses general descriptions such as "Niglenglish" and "the Nigerian version of mall English"; yet the examples he provides clearly indicate that he is referring to the usage of Nigerian Pidgin. Thus *abi*, *(o)jare* and *shay* are commonly used as tag questions in NigP, whereas *sha* is placed after constituents to mark them as sentence topics (Faraclas 1996: 121). And sure enough, the ensuing discussion revolves mainly around the role of NigP and its usage in Nigeria and around the globe. The attitudes towards NigP cover a broad spectrum, from the skeptical stance presented in the opening post to calls for making NigP an official language of Nigeria.

Of the many contributions in this thread that would warrant a closer discourse analysis, only two are quoted here, because they offer a globalized take on the perception of NigP. The first is by iice; while her background and location cannot easily be pinpointed, it can be inferred from many of her statements that she is a Nigerian emigrant in a Western country.

(3)   Abegi leave ma pidgin o! 😊
      Na berra language o jare! 😊
      Even some of ma friends speak it
      My bro's gf is not nigerian but she speaks pidgin
      Has to, being around naija people all the time 😊

      Na wonderful language o! 😊😊

      [Please leave my pidgin + PHRASE-FINAL PARTICLE
      It is a very good language, you know.
      ...
      It is a wonderful language + PHRASE-FINAL PARTICLE]
      (http://www.nairaland.com/75696/terrible-state-english-language-nigeria)

The second quote comes from soulpatrol, whose own narrative of belonging describes her as "a nigerian student living in the eastern part of canada (the maritimes)":

(4)   my own be say, as long as u try to put a sentence together that makes sense and is understandable, then u're good. no need for fone or trying to acquire an accent. me i flow better when i'm speaking in my natural state, as long as u can hear me well, no need to please everbody. and for goodness sake, there's aboslutely nothing wrong with speaking pigdin when u're talking to your country people. English is so over-rated! very boring on its own, and believe it or not, other countries actually appreciate it and want to learn. thank the lord for Ebonics to spice things up! there is always a place and time to speak it of course.
      [**My opinion is that** as long as you try to put a sentence together that makes sense and is understandable, then you're good. No need for **an artificial foreign accent** (NigP *fone* ← Engl. *phonetics*) ...]
      (http://www.nairaland.com/75696/terrible-state-english-language-nigeria/2)

Both commenters appear to be skilled in the usage of NigP features. iice relies on the NigP repertoire very strongly, in particular in the first two and final lines of her posting, whereas soulpatrol only uses NigP to open her turn and then continues in a very informally spelled but stylistically relatively neutral Americanized English. In terms of metalinguistic commentary, both posters display a positive stance toward NigP; soulpatrol's stance is somewhat more leveled as she takes into account factors such as appropriateness and communicative context. Interestingly, both users also touch on the subject of NigP as a globalized vernacular. Thus iice mentions the appropriation of NigP by outsiders: "Even some of ma friends speak it (...) My bro's gf is not nigerian but she speaks pidgin".[5] And soulpatrol hints to the possibility of vernacular mixing by bringing AAVE into the picture: "thank the lord for Ebonics to spice things up!"

While these examples of usage of and commentary on vernacular mixing and appropriation strike us as 'authentic' and unproblematic, this may not be the case for all of them. In a discussion titled "Is It Necessary To 'try' And Adapt An American, west Indian Or British Accent?", the user deedami provides the following response:

(5) Well guess wat ! i speak Patois ! and i live in killafornia, I just cant help but blendin ma Naija accent wit Patois, gives me and identity, different from dem Bay Area N!ggas, everyone that walks up to me always make that perfect guess, and the reason why i picked on Patois is its African origin,
it was a languaged coined by slaves who needed an identity, and it still shows the connection to our roots, and besides i love the way English is murdered in Patois so i speak it, and of course, Ma naija accent very obvious, and ma Naija flag on ma backpack. I never tried to be what am not,
to all thosr guys that come out here and try to act all Americanised . . . . Loosers,
Yankee people can tell theirs when they see theirs, sooo i gets ma respect from homies cos am reppin where am from faithfully,
(http://www.nairaland.com/92531/it-necessary-try-adapt-american%2Cwest/2)

---

5 In another metalinguistic discussion thread, „How many of you speak pidgin to your parents?", iice elaborates on this case of Pidgin appropriation – strikingly, the 'gf' in question is labeled as Asian:
I speak a mixture of english, pidgin and Tagalog 2 my mom, but if she doesn't want d peeps here 2 know what we r talking about, we do a mixture of pidgin and hausa , (...) **Case in point: my bro girlfriend never go naija, she na chinko, but she dey speak pidgin because we dey blast am anyhow 4 her wey she gas learn am oh** [*My brother's girl friend has never been to Nigeria. She is Chinese, but she speaks Pidgin because we use it anyhow for her where she can learn it*] (http://www.nairaland.com/15282/how-many-you-speak-pidgin)

Deedami is a young college student who, according to information on his profile and Myspace pages, was born in Nigeria, emigrated with his parents and was raised in Sacramento, CA. In this posting, he self-identifies with two ethno-linguistic repertoires: Jamaican Creole ("Patois") and his "Naija accent" – it is unclear whether this refers to pronunciation alone or to actual use of NigP features as well. At the same time, he takes on a highly critical stance toward accommodation to American English: those who "act all Americanised" are judged as inauthentic.

In this example, the discrepancy between metalinguistic belief and self-assessment, on the one hand, and the participant's actual use of a linguistic repertoire is striking. Thus deedami's utterance quoted here does not contain distinctive features of either Jamaican Creole or Nigerian Pidgin. Instead, he uses a number of features that are indexical of young American male speech, and/or of AAVE – for example the use of "homies", as well as "ma" instead of "my". In other utterances in the corpus, deedami also uses features that are typical of AAVE (e.g. "yadig" as a tag question), of Californian English ("hella"), or that originate in American Hip Hop ("haters" and "hatin"), but no distinctive JC or NigP features. Of course, the corpus naturally limits our access to deedami's utterances in the CMC context, and it is not impossible that his real-life linguistic profile may differ from his digital usage; nevertheless, the linguistic evidence found here suggests that "reppin where am from faithfully" for this user in fact amounts to a thoroughly Americanized ethnolinguistic identity.

3.2 The web as a classroom: Cataloguing and teaching pidgin

Nairaland is not only used by participants to showcase their own NigP usage. The forum also serves as a platform to inquire about questions of vocabulary, pronunciation, and proper NigP usage in general. Occasionally, these discussions are taken one step further, so that users openly express the wish to learn Pidgin with the help of the forum.

These exchanges are afforded by the community structure of the forum as described in the introduction: it serves as a meeting place for Nigerian locals – who are usually viewed as the authorities on proper Pidgin usage – and other, more heterogeneous participants in the diaspora: first and second generation emigrants and people whose affiliation with Nigeria is even more indirect, for example through a spouse or people in their peer group. As a consequence, the desire to learn Pidgin is often motivated to a certain degree by the participants' Nigerian heritage; but another, frequently expressed motivation is the wish to speak Pidgin in their offline interactions, e.g. with friends who are fluent in

Pidgin. As a consequence, the forum not only functions as a repository for knowledge about written NigP, but it simultaneously works as a place to ask for online help in understanding and producing NigP; and as a sounding board where NigP skills can be explored.

Again, there are a number of metalinguistic discussion threads on the forum which facilitate these exchanges. Indeed, it is an established tradition of the forum to maintain metalinguistic threads where the individual Nigerian languages can be performed and shared. Typical thread titles include "Be Proud To Speak Hausa Language Here"; "If You Can Speak Yoruba, Talk It In Here!" or "Igbo Kwenu ! Kwenu Kwezo Nu ! Join Us If You Proud To Be An Igbo Guy/lady". In the same vein, there is a thread on NigP with the title "People Wey Sabi Write Pidgin: Make Una Show Una Skills" [*People who know how to write Pidgin: show your skills!*], which is opened by this invitation to participate:

(6) eventhough pigin no be our offcial langauage, at least na our hood language, make we speak am here, talk your pigin proverbs, yarns, as for me i do yarn
[*Even though Pidgin is not our official language, at least it is our community / neighborhood language. Let us speak it here. Say your Pidgin proverbs, tales. As for me, I speak*]
(http://www.nairaland.com/109915/people-wey-sabi-write-pidgin)

Even though the thread is comparatively short with 169 contributions, it contains a wealth of different motivations for and approaches to teaching and learning NigP. The following examples give a brief overview of these different takes.

After the thread has started with a number of contributions by highly skilled NigP speakers, the user drrionelli puts forward this request:

(7) Since I've been here at nairaland.com, I've tried to familiarize myself with Pidgin. Several fine people whom I've encountered here have been helpful to me in that regard. To those persons I am, and shall remain, grateful.
However, allow me to address this to everybody. I would like to learn Pidgin, so that I may more readily understand some of the postings made here (and for a possible trip to Nigeria, as well).
Is there a good method of learning it? Do I have to simply struggle through reading it and trying to approximate its pronunciations?
What do you suggest?
(http://www.nairaland.com/109915/people-wey-sabi-write-pidgin/1)

The overall style and stance of this posting are strikingly deviant from the typical writing style in an online discussion forum, and seem even more out of place in a pidgin performance thread. As a consequence, the poster's sincerity and motives are questioned by the other participants. However, his writing style is consistent with all his other postings on Nairaland,[6] and eventually the other participants take his eagerness to learn NigP at face value. For example, ikamefa replies with the following suggestion:

(8) @ drrionelli
     try learning Hawaiian pidgin English , that is the closest thing to Nigerian pidgin English, i
     think you will be better able to understand 9 j a [= Naija = Nigeria(n), TH & CM] pidgin then
     (http://www.nairaland.com/109915/people-wey-sabi-write-pidgin/1)

Drrionelli then addresses ikamefa with more specific questions about spoken NigP:

(9) (...)Is the language pronounced in a phonetic way, i.e., is it largely pronounced the way it
     would seem to be in proper English?

     Example:? Is "sabi" pronounced sah-bee??
     ? ? ? ? ? ? ?? ? Is "una" pronounced ooo-nah or yoo-na?? ?
     (http://www.nairaland.com/109915/people-wey-sabi-write-pidgin/1)

Again, ikamefa replies:

(10) (...)
     as to the second part of your question : erhmmmmmmmmm i nor sabi oh " "

     for real though! i grew up listening to and then being able to speak pidgin, never went to
     schoo to learn it (like any other 9 j a child)
     so that pronounciation thingy up there " i nor sabi"
     like i once told yah get a good book on pidgin english or prolly some other folks in here can
     help you clarify that dear!
     (http://www.nairaland.com/109915/people-wey-sabi-write-pidgin/1)

In this exchange, the users drrionelli and ikamefa represent the extremes in the broad spectrum of learning pidgin. Thus drrionelli is the outsider to the language and culture; his knowledge of NigP is theoretical only and his approach to learning it is almost academic in nature. By contrast, ikamefa is the quintessential native speaker of NigP; indeed, her NigP competence is so ingrained and intuitive that drrionelli's questions about pronunciation seem too abstract for her to answer.

---

6 According to self-description, drrionelli is black, of Franco-Canadian origin, and lives in Michigan.

Yet another facet of learning NigP can be seen in the contributions by zandra1 in the same thread. A young woman who came to the US with her parents at high school age, she writes:

(11) Me I know sabi speak pidgin . The small wey I speak na the basics wey I learn from nai-raland and some friends but I still dey learn sha. I love seeing people wey dey speak pidgin or when they write with am esp. on nairaland. I go come back when I sabi speak more. I troway salute and hail una.
[*I don't know how to speak Pidgin. The little that I speak is the basics which I learned from Nairaland and some friends, but I am still learning. I love seeing people who speak Pidgin or write it, especially on Nairaland. I will come back when I can speak more. I greet you all!*]
(http://www.nairaland.com/109915/people-wey-sabi-write-pidgin)

At first glance, this posting contains a great number of NigP features – zandra1 uses *sabi* for "know / be able to", the relativizer particle *wey*, *am* as a third person pronoun, and similar features; the greeting formula at the end is adopted from the previous posters in the thread. However, it quickly becomes apparent that these features are mostly lexical additions to an otherwise ethnolinguistically unmarked utterance. Indeed, all of zandra1's other contributions in the corpus are either in Igbo or in English. According to her self-description – "the basics wey I learn from nairaland" – zandra1 is indeed a case where digital mediation of NigP through the discussion forum is the primary source for ethnolinguistic knowledge and learning. The boundaries of her knowledge become visible further down the discussion thread; after a few postings by other NigP speakers, zandra1 returns to unmarked English and notes that

(12) I guess some people are speaking the 'real' pidgin and, I dont get some of the stuff they said.
(http://www.nairaland.com/109915/people-wey-sabi-write-pidgin/1)

In sum, these examples show that there is a grassroots 'market' for learning NigP online. The underlying motivations and strategies, however, can vary. For some, the goal appears to be using the forum as a facilitator for offline language skills (as in the case of drrionelli, who is interested in the finer points of NigP pronunciation). For others, such as zandra1, acquiring the digitized vernacular may be an end unto itself: they are particularly interested in learning, and participating in, the online usage of NigP. For all of these scenarios, the metalinguistic components of Nairaland provide a platform.

3.3 The web as a linguistic resource: Pidgin and netspeak features

In the first two scenarios, we have considered more general, macrolinguistic strategies of NigP usage and metadiscussion. In a narrower sense, the mediatization of NigP, and its use as a digital vernacular, also touches on the linguistic inventory of NigP itself. Does the usage of NigP in CMC bring forth new lexical items or expressions? More specifically, does the digitally mediated use of NigP result in the emergence of NigP-based Netspeak features?

In discussing the notion of Netspeak, it should be noted that this concept is at the center of an ongoing debate in CMC studies. Coined by David Crystal (2006), who put it forward as an encompassing description for online language use in general, the term was subsequently criticized for being an over-generalization; many studies since have found that typical Netspeak items are in fact relatively infrequent even in adolescent CMC use (Tagliamonte & Denis 2008). In a more balanced view, for example a recent study by Squires (2010), Netspeak is seen as a typical product of enregisterment – where an array of linguistic features comes to be symbolically linked to a speaker community. With this caveat in place, Netspeak can be described as an inventory of features that are typically used to index 'doing CMC'. This essentially includes a bundle of highly visible and recognizable features, predominantly on the level of orthography and typography: non-standard spelling and punctuation; abbreviations and acronyms; emoticons, and the like.

In the context of our data, two questions seem particularly relevant: What are the patterns of usage for typical Netspeak features in the Nairaland data? And are there features that are specific to NigP/specific to the forum? The first question is part of a larger, ongoing study, but the following examples provide a first insight into Netspeak usage on Nairaland.

A first case in point is the use of the forms "Naija", as well as variants such as "9ja", "9-ja" or "9ija". *Naija* is a widely used localized informal spelling for the word *Nigeria*, which was originally probably meant to capture an indigenized English or NigP pronunciation of the country's name. While not restricted to such contexts, the spellings are of course extremely frequent in CMC:

(13) I'm proud n happy being a 9ija man.
  (http://www.nairaland.com/7049/nine-oil-workers-kidnapped-niger/1)

(14) my 9-ja people, get set for the year 2007 is the year for you and for me.
  (http://www.nairaland.com/13003/senate-throws-out-third-term)

(15) is it in built or wat? every babe in 9ja 2day is cheating.why, why n why?
  (http://www.nairaland.com/757164/y-cant-9ja-women-stop)

Replacing syllables with digits is a very common practice in Netspeak, and particularly in texting. It is also often associated with Hip Hop culture; the number 9 also figures in Nigerian popular culture, for example the name of Hip Hop musician 9ice. This convergence of globalized Netspeak conventions[7] on the one hand, and a pop cultural frame of reference may account for the rising popularity of this alternate spelling.

The other two examples are more conventional abbreviations that have become widespread in Nigerian Netspeak: ITK and JJC. Both are ascriptions used to characterize others and to point out particular personality traits; as such, both carry a more or less overt negative connotation, as the following examples demonstrate:

(16) @Farriel, U too should be unwilling to continue then. If their uncooperative or itk attitude will undermine your job, why not tell them so. @ the end of the day, you will get the big stick if things don't work out as expected
(http://www.nairaland.com/10356/www.enyimbafc.net)

(17) i'm Igbo and proud of it can't nobody change that! . yoruba people in general r da ITK(i 2 know) type they've always been always will be, (no offence) we igbos just keep it real and on da low that is y we get tribes hatin(yorubas in particular) . dnt get me wrong peeps i like yoruba people and i got friends who r yorubas(but they act itk so much damn).... reppin da igbos fa sho igbo gurl 4 lyfe he big stick if things don't work out as expected
(http://www.nairaland.com/5122/where-igbos-hausas-other-non-yorubas)

(18) yes o omoge. some just over do it to fit in. you'll hear of one emeka person (jjc) that just landed in yankee and within 1 month, he has changed his name to micky or mekhi and starts speaking yeye english like gerrout, mothafu$ka, shit men, wharabout, yels etc. pitiful. no be by force o. naija peeps to dey overmurder English
(http://www.nairaland.com/54330/nigerians-foreign-accents/1)

(19) Goodguy you be JJC, abeg, this is a forum and i can voice my opinion, shey you dey for Chicago here [isn't it the case you are here in Chicago ...] and see how many Nigerians are in jail waiting to be repatriated for conspiracy crimes? This are all people I see in the club and Nigerians gathering. So don't tell me we are doing good when about 20 % of youngstars in Chi town are in jail
(http://www.nairaland.com/2359/nigerians-most-corrupt-people-world)

As can be seen in the second excerpt, ITK is short for "I too know", an established NigP description for a smart alec or know-it-all. Interestingly, the abbreviation

---

7 See Blommaert (2011), where the language of texting is discussed as an instantiation of "supervernaculars".

ITK is also sometimes found in general English Netspeak / texting to refer to "in the know" – which is semantically quite similar to the NigP meaning, but probably holds less of a negative connotation. The second excerpt also alludes to the notion that an ITK attitude is not just associated with individual personality, but is perceived as a cultural or tribal stereotype in Nigerian society; here, to "act ITK" is associated with "Yoruba people".

The second abbreviation, JJC, is short for "Johnny just come": an expression in NigP that semantically forms an antonym to the concept of ITK. This negative description is usually used for recent Nigerian emigrants who are perceived as clueless and naïve, as in the upper example, where jjc refers to Nigerian emigrants to the US as the quintessential "emeka person (...) that just landed in yankee". The readiness to give up the Igbo name *Emeka* for the American *Micky* is criticized as a symbol of lacking cultural pride. As may be noted, the rest of this first excerpt offers a critique of "yeye English", stupid English – the linguistic accommodation that is perceived to be typical for emigrants.

In online usage, the notion and implication of JJC has been metaphorically extended to include newcomers to another space, namely the discussion forum, or even the Internet in general. This strategy can be seen in the final excerpt, where a disagreeing participant is first called out ("Goodguy you be JJC") and then reprimanded ("this is a forum and I can voice my opinion"). In other words, JJC has become a specifically Nigerian derogatory term for calling out newbies. In this sense, JJC is a striking example of the development of CMC norms and conventions that are specific for a specific ethnolinguistic community: while digital (il)literacy and the associated experience and prestige or lack of it are essential notions in all online communication, the community that is investigated here has coined its own Netspeak term that is rooted in a culturally relevant and well-known practice.

3.4 The web as an infrastructure: NigP in digital interfaces

The final scenario is an attempt to widen the scope from the forum data to more general, and also more visible, areas of the Web. The vernacular usage that has been described so far is quite grass-roots, spontaneous, and bottom-up in its nature. Although we have seen it in several instances to be highly mediated, self-reflective and stylized, it still takes place on the level of individual users and is in fact discouraged by the forum guidelines, as this quote from the Nairaland forum netiquette makes clear:

(20) 1. Nairaland is an English language forum. English happens to be our official language in Nigeria. it also happens to be the language of the web. Please make every effort to use clear English at all times:
Avoid 'netspeak' or 'SMS-language'. 'You' is spelled Y-O-U, not u!
Avoid pidgin English, but 'put am inside italics' if you need to use pidgin English. (...)
(http://www.nairaland.com/6/nairaland-forum-participation-guidelines)

As these metalinguistic guidelines indicate, the widespread usage and discussion of NigP on Nairaland in fact take place in spite of being officially discouraged within the forum framework. This leads on to the question whether there are instances and emerging practices where NigP use is not only encouraged, but where it is in fact used in a more institutionalized, well-planned and top-down manner. Specifically, are there instances of online language use where NigP is inbuilt into the digital infrastructure of the website, program, or digital interface?

Such instances of 'officialized' NigP usage on the Web have only begun to emerge recently (whereas forums such as Nairaland have been used for the spread of NigP for a decade or longer). In this sense, the commodification of NigP in digital interfaces has only just begun. Two examples to illustrate this trend are Google Naija and the social networking site naweown.com.

Figure 1: Google Naija in Nigerian Pidgin.

The first example refers to the language settings that are available for Google. While the Nigerian Google domain, http://www.google.com.ng, has been online for quite a while, the language settings for the search interface have recently been extended: in addition to English, Hausa, Yoruba and Igbo, users can also choose Nigerian Pidgin since October 2011. Choosing the "Pidgin" version leads to the search interface depicted in Figure 1. The changes are subtle, but pervasive and touch on all linguistic features on the site. Thus "Google Nigeria" becomes "Google Naija"; "Google Search" becomes "Google Find"; "I'm Feeling Lucky" is rendered as "I Dey Feel Lucky"; and "Google.com.ng offered in" translates as

"Google.com.ng wey dem don give". Interestingly, the NigP glossing extends into some – but not all – further Google pages that are accessible through the Options button on the top right hand corner. Thus the instructions on the Advances Search page remain in Standard English, but the Language Options site reads: "Make you arrange Google homepage, message, and button to show am for de language wey you want through our Preferences page. Google don start to dey offer interface language:" [Followed by a list of languages]

It is important to note that these changes to the search interface are (as of yet) only of a cosmetic nature: the search process itself is not language-specific, nor are the results that it yields. It should also be noted that the addition of languages for search preferences is not an entirely serious endeavor for Google, and that a playful element is involved. Thus the language catalog includes extinct languages, such as Latin; artificial languages, such as Esperanto and Interlingua; fictional languages such as Klingon or "Bork Bork Bork" (the vernacular spoken by the Swedish Chef from the Muppets); and, finally, a Leetspeak version of the interface. Nevertheless, the inclusion of vernaculars such as Krio, Seychellois and Haitian Creole speak to the fact that these ethnolinguistic repertoires are becoming visible on a global and digital scale; and that, ultimately, their usage may be a factor that can be monetized.

Figure 2: The social network naweown.com

An example that takes the use of NigP far more seriously, and one step further, is the website www.naweown.com which has been online since September 2011 (see Figure 2). Naweown – a phrase from NigP that roughly translates as "it is our own" – is designed as a social networking site that is explicitly geared to the NigP-speaking community. Thus it contains many features that are inspired by networking platforms such as Facebook: users have profile pages, they can friend and follow other users and comment on their updates. However, all of these communication options that are inbuilt to the system are in NigP: thus friends are called "padis"; the wall with recent comments is titled "As e De Hot"; and status updates by users have labels such as "don join" or "don add a new story".

This NigP-based interface is thus designed as a digital space where the use of NigP is not only tolerated, but in fact actively encouraged. The title of the site suggests this positive and embracing attitude, and it becomes even more evident in the "rules & conditions" that new users agree to upon registering:

(21) Rules & Conditions (abi na constitution sef)
     This social network na we own. So make sure say majority of everything wey you de do (whether na to connect, share, upload, yan) na for we own mother tongue, pidgin.

     You fit yan oyinbo. But keep am minimal. This na we own!
     [*This social network is our own. So make sure that most of what you do (whether it is to connect, share, upload, chat) is in our own mother tongue, Pidgin. You can speak the white man's language, but keep it minimal. This is our own.*]
     (http://naweown.com/member/signup)

The contrast to the language policy on nairaland.com, quoted earlier, is striking; it can be speculated whether a platform such as naweown.com is at least partially motivated by such restrictive attitudes toward NigP. It is too early to judge whether the integration of NigP features into the infrastructure of digital interfaces will become more widespread and established; for the time being, the examples shown here can be taken as an indicator of at least early-stage mediatization and commodification of the repertoire.

4 Discussion and outlook

The present study has investigated the use of Nigerian Pidgin in a diasporic web forum, focusing on its role in indexing ethnicity. We have argued that the most productive approach to this phenomenon is **not** to describe "cyber-Pidgin" as a variety or even to compare it to the Pidgin attested in face-to-face interaction in Nigeria, but to treat it as part of a rich and complex inventory of linguistic resources which Nigerians – whether they are locals resident in the country itself or members of the global diaspora – have at their disposal to vernacularize and thus appropriate the neutral domain of cyber-space for their purposes. In doing so, members of the Nairaland forum constitute a community of practice, and cyber-Pidgin is a central element in their "digital ethnolinguistic repertoire", a central analytical notion which we have developed from recent work on ethnic minority communities in Britain and the US by Benor (2010) and Sharma (2011).

The consequences of deterritorialization, mediatization and commodification which we have described for Nigerian Pidgin are not specific to this case but can be observed for many other vernaculars which have been "mobilized" in physical space through migration or have made it into the global "mediasphere" (Appadurai 1996) because of their association with transnational counter-cultural movements, popular musical traditions or the entertainment industry.

Our contribution is relevant to *indexing authenticity*, the theme of the present volume, because we show that the vernacular used in face-to-face interaction in tightly circumscribed local speech communities is not the only authentic vernacular. We have adopted Blommaert's (2010) model of the "sociolinguistics of globalization," defined as a "sociolinguistics of mobile resources, not one of immobile languages" (2010: 102), in order to show that elements of a local vernacular – whether transformed through transposition into a different medium or displaced through migration in physical space – survive as authentic indexes of macro-categories such as ethnic affiliation, but also on the micro-level of expressing stance in interaction. In this sense, we hope to have made an empirical and a theoretical contribution to the emerging sociolinguistics of CMC.

References

Alo, M. A., & Rajend Mesthrie 2004: Nigerian English: morphology and syntax. In Bernd Kortmann and Edgar Schneider (eds.), *A Handbook of Varieties of English*, 813–827. Vol. 2. Berlin/new York: Mouton de Gruyter.

Androutsopoulos, Jannis 2006: Multilingualism, diaspora, and the Internet: Codes and identities on German-based diaspora websites. *Journal of Sociolinguistics* 10: 429–450.

Appadurai, Arjun 1996: *Modernity at Large: Cultural Dimensions of Globalisation*. Minneapolis, MI: University of Minnesota Press

Bailey, Richard & Manfred Görlach (eds.) 1982: *English as a World Language*. Ann Arbor, MI: University of Michigan Press.

Benor, Sarah Bunin 2010: Ethnolinguistic repertoire: Shifting the analytic focus in language and ethnicity. *Journal of Sociolinguistics* 14: 159–183.

Blommaert, Jan 2010: *The Sociolinguistics of Globalization*. Cambridge: Cambridge University Press.

Blommaert, Jan 2011: Supervernaculars and their dialects. *Working Papers in Urban Language and Literacies* 81.

Bucholtz, Mary & Kira Hall 2008a: All of the above: new coalitions in sociocultural linguistics. *Journal of Sociolinguistics* 12(4):1–31.

Bucholtz, Mary & Kira Hall 2008b: Finding identity: theory and data. *Multilingua* 27(1–2): 151–163.

Coupland, Nikolas 2003: Sociolinguistic authenticities. *Journal of Sociolinguistics* 7(3): 417–431.

Coupland, Nikolas 2007: *Style: Language, Variation and Identity*. Cambridge: Cambridge University Press.

Coupland, Nikolas (ed.) 2010: *The Handbook of Language and Globalization*. Malden, MA: Blackwell.

Crystal, David 2006: *Language and the Internet*. 2nd edition. Cambridge: Cambridge University Press.

Danet, Brenda & Susan C. Herring (eds.) 2007: *The Multilingual Internet: Language, Culture, and Communication Online*. Oxford: Oxford University Press.

Eckert, Penelope 2005: Three waves of variation study: the emergence of meaning in the study of variation. http://www.stanford.edu/~eckert/PDF/ThreeWavesofVariation.pdf.

Eckert, Penelope 2008: Variation and the indexical field. *Journal of Sociolinguistics* 12: 453–476.

Eckert, Penelope 2006: Communities of practice. *Encyclopedia of Language and Linguistics*. London/Amsterdam: Elsevier.

Faraclas, Nicholas 1996: *Nigerian Pidgin*. London: Routledge.

Gilroy, Paul 1993: *The Black Atlantic: Modernity and Double Consciousness*. Cambridge, MA: Harvard University Press.

Gut, Ulrike 2004: Nigerian English: phonology. In Bernd Kortmann and Edgar Schneider (eds.), *A Handbook of Varieties of English*, 813–830. Vol. 1. Berlin/New York: Mouton de Gruyter.

Heller, Monica 2003: Globalization, the new economy, and the commodification of language and identity. *Journal of Sociolinguistics* 7(4): 473–492.

Hinrichs, Lars 2006: *Code-Switching on the Web: English and Jamaican Creole in E-mail Communication*. Amsterdam: Benjamins.

Kachru, Braj B. 1982: *The Other Tongue: English Across Cultures*. Urbana, IL: University of Illinois Press.

Kortmann, Bernd & Edgar Schneider (eds.) 2004: *A Handbook of Varieties of English*. Berlin/ New York: Mouton de Gruyter.

McArthur, Tom 2003: World English, Euro-English, Nordic English. *English Today* 19(1): 54–58.

Mair, Christian 2003: Language, code, and symbol: the changing roles of Jamaican Creole in diaspora communities. *Arbeiten aus Anglistik und Amerikanistik* 28: 231–248.

Mair, Christian 2011: Corpora and the New Englishes: using the 'Corpus of Cyber-Jamaican' (CCJ) to explore research perspectives for the future. In Fanny Meunier, Sylvie De Cock, Gaëtanelle Gilquin and Magalie Paquot (eds.), *A Taste for Corpora: In Honour of Sylviane Granger*, 209–236. Amsterdam: Benjamins.

Mair, Christian & Stefan Pfänder 2013: Using vernacular resources to create digital spaces: towards a sociolinguistics of diasporic web forums. In Peter Auer, Martin Hilpert, Anja Stukenbrock and Benedikt Szmrecsanyi (eds.), *Space in Language and Linguistics: Geographical, Interactional, and Cognitive Perspectives*, 529–555. Berlin/New York: de Gruyter.

Mann, Chris & Fiona Stewart 2002: *Internet Communication and Qualitative Research: A Handbook for Researching Online*. London: Sage.

Mesthrie, Rajend 2006: World Englishes and the multilingual history of English. *World Englishes* 25: 381–390.

Mesthrie, Rajend & Rakesh M. Bhatt 2008: *World Englishes: The Study of New Varieties*. Cambridge: Cambridge University Press.

Meyerhoff, Miriam 2008: Community of practice. In J. K. Chambers, P. Trudgill and N. Schilling-Estes (eds.), *The Handbook of Language Variation and Change*, 526–548. Oxford: Blackwell.

Mufwene, Salikoko 2010: Series editor's foreword. In Jan Blommaert (ed.), *The Sociolinguistics of Globalization,* xi–xii. Cambridge: Cambridge University Press.

Rampton, Ben 1995: *Crossing: Language and Ethnicity Among Adolescents*. London: Longman.

Schneider, Edgar 2007: *Post-colonial English: Varieties Around the World*. Cambridge: Cambridge University Press.

Sharma, Devyani 2011: Style repertoire and social shift in British Asian English. *Journal of Sociolinguistics* 15: 464–492.

Siebenhaar, Beat 2006: Code choice and code-switching in Swiss-German Internet Relay Chat rooms. *Journal of Sociolinguistics* 10: 481–506.

Squires, Lauren 2010: Enregistering internet language. *Language in Society* 39: 457–492.

Tagliamonte, Sali & Derek Denis 2008: Linguistic ruin: Lol! Instant messaging and teen language. *American Speech* 83: 3–34.

Trudgill, Peter & Jean Hannah 1982: *International English: A Guide to Varieties of Standard English*. 1st ed. London: Arnold.

Wenger, Etienne 1998: *Communities of Practice: Learning, Meaning, and Identity*. Cambridge: Cambridge University Press.

Akinmade T. Akande
Hybridity as authenticity in Nigerian hip-hop lyrics

1 Introduction

As nobody ever wants to be accused of being fake, there is always an attempt to lay claim to authenticity in whatever one does. In everyday life, originality and creativity not only matter, they are often seen as a mark of success in everything we do. Especially crucial to popular culture generally, and hip-hop specifically, is the philosophy of 'keeping it real', which is synonymous to *authenticity*. While there is no doubt that hip-hop can be found worldwide (Krims 2000; Lee 2010), its origins can be linked to African American communities in the USA as well as to the language of these communities (i.e. African American Vernacular English). This implies that, since African American Vernacular English (AAVE) is the original language of hip-hop (Alim 2004), performing in such a code is one of the ways through which hip-hop artists in other parts of the world could express legitimacy and authenticity (see Lee 2011).

In spite of the strong connection, both in form and content, that various national hip-hops have with their African-American counterpart, Pennycook (2009: 231) has pointed out that 'it is common in many contexts to see the growth of hip-hop in local languages, the localization of English, and then a composite interplay between local, regional and global flows of languages and culture.' What Pennycook's view here seems to suggest is that authenticity is context-dependent and can vary from place to place depending on a number of factors which may include the socio-political reality and the economy of the setting as well as the mixing and re-mixing of English and indigenous languages. As will be demonstrated in this chapter, authenticity primarily involves the fusion of local and global elements, a phenomenon which Robertson (1995) has described as "glocalization". Thus, one could submit that being authentic for hip-hop artists who are non-Americans means engaging in the hybridity of both the local and the global.

In this chapter, our aim is to investigate how Nigerian hip-hop (NHH) artists perform authenticity and establish legitimacy for their brand of hip-hop. One of the arguments in this chapter is that the hybrid use of AAVE and other Nigerian languages like Nigerian Pidgin English (NPE), Yoruba, Idoma, Hausa and Igbo bestow NHH artists with originality and legitimacy. In fact, Omoniyi (2006) has described NHH as a hybrid rap that integrates NPE. Apart from the use of global and local linguistic resources as a means of performing authenticity and (re)constructing a distinct identity, another argument is that the content of NHH music often reflects the endemic social problems in the country. These problems include corruption and the use of hired assassins to get rid of political enemies coupled with the way some of them have often criticized the government on account of misrule. Depicting and representing these social problems is one important way through which hip-hop in Nigeria could be tagged authentic.

2 On the notion of authenticity

Authenticity, or *keepin' it real*, is a complex concept which does not lend itself to a fixed definition (Rose 2008). Its complexity is rooted in the fact that due to linguistic and socio-political differences of various settings, what is authentic in one setting may not be in another setting. Rose (2008: 134) says:

> ONE OF THE MOST COMMON CLAIMS heard among rappers, their corporate managers, and fans of rap music is the idea that hip hop/rap music is *"just keeping it real."* This phrase can mean many things, but generally speaking, it refers to talking openly about undesirable or hard-to-hear truths about black urban street life.

Rose's view, in a way, confirms Alim's (2004: 86) assertion that authenticity consists in not just the ability to express one's opinion freely but in 'you allegedly speakin the truth as you see it, understand, and know it to be.' Rickford and Rickford (2000: 24) remark that 'Authenticity in African American art and life is paramount. Within hip-hop circles, the mantra is "keep it real", but the same notion exists wherever black people meet ...authenticity is the highly valued sense of what is genuine' (Rickford & Rickford 2000: 4). Coupland (2003: 417), agreeing with Rickford and Rickford (2000), also notes that authenticity is not only highly valued, our lives are often monitored based on criteria like truthfulness, reality, consistency and coherence. He goes further to say that authenticity can be achieved or discredited through language as '[S]pecific ways of speaking and patterns of discursive representation can achieve the quality of experience that we define as authentic' (Coupland 2003: 417–418). For Mitchell (2003), authenticity is 'a linguistically, socially, and politically dynamic process which results in complex modes of indigenization and syncretism' while Stylianou (2010) claims that authenticity in hip-hop is achieved through 'the appropriation and adaptation of hip-hop culture to express the unique identities of new locales.'

While it is true that an important way of constructing authenticity by artistes around the world is the adoption of the linguistic features and cultural patterns of

African Americans, there are some aspects of the African American culture which, if adopted, could render hip-hop artistes outside the US inauthentic. Omoniyi (2006: 198) observes that 'Nigerian hip-hop departs significantly from mainstream norms by excluding features such as gangsta, heavy sexualization, misogyny, politics and monolingualism.' What then becomes important for artistes is not only the ability to be native even while making use of global linguistic and cultural features but also the deliberate attempt to localize these global features. As Lee (2010: 156) has noted, '[B]ehaving just like American gangsta hip hoppers is not real, but not incorporating some features from the global hip-hop scene is likewise not real.' Striking a balance in the use of the features that belong to the two worlds (i.e. the periphery and the centre) is, therefore, especially germane to non-American hip-hop artistes if they must be seen as authentic rappers. In Hess's (2005: 372) view, 'hip-hop's imperatives of authenticity are tied to its representations of African-American identity, and white rap artists negotiate their place within hip-hop culture by responding to this African-American model of authenticity.' In contrast to Hess's view, black or non-American hip-hop artistes do not necessarily have to copy the 'African-American model of authenticity' in its entirety as various national hip-hops around the world have shown that there are different models for authenticity. Finally, Akande (2012a: 109–110) claims that authenticity:

> ...could be defined in terms of being true to oneself by singing songs that reflect one's true experience and represent one's personal identity, in terms of abhorring foreign elements which manifest mainly in the style of dressing, walking and talking, and one could look at it from the perspective of language use: using local languages as opposed to a foreign one. More importantly is the expression of authenticity through a fusion of both foreign and local resources so that it becomes difficult to actually say that a particular song is completely foreign or local.

In another study, Akande (2012b) argues that 'If rappers drawing on foreign and local linguistic resources combine imitation and creative adaptation in an imaginative way, this will not undermine the authenticity of their performances. However, if language material is borrowed with insufficient understanding of its original context of use, the result may be problematical.'

3 Data analysis and discussions

The data for this study are drawn mainly from the lyrics of NHH artistes. These artistes have different ethnic, educational and religious backgrounds. For instance, while some of them are Christians, some are Muslims. In addition, there are Nigerian rap artistes who are university graduates just as we have some who dropped out of school. However, what seems to be common to all of them is the use of NPE. In most cases, they use NPE to ensure that fans outside their ethnic group understand their lyrics. The songs used here were listened to and transcribed. In the following songs, Standard English (SE) is unmarked, elements borrowed from AAVE (or Jamaican Patois) are underlined; NPE expressions are in italics and also underlined while expressions from indigenous languages are in bold fonts.

4 Content analysis of NHH lyrics: Some examples

As noted above, the authenticity of hip-hop lyrics, and by extension hip-hop artistes, could be gauged by examining how locally relevant the themes of the songs are. This means that for a rap song to be considered thematically authentic, it should reflect, at least, a social problem that could be found within the country. Many NHH artistes have demonstrated in their lyrics that they are not just very familiar with the social problems in Nigeria; they are prepared to speak out and protest against uneven distribution of wealth, corruption, assassination and injustice. I provide some songs whose themes mirror Nigerian socio-political problems.

Song 1: (Verse 3 of Eedris 'Jagajaga')

Won ti ko owo wa ja	– They have gone away with our money
NEPA, won ti di regular 419 in Nigeria	– NEPA has become regular 419 in Nigeria
Agege to Ikeja na 100 naira	– Agege ti Ikeja is N100
Fuel scarcity na popular	– Fuel scarcity is popular
Action film for Nigeria	
[Eedris, where Charles Taylor dey now?]	– He is living a flamboyant life
He dey live big life	– He is living a big life
Fine estate for Calabar	– Fine Estate in Calabar
That na Liberian mafia	– That is Liberian Mafia
For Nigeria	– In Nigeria
Everything jaga jaga	– Everything is chaotic
Everything scatter scatter	– Everything is scattered
Poor man dey suffer suffer	– Poor men are suffering
(Eedris 2004)	

In Song 1, there are references to some of the problems that characterize Nigeria as a country. Among these crises is fuel scarcity in spite of the fact that Nigeria is undoubtedly one of the biggest oil producing countries in the world. An Internet report posted on September 16, 2011 states as follows:

Nigeria produces 2.2 million gallons of oil per day, placing them 12th among producers. But they are the 4th biggest exporter, exporting 2.1 million barrels each day. Much controversy has surrounded oil production in Nigeria. Most recently Royal Dutch Shell is on the defensive following a $100 million fine imposed by a Nigerian court for a 1970 oil spill. Also, past reports show that militants have attacked pipelines and kidnapped oil employees, cutting into Nigeria's oil production. Last year, a military attack in Nigeria's Oil Delta killed up to 150 people.

http://www.therichest.org/business/highest-oil-producing-countries/

The incessant fuel scarcity often occasioned by the decision of the government to hike the price of oil products has led to loss of lives and property in the country.

This song is a protest song at its best. The first line of the song, which is rendered in Yoruba, refers to the practice of money laundering by people in power. Money laundering, although being a criminal offence in Nigeria, is very common among Nigerian politicians. What most politicians in Nigeria do when they get to power is to siphon the treasury and either save the money in foreign accounts or use it to acquire property abroad. For instance, a few months ago, a former governor of Delta State in Nigeria was jailed for thirteen years in London for offences related to corruption and money laundering. On April 17, 2012, *This Day Live* reports as follows:

The court went for a recess at about 12.30pm and reconvened at 2.25pm after which his sentence was read.

Ibori had earlier pleaded guilty to a number of corruption and money laundering charges against him put at about $250million before Judge Pitts. This includes the V-Mobile and Bombardaire scams which amounted to $50million. Ibori and Victor Attah, former Akwa Ibom state governor also formed a phantom company called ADF to siphon US$37.5million from Delta and Akwa Ibom states' shares in V-Mobile. He was accused of embezzling these funds during his tenure as governor and using most of them to live a lavish lifestyle and acquire property and assets around the world. (Italics mine)

http://www.thisdaylive.com/articles/money-laundering-uk-court-gives-ibori-13-ye-ars/113938/

Eedris also refers to the fraudulent practices of NEPA (National Electric Power Authority), which was in charge of electricity in Nigeria until 2005. NEPA was notorious for rolling out large bills to customers without any stable power supply. Sometimes, houses whose connections had been cut off for several months could still receive bills. There are cases where NEPA officials would receive bribes from individuals who did not pay their electricity bills and their houses would be spared of being disconnected.

The irony of Nigeria as reflected in the song above is that while the majority of Nigerians are languishing in poverty and cannot afford three square (or rectangular) meals daily, the government of Nigeria spent millions of naira on

Charles Taylor, a world-rate criminal. Charles Taylor, the former leader of Liberia, was given asylum under the President Olusegun Obasanjo-led administration. Eedris is simply saying that Nigeria is a country where hardened criminals could be protected and hero-worshipped. Using the expressions '*Everything jaga jaga/ everything scatter scatter/poor man dey suffer suffer*', Eedris paints a picture of a country where there is no security, a country where prices of goods skyrocket as the expression '*Agege to Ikeja na 100 naira*' meaning '*Agege to Ikeja is N100*' suggests.

Song 2 (An Extract from P-Square's 'Oga Police')

> Tell me
> *Na wetin you go do for this life*   There is nothing you will do in this life
> *Wey police no go come harass you*   That police will not harass you
> *I no know oh*   I do not know
> *Even though you be superstar*   Even if you are a superstar
> *Them go still come embarrass you*   They will still embarrass you
> Tell me
> *Na wetin you go do for this life*   There is nothing you will do in this life
> *Wey police no go come harass you*   That police will not harass you
> (P-Square 2005)

What is generally typical of the Nigerian police is the harassment of civilians. Whenever there is a quarrel between two parties, without any thorough investigation, a party which is richer can use the police to arrest and harass the one which is poor. Sometimes innocent citizens get beaten up even while conducting their lawful business. Song 2 therefore represents the typical behavior of the Nigerian police and it underscores the fact that citizens could still get arrested even when no case has been established against them.

Song 3 (Verse 2 of Timaya's 'Them Mama')

> *Na so them march dey go iyo*   That is how they marched
> Ten thousand soldiers *for road iyo*   Ten thousand soldiers on the road
> Ask them where *them dey go*   Ask them where they are going
> *Them say them dey go Bayelsa oh*   They say they are going to Bayelsa
> *Which place for Bayelsa*   Which place in Bayelsa?
> One village they call Odi oh   A village they call Odi
> *Na im them enter our village*   That is how they enter the village
> And rape our young girls
> And make us homeless oh [chai]
> *Them kill our mama iyo*   They killed our women
> *Them kill our papa iyo*   They killed our fathers

Them kill our brothers	They killed our brothers
Them kill our sisters	They killed our sisters
And make us homeless oh	
Wetin we go do iyo?	What are we going to do?
Do iyo	Do
Say do iyo	
Everybody dey cry oh	Everybody is crying oh
I say Government them bad oh	I tell you, the government is bad.
(Timaya 2007)	

The song above makes a reference to a true-life story of what happened in Odi, a town in Bayelsa State. In 1999, there was anarchy and lawlessness in Odi as some criminals were killing people and raiding the town. The lawlessness got to its peak when twelve policemen were killed by these criminals and when it became obvious that the state could no longer control the situation, the federal government under the leadership of former President Olusegun Obasanjo ordered the army to go there and restore normalcy. In an attempt to restore normalcy, the soldiers killed many people, raped hundreds of girls and women and destroyed properties worth millions of naira. Concerning this ugly incident, New York Times of October 30, 2001 entitled 'Nigeria Army Said to Massacre Hundreds of Civilians' states:

> President Obasanjo finally commented over the weekend, seeming to suggest on state television that the soldiers had acted in self-defense.
>
> "Whatever they are taught to do or not to do, soldiers fight in self-defense," he said, adding that he was not "justifying any killing."
>
> In late 1999, Mr. Obasanjo ordered hundreds of troops to Odi, a town in the Niger Delta, after 12 police officers were killed. The soldiers flattened Odi and killed many civilians. Later, Mr. Obasanjo expressed regret.
> http://www.nytimes.com/2001/10/30/world/nigeria-army-said-to-massacre-hundreds-of-civilians.html?pagewanted=all

What Timaya has done, being a member of that community (i.e., the Niger Delta community), is to reflect this real life story in his song. As we have shown above, the themes in the lyrics of most NHH artistes are issues that deal with things that are verifiable within Nigeria. A rapper who sings about events and issues happening in other countries without depicting the social, economic and political situations of his country cannot be taken to be a serious and *real* rapper. Represented in many of the NHH artistes' songs are Nigerian social realities which include corruption, politics, and harassment. As far as the contents of their lyrics are concerned, therefore, their performances are authentic and legitimate.

5 Linguistic analysis of NHH lyrics

The second major aspect of authenticity, apart from content, is the use of language. The most important concept to emphasize is the hybrid use of language
evident in the deployment of both global and local linguistic resources. As far as
the use of language is concerned, for NHH rappers to be seen as being authentic,
they must necessarily be bi/multilingual in their lyrics since they operate within
a multilingual setting. Some scholars have observed that language mixture is an
essential feature of multilingual rap music (Androutsopoulos 2010; Pennycook
2010). I propose a discussion of language use in lyrics under the following head-
ings:
a)   the adoption of pseudonyms and the use of universal tropes
b)   the use of a hybrid accent
c)   the employment of global communicative strategies
d)   the appropriation of syntactic patterns typical of AAL
e)   code-switching and the use of indigenous languages
f)   references to local places
g)   the use of slang expressions.

5.1 The adoption of pseudonyms and the use of universal tropes

An important way through which NHH artistes have demonstrated some sem-
blance and connectivity with other rap artistes around the world is the adoption
of stage names as well as the use of universal tropes in their lyrics. Like other
rap artistes elsewhere, NHH artistes bear names like Modenine, Tuface, P-Square,
Nigga Raw, Waconzy, Weird MC, Ruggedman and so on. These names are certainly
similar to names like Eminem and Tupac which are popular American rappers.
So, by adopting names similar to the names of American rappers, NHH rappers
seem to be affiliating with the universal practice within the hip-hop world and,
by so doing, stamping their practice as being real. Similarly, NHH artistes use
universal tropes (see Omoniyi 2006) like other rappers. For instance, Faze sings:

Song 4 (An Extract from Faze's 'Kolomental')

> Start to craze **eh**
> Scatter the place **eh**
> Show yourself **eh**
> All the boys **eh**
> Scatter the place **eh**

Show yourself **eh**
Show your craze for this place, kolomental
(Faze 2006)

Other universal tropes that are also commonly found in NHH lyrics are *yeah, o(h)* and *yo(h)*. Pennycook (2003) argues that the use of universal tropes is indexical in that it often indicates identification with certain cultural affiliations.

5.2 The use of a hybrid accent

A crucial aspect of language use by NHH rappers is the accent they use in their lyrics. There are some of them who sometimes sporadically imitate an American accent without having ever lived in America. Although some of these rappers do go on concert tours and short visits to the US, brief visits to America cannot guarantee a good mastery of an American accent by these rappers. The use of this 'foreign' accent questions the legitimacy of these rappers especially when it is clear that it is often difficult for them to sustain this accent for a long time without switching to their 'native' accent. Akande (2012b) observes that:

> ...the majority of Nigerians neither identify with nor fully understand songs rendered in this [American] accent. If they parade themselves as Nigerian rappers and most Nigerians do not understand them because of the accent they use, their authenticity can indeed be questioned. If they are not understood by Nigerian audience, who are they singing for then? Would Americans, whose accent the artists use, readily accept their accent as the original, authentic American accent? Certainly not. And this means that, as far as the use of accent is concerned, most of these rappers are neither here nor there.

Examples of foreign accent are numerous in the lyrics of NHH. The pronunciation of *got* as [gat] by Eedris in one of his lines '*Them say I ain't gat no game*' as well as the pronunciation of *my* as [ma] by Wizkid are good examples of the adaptation of American accent. While rappers who use foreign accents usually get criticized, those who use Nigerian accent are considered as being real and original.

The Nigerian accent is characterized by certain phonological features which include (th) and (dh) stopping, monophthongization of diphthongs, lack of distinction between the lax and tense vowels, realization of schwa as a full vowel and placement of stress on almost every syllable in words (Akande 2008; Josiah & Babatunde 2011). Omoniyi (2006: 198) reports the substitution of voiced labiodental fricative /v/ with [f] as well as the substitution of interdental fricatives /θ, ð/ with [t, d] in the lyrics of Nigerian rap artistes. Many of these features manifest in the lyrics of NHH artistes. In their songs, they often pronounce *the* and *thank* as [di] and [tank] respectively. Tuface Idibia, in *The Unstoppable*, pronounces the word *something* as [sɔmtin] in 'Something in my mind' while the word *sister* is pronounced as [sista] by Wizkid. As shown in the pronunciation of *something*, the tense vowel [i] replaces the lax vowel while the back vowel [ɔ] replaces the central vowel /ʌ/. Pronunciations like these are common in the lyrics of NHH.

5.3 The employment of global communicative strategies

In every brand of hip-hop, rappers do make use of global communicative strategies which include *call and response, narrativity, preaching, boasting* and *dissing*. While *call and response* serves the pragmatic function of inviting the listener/ hearer to join the rapper in the performance by carrying out one task or the other, boasting enables the rapper to assert 'his or her superb and many times exaggerate characteristics or abilities' (Richardson 2006:11). Dissing occurs when rappers engage in verbal wars by insulting one another (Smitherman 1997). All of these are present in NHH lyrics. For instance, when there was a quarrel between 9ice and Ruggedman some years ago, they openly insulted each other in their performance to the extent that other artistes had to mediate between the two of them. As communicative strategies of NHH artistes have been discussed elsewhere (Akande 2012a), I will just provide an example of *call and response* here.

Song 5 (Chorus in P-Square's 'Game Over')

> Put your hands up now [hands inna the air]
> My sister
> *Make we stand up now* [hands inna the air]
> *Because everything done change oh*
> *E done change oh*
> *E don spoil eh*
> *No mind them*
> *No mind them*
> *No mind them*
> Eh Eh
> (P-Square 2007)

The song above illustrates the use of *call and response* technique. In the song, P-Square invite their fans and listeners to do two things. First, they are supposed to put their hands up and secondly P-square also want their fans to stand up. In other words, the fans are indirectly invited to join the artistes by clapping and dancing. This is certainly an oral tradition through which both the artistes and the listeners are supposed to collaborate together in any performance.

5.4 The appropriation of African American vernacular English

The appropriation of AAVE by NHH artistes does not completely show that these artistes are authentic. As I have shown elsewhere (Akande 2012a, 2012b), when NHH artistes borrow elements from AAVE and Jamaican Patois (JP), they do not always have a full understanding of both the linguistic and cultural contexts of the borrowed elements. Akande (2012b) demonstrates that NHH artistes are not likely to be aware of the cultural contexts of the use of JP words like *batty, wine* and *rudeboy* which they often use freely in their music just as they might be unfamiliar with the linguistic and the social milieu that surround the use of terms like *nigga* and *booty*. At the level of grammar, the appropriation of syntactic patterns by NHH artistes becomes more complex and problematic as, in some cases, there is no neat line of demarcation between AAVE, JP and NPE. Akande (2012b) says, '[t]he **grammatical** embedding of AAVE and JP borrowings in NHH lyrics is an even more complex process – not least because the dividing line between AAVE, JP and NPE can become fuzzy at times.' First, there are syntactic features that are clearly NPE. These features include the TMA auxiliaries like *sabi*, the focus particle or copula *na* as well as the pronouns *am* and *una*. Secondly, there are syntactic features that are typical of AAVE and examples of these are the TMA marker *fiinna* and the negator *ain't* while, lastly, some syntactic features seem to be common to both codes and it is only the context that can show whether these features are used as NPE or AAVE features. Examples of these are the TMA *don(e)*, the use of *them* as the subject of a sentence and the complementizer *say*. Apart from these features, we also quickly notice *auxiliary BE deletion*, *copular BE deletion*, *habitual BE*, *intensified equative BE* and the use of *ain't* as a negator - all of which are AAVE syntactic features. However, these features are just too few out of the numerous AAVE syntactic features that scholars have identified (see Wolfram 2004). What this suggests is that the range of AAVE syntactic constructions available for borrowing is not often fully explored; thus, it could be inferred that the artistes are very selective in their use of AAVE syntactic constructions. Be this as it may, the co-existence of NPE and AAVE features and how they are usually properly blended in the lyrics demonstrate some degree of realness on the part of these artistes.

5.5 Code-switching and the use of indigenous languages

Nigeria is a country which is characterized by both linguistic and ethnic diversity. It is a country where we have three major indigenous languages (Yoruba, Hausa, Igbo) and well over three hundred 'minor' languages (see Adegbija 1994). This linguistic scenario is further made complex by the domineering roles that English plays within the linguistic polity of Nigeria. As our data and even recent works on NHH have shown (Akande 2013; Omoniyi 2006, 2009), code-switching is an essential feature of NHH lyrics. Omoniyi (2009:128) notes that '[C]ode-switching is an identity marker for the Nigerian brand within the global Hip Hop community.' And he goes further to observe that code-switching in NHH should not be narrowed down to language and communicative competence alone but it should be extended to modes of dressing, walking and patterns of behavior. As has been observed, the choice of language in hip-hop usually coincides with genre boundaries (Androutsopoulos 2010).

Apart from the use of English and NPE, NHH artistes do make use of indigenous languages in their lyrics (see Liadi and Omobowale 2011). Thus, rather than being characterized by bilingual code-switching, their music is often characterized by multilingual code-switching. NHH artistes have to freely mix several languages together in their lyrics so as to reflect the multiethnic and multilingual nature of the country.

Song 6 (A Verse in Eldee lyrics entitled 'Me I go yarn')

Me, I go yarn	I will speak out
It's time to say no	
It's time to fight	
Me, I go yarn	I will speak out
It's time to break forth	
And time to bite	
Make we yarn	Let us speak out
It's time to make advances	
It's time to get some answers	
It's time to separate this wrong from right	
Me, I go yarn	I will speak out
It's time to say no	
It's time to fight	
Me, I go yarn	I will speak out
....	....
(Eldee 2006)	

As we can see in Song 6, the codes that participate in the mixing are SE and NPE. Although the song is dominated by SE, there is a recurrent insertion of the NPE expression *Me, I go yarn*. One thing that seems to be foregrounded in the song above is syntactic parallelism which is evident in the repetition of the SPCC pattern in sentences like 'It's time to say no/It's time to fight/It's time to break forth.' This repetition is a way of getting his listeners to protest against injustice and oppression in their society.

Song 7: (D'Banj's 'Booty Call')

When we step into the party	When we step into the party
Oh they say Oh they say	
Yo, its Wande Yo its Wande	
Make una applaudise	You should applaud us
I really <u>wanna</u> see the <u>chicks</u> with bakassi	I really want to see the chicks with bakassi
Come out and play	Come out and play
With no delay	With no delay
We got to pay We got to pay	
From far away From far away	
Cos **gbogbo wa mo pe atun ti de** –	Because all of us know we have come back
Je a pade Let us meet	
Je a sere Let us play	
And you go know wetin dey today today	And you will know what is happening today
I'm calling on the booty girls	I'm calling on the booty girls
Make them come outside, come outside **yeah**	Let them come outside, come outside yeah
I'm calling on the booty girls	I'm calling on the booty girls
Make them come outside, come outside **yeah**	Let them come outside, come outside
Girl, if you love me, it's your one opportunity	Girl, if you love me, it's your one opportunity
You know, Don Jazzy got the Booty community	You know, Don Jazzy got the Booty community
Your booty is like a gift to humanity	Your booty is like a gift to humanity
That's why you got a booty immunity	That's why you got a booty immunity
(D'Banj 2008)	

In the song above, D'Banj switches between NPE, Yoruba and English. The switches are both at the intra-line and inter-sentential positions. D'Banj uses *wanna*, an informal American expression, and *chicks* (a slang expression for women) in the lyrics in order to show his affiliation with the language of global hip-hop. To further strengthen the loyalty to AAVE, he uses two universal tropes: *yo(h)* and *yeah*. The NPE expressions in the song are marked by such features as the pronoun *una*, the preverbal marker *go*, *wetin* and the reduplication of *today* as the sentence *And you **go** know **wetin** dey **today today*** illustrates. In the same vein, there are inflectional markers such as the present progressive marker *–ing* and the plural marker *–s* (as in '*I'm **calling** on the booty **girls***') and the past tense marker in *got* (as in '*That's why you **got** a booty immunity*.'); all of which are markers of SE. Lines 10 to 12 are almost completely rendered in Yoruba except for the shortened form of the English word *because*. Thus, in a song consisting of about twenty lines, D'Banj switches between three languages apart from the elements he borrows from AAVE.

5.6 References to local places

One of the ways through which authenticity is often achieved in hip-hop globally is "glocalization" (see Robertson 1995). NHH is not an exception in this respect as it makes references to both local and global names and cultural items. Sometimes, NHH artistes make references to not only Nigerian or foreign rappers but also to other dignitaries in their music. Omoniyi (2009: 132) uses the term bridging to describe how rappers in one part of the world refer to rappers in other parts of the world. He says bridging consists of 'the practice of claiming or tracing links between established artistes in one Hip Hop community and those in another community who may themselves not have declared the same publicly. This is often a periphery practice' (Omoniyi 2009: 132). As an example, Eedris in *Koleyewon* refers to three Nigerian artistes namely *Charly Boy*, *Tuface* and *Fela Anikulapo Kuti* of blessed memory and also to *50 Cent*, an American rapper. The reference to both local and foreign rappers is a way of demonstrating that he is familiar with other rappers within and outside Nigeria. This is in addition to referring to the former President Olusegun Obasanjo. Obiwon, another rapper in Nigeria, also refers to many places within Lagos in *Streets of Lagos* by referring to Lekki, Ikeja, Oshodi, Ojuelegba and Ozumba Mbadiwe street. Similarly, in *Nigerian Girls*, Modenine refers to different places when he sings:

> KD, Jos, Abuja, Lagos, Osun, Kwara
> Maidugiri, Katsina, etc, etc
> I love y'all
> Thank you for coming out
> Goodnight, muah!

A foreigner who is familiar with Lagos, Jos and Abuja will probably think that Osun and Kwara too are names of cities like Lagos, Jos, Abuja, KD (Kaduna) and Maiduguri but they are names of states and no towns in Nigeria bear the names Osun and Kwara. This is where he has effectively localized his references here. Lastly, 9ice makes reference to foreign drinks such as *hennessy*, *moet*, *baccardi* and *scordi* all of which are drinks distilled in Europe when he sings '*Everywhere weh i deh na party/Hennessy nlo, Moet nlo, Baccardi nlo/ ... /Fidi gbodi, make u shark scordi/Make ur eye dirty/From now till eternity*' [*Anywhere I am, there is a party/ We drink Hennessy, moet and Baccardi/ .../Local gin, you better drink scordi/ Let your eyes be dirty (red)/ From now till eternity*].

5.7 The use of slang expressions

Slang is very common in everyday conversations especially among adolescents and its most important quality is its instability as it changes rapidly (Thorne 1997). As common as it is, it is a term which is very difficult to define in any precise manner as its formation and use involve certain complex sociolinguistic factors (Eble 1996). Dumas and Lighter (1978: 13) say slang can be used "to name a body of lexemes that are distinct from standard English, jargon, and all other kinds of informal uses such as regionalisms and colloquialisms and which are identifiable primarily by the intent (or the perceived intent) of the speaker or writer to break with established linguistic conventions." Eble (2004: 379), who describes slang as the "deliberate alternative vocabulary that sends social signals", lists four characteristics of slang as follows: (a) it is ephemeral, (b) it is used in informal settings where spontaneous language is given priority over planned language, (c) it identifies its users with a group or an attitude and (d) slang projects a degree of irreverence or defiance toward what is proper.

Slang terms are profusely used in NHH lyrics. Although there could be some overlap, the slang they use can be classified into non-derogatory slang, swearing and derogatory slang, slang for body parts, and slang for compliments. The table below provides examples of slang from NHH lyrics.

Types	AAVE origin	Meaning	Nigerian-origin	Meaning
Non-derogatory	cool	good, nice	–	–
	dude/fella	a man	–	–
	chick	a lady	–	–
	nigga	a male or a female friend	–	–
Derogatory	motherfucka	an abusive term	múgùn/ mùmú	A fool
	(bull)shit/beef talk	rubbish, nonsense	àpà	A wasteful person
	ass-hole	an abusive term	omota	A scoundrel
Slang for body parts	booty	sizeable buttocks	ikebe/kaka/ bakassi	
	–	–	banana/bulala	Penis
Slang for compliments	–	–	kokokets	A beautiful woman
	–	–	lepa	A beautiful slim woman
	–	–	orobo	A beautiful woman who is physically huge

Table 1: Slang in NHH lyrics

Table 1 above shows that while some of the slang terms used by NHH artistes have their origin in AAVE, there are some whose origin can be traced to Nigerian languages especially Yoruba. Many of the AAVE slang expressions are used by NHH artistes exactly the way they are used in AAVE or in American hip-hop. For instance, in both NHH and American hip-hop, terms like *dude, fella* and *cool* have the same meanings and this shows that NHH artistes have mastered this slang to a large extent. However, Nigerian rappers do use local slang so as to portray their music as being both locally and globally relevant. Hybridity is thus played out in the use of slang by NHH artistes.

6 Conclusion

The major aim of this paper has been to show how NHH artistes express authenticity in their lyrics. The major argument of the paper is that hip-hop in NHH is expressed through hybridity. First of all, the paper shows that as far as the contents of their music are concerned, their music is highly authentic and real in that the themes they engage with in their lyrics are those that represent the realities in the country. Secondly, the paper reveals that their music is characterized by a combination of both local and global elements. The global elements in their music include the adoption of pseudonyms, the use of universal tropes and the employment of global discourse practices while local slang terms as well as references to local names and places serve to localize their lyrics. Lastly, the use of hybrid language which is evident in the alternation between English and indigenous languages depicts NHH lyrics as authentic.

References

Adegbija, Efurosibina 1994: Language *Attitudes in Sub-Saharan Africa: Sociolinguistic Overview*. Clevedon: Multilingual Matters.

Akande, Akinmade T. 2008: Investigating Dialectal Variation in the English of Nigerian University Graduates: Methodology and Pilot Study. *Studia Anglica Posnaniensia* 44: 431–456.

Akande, Akinmade T. 2012a: *Globalization and English in Africa: Evidence from Nigerian hip-hop*. New York: Nova Publishers.

Akande, Akinmade T. 2012b: The appropriation of African American Vernacular English and Jamaican Patois by Nigerian hip hop artists. In Véronique Lacoste and Christian Mair (eds.), *Authenticity in Creole-Speaking Contexts. Zeitschrift für Anglistik und Amerikanistik* 60, 3. Würzburg: Königshausen & Neumann.

Akande, Akinmade T. 2013: Code-switching in Nigerian hip-hop lyrics. *Language Matters: Studies in the Languages of Africa* 44(1): 39–57.

Alim, Samy H. 2004: Hip-hop Nation Language. In E. Finegan and J. Rickford (ed.), *Language in the USA: Themes for the Twenty-first Century*, 387–409. Cambridge: Cambridge University Press.

Androutsopoulos, Jannis 2010: Multilingualism, ethnicity and genre in Germany's migrant hiphop. In M. Terkourafi (ed.), *Languages of Global Hip Hop*, 19–43. London: Continuum.

Coupland, Nikolas 2003: Sociolinguistics and globalization. Special issue of *Journal of Sociolinguistics* 7(4): 465–623.

Dumas, Bethany K. & Jonathon Lighter 1978: Is slang a word for linguists? *American Speech* 53: 5–17.

Eble, Connie 1996: *Slang and Sociability: In-Group Language among College Students*. Chapel Hill, NC: University of North Carolina Press.

Eble, Connie 2004: Slang. In Edward Finegan and John R. Rickford (eds.), *Language in the USA: Themes for the Twenty-first Century*, 375–386. Cambridge: Cambridge University Press.

Hess, Mickey 2005. Hip-hop realness and the white performer. *Critical Studies in Media Communication* 22(5): 372–389.

Josiah, Ubong E. & Sola T. Babatunde 2011: Standard Nigerian English phonemes: The crisis of modelling and harmonization. *World Englishes* 30(4): 533–550.

Krims, Adam 2000: *Rap Music and the Poetics of Identity*. New York: Cambridge University Press.

Lee, Jamie S. 2010: Glocalizing keepin' it real: South Korean hip-hop playas. In Marina Terkourafi (ed.), *Languages of Global Hip Hop*, 139–161. London: Continuum.

Lee, Jamie S. 2011: Globalization of American Vernacular English in Popular Culture: Binglish in Korean Hip Hop. *English World-Wide* 32: 1–23.

Liadi, Olusegun. F. & Ayokunle O. Omobowale 2011: Music multilingualism and hip hop consumption among youths in Nigeria. *International Journal of Sociology and Anthropology* 3(12): 469- 477.

Mitchell, Tony 2003: Doin' damage in my native language: The use of 'resistance vernaculars' in hiphop in France, Italy, and Aotearoa/ New Zealand. In H. Berger and M. Carroll (eds.), *Global Pop, Local Language*, 3–17. Jackson, MS: University Press of Mississippi.

Omoniyi, Tope 2006: Hip-hop through the world Englishes lens: A response to globalization. *World Englishes* 25(2): 195–208.

Omoniyi, Tope 2009: 'So I choose to do am naija style': Hip hop, language, and postcolonial identities. In H. S. Alim, A. Ibrahim and A. Pennycook (eds.), *Global Linguistic Flows*, 113–135. New York/London: Routledge.

Pennycook, Alastair 2009: Refashioning and performing identities in global hip-hop. In N. Coupland and A. Jaworski (eds.), *The New Sociolinguistic Reader,* 326–340. New York: Palgrave.

Pennycook, Alastair 2010: Popular cultures, popular languages, and global identities. In N. Coupland (ed.), *The Handbook of Language and Globalization*, 592–607. Oxford: Blackwell.

Richardson, Elaine 2006: *Hiphop Literacies*. London: Routledge.

Rickford, John R. & Russel J. Rickford: 2000. *Spoken Soul: The Story of Black English*. New York: Wiley.

Robertson, Roland 1995: Glocalization: Time-space and Homogeneity-Heterogeneity. In Mike Featherstone et al. (eds.), *Global Modernities*, 25–44. Thousand Oaks: Sage.

Rose, Tricia 2008: *The Hip Hop Wars*. New York: Basic Civitas Books Publishers.

Smitherman, Geneva 1997: 'The chain remain the same': Communicative Practices in the Hip Hop Nation. *Journal of Black Studies* 28: 3–25.

Stylianou, Evros 2010: Keeping it Native (?): The Conflicts and Contradictions of Cypriot Hip-Hop. In Marina Terkourafi (ed.), *Languages of Global Hip Hop*, 194–222. London: Continuum.

Thorne, Tony 1997: *Dictionary of Contemporary Slang*. London: Bloomsbury.

Wolfram, Walt 2004: Urban African American Vernacular English: Morphology and Syntax. In Bernd Kortmann, Kate Burridge, Rajend Mesthrie, Edgar W. Schneider and Clive Upton (eds.), *A Handbook of Varieties of English*. Vol. 2: *Morphology and Syntax*, 319–340. Berlin/New York: Mouton de Gruyter.

Discography

Abdulkareem, Eedris. 2004. Jagajaga [Recorded by Eedris Abdulkareem]. In *Jagajaga*. Nigeria: Kennis Records.

Babatunde, Olusegun. 2007. 'Nigerian Girls' [Recorded by Modenine]. In *Nigerian Girls*. Nigeria: REDEYEMUZIK.

Dabiri, Lanre 2006. I go yarn [Recorded by Eldee]. In *Long Time Coming*. Nigeria: Trybe Records.

Odom, Enetimi Alfred. 2007. Them Mama. [Recorded by Timaya]. In *True Story*. Nigeria: Black Body Entertainment.

Oji, Chibuzor 2006. 'Tattoo Girls' [Recorded by Faze]. In *Independent*. Nigeria.

Okoye, Paul and Okoye, Peter. 2005. Oga Police. [Recorded by P-Square]. In *Get Squared*. Nigeria : Square Records.

Okoye, Paul and Okoye, Peter. 2007. Game Over [Recorded by P-Square]. In *Game Over*. Nigeria: Square Records.

Oyebanjo, Dapo Daniel. 2008. Booty Call. [Recorded by D'Banj and others]. In *Mo Hits*. Nigeria : MO' HITS Records.

Section 3:
Authenticity construction in other mediatised contexts

Florian Coulmas
Authentic writing

Writing means revealing oneself to excess.[1]
Franz Kafka

1 Introduction

While the primacy of speech is a given of modern linguistics, modern linguists base their theories on concepts that are derived from writing. *Authenticity*, for example. Already in medieval times Greek αὐθεντικός 'reliable, established' was conflated with Latin *auctor* 'originator, creator, instigator', reflecting the perceived conceptual proximity of the true and the written that remains a lexicalized topos in many European languages to this day. The fickle nature of speech has proverbially been contrasted with the more stable and hence reliable written word: *verba volant, scripta manent*. Except for linguists, people tend to regard writing as more genuine and trustworthy than speech, which is not surprising in a society that relies so much on literacy. This general attitude manifests itself in various practices and institutions some of which will be reviewed in this paper. It demonstrates that both on the individual and on the collective level writing relates to the expression, recognition and affirmation of authenticity as much as speech, if not more so.

2 Individual authenticity

First, consider individual handwriting. Its analysis is employed to establish a document's author and to determine forgery or authenticity. Graphologists have, moreover, claimed that a person's character, mental health, reliability, diet and sex, if not sexual appetite, not to mention handedness, gender and weight can be inferred from the formation, size and connectedness of their letters. They are convinced that erratic handwriting reveals an erratic personality and advise clients who suffer from low self-esteem to 'raise the crossbar on their ts'. Many employers require applicants to submit handwritten CVs for graphological analysis to

---

1 Schreiben heißt ja, sich öffnen bis zum Übermaß. Franz Kafka, Briefe an Felice, 14 January 1913.

detect flaws in their personality, discover their strengths and weaknesses and thus determine their suitability for the job. Where in this hazy terrain psychology merges with quackery is a question that may not have a clear answer, but on a more prosaic level it is generally accepted that handwriting is linked to the writer's identity. Signing all sorts of documents to demonstrate that they are ours or reflect our intentions, we reconfirm the validity of this notion on a daily basis. For instance, to be valid, a will must be signed and, in some jurisdictions, handwritten entirely by the testator. Notaries public and other professionals make a living witnessing and authenticating signatures. Only we can produce our 'real' signature.

It is worth noting, however, that the great significance attributed to the handwritten signature is indexed to contemporary Western individualistic culture. As a matter of fact, the desire for more reliable identity verification in the urban *mixophobia* in which we live (Bauman 2007: 86) in combination with technological progress concerning biometric measuring devices such as retinal photography are on the way to render the signature obsolete as a means of authentication. Legal recognition of the handwritten signature presupposes a literate populace (or social discrimination) and an established convention of signing legally binding documents. In cultures where the universe is not framed as extending from α to ω, the handwritten signature never enjoyed the importance and trust alphabetic cultures place in it. Everybody can forge a signature, whereas my personal seal cut in jade, horn or ivory only I possess. This rationale for relying on seals is the exact opposite of what lends credibility to the handwritten signature in the West. In China seal stamps in red have been the originators' authentic mark on works of art and bureaucratic documents at least since the Qin Dynasty of the third century BCE (Lurie 2011: 70). Japan was first to adjust the system of name seals to the needs of the modern state. Important business and administrative transactions require a seal which, however, must be registered at the city office to preclude any possible forgery.

These practices demonstrate how the functions and forms of writing are subject to cultural modulation; however, there are also commonalities that derive from the physical properties of the medium. Thanks to its permanence linguistic expression perceived by the eye universally accrues veneration both by the literate and, more so, the illiterate. For, wherever it emerged, writing has inevitably been associated with power. The symbolic expression of authority through writing is a feature of every literate civilization.

Writing is no child's play. It must be learnt deliberately, almost universally following the acquisition of speech. Young children are more adroit with their speech organs than with their hands. The enormously complex coordination of their lungs, larynx, pharynx, epiglottis, uvula, tongue and lips to produce their first words they seem to master, yes: naturally, at a very early age, whereas setting pen to paper takes them more time and effort, probably because evolution has not taught them to do so. Coordinating brain, language, eye and muscle movements of arm, wrist and fingers to produce a sequence of letters is as complex as producing speech sounds. Printing, from a mechanical point of view, is easy, but simulating handwriting movements by means of a computer requires algorithms as elaborate as those needed for speech synthesis. On the recognition side enough knowledge has been accumulated for various standard organisations, such as for example, the International Organization for Standardization (ISO), the American Society for Testing and Materials (ASTM), and the Deutsches Institut für Normung e.V. (DIN) to publish guidelines for the examination of handwriting. For instance, ISO 10667, entitled 'Assessment service delivery – Procedures and methods to assess people in work and organizational settings', and DIN 33430, 'Requirements for procedures and their application in job related proficiency assessment', constitute attempts to objectify psychological proficiency tests based on handwriting analysis. Another important application is for forensic purposes, as exemplified by ASTM E2290–07a, 'Standard Guide for Examination of Handwritten Items', which defines procedures for reliably reaching 'an opinion concerning whether two or more handwritten items were written by the same person(s)'.

In short, the analysis of handwritten signatures and pieces of text may reveal the author's identity at a high degree of certainty – much like spectrographic voice analysis (which is why blackmailers and extortionists prefer using letters cut from newspapers and magazines for writing their ransom notes and speak with a pencil in their mouth or use voice changer software when making ransom calls). Thus, what voice is to speech, one's hand is to writing. Linguists tend to consider both external to language. However, as Anne Karpf has demonstrated in her wonderful 2006 book, the infinitely differentiated human voice is crucially important for our ability to communicate. Handwriting, too, is minutely discerning and expressive, but whether or to what extent the individuality of one's hand is exploited for authentication is a cultural choice.

3 Style

Shakespeare's handwriting has been an object of curiosity and research since the 19th century when debate emerged over the authorship of the play *Sir Thomas More*. Ever since, the question of *Hamlet*'s and *Romeo and Juliet*'s author's identity has intrigued legions of scholars eager to establish beyond doubt whether or not the great bard from Stratford on Avon was the author of a given poem or play. On the whole, those who occupy themselves with questionable authorship study style rather than handwriting, coming closer to what linguists consider their proper territory (Ravassat, and Culpeper 2011). The fascination with forgery is many-facetted, both on the part of those who get a kick out of passing their products off as someone else's and those bent on revealing a fake as what it is. It isn't necessarily the promise of material profit or fame that motivates counterfeiters, fooling the experts may be just as strong an impulse (Whitehead 1973). In any event, for those interested in deception, literature and scholarship are vast fields[2] to plough by historians, philologists and linguists alike (Grafton 1990). This field is not really of our concern here, except that the furrows are lines of text. It is also worth noting that notions of what is and what isn't authentic, real, true, original or, in the contrary, fake, counterfeit and make-believe are not universal, but subject to variable historical and cultural understanding.

In the Western world of letters individuality of style is highly valued, and it is expected that writers differ not just in what they compose, but also in how they do it. A rather consequential case of stylistic identity involves the apprehension in 1996 of the mathematical genius gone astray and murderer Theodore Kaczynski. To express his misgivings about the abuse of technology in modern society he started bombing universities and airlines in the 1980s. During a protracted investigation he was therefore known as the Unabomber. Threatening more bombs, he forced the publication of his manifesto 'Industrial Society and Its Future' – which gave him away. His brother recognized his style of writing and linguistic analysis comparing some of Kaczynski's earlier texts with the manifesto determined that he was most probably its author (Chase 2003).

In the meantime technological innovations have led to the development of powerful data processing tools triggering a surge in quantitative studies in linguistics. Corpus linguistics, that is, the study of linguistic phenomena on the basis of large collections of machine-readable texts, has attracted scholarly attention. Huge corpora of written text are available and can be subjected to lexical and structural frequency analyses, compared to each other, searched for specific features, such as length of phrases and sentences, vocabulary range, type-to-ken relations, spelling consistency and variation, etc., on a scale impossible by manual count (e.g., Michel et al. 2010). As might be expected, forensic linguistics is one of the fields where these tools are put to use, for 'linguistic fingerprinting' (Coulthard 2004), as it were, that is, author identification.

A relatively new application of quantitative stylistic analysis is in the area of plagiarism detection. It is based on two ideas. The first is that every writer has his or her unique style which is unlike any other. The second is that using another's

---

2 Cf. e.g., the Forgeries Bibliography at http://www.bibliopath.com/forgebib.html

text or a portion thereof without properly attributing it to its originator is reprehensible. Both depend on a notion of language that is grounded in writing. In oral culture, if other speakers' messages are reported, it is what they meant rather than what they said. Verbatim rendition is a literate practice that presupposes a self-contained immutable original in the sense of a unique form, the kind of language manifestation writing affords. That such a form should not be reproduced or reused at discretion in a different context is a relatively new concept that evolved in conjunction with the integration of intellectual property rights into codified law, which as the term 'copyright' suggests, first referred to the right to copy text.

Shakespeare Apocrypha is a collection of texts that have been attributed to, but not proven beyond doubt to be by, Shakespeare. Its existence is testimony to the fact that intellectual property rights are a modern phenomenon that evolved together with ever more complex judicial systems. *Pericles, Prince of Tyre* is a play first published in 1609 under Shakespeare's name. Literary scholarship has raised doubts about its authenticity, arguing on stylistic grounds that a disciple or collaborator of Shakespeare's, George Wilkins, perhaps, must have penned the first two acts. At the time, no one seems to have cared much. For one thing, plays were a spectacle meant to be watched and listened to rather than read, and they were presented to a particular audience the stage director and the actors may take into account in one way or another. The many surviving versions of Shakespeare's plays that keep a cottage industry of literature detectives gainfully employed suggest that adjustments were often made, and that the difference between the one and only authentic original and more or less corrupted copies was then less important than it now is. This notion is a spin-off from mechanical reproduction technology, the printing press, in particular, and it is interesting to see that in the wake of a new reproduction technology the very idea of intellectual property is coming under attack by Internet freebooters. Copy-and-paste and world-wide posting at a mouse click change conditions of ownership leading to a re-evaluation of knowledge and other intangible things as public goods of which no one can claim proprietorship.

'The exact same phrase' is a notion born by the literate mind. In speech we are less likely to repeat 'literally' the same words we or others said before, and in the event that it does happen it is likely on the basis of a written text. In Shakespeare's day collections of standard epithets and commonplaces were widely used, and some of his best known poems just pile one upon the other. Repeating phrases that had been used before was not disreputable. But in Renaissance Europe when the printing press had just started to move, the management of knowledge and information was not what it is today. As Ong perceptively put it a generation ago,

'Information could not be codified so neatly as it can in our superindexed books and super-catalogued libraries and superprogrammed electronic computers' (Ong 1977: 187).

The gist of Ong's argument is that the way we *see* language profoundly affects our conception of language. If someone said what I said, no: wrote above, 'The notion [of the original] is a spin-off from mechanical reproduction technology', I wouldn't take him to court. Or suppose, to carry this a little bit further, someone said, 'the notion is a spin-off'. It would be rather absurd for me to say, 'hey, wait a second, if you want to say that you should give me credit because I said it first.' But students who lift the sentence from this text and put it into their term paper without attribution may get into trouble, because technology makes it so easy to detect the self-same phrase and because the same technology has taught us that 'the written word is the authorized version, the authenticated truth' (Illich & Sanders 1988: 90) that has an owner. I must say 'may' because it is not self-evident when recycling constitutes plagiarism. It is convention and legal definition that draw a line where no line naturally exists.

4 Collective authenticity

Turning to the collective aspects of the nexus between writing and authenticity, we can once again start with handwriting. A French, Spanish or English hand can be identified as such not just because their respective alphabets include distinctive letters such as **Ç**, **Ñ**, etc., but also because teaching methods and models of the form and slant of letters, letter proportion, starting and stopping points of letters, ligatures, etc. differ from one country to another. Just as children acquire the speech variety spoken around them they learn the movements that produce the characteristic features of their community's handwriting. And, while the way they write individual characters and how they connect them to form words is structurally similar, every person still has a distinctive hand. Much like a national language, a national script exhibits many common features shared by the community of users at large which, however, within a range of possible variation are individually shaped. As a result the relationship that obtains between national script and individual handwriting is analogous to that between language and idiolect.

Handwriting styles, such as, French book hand, English chancery style and Italian legal cursive have been national long before the advent of the modern nation state, and even in current word processing software fonts such as 𝒮𝒸𝓇𝒾𝓅𝓉, *Italic*, and 𝔒𝔩𝔡 𝔈𝔫𝔤𝔩𝔦𝔰𝔥 𝔗𝔢𝔵𝔱 bear witness to the emblematic nature of scripts and their use as indices of national graphic identity. Over the past two decades, great advances have been made in developing handwriting recognition technology which is very elaborate now and commercially available for many languages. Country specific prototypes of letters, their frequencies, sequences, and ligatures have been integral parts of handwriting recognition engines from the beginning. I mention this here just in passing to emphasize the fact that handwriting systems combine collective with individual dimensions.

Beyond the shape of handwritten characters and printed fonts norms and spelling conventions are for many a matter of symbolic significance and emotional attachment. 'In nineteenth and twentieth century schools spelling was framed in terms of character formation, morality and national pride and distinction' (Coulmas 2013: 108). For instance, American nationalist Noah Webster considered a spelling system that diverged from the British as important as a national flag and anthem. Accordingly, his *American Spelling Book* included a moral catechism and a patriotic catechism. Almost two centuries later a minor German spelling reform enraged large parts of the German public including leading writers and hundreds of other opinion leaders who signed the *Frankfurter Appell* calling to rescind it in the name of 'democratic culture'. The ultimate decline of the German language seemed imminent because of a few modified rules that basically changed nothing. But no matter how trivial a reform, tinkering with what people have learnt, many at great pains, in early childhood is rarely welcomed and more likely to be perceived as desecration of a hallowed tradition. Defenders of the established and time-tested never have problems mobilizing scientific experts who prove beyond any reasonable doubt not just that the traditional is best but that the proposed changes will bring ruin to the language and undermine the mental health of the nation. Irrespective of the technical merits of any particular spelling reform it is remarkable how much importance people attach to the written form of their language. Writing language X without character Y or rule Z is not really X because, as Sebba (2007) illustrates with many examples, orthography is a very salient marker of identity. The fact that in Switzerland German is written without the ligature ß (derived from s and z and accordingly called 'esszett') in place of which **ss** is used without causing any confusion cannot convince traditionalists to do away with the esszett for one and only one reason: It is distinctly German. However, since in our age and day nationalism is not highly regarded, linguistic arguments for keeping the flag-bearing letter are put forth.

The irrationality of debates about spelling and writing reforms – for more examples see my above quoted book – can only be explained if the emblematic as opposed to the functional aspects of writing and the ideological scaffolding built around them are taken into consideration. It is the rare exception that spelling reforms are dealt with dispassionately as mere technicalities by their writing communities, for practical utility tends to be overshadowed by emblematic significance. Traulsen discusses the 'linguistic- nationalistic dimension' of Korean writing pointing out that 'it was the Korean alphabet that served best for a national-linguistic self-esteem' (Traulsen 2012: 104). Simple, beautiful and suitable for the Korean language, it was first promulgated in 1443, intended as a system for 'enlightening the people'. However, at the time it was opposed by the literate elite and neglected for centuries, because it was so easy that it could be learnt in a day and would thus undermine the value of the traditional Chinese script which took years to master. It was only when, early in the 20th century, Japan where Chinese characters were also used occupied Korea, that Koreans embraced the Korean alphabet, now called *Hangul* ('great script'), as a symbol of identity and opposition to Japanese rule (Rhee 1992).

Functionality is often of secondary importance at best where writing reforms are promoted or resisted. At the periphery of the Sinocentric world the Chinese script was adapted to local languages, Vietnamese, Korean and Japanese. While Chinese characters are ill-suited for the latter two, both of which are agglutinating languages and typologically very different from isolating Chinese, Vietnamese, being typologically very similar to Chinese, can be written with Chinese characters more easily. Yet, the desire to modernize and resist Chinese domination of Vietnamese culture led Vietnamese reformers early in the 20th century to adopt a Romanised orthography originally designed by French missionaries. That China, Vietnam's donor culture for centuries, had fallen into discredit for its weakness in the face of Western aggression was another factor in favour of Romanisation.

Spelling reforms and script reforms arouse emotions because, in modern societies, they concern everyone and compel even the educated to relearn, especially script reforms which have more far-reaching implications for the community's intellectual infrastructure than a few altered spelling rules. The results of spelling reforms cannot be overlooked or ignored, because there is much less leeway in writing than in speech for people to use the language as they please. Industrial society is characterized among other things by the omnipresence of standards, orthographies being a paradigm case. By regulating a kind of behaviour authoritatively and uncompromisingly they create a community bond that can be ignored only at the peril of being excluded. In the literal and in the metaphorical sense, orthographies are part of the linguistic landscape and therefore, not surprisingly, closely tied to collective identity. In any event, the question with whom a community wants to align itself culturally and politically plays an important role. Fereydoun Safizadeh (quoted in Hatcher 2008: 105) asks, for example, 'how can you speak about the identity of a people whose alphabet has been changed four times in the last seventy-five years?' Alluding to Le Page and Tabouret-Keller's (1985) work on creating group affiliations, Hatcher in a paper entitled 'Script change in Azerbaijan: acts of identity' notes, 'as people choose which script to use in writing their language, they are visibly projecting an identity [...], choosing to claim an identity based on factors similar to those linked with choices of spoken languages, such as ethnicity, nationality, religion, level of education, etc.' (Hatcher 2008: 105).

What is or isn't authentic X-ish can always be turned into scholarly dispute about roots, patrimony, heritage, etc., and this holds equally for lexicon, grammar and pronunciation. However, what makes the written form of a language, its writing system and its orthography, particularly serviceable for such designs is that it is visible everywhere and that it can be prescribed. To enforce a standard pronunciation is more difficult than imposing an orthographic norm. By penalizing non-standard spellings compulsory education works as a powerful authority and norm-enforcing agency, producing an output of users who rarely have reason to reflect on the validity and rationality of the system they were taught to take and respect as the correct form of their language rather than one among several conceivable varieties. What is more, in contradistinction to co-existing dialects, there is typically just one written norm of the national language, unification being the very point of establishing a norm. It should be remembered, however, that this is a modern phenomenon which may be on its way out again already. Just a couple of centuries ago much more variation in spelling was quite common, and the availability of spellcheck software has softened the rigidity of 19th century precepts about orthographic norms. Word-processing software for English, French, Spanish, German, Portuguese, Chinese and a host of other languages come with several alternative spellcheckers manifesting the variable and in this sense arbitrary nature of spelling conventions to everyone.

Yet, the evident possibility of choice does not weaken emotional attachments or the potential to serve as an emblem of collective identity, quite the contrary. In some cases different writing conventions brought about by reforms that were implemented in parts of the language area only quickly became markers of identity and affiliation, e.g., China vs. Taiwan and Rumania vs. Moldavia. In other cases the absence of a unified spelling standard was seen or continues to be seen as an obstacle to claiming language status, as for instance, for Flemish, as distinct from Dutch (Willemyns 2003) and Valencian, as distinct from Catalan (Lledó 2011). To most people other than linguists it is a matter of course that their language is written in its proper script which they consider an integral part of it rather than an exchangeable form, assuming, quite correctly and not just because they cannot read any other, a substantial rather than a superficial relationship between their language and its writing system.

Lay theories (folk beliefs) are in agreement across linguistic and cultural borders in this regard: My language transcribed in a system other than its proper script is not my language. Even if it is just the shape of the characters that is different, while their phonetic interpretation and sequencing can be largely isomorphic, as between Greek, Cyrillic and Roman letters, a transfer is not acceptable. Greek in Latin script is not authentic to most Greeks today, and wasn't in earlier times when, for example, medieval scribes character-switched, recording Greek quotes in Latin manuscripts in *ipsae authenticae litterae* (Pelttari 2011). This seemed the proper thing to do, as for the reader a change of script most obviously indicated a change of language. The identification of both is still a matter of course to many speakers today who believe not just that language X should not be written with anything but the X-script, but that it would be outright impossible to do so.

ιτ ισ εασι το ρεκογνιζε θισ ασ ενγλισ, βυτ μανι ωιλλ νοτ αξεπτ ιτ ασ αυθεντικ.[3]

In linguistics this problem is often brushed aside as, fortunately, we have an objective instrument for the description of languages at our disposal, IPA, or so it seems. However, the underlying assumption is not different in principle from imposing a Western perspective as objective and universal, for example, on the reading of the history or the analysis of the social structure of non-Western nations. To avert any misunderstanding: This is not to argue the case of unqualified relativism, but just a plea to recall that IPA is an offshoot of the Latin alphabet rather than the other way around, with which, moreover, Western linguists have been socialized from early childhood and which can, therefore, be assumed to have an influence on the way they see language.

	Tones	
1. level *(không dấu)*	a ă â e ê i o ô ơ u ư y	ma [mā] = ghost
2. high rising *(dấu sắc)*	á ắ ấ é ế í ó ố ớ ú ứ ý	má [má] = cheek
3. low/falling *(dấu huyền)*	à ằ ầ è ề ì ò ồ ờ ù ừ ỳ	mà [mà] = but
4. dipping-rising *(dấu hỏi)*	ả ẳ ẩ ẻ ể ỉ ỏ ổ ở ủ ử ỷ	mả [mả] = tomb
5. high rising glottalized *(dấu ngã)*	ã ẵ ẫ ẽ ễ ĩ õ ỗ ỡ ũ ữ ỹ	mã [má] = horse
6. low glottalized *(dấu nặng)*	ạ ặ ậ ẹ ệ ị ọ ộ ợ ụ ự ỵ	mạ [mà] = rice seedling

Table 1: Diacritics for Vietnamese vowel letters

For an illustration of how ill-suited the Latin alphabet is for many languages consider the paucity of vowel letters that for writing Vietnamese necessitates dozens

---

3 It is easy to recognize this as English, but many will not accept it as authentic.

of diacritics (Table 1) because the Latin alphabet, derived from its Semitic origin and adapted to Indo-European languages, does not provide for the phonological dimension of tone that characterises many Asian languages. Writing systems, including the Roman alphabet, came into existence in the context of particular languages and reflect some of their features, adapted and expanded to others though they may be. Keeping this in mind, the lay theory that the writing system is a subsystem of the language is less implausible than the lack of attention to writing in linguistics textbooks suggests.

In some linguistic traditions the conceptual association of language and writing is particularly strong as, for instance, in Arabic. According to Baalbaki (2008), the oldest systematic description of the (written) language, al-Kilab by Sibawayh's (born ca. 760 CE), which he calls 'the first unequally authentic Arabic grammar', became a repository of the DNA of the nation; never mind that Sibawayh was Persian. Metaphors are patient.

As the above example may illustrate, writing systems, scripts, orthographies and even fonts serve powerful emblematic functions reminding us, as all of these are artefacts, that the authentic is constructed and can be enlisted for purposes of the individuation of languages, identity, uniqueness and distinctiveness at will.

5 Epics and myths

The metaphor of language as 'the DNA of a nation' is a contemporary reformulation of an idea made popular in Europe by the Romantic movement of the late eighteenth century. Its preeminent representative was the German philosopher Johann Gottfried Herder (1744–1803) who, under the impression of the domineering role of French as the preferred language of the German intellectual elite and the lack of political unity of German principalities at the time, elevated linguistic heritage to the principal badge of nationality. After his seminal essay 'On the Origin of Language' (1772), the notion that a language is the repository of national character became accepted wisdom among philologists, philosophers and lay people alike. Wilhem von Humboldt wrote extensively about the diversity of human languages and their function for attaining a worldview. He maintained that 'language is the formative organ of thought' (Humboldt 1988: 54), a view that implies that if languages differ the ways of thinking of their speakers would also differ. Transposed to the political level this idea served as the foundation of linguistic nationalism, an ideology insisting that political boundaries should coincide with linguistic boundaries. In the 19th century it swept through Europe first to be subsequently embraced in other parts of the world, too.

Romantic nationalism paved the way for ethnic-based solidarity and the idealization of the monolingual state which posed a counter model and a threat to the great multilingual empires of the Ottomans, the Hapsburgs and the Romanovs. In the process of awakening national consciousness language played an important role, especially as embodied by national epics that could be cited as witness to authenticity and claims to independence whenever useful. Both civic (e.g., France) and ethnic (e.g., Sweden) models of national identity made use of this device (Oakes 2001), as in the course of the 19th century many new nation states were born (Kloss 1967).

Harking back to the past, to the authentic language of the nation, is 'a powerful source of legitimacy for those who would change the present for a new future' (McCrone 1998: 52). A paradigm case is the renewed attention bestowed on the Iliad and Odyssey during the Greek War of Independence which also saw the emergence of an archaizing variety of Greek that was cleansed of the corrupting influence of foreign loan vocabulary, mainly Turkish and Arabic, that had entered the language during four hundred years of Ottoman rule. Katharevousa, the 'pure', was promoted as genuine Greek and codified by philologist Adamantios Korais whose knowledge of authentic Greek in the sense of the language actually spoken by the people was however limited, as he spent most of his adult life in Paris; but that was of secondary importance. What counted was a credible myth of authenticity. Needless to say, the sources Korais drew on as models for the Katharevousa were exclusively written.

In other cases this was not so obvious. In Germany, much in the spirit of Herderian Romantic nationalism, Jacob and Wilhelm Grimm set out as young men to collect fairy tales that were portrayed as representing the wisdom, fears and aspirations of the common people handed down orally from the distant past. As a matter of fact, however, the brothers did what editors do, cleansing their material of unnecessary stuff and pressing it into a format that suited their purpose. It is worth noting in passing that the same Grimm brothers erected what was meant to be a monument to the German language, the most comprehensive dictionary, which consists of quotes of (non-contemporary) literary works entirely: The treasure of the authentic language that tells us '"whence we came" which is central to the definition of "who we are"' (McCrone 1998: 53).

Another 19th century example is the Kalavala, a collection of Finnish verse compiled by Elias Lönnrot, which came to be regarded as the national epic of Finland and is thought to have propped up the Finns' sense of nationality that resulted in independence from Russia. Many other 'national epics' came into existence in that century, hailed as embodying the nation's authentic heritage and thus serving to express, claim, or consolidate a speech community's national aspirations. Beowulf (8th to 11th century), the Niebelungenlied (11th century), the

Song of Roland (12th century), the Divine Comedy (14th century), Don Quixote of La Mancha (1605/1613) were known as great literary works previously; in the 19th century they became national epics and their authors, if known, national heroes: Dante Alighieri, *il padre della lingua italiana*, for example. The language of national epics was said to be rooted in and giving expression to the genius of a people, representing the best of its intellectual heritage.

Ethnicity-based solidarity as the foundation of political boundaries and organisation presupposes a pre-existing clearly delimited language, the natural fountain of nationhood, as it were. Yet, in the event, naturalness and authenticity were not quite what they were said to be. Authentic language, real French, Italian, Greek, etc. would be as people speak under 'normal' circumstances, unguarded, not deliberately observing their pronunciation or grammar, in a word: unedited. This kind of authentic speech is virtually never seen in print and hence cannot be put in the service of ideology. The authenticity that was needed was created – by writers and grammarians. Before the fairy tales were published they had to be made palpable to the reader whose communication needs differ in many ways from those of the listener. The 'nation-forming power of language' asserted by Dominian (1917, quoted by Fishman 1972: 50) could be realised only through the medium of what Anderson (1983) called 'print-language'. The advance of literacy aided by a unified educational system taught people what their languages were and weren't (dialects, for instance, which might suggest fuzzy criteria of belong-ingness), turning them into markers of authenticity defining boundaries that were conceptually as hard to cross as were casts in India's rigid social hierarchy or religions in communities anchored in faith. The epics that were recruited as witnesses to nationhood were, of course, written works.

Because of the ephemeral nature of speech it is very difficult if not impossible to assert and verify linguistic authenticity without writing. Where nowadays 'cul-tural and/or linguistic authenticity' is advocated for purposes of education, espe-cially in multicultural societies and in foreign language classrooms (cf., Kilickaya 2004 for some references) this is still true.

6 Coda

Authenticity in language is a protean notion, used in different ways in schol-arly and ideological contexts. Both are not always distinct. How it functions and impacts the behaviour of social groups and individuals are, therefore, questions that cannot be answered without considering social processes. Authenticity, rather than being a naturally given quality, is a means whereby communities shape their identities in an active fashioning. Language serves as an important instrument to this end, that is, the individuation of languages which, as I have tried to demonstrate here, is hard to conceive without taking writing into consideration. Both on the micro level of individual skills and on the macro level of collective decisions and possessions script, spelling, written style, and literary heritage hold the potential of exhibiting authentic language. Rather than being a representation of speech, in whatever vague sense, it is a model that, not just in literate societies, shapes people's perception of languages and what they consider authentic.

References

Anderson, Benedict 1983: *Imagined Communities. Reflections on the Origin and Spread of Nationalism.* London: Verso.

ASTM E2290–07a: Standard Guide for Examination of Handwritten Items. http://www.astm.org/Standards/E2290.htm

Baalbaki, Ramzi 2008: *The Legacy of the Kilab: Sibawayhi's Analytical Methods Within the Context of the Arabic Grammatical Theory.* Studies in Semitic Languages and Linguistics, 51. Leiden: Brill.

Bauman, Zygmunt 2007: *Liquid Times. Living in an Age of Uncertainty.* Cambridge: Polity Press.

Chase, Alsoton 2003: *Harvard and the Unabomber: the Education of an American Terrorist.* New York: W.W. Norton.

Coulmas, Florian 2013: *Writing and Society.* Cambridge: Cambridge University Press.

Coulthard, Malcom 2004: Author identification, idiolect and linguistic uniqueness. *Applied Linguistics* 25: 431–447.

Dominian, Leon 1917: *The Frontiers of Language and Nationality in Europe.* New York: Holt.

DIN 33430: Requirements for procedures and their application in job related proficiency assessment. http://www.nadl.din.de/cmd?artid=51198265&contextid=nadl&bcrumblevel=1&subcommittee id=117160658&level=tpl-art-detailansicht&committeeid=117152656&languageid=en

Frankfurter Appell 2004: http://www.schriftdeutsch.de/orth-a11.htm

Grafton, Anthony 1990: *Forgers and Critics: Creativity and Duplicity in Western Scholarship.* Princeton: Princeton University Press.

Hatcher, Lynley 2008: Script change in Azerbaijan: acts of identity. *International Journal of the Sociology of Language* 2008(192): 105–116.

Herder, Johann Gottfried 1772: Über den Ursprung der Sprache [Treatise on the origin of language. *Johann Gottfried Herder, Philosophical Writings*, translated and edited by M.N. Forster, 65–165. Cambridge: Cambridge University Press, 2002].

Humboldt, Wilhelm von 1988 (1836): *Über die Verschiedenheit des menschlichen Sprachbaues und ihren Einfluß auf die geistige Entwicklung des Menschengeschlechts.* Paderborn: Schöningh [*On Language. The Diversity of Human Language Structure and its Influence on the Mental Development of Mankind*, translated by Peter Heath. Cambridge: Cambridge University Press, 1988.]

Illich, Ivan & Barry Sanders 1988: *The Alphabetization of the Popular Mind.* San Francisco: North Point Press.

ISO 10667–1:2011: Assessment service delivery – Procedures and methods to assess people in work and organizational settings. (http://www.iso.org/iso/catalogue_detail. htm?csnumber=56441)

Karpf, Anne 2006: *The Human Voice. The story of a Remarkable Talent*. London: Bloomsbury.

Kilickaya, Ferit 2004: Authentic materials and cultural content in EFL classrooms. *The Internet TESL Journal, Vol. X, No. 7,* http://iteslj.org/Techniques/Kilickaya-AutenticMaterial.html

Kloss, Heinz 1967: 'Abstand languages' and 'Ausbau languages'. *Anthropological Linguistics* 9(7): 29–41.

Lledó, Miquel Àngel 2011: The independent standardization of Valencian: From official use to underground resistance. In J.A. Fishman and O. Garcia (eds.), *Handbook of Language and Ethnic Identity, Vol. 2*, 336–348. New York: Oxford University Press.

Lurie, David B. 2011: *Realm of Literacy. Early Japan and the History of Writing*. Cambridge, MA: Harvard University Press.

McCrone, David 1998: *The Sociology of Nationalism*. London/New York: Routledge.

Michel, Jean-Baptiste et al. 2010: Quantitative Analysis of Culture Using Millions of Digitalized Books. www.sciencexpress.org / 16 December 2010 / Page 1 / 10.1126/science.1199644

Oakes, Leigh 2001: *Language and National Identity. Comparing France and Sweden*. Amsterdam: John Benjamins.

Ong,Walter J. 1977: *Interfaces of the Word. Studies in the Evolution of Consciousness and Culture*. London: Cornell University Press.

Pelttari, Aaron 2011: Approaches to the writing of Greek in Late Antique Latin Texts. *Greek, Roman, and Byzantine Studies* 51: 461–482

Ravassat, Mireille & Jonathan Culpeper 2011: *Stylistics and Shakespeare: Transdisciplinary Approaches*. London: Continuum

Rhee, M.J. 1992: Language planning in Korea under the Japanese colonial administration, 1910-1945. *Language Culture and Curriculum* 5: 87–97

Schmid, Peter F. 2001: Authenticity: The person as his or her own author. *Dialogical and Ethical Perspectives on Therapy as an Encounter Relationship. And Beyond*. In Gill *Wyatt* (ed.), *Congruence*, 217–232. Ross-on-Wye: PCCS Books.

Sebba, Mark 2007: *Spelling and Society: The Culture and Politics of Orthography Around the World*. Cambridge/New York: Cambridge University Press.

Traulsen, Thorsten 2012: Han'gŭl reform movement in the twentieth century. Roman pressure on Korean writing. In Alex de Voogt and Joachim Friedrich Quack (eds.), *The Idea of Writing. Writing across borders*, 103–130. Leiden: Brill.

Whitehead, John 1973: *This Solemn Mockery: The Art of Literary Forgery*. London: Arlington Books.

Willemyns, Roland 2003: *Het verhaal van het Vlaams – De geschiedenis van het Nederlands in de Zuidelijke Nederlanden*. Antwerpen: Standaard Uitgeverij.

Anna Kristina Hultgren

Lexical variation at the internationalized university: Are indexicality and authenticity always relevant?[1]

1 Introduction

When people communicate they convey meaning on more than one level. They exchange information (transactional/referential meaning) and they negotiate social relationships (interactional/social meaning) (Brown & Yule 1983; Lakoff 1989; Kasper 1990). Thus, when a lecturer in computer science at a Danish university chooses the term *regular expressions* over the co-existing Danish equivalent *regulære udtryk*, they not only inform students of the topic of the class, their choice may also be socially meaningful – it may have indexical value. As social meaning is multiple, variable and contextually contingent, it cannot be established *a priori* of careful contextual analysis. Thus, in choosing the English over the Danish lexical variant in the example above, the lecturer may try to signal that they are cosmopolitan, trendy and globally-oriented, but they may well be perceived by hearers as being pretentious, uncultivated or even ridiculous. Or possibly, as I shall argue in this chapter, their choice may not be associated first and foremost with any social meaning at all. While both referential and social meanings co-exist in any given utterance, it is probably fair to say that most linguistic scholars (pragmaticians, linguistic anthropologists and sociolinguists, e.g. Wilson & Smith 1992; Silverstein 2003; Eckert 2008) have been primarily interested in social meaning, perhaps perceiving of the other as too self-evident or uninteresting to warrant any serious scholarly attention.

In this chapter, I shall make a case for keeping referential meaning firmly within the analytic and theoretical toolkit of linguists of all sub-disciplines. I shall base this argument on qualitative data in the form of English/Danish lexical variation in the scientific vocabulary of Computer Science, Chemistry and Physics

---

1 The author wishes to thank the organizers and the participants of the conference "Indexing Authenticity: Perspectives from linguistics and anthropology" held in Freiburg, 25th–27th of November 2011, for their feedback on an oral version of this paper. The Danish Research Council for Independent Research (grant number 09–070588) is gratefully acknowledged for financial support and the research participants who gave so generously of their time are warmly thanked.

in spoken Danish. Because English is widely used as an international language of science (Ammon 2001), many scientific terms, especially in the relatively recent discipline Computer Science, exist only in English, or in both English and Danish. When there is a choice between an English and a Danish lexical variant, current theory on indexicality would assume that the choice is socially meaningful. While this is certainly corroborated by my data, it does not appear to account for what goes on in all cases. More specifically, I shall show that when asked about their rationale for choosing a Danish over an English term or vice versa, the scientists themselves seem to place greater emphasis on referential meaning (specifically, communicative efficiency) than social meaning. I shall suggest that this may be explained by two factors: 1) that the goal-orientedness (Drew & Heritage 1992) of the type of talk that is focused on here (institutional talk) inherently prioritizes referential over social meaning, and 2) that the epistemological orientation of this chapter, which accords greater significance to participants' own interpretations of their language use than to those of the analyst, also entails that greater priority is assigned to referential than social meaning.

Having first provided an account of the theoretical and socio-cultural context of the study, I shall describe my data and methodology, making an important distinction between emic (insider) and etic (outsider) perspectives. I shall then proceed to test my data on the current theory of indexicality. The main part of this section will be devoted to showing how the theory is well-suited to account for a considerable proportion of the data. This shall be followed by a shorter section providing some examples which do not seem to fit into the current theoretical framework. This imbalance is deliberately intended so as not to deny the significance of social meaning but to take on the role of the devil's advocate and point out some examples which do not first and foremost seem to be captured by an explanation in terms of social meaning. I shall consider some possible explanations for why these examples do not fit the theory before I go on, in the conclusion, to ask whether a theory of indexicality should be able to account also for cases in which the choice between two linguistic variants may not primarily be socially motivated.

2 Theoretical background

2.1 A state of the art of the theory of indexicality

In the early days of modern sociolinguistics, scholars were typically concerned with correlating linguistic variables with demographic variables (see Figure 1).[2] Thus, in Labov's (1966) classic New York department store study, the linguistic variable postvocalic rhoticity was correlated with the demographic variables class and socio-economic status of the speaker. Since the early 2000s, however, there has been a consolidated theoretical move away from such direct correlations between linguistic and demographic variables to a more indirect correlation, instigated jointly by variationist sociolinguists and anthropological linguists: "Variables index demographic categories not directly but indirectly (Silverstein 1985), through their association with qualities and stances that enter into the construction of categories" (Eckert 2008: 455). Such associated meanings are referred to in different ways, e.g. as qualities, stances (Eckert 2008) or attributes (Agha 2005), but here I shall use the term *associated meaning* because it is broader and allows for an interpretation of meaning that does not necessarily have anything to do with speaker qualities, stances or attributes, which I shall demonstrate later on. First, though, to illustrate more concretely the theoretical reorientation from demographic variables to associated meanings, I shall use the example of the speech style prescribed to call centre agents.

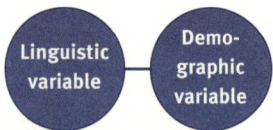

Figure 1: The semantic relationship between linguistic and demographic variables in early sociolinguistics

The speech style which call centre agents are instructed (by their managers and in communication training courses) to use in their interaction with customers has

---

2 Where variationist sociolinguists and some linguistic anthropologists typically work with a restricted set of variants for each variable given their focus on phonological, lexical or morphosyntactic variation, I include in this category also pragmaticians and discourse analysts who work with infinite sets of variants. Nevertheless the latter group too will assume that the preference of a speaker to say *something* in favour of something else will be socially meaningful if one way or another.

many features in common with what has traditionally been associated with the demographic variable white, Anglo-Saxon, heterosexual woman. For instance, call centre agents are supposed to ask questions, show empathy, create rapport and use expressive intonation (Cameron 2000). In the early days of research into language and gender, a subfield of sociolinguistics, this way of speaking was interpreted as a normative woman's way of speaking (Lakoff 1973). In current theory, it is more common to relate it, not to the demographic variable woman, but indirectly to the stances or qualities that are associated with women by social convention. In this interpretation, call centre agents are supposed to speak this way, not to show that they are women (indeed, many men work as call centre agents too), but to signal or index that they are caring, nurturing and empathetic (Cameron 2000). Thus, in current theory, the social meaning (or indexicality) of a linguistic variable is interpretable *qua* its indirect association with the demographic variable it also indexes (see Figure 2).

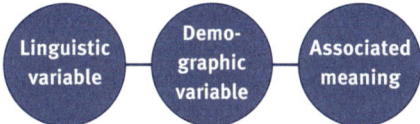

Figure 2: The semantic relationship between linguistic variables and meaning in modern sociolinguistics

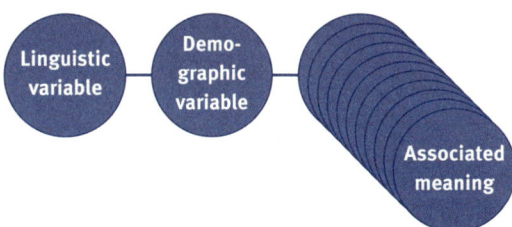

Figure 3: The multiplicity and variability of associated social meanings in modern sociolinguistics

The second identifying feature of current theories of indexicality is that the associated meanings are multiple and variable and contextually contingent: "[T]he meanings of variables are not precise or fixed but rather constitute a field of potential meanings – an *indexical field*, or constellation of ideologically related meanings, any one of which can be activated in the situated use of the variable" (Eckert 2008: 453). Johnstone and Kiesling point out that "[T]he indexical meanings of speech features can vary widely within a community, and we illustrate the danger of confusing the meaning assigned by hearers to a linguistic form with the meaning users would assign to it (2008: 5). To illustrate this with an example: the two lexical variants *regulære udtryk* and *regular expressions* are in free variation in spoken Danish. While the speaker may have wished to come across as cool in their choice of an English lexical variant over a Danish one, the hearer may well have interpreted this stance as something entirely different, e.g. pretentious. This variability – an entire "field" of potential meanings (Eckert 2008) – means that the analyst must be aware of a range of different possible meanings of any linguistic variant.

To sum up, I have suggested that there are two particularly important features of the current theory of indexicality. First is an explicit concern with associated meanings of linguistic variables over demographic categories. Second is a recognition that such associated meanings are multiple, variable and contextually contingent. Underlying these explicitly declared interests, there is, I suggest, in current theory a tacit assumption that linguistic variables *have* a social meaning. It is assumed, in other words, that given the choice between two variants, a speaker's decision in favour of one of those variants will be socially meaningful (Silverstein 2003). Very little, if any attention, is devoted in current theory to discussions about whether the variants actually have any social meaning at all. This is, of course, to a certain extent to be expected of a field which self-identifies as being primarily concerned with the social uses of language, but in this article, questions shall be raised about whether this assumption is always valid. I shall ask, more precisely, if there are situations in which a non-social meaning, such as referential meaning, takes precedence.

2.2 Delimitation of terms: Lexical variation and authenticity

In this paper, I shall test the theory of indexicality on instances of Danish/English lexical variation in the scientific vocabulary of spoken Danish. Lexical variation is here understood as Danish-speaking computer scientists' choice between using an English or a Danish variant for concepts such as the following: *regular expression* vs. *regulært udtryk*, *source code* vs. *kildekode*, *curly brackets* vs. *tuborgklammer* in undergraduate teaching sessions.[3] I shall use the term lexical variants instead of code-switching as the latter normally implies that the choice between

---

3 In the first two of these sets, the Danish variant is a literal translation of the English variant. In the last one, *tuborg* is a jocular, colloquial way of referring to *curly* by alluding to the curly-shaped logo printed on Danish Tuborg beer bottles.

codes (in this case Danish and English) has social significance (Myers-Scotton 1988), which I shall argue is not necessarily the case.

It may be argued that in testing the theory of indexicality on instances of *inter*-language variation, i.e. cases in which lexical candidates come from two different languages, I am overstepping my mark. Indeed, it may be objected that the theory of indexicality has been built on evidence of *intra*-lingual variation only, particularly perhaps, that on the phonological level (e.g. Eckert 2008; Johnstone & Kiesling 2008). In line with an increased realization of the artefactual nature of language boundaries[4], however, there have been calls for considering instances of language mixing – or to use a term from the literature: hybridity – as the unmarked norm (Otsuji & Pennycook forthcoming; see also Auer 2007). Attention in such work is drawn to the fact that nameable languages are historical constructs that do not necessarily agree with the way in which code-switchers themselves consider the situation. Analysing instances of workplace talk between highly proficient English-Japanese speakers in a Japanese company, Otsuji and Pennycook (2013) argue that these speakers sometimes do not even realize that they switch codes and that there seems to be no special meaning attached to using one or the other. (Though they do point out the methodological issue that this lack of awareness does not necessarily mean that the choice is not meaningful, merely that the participants are not able in follow-up interviews to recall any meaning attached to it.) Auer and Eastman too argue for according priority to code-switchers' own interpretations of their language use and suggest amending Gumperz's definition of code-switching thus "the juxtaposition within the same speech exchange of passages of speech belonging to two different grammatical systems or sub-systems *which the participants perceive as such*" (2010: 86, emphasis added). In other words, if it is accepted that boundaries between languages are ideologically constructed artefacts that do not necessarily have any empirical or cognitive reality, it may be argued that *inter*-lingual lexical variation should be equally well captured by a theory of indexicality.

A final notion that needs to be considered briefly before we turn to the analysis proper is authenticity. This is a notion which has received attention (see, e.g. special issue in the *Journal of Sociolinguistics* (Coupland 2003) and the present volume) but it sits somewhat uneasily within the theoretical framework of indexicality. While indexicality moves away from the stasis implied by

---

4 This is of course a truism which has always underpinned sociolinguistics (Haugen 1972), but it seems that it is only relatively recently in the context of intensified global interconnectedness that it has become more exposed and consequently accorded the attention that it deserves (see, e.g. Heller 2008; Blommaert 2010; Pennycook 2010).

demographic variables, authenticity is, arguably, contingent upon such stasis. Authenticity is only meaningful, in other words, if there is something static to evaluate it against. A speaker can speak more or less authentically as, say, a Dane or a Brit, but in every case, authenticity is evaluated against the demographic category that it is thought to be authentic of, in this case the category of nationality. When the notion of authenticity is drawn upon in this paper, it is because there is evidence to suggest that it has gained increased significance. This is especially true, perhaps, of the authenticity that relates to the demographic variable of place, which appears to have become more salient as a result of intensified global interconnectedness and mobility. For instance, Johnstone, Andrus, and Danielso (2006) argue that the dialect of Pittsburghese is now primarily interpreted as a marker of regional place rather than of socio-economic class as it was before. As we shall see, the data which forms the basis of this chapter also (partly) suggests an interpretation of authenticity, specifically in relation to the demographic variable of nationality.

3 Socio-political background: Internationalized universities of Denmark

In order to understand why English/Danish lexical variation is an issue at Danish universities, it is necessary to briefly describe the socio-political background. Over the past 15–20 years universities across the Western world have undergone significant transformation (Hazelkorn 2011; Guruz 2008; Becher & Trowler 2001). Universities today are significantly affected by the neoliberal ideology which promotes competition and reduces governmental interference. This happens across the world but the linguistic consequences are arguably particularly noticeable in countries in the "expanding circle" (Kachru 1985) in which English is not the official language but is increasingly being used in certain areas of society. In Northern Europe and in the Netherlands, e.g., the neoliberalist practice to allocate funding on the basis of measurable research output prompts researchers with other first languages than English to publish in high-ranking international, *de facto* English-medium, journals. Moreover, the common European framework for higher education, established to make the EU competitive *vis-à-vis* the US, has led to increased intra-European mobility and necessitated a common language, which again defaults to English. In Northern Europe, the linguistic consequences of this political ideology is that in some disciplines, notably in the natural, technical and medical sciences, English is now being used increasingly alongside the local national languages as the language of publication and teaching above graduate level (Bolton and Kuteeva 2012).

The widespread use of English in higher education and research has prompted concerns in the Nordic countries over whether the national Nordic languages will eventually cease to be *"komplet og samfundsbærende* [complete and society-bearing]", i.e. equipped to serve all societal functions (Nordic Council of Ministers 2007: 11, emphasis in original). Such concerns have been expressed across Scandinavia and are reflected in an upsurge of language policy documents (Norwegian Department of Cultural and Ecclesiastic Affairs 2008; Danish Ministry of Culture 2008; Swedish Department of Culture 2002). Despite a frequent overt denial in Nordic language policy discourses that lexical borrowing from English is ominous, there is plenty of evidence in the language policy documents to suggest that an underdeveloped terminological repertoire in the national language is a problem in need of rectification. Indeed, a cornerstone of the notion of a "complete" and "society-bearing" language is to ensure that the local languages have a well-developed scientific vocabulary (Danish Ministry of Culture 2008). In Denmark and in Norway, there have been suggestions to create terminological databases to ensure that national terminological equivalents are established and updated as alternatives to English ones (Danish Ministry of Culture 2008; Norwegian Department of Cultural and Ecclesiastic Affairs 2008). In Denmark, the focus of this chapter, a lack of national terms has been considered, by influential linguists, a problem either in its own right (Davidsen-Nielsen 2005) or because it may eventually reinforce the dominance of English as speakers will prefer to speak a language which provides them with the lexical items they require (Kirchmeier-Andersen 2008).

4 Presentation of data and methods

4.1 Etic and emic data

The data that informs the analysis in this chapter can be divided into two types: etic and emic (see Table 1). This refers to a distinction originally made by the linguist Kenneth Pike (1967) between, respectively, an outsider and an insider perspective of human behaviour. The rationale for including both types of data in the study is to develop an understanding of possible differences in the way in which the much-talked about phenomenon of English in Danish higher education and research is viewed by outsiders on the one hand and insiders on the other. The outsiders in this case are those who have commented on the situation in national newspapers and contributed to the development of language policies.

They include leaders of the Danish Language Council[5] and of the Danish Language and Literature Society[6], other professional linguists and a few politicians. The insiders are those who represent the focus of discussion: 10 scientists in the three disciplines physics, chemistry and computer science at the University of Copenhagen. Each type of data will be further described below.

Etic data	Emic data
62 newspaper contributions in national and regional Danish newspapers on the topic of language policy in higher education and research	10 recordings and transcripts of undergraduate teaching sessions delivered by chemists, physicists and computer scientists at the University of Copenhagen
4 key Danish language policy documents issued by the Danish government	7 open-ended questionnaires with the recorded scientists

Table 1: Etic and emic data drawn on in this study.

4.1.1 Etic data and methods

62 newspaper contributions in major Danish national and regional newspapers were extracted through a publically available database using keywords related to the topic of English at Danish universities. The articles were written between the 1st of August 2000 and the 1st of August 2010. The corpus was analysed qualitatively (by coding articles thematically) and quantitatively by extracting a list of keywords (i.e. words that occur with a higher frequency than would be expected by chance in comparison with a reference corpus) to cross-check the qualitative coding. In combination, the methods used can be described as a corpus-assisted discourse analysis, which exploits the claim to objectivity afforded by the corpus linguistic keyword analysis while also making use of the uniquely human capacity to interpret tokens in their appropriate socio-political context (Baker et al. 2008). The policy documents, four in total, are: *Sprog på Spil [Language at Stake]* and *Sprog til Tiden [Language in Time]* published in 2003 and 2008, respectively, and written by expert committees appointed by the Danish Ministry of Culture as

---

5 The Danish Language Council is a governmental unit in Denmark whose most important tasks consist of monitoring the development of the Danish language, publish and update the most authoritative Danish dictionary for orthography, and to provide telephonic and email guidance to people who contact them about language-related questions.
6 The Danish Language and Literature Society publishes and documents Danish language and literature from the olden days to now.

well as two follow-up documents written by the Danish Ministry of Culture published in 2004 and 2009. The policy documents were analysed critically with the aim to expose hidden and taken-for-granted assumptions about language and its social meaning.

4.1.2 Emic data and methods

A total of ten undergraduate teaching sessions conducted in Danish and spread out across the three disciplines physics, chemistry and computer science were recorded in November and December 2010 at the University of Copenhagen. The teachers included both permanent staff and graduate students. As is customary for highly-educated Danes, all participants had high oral proficiency in English. The teaching sessions were partially transcribed and analysed for instances of lexical variation. This required determining whether a lexical item has a counterpart with which it is in free variation, which is a matter of judgment. More specifically, the decision on whether to consider something a lexical variable was taken through a combination of introspection, Internet searches and consultancy with the participants. Open-ended, tailor-made questionnaires were sent out to the speakers subsequent to the recordings to shed further light on their reasons for favouring one lexical variant over another. Online questionnaires were favoured over face-to-face interviews to allow more time for the participants to reflect upon their practices. The questionnaires were tailor-made to the specific scientist enabling the researcher to ask specific questions about their prior linguistic behaviour. They were also open-ended, thus enabling the scientists to comment on the situation in their own words. In addition to this, respondents often provided additional examples of Danish/English lexical variation which did not occur in the specific teaching session which was recorded. In this way, it was possible to build up a picture of the underlying rationale for choosing one lexical variant in favour of another.[7]

5 Testing data on theory

5.1 Where the theory fits: The variability of associated social meanings

In this section, I shall provide examples from the data which support the previously described features of the theory of indexicality, i.e. the shift away from

---

7 Seven out of ten invitees responded to the questionnaire..

demographic variables to the social meanings that are indirectly associated with them and a recognition that such associated meanings are multiple and contextually variable. Drawing on the notion of authenticity, I shall begin, however, by arguing that despite the move away from the stasis implied in demography, there is evidence to suggest that it gains renewed appreciation in light of increased transnationalism, global interconnectedness and mobility.

In a contribution to a national Danish newspaper, the then chairman of the Danish Language Council, Niels Davidsen-Nielsen, responds to a charge by a professor of biochemistry (Olesen Larsen) that the Council are too complacent in their position towards the English influence on Danish scientific terminology.

> Olesen Larsen wants systematic work to bring *international/English* scientific vocabulary into the *Danish* language to avoid a mixture of *English* and *Danish* which will eventually be so confusing that *Danish* will be dispreferred when scientists talk and write about the sciences [...] what the author wants is an adaptation of the words so that they are spelled, pronounced and inflected in *Danish* and that they thereby cease to be *foreign* (Davidsen-Nielsen 2005: 12, my emphasis).

In this citation, the chairman makes an unquestioned assumption about lexical variants being either authentically Danish or not (all words which refer explicitly to national origin have been italicized). It is clear to the author not only that orthographic, phonological and morphological assimilation of international/English/foreign words into Danish is *desirable*, but also that it is indeed possible to make an operational distinction between Danish and non-Danish words, despite considerable problems associated with this (see Hultgren 2013). Just to mention one problem, it will depend on how far back in history one goes, a decision which is ultimately, however well justified, arbitrary. The view expressed here is not idiosyncratic but reflects the aforementioned idea of a "complete" and "society-bearing language", which underpins Danish language policy discourses, and which rests on an idea that the Danish language should be fully elaborated in all registers. It is possible to interpret this quotation as corroboration of the importance accorded to authenticity in current theory (see, e.g. Coupland 2003; Johnstone, Andrus & Danielson 2006). More specifically, it would seem that in the context of increased mobility and trans-nationalism, the choice of an authentically Danish lexical variant over an inauthentically English one is perceived to be inherently preferable.

An obvious next question is what social meaning is assigned to, respectively, Danish and English variants. Why is it perceived to be important, in other words, to use a Danish variant in favour of an English one if both, referentially, denote the same? To understand this, we need to consider the underlying ideologies associated with using each language. The Danish debate on the use of English at

Danish universities can be described as being a struggle between three political/ ideological positions (see, e.g. Thøgersen 2009). This is in spite of the fact that, overtly, there is wide agreement on the importance of *parallellingualism*, i.e. to ensure an equitable use of English and Danish without the former encroaching on the latter. Those who favour English typically include universities themselves and the right-wing and liberal political parties in Denmark. Their ideological orientation and economic rationale favour elitism, economic gain, a free market, free movement, international benchmarking and European standardization. In contrast, those who favour Danish typically include two internally heterogonous groups. One includes the Danish Language Council, the Danish Language and Literature society, intellectuals (including professional linguists) and politicians left of the political centre. Their political ideology typically attributes less importance to economic gain and acknowledges other values, such as cultural and linguistic diversity. They also often invoke egalitarianism as an ideal arguing that the increasing use of English constitutes a threat to democracy by disenfranchising large segments of the population whose English proficiency is not sufficiently high. The other group is constituted by the far right nationalist parties who advocate Danish on more or less explicitly pronounced xenophobic grounds. In the Danish debate on the use of English at Danish universities, language has become, as is not unusual, the centre of an ideological and political battle (Cameron 1995; Blommaert 1999; Duchêne & Heller 2007).

It seems that on word-level too, these ideological associations are at work. Thus, there is emic evidence to support the interpretation of the use of Danish lexical variants as connoting traditionalism, national pride and intellectualism.

> I min studietid var normen, at der blev brugt danske fagtermer, og det har jeg forsøgt at holde, selv om jeg ikke er helt konsekvent. F.eks. [...] siger jeg *tabel* i stedet for *array*, *lager* i stedet for *memory*, *tegn* i stedet for *character* [...], *kant* og *knude* i stedet for *edge* og *node* (i grafer), *oversætter* og *fortolker* i stedet for *compiler* og *interpreter*, *beregning* i stedet for *evaluation* osv.
>
> When I was a student [at DIKU, the Institute of Computer Science at the University of Copenhagen], the norm was to use Danish terms, and I have tried to maintain this though not entirely consistently. For instance [...], I say *tabel* instead of *array*, *lager* instead of *memory*, *tegn* instead of *character* [...], *kant* and *knude* instead of *edge* and *node* (in graphs), *oversætter* and *fortolker* instead of *compiler* and *interpreter*, *beregning* instead of *evaluation*, etc. (Lecturer in computer science).

> [u]den for DIKU (blandt alm. nørder og på arbejdsmarkedet) blander man bare engelsk ind lige så meget man vil.
>
> [o]utside of DIKU (among ordinary nerds and at the job market) you just mix it up with English as much as you want]. (Teaching assistant in computer science).

These quotations suggest that Danish lexical variants are preferred over English at the Institute of Computer Science at the University of Copenhagen. This was repeatedly pointed out to me during my observations and informal talk with participants, who talked about their pride in using Danish terms, a tradition, I was told, which dates back to the establishment of the Institute in 1970. Interestingly, the preference for Danish terms was often contrasted with practices at comparable institutions: "outside of DIKU (among ordinary nerds and at the job market) you just mix it up with English as much as you want". The reported preference for using Danish variants over English ones is supported by evidence from language use; in cases where there is more than one way of referring to the same thing, it is consistently the Danish variant that is used. It is possible to interpret this widespread preference for and apparent pride in using Danish variants as a way for participants to distance themselves from the more market-driven and applied rationale of other computer science institutions and professions. Compared to the IT University of Denmark, for instance, the Institute of Computer Science at the University of Copenhagen is more academically than vocationally oriented, its scientific foundation more pure than applied, something which employees at this institution may take pride in.

This apparent local pride in Danish variants at DIKU might be explained by invoking Michael Silverstein's notion of "higher order indexicality", which is well-developed in his description of oinoglossia, or "wine talk" (Silverstein 2003). Against the backdrop of "first" and "second order indexicalities", which may be broadly understood as, respectively, referential and social meanings, Silverstein describes wine talk as drawing on "higher order indexicalities" where the meaning of certain words is neither referential nor social (in the sense of being shared by most people) but very specific to that particular context and the particular language users in it. Thus, when wine tasters refer to a specific wine as having, say, "blueberry aromas merging with touches of spice, vanilla and chocolatey notes", this is a highly conventionalized register, in which the words have very specific meanings with which few others than oenologists are familiar. While the preference for Danish over English terms by computer scientists at DIKU is slightly different in that most terms used would probably be familiar also to people outside of DIKU, there are certain commonalities with Silverstein's oinoglossia in that the register is "professionally terminologized" (2003: 226), i.e. the words used are associated with a particular profession which appears to self-identify with a certain degree of pride.

Importantly, though, the apparent prestige accorded to Danish variants at the Institute of Computer Science at the University of Copenhagen may be restricted to this particular local context. Many participants pointed out that they would be wary of using Danish terms outside of the institute. One pointed out that this might make him come across as "eccentric". Examples in which English variants are preferred are certainly both plentiful and well-documented (Rathje 2010; Heidemann Andersen 2004; Preisler 1999). Thus, since the social meaning of a given variable is multiple and variable, where one may perceive an English variant as trendy, cosmopolitan and outward-looking, others might see as pretentious, uncultivated, or even ridiculous (see, e.g. Davidsen-Nielsen 2009).

Above, I have tried to show that as regards the three identifying features of the theory of indexicality, they are all empirically corroborated by the data analysed here. Firstly, authenticity seems to be important if we understand this as lexical items being perceived to be authentically or inauthentically Danish. Secondly, the choice between Danish and English lexical variants clearly has more than referential meaning; it matters whether one uses the Danish or the English variant. The choice may be seen to be associated with a range of ideological meanings, which are always contestable and contextually variable. Having now focused on the way in which the data supports current theory, the remainder of the data section will consider some examples in which the theory is not supported.

5.2 Where the theory does not fit: The importance accorded to referential meaning

In this second and final data section, I shall provide evidence from the emic perspective to suggest that social meaning is not always relevant or at least not the primary type of meaning in all situations. Three extracts from the open-ended questionnaires suggest instead that the primary factor motivating the choice between an English and a Danish variant seems to have to do, not primarily with *social* but with *referential* meaning. Thus, when asked whether it is important to find Danish equivalents of new (often English) scientific terms in their field of research, a teaching assistant in chemistry replies:

> Nej det er ikke vigtigt for mig, da jeg ikke mener at det er det centrale. Det vigtige er at blive forstået, men hvilke ord man bruger er i princippet underordnet synes jeg!
> No, it is not important to me, because I don't think it is central. The important thing is to be understood, but which words you use are in principle unimportant, I think! (Teaching assistant in chemistry)

This teacher apparently places emphasis on the need to be understood and does not accord any significance to whether an English or a Danish term is used. Asked the same question, a teaching assistant in computer science replies

> [...] hvis en dansk oversættelse til et begreb er oplagt, men [...] en som ingen benytter [...]
> [ville det] være svært at formidle informationen om emnet uden at inkludere det engelske
> ord. For eksempel det engelske ord *tag*, som kan oversættes til *mærkat*. [...] Jeg kunne bruge
> [det ord] men hvis jeg siger *tagge* (udtalt engelsk) er en hel kontekst givet uden meget for-
> klaring.
> [...] if a Danish equivalent of a concept is obvious, but [...] one that no one uses it would be
> difficult to communicate information about that topic without including the English word.
> For example, for the English word *tag*, which is translatable as *mærkat*. [...] I could use this
> word but if I say *tagge* (pronounced in English) a whole context is given without a lot of
> explanation. (Teaching assistant in computer science)

Again, what is emphasized here is communicative efficiency as a guiding principle in the choice between a Danish and an English variant. The teaching assistant
suggests that he would use the English word *tagge* instead of the Danish co-existing term *mærkat* because the former would exempt him from having to explain
the context. Thus, it seems that communicative efficiency is valued higher here
than any social meaning in spite of the aforementioned pride accorded to Danish
variants. The final example is offered in response to the researcher's request for
examples in which an English lexical variant would be preferred over a Danish
and why:

> *Editor* eller *teksteditor* i stedet for *tekstredigeringsværktøj*, *CPU* i stedet for *centralberegning-
> senhed*, *harddisk* i stedet for *fastpladelager*. I disse (og andre) tilfælde er oversættelsen ikke
> særligt kendt, eller god.
> *Editor* or *text editor* instead of *tekstredigeringsværktøj*, *CPU* instead of *centralberegnings-
> enhed*, *harddisk* instead of *fastpladelager*. In these (and other) cases the translation is not
> particularly well-known or good. (Teaching assistant in computer science)

The teaching assistant here refers to the importance of a Danish variant to be
"well-known" or "good" if it is to be considered a viable alternative. This again is
interpretable as a way of prioritizing communicative efficiency since if a term is
not established, it might threaten communicative success. All in all, then, despite
the possibility to assign social meaning to the respective use of Danish and English
variants, what seems to be pivotal in these extracts is referential meaning, more
specifically, the potential of a given variant to hinder or enhance communication.
    One possible explanation for the apparent concern with referential meaning
in these examples has to do with the type of talk investigated. This is describ-
able as institutional rather than casual talk, more specifically as a technical register. It is to be expected that such talk is more referentially than socially oriented
(Partington 2006), given its goal-orientedness (Drew and Heritage 1992). In connection with the use of English as a Lingua Franca, House (2003) has made a
distinction between "languages for identification" and "languages for commu-

nication". Although this is perhaps a distinction which partly falls into the same trap as current theory, namely of assuming that social and referential meaning can be teased apart, it certainly seems to be useful in explaining how English is perceived by Danish university employees. Many of those taking part in this study regarded English as a tool for communication first and foremost. The observation that workplace talk has been much less studied by sociolinguists than, e.g. community or education talk (Roberts 2012) may help explain why referential meaning has received far less attention than social meaning.

Another possible explanation for why referential meaning is given priority here has to do with epistemological orientation, i.e. what we count as valid ways of obtaining knowledge. The interpretation in terms of the referential meaning argued for here, accords greater priority to participants' own interpretation of their language use than to the analysts. It also rests on the assumption that it is possible to take at face value what participants express in open-ended questionnaires, which is of course debatable (Talmy 2010). It may be objected, for instance, that just because participants themselves do not think of social meaning as the primary (or, put in a weaker form: do not communicate this in the questionnaires), it does not mean that social meaning may not be accorded to the choice *post hoc* (by the analyst or indeed by the participants themselves.) Nor can it be denied that the sociolinguist expert will possess knowledge, skills and analytic tools and theories to interpret language behaviour at a higher level than non-experts. Nonetheless, it seems to me that in a theoretical framework which emphasizes fluidity of meaning, it should be possible to at least consider the possibility that the choice between two linguistic variables may not for all types of talk or from all perspectives be socially meaningful.

6 Conclusion:
The negligence of referential meaning in current theory

In this study, I set out to test the most central features of the theory of indexicality on data in the form of Danish/English lexical variation at the internationalized University of Copenhagen. While I suggested that it is certainly possible to interpret the choice between English and Danish variants in terms of social meaning, there were also examples in which the most important factor guiding the choice was not primarily social but whether the variant in question hindered or enhanced communicative efficiency. This came across in participants' own accounts of their reasons for favouring one term over another. While this does not of course invalidate the theory of indexicality, it does perhaps raise questions about the assumption that when there is more than one way of saying the same thing the choice will be socially meaningful. Whilst it is perhaps unsurprising that sociolinguists' deliberate dissociation from the Chomskyan cognitive and structural paradigm has made them primarily interested in the social aspects of language, it seems that, if the findings in this studies are anything to go by, we should keep an eye out for the potential of referential meaning to, in some contexts at least, override the importance of social meaning. At the very least, the findings suggest that teasing apart social from referential meaning, which current theory to a certain extent relies upon, may not be tenable (a point also made by Eckert 2008). Rather, social and referential meaning always co-exist and which one is granted interpretative priority depends on a range of factors, including as we have seen here type of talk (institutional vs. casual) and epistemological orientation (emic or etic).

References

Agha, Asif 2005: Voice, footing, enregisterment. *Journal of Linguistic Anthropology* 15(1): 38–59.

Ammon, Ulrich 2001: *The dominance of English as a Language of Science: Effects on Other Languages and Language Communities*. Berlin/New York: Mouton de Gruyter.

Auer, Peter 2007: The monolingual bias in bilingualism research, or: Why bilingual talk is (still) a challenge for linguistics. In Monica Heller (ed.), *Bilingualism: A Social Approach*, 319–339. London: Palgrave.

Auer, Peter & Carol M. Eastman 2010: Code-switching. In Jürgen Jaspers, Jef Verschueren and Jan-Ola Östman (eds.), *Society and language use*, 84–113. Amsterdam/ Philadelphia: John Benjamins.

Baker, Paul, Costas Gabrielatos, Majid Khosravinik, Michal Krzyzanowski, Tony McEnery & Ruth Wodak 2008: A useful methodological synergy? Combining critical discourse analysis and corpus linguistics to examine discourses of refugees and asylum seekers in the UK press. *Discourse & Society* 19(3): 273–305.

Becher, Tony & Paul Trowler 2001: *Academic Tribes and Territories: Intellectual Enquiry and the Cultures of Disciplines*. Milton Keynes: Society for Research into Higher Education & Open University Press.

Blommaert, Jan 2010: *The Sociolinguistics of Globalization*. Cambridge: Cambridge University Press.

Blommaert, Jan 1999: *Language Ideological Debates*. Berlin/New York: Mouton de Gruyter.

Bolton, Kingsley & Maria Kuteeva 2012: English as an academic language at a Swedish university: parallel language use and the 'threat' of English. *Journal of Multilingual and Multicultural Development*. 33(5): 429–447.

Brown, Gillian & George Yule 1983: *Teaching the Spoken Language: An Approach based on the Analysis of Conversational English*. Cambridge: Cambridge University Press.

Cameron, Deborah 2000: Styling the worker: Gender and the commodification of language in the globalized service economy. *Journal of Sociolinguistics* 4(3): 323–347.

Cameron, Deborah 1995: *Verbal Hygiene*. London/New York: Routledge.

Coupland, Nikolas 2003: Sociolinguistic authenticities. *Journal of Sociolinguistics* 7(3): 417–431.

Danish Ministry of Culture 2009: *Sprog til tiden - Regeringens opfølgning på sprogudvalgets rapport* [Language in time – the government's follow-up to the language committee's report] http://kum.dk/Documents/Publikationer/2009/Sprog%20til%20tiden%20-%20 Regeringens%20opf%C3%B8lgning%20p%C3%A5%20sprogudvalgets%20rapport/pdf/ KUM_Sprogtiltiden_web_NY.pdf

Danish Ministry of Culture 2008: *Sprog til tiden* [Language in time]. Copenhagen: Danish Ministry of Culture. http://kum.dk/Documents/Publikationer/2008/Sprog_til_tiden%20 -%20Rapport%20fra%20Sproguvalget/pdf/sprog_til_tiden_netpub.pdf (accessed 6 July 2012).

Danish Ministry of Culture 2004: *Sprogpolitisk redegørelse* [Language Policy Review]. Copenhagen: Danish Ministry of Culture. http://kum.dk/Documents/Publikationer/2003/ Sprogpolitisk%20Redeg%C3%B8relse/Sprogpolitisk%20Redeg%C3%B8relse.pdf (accessed 7 July 2012).

Danish Ministry of Culture 2003: *Sprog på spil – Et udspil til en dansk sprogpolitik* [Language at stake – An initiative towards a Danish language policy]. Copenhagen: Danish Ministry of Culture. http://kum.dk/Documents/Publikationer/2003/Sprog%20p%C3%A5%20spil/ Sprog%20paa%20spil.pdf (accessed 6 July 2012).

Davidsen-Nielsen, Niels 2009: *Moders stemme, fars hammer: En debatbog om dansk sprogpolitik* [Mother's voice, father's hammer: A debate book on Danish language policy]. Copenhagen: Dansklærerforeningens forlag.

Davidsen-Nielsen, Niels 2005: Debat: Fagsprog skal Assimileres [Debate: Scientific language should be assimilated]. *Berlingske Tidende,* 19th May 2005: 12.

Drew, Paul & John Heritage 1992: *Talk at Work: Interaction in Institutional Settings*. Cambridge: Cambridge University Press.

Duchêne, Alexandre & Monica Heller 2007: *Discourses of Endangerment: Ideology and Interest in the Defence of Languages*. London: Continuum.

Eckert, Penelope 2008: Variation and the indexical field. *Journal of Sociolinguistics* 12(4): 453–476.

Guruz, Kemal 2008: *Higher Education and International Student Mobility in the Global Knowledge Economy*. New York: State University of New York Press.

Haugen, Einar 1972: *The Ecology of Language*. Stanford, CA: Stanford University Press.

Hazelkorn, Ellen 2011: *Rankings and the Reshaping of Higher Education: the Battle for World-class Excellence*. Basingstoke: Palgrave Macmillan.

Heidemann Andersen, Margrethe 2004: *Helt vildt sjovt eller wannabeagtigt og ejendomsmæg-lerkækt?* [Hilariously funny or wannabeish and estate agent smart?] Copenhagen: Danish Language Council.

Heller, Monica 2008: Language and the nation-state: Challenges to sociolinguistic theory and practice. *Journal of Sociolinguistics* 12: 504–524.

House, Juliane 2003: English as a lingua franca: A threat to multilingualism? *Journal of Sociolinguistics* 7(14): 556–578.

Hultgren, Anna Kristina 2013: Lexical borrowing from English into Danish in the sciences: An empirical investigation of "domain loss". *International Journal of Applied Linguistics* 23(2): 166–182.

Johnstone, Barbara & Scott F. Kiesling 2008: Indexicality and experience: Exploring the meanings of /aw/-monophthongization in Pittsburgh. *Journal of Sociolinguistics* 12(1): 5–33.

Johnstone, Barbara, Jennifer Andrus & Andrew E. Danielson 2006: Mobility, indexicality, and the enregisterment of 'Pittsburghese'. *Journal of English Linguistics*. 34(2): 77–104.

Kachru, Braj B. 1985: Standards, codification and sociolinguistic realism: The English language in the outer circle. In Randolph Quirk and Henry G. Widdowson (eds), *English in the World: Teaching and Learning the Language and Literatures*, 11–36. Cambridge: Cambridge University Press.

Kasper, Gabriele 1990: Linguistic politeness: Current research issues. *Journal of Pragmatics* 14(2): 193–218.

Kirchmeier-Andersen, Sabine 2008: Lov til dansk? *Jyllands-Posten*, 7th April 2008.

Labov, William 1966: *The Social Stratification of English in New York City*. Washington, D.C.: Center for Applied Linguistics.

Lakoff, Robin 1989: The Limits of Politeness: Therapeutic and Courtroom Discourse. *Multilingua* 8(2–3): 101–129.

Lakoff, Robin 1973: Language and woman's place. *Language in Society* 2: 45–79.

Myers-Scotton, Carol 1988: Code switching as indexical of social negotiations. In Monica Heller (ed.), *Code-switching*, 151–186. Berlin/New York: Mouton de Gruyter.

Nordic Council of Ministers 2007: *Deklaration om nordisk språkpolitik* [Declaration on Nordic Language Policy]. Copenhagen: Nordic Council of Ministers http://www.norden.org/en/publications/publikationer/2007-746/at_download/publicationfile (accessed 6 July 2012).

Norwegian Department of Cultural and Ecclesiastic Affairs.2008: *Mål og meining – ein heilskapleg norsk språkpolitikk [Tongue and Opinion: A comprehensive Norwegian Language Policy]*. Oslo: Norwegian Department of Cultural and Ecclesiastic Affairs.

Otsuji, Emi & Alastair Pennycook 2013: Unremarkable hybridities and metrolingual practices. In Rani Rubdy and Lubna Alsagoff (eds.), *The Global-Local Interface, Language Choice and Hybridity*, 83–99. Bristol: Multilingual Matters.

Partington, Alan 2006: *The Linguistics of Laughter: A Corpus-assisted Study of Laughter-talk*. London: Routledge.

Pennycook, Alastair 2010: *Language as Local Practice*. Abingdon: Routledge.

Pike, Kenneth Lee (ed.) 1967: *Language in Relation to a Unified Theory of Structure of Human Behavior*. (2nd ed.) The Hague: Mouton.

Preisler, Bent 1999: *Danskerne og det engelske sprog [The Danes and the English language]*. Roskilde: Roskilde Universitetsforlag.

Rathje, Marinne 2010: *Generationssprog [The Language of Different Generations]*. PhD dissertation. Copenhagen: The Danish Language Council.

Roberts, Celia 2012: Review of Bernd Meyer and Birgit Apfelbaum (eds.), *Multilingualism at Work: From Policies to Practices in Public, Medical and Business Settings*. Amsterdam/Philadelphia: John Benjamins. 2010. *Journal of Sociolinguistics* 16 (3): 444–446.

Silverstein, Michael 2003: Indexical order and the dialectics of sociolinguistic life. *Language and Communication* 23(3): 193–229.

Silverstein, Michael 1985: Language and the culture of gender: At the intersection of structure, usage and ideology. In Elizabeth Mertz and Richard Parmentier (eds.), *Semiotic Mediation: Sociocultural and Psychological Perspectives*, 219–259. New York: Academic Press.

Swedish Department of Culture 2002: *Mål i mun – Förslag till handlingsprogram för svenska språket* [Keep Your Tongue – Proposition for an action plan for the Swedish language]. Stockholm: Swedish Department of Culture.

Talmy, Steve : 2010: Qualitative interviews in applied linguistics: From research instrument to social practice. *Annual Review of Applied Linguistics* 30: 128–148.

Thøgersen, Jacob 2009: Den danske debat om sprog på universiteterne – og CIP. [The Danish debate on language at the universities – and at CIP] Talk given at Hanaholmen, March 2009.

Wilson, Deirdre & Neil V. Smith 1992: *Relevance Theory*. Amsterdam: Elsevier Science Publishers B.V.

Martin Gill

"Real communities", rhetorical borders: Authenticating British identity in political discourse and on-line debate

> Great news. At last some common sense from the Government. Why should we have to provide translation services for people who choose to come and live here of their own voli-tion The language of our country is English. If they can't don't [sic] understand it that is their problem not ours. Great way to save money. When I lived in Germany I had to learn German. They didn't provide translators for me.
> [Data set 2, post 10]

1 Introduction

1.1 Authenticity and nation

Despite the doubts sometimes expressed about its continued relevance, the ter-ritorial nation-state shows no sign of declining as the preferred unit of political self-realisation for aspiring national groups. When the President of the European Union, Herman Van Rompuy, suggested that "the time of the homogenous nation state is over" (Martin 2010), his comments provoked heated responses in Britain, with the leader of the UK Independence Party, as quoted by the *Mail Online*, warning darkly that Van Rompuy "wants to abolish our nation". While the chang-ing social realities of late modernity, and the growth both of transnational net-works and sub-national identities and allegiances, have undoubtedly affected its scope for independent action, the nation state continues to be experienced as an authentic "common sense" object of popular identification and to make undi-minished (if anything, increased) rhetorical efforts to defend its borders, not least with regard to issues of immigration and language policy.

Language is central to debates about immigration. Under pressure from a popular political discourse dominated by negative assessments of migration and multiculturalism and the threats they pose to the supposed integrity of national polities, many hybrid, heteroglossic contexts across the world are witnessing the resurgence of monocultural ideologies, including (re)enforcement of regulated language norms and an increased determination to regard the national speech community as stable, homogeneous and monolingual: in short, "'modernist' responses to 'postmodern' conditions" (Blommaert et al. 2009: 204). The Official English movement in the United States is a prominent example.

In an era of mass migration and social/demographic change on a global scale, the continued currency of these responses and their political implications calls for scrutiny. For one thing, we should ask whose interests they serve; not, we can be sure, those on whom their consequences fall most heavily. As Blommaert has observed, for example: "In the context of asylum application procedures, the imagination of language, notably, is dominated by frames that refer to static and timeless (i.e., uniform and national) orders of things" (Blommaert 2009: 415), constraining a transnational phenomenon within concepts at a national scale, with consequences for the treatment of migrants themselves.

It is likely that modernist conceptions of language and nation were always idealizations for particular ends; above all, it seems, they serve to naturalize inequalities. By regarding nations as stable, coherent entities, and their languages as purified autonomous codes, detachable from their contexts – what Blommaert and Verschueren (1992: 361; 1998: ch. 5) refer to as "homogeneism" – state policies render suspect the presence and everyday linguistic practices of many migrants, including multilingualism and code-mixing, and erase their own language competences, turning them instead into indices of disadvantage and obstacles to "integration". As Blommaert and Verschueren point out, these views have also had the effect of turning language into an interethnic battlefield (1992: 370).

At the same time, thanks largely to the survival outside academic contexts of a broadly Herderian conception of the nation state as an ethnolinguistically distinct, organic whole, the proposition that language indexes the true essence of the nation seems too obvious to question in many contexts. As a result, knowledge of "our" language becomes an apparently common-sense criterion for the admission of "outsiders" into "our" community – not just for instrumental reasons (although this often provides its surface justification), but in order for them to prove that they deserve to be regarded as authentic members; as "one of us".

Issues of national and linguistic identity become salient at state frontiers, where transition is officially regulated. As rhetorical constructs, however, state frontiers and the polities they demarcate are constantly (re-)imagined and naturalized in everyday discourse, and in the ideological / semiotic work done both by policy makers and by "ordinary" members of the public to draw the boundary between "us" and "them". Through an almost endless variety of means, formal and informal, on scales ranging from macro-level official legislation to micro-level incidental interactions, the criteria for authentic belonging and norms for its proper performance are maintained and policed, repeated and recontextualized, making it relevant to examine the nature of the "us" that is created, how its authenticity is constructed and contested; and how discourses at different levels work to maintain it. As we shall see, what then appears is a closed category; one that "outsiders" are not automatically free to join, even if they are under continuous pressure to do so from state agencies, political discourse and the media, and even if their not joining is interpreted as a free choice on their part, hence, at best, indicative of dubious commitment.

In this paper my main focus will be on two instances of discursive boundary maintenance at opposite ends of the rhetorical scale: the first, a speech to Conservative party members by British Prime Minister David Cameron on the topic of immigration to Britain, which deploys a familiar narrative of Britishness under threat to position "new people" as unwelcome outsiders; the second a corpus of posts to a forum linked to the BBC online news pages, which invites readers to "Have Your Say" (henceforth, HYS) on controversial questions in the news, in this case English language requirements for immigrants. In this context, discussion centres on the real nature of "Britishness"; for many contributors the apparently instrumental issue of proficiency in English is transformed into a criterion for membership in an imagined British ethnolinguistic community.

1.2 Authenticity in sociolinguistics

Work in various fields during the past two decades (e.g. Bendix 1997; Lindholm 2008; Taylor 1991) has made clear the extent to which notions of authenticity have helped to shape the post-Romantic conceptual landscape, including many taken-for-granted landmarks in linguistics and sociolinguistics (see, for example, Bucholtz 2003; Coupland 2003; Gill 2011; Johnstone, this volume). Much of this work can be seen as a response to dynamic late modern social contexts, to the detachment of voices from social formations previously treated as stable and explanatory, and the processes of transposition and recontextualization that result, not least in new media and CMC, which have created new bases for identity construction and authentication. Recent discussion of authenticity within sociolinguistics, in what Eckert (2009) refers to as "third wave" studies, has highlighted the internal dynamics of communities and explored the ways in which speakers fashion authentic identities from the semiotic resources at their disposal, and position themselves in relation to normative associations between linguistic forms and social meanings. In the process, it has traced transient meanings and unstable "authenticity effects", and foregrounded speakers' agency in relation to their linguistic and stylistic choices. This work has naturally tended to concentrate on contexts of maximum hybridity and layered indexicality, in which identities are styled, often ironically, and claims to authenticity are evaluated in a context of social action.

All this has helped to de-essentialize the concept; yet features of the old landscape remain stubbornly visible. Despite the shifts of focus described here (the very shifts that have illuminated the "elephants in the room" (cf. Eckert 2003) and raised authenticity as a topic of interest in its own right), authenticity talk goes on unabated, still projecting a kind of essentialist aura across the range of its uses. (In)authenticity effects can, of course, be strategically deployed for various purposes: but the promise the term seems to offer of an unambiguous, non-negotiable, morally secure position, and resistance to the rising tides of relativism, remains as compelling as ever; indeed, to those nostalgic for old certainties, not least in debates about national identities and legitimacy, we can suspect that this is its main appeal. As Coupland (2003:429, note 2) notes: "The power of the term 'authentic' is to succeed in asserting absolute values in necessarily relative circumstances, and in asserting a singular essence when competing criteria for authenticity exist". Moreover, by virtue of its apparent common-sense anchoring in the "real world", it serves to validate the particular ideological constructions it purports to describe.

Directly or indirectly, ideas of authenticity have shaped the ideological discourses in which the connections between language and nation are constructed, prompting us to ask what indexical resources are deployed to this end, and how; and what it is that is supposed to be indexed; specifically, what "Britishness" is taken to be, and how it is deployed in different contexts.

2 David Cameron's "real community"

In a speech to members of his own Conservative party in April 2011, British Prime Minister David Cameron (2011a) said:

> [R]eal communities aren't just collections of public service users living in the same space. Real communities are bound by common experiences ... forged by friendship and conversation ... knitted together by all the rituals of the neighbourhood, from the school run to the chat down the pub. And these bonds can take time. So real integration takes time.

> That's why, when there have been significant numbers of new people arriving in neighbourhoods ... perhaps not able to speak the same language as those living there ... on occasions not really wanting or even willing to integrate ... that has created a kind of discomfort and disjointedness in some neighbourhoods.

> This has been the experience for many people in our country – and I believe it is untruthful and unfair not to speak about it and address it.

This was not the first time that Cameron had chosen to focus on issues of language and multiculturalism (for detailed analysis of an earlier speech on this theme, and its subsequent recontextualization in the media, see Blackledge 2009). In February 2011, he had again faced controversy head-on by criticizing the prevailing "doctrine of state multiculturalism" and the divided, non-inclusive vision of society (and extremism, ultimately terrorism) to which, in his view, it had led (Cameron 2011b). Predictably enough, his presupposition was that only a culturally and linguistically homogeneous society could hope to achieve true security.

The construction of reassuring visions of "Britishness" (or "Englishness") in times of crisis belongs to a long tradition. Two earlier examples – Orwell's wartime evocation, echoed here, of "[t]he clatter of clogs in the Lancashire mill towns, the to-and-fro of the lorries on the Great North Road, the queues outside the Labour Exchanges, the rattle of pin-tables in the Soho pubs, the old maids biking to Holy Communion through the mists of the autumn mornings" (Orwell 1954: 193), and John Major's (1993) consciously Orwellian description of "Britain" as "the country of long shadows on cricket grounds, warm beer, invincible green suburbs, dog lovers and pools fillers" – were both responses to perceived external dangers: Orwell's to devastation by Hitler's forces, Major's, half a century later, to the imagined encroachment on British liberties of post-Maastricht Europe. As such, both were no less concerned with the creation of a distinct idea of the "others" on whose exclusion the survival of authentic "Britishness" depended. Cameron's unsubtle piece of political fiction in this same genre opposes a defiantly ordinary image of the timeless folkways, the homely local routines of Britain's "real" natives to the sudden jarring presence of migrants who have no knowledge of them or intention of adapting to them, who are not merely unable to understand but culpably determined not to understand – as Cameron's remarks illustrate, agency and intentionality are usually attributed to "others" in cases like this, meaning that their failure to meet these criteria is also their fault, for which typical explanations are likely to involve stereotypes such as laziness, pride, disdain for British culture, and so on. As we shall see, full agency is also a regular trope in the HYS data I have looked at.

In all three texts, the image presented contrasts the details of authentically happy vernacular life with the hideous – and already present – spectre of vast forces about to crash in upon it and sweep it away: and in each case, we know, these local ways will ultimately prevail. "Britishness" will win through.

Britishness in these visions is indexed by reference to its diversity, its appealing quirkiness (qualities that by implication outsiders must be supposed to lack), yet diversity is not held up to invite the possibility of change or enlargement; on the contrary, it is just these qualities – vulnerable as they may be – that have ensured its ability to resist outside influence. They are the authentic features that can be counted on to preserve the spirit of the nation.

Authenticity is central to the frame in which Cameron's ideological position is articulated; and the image it invokes – prelapsarian, local, nostalgic, already slipping away for ever – draws on exactly those qualities to which, in the post-Romantic world, the notion of authenticity has attached most firmly. The "real community" invoked here, masquerading as an objective category, is an ideal against which almost any slice of contingent everyday experience is likely to be found wanting; but its most pressing rhetorical function is to bring into existence for us the category of the "inauthentic community" – alien, rootless, urban, overwhelming, and above all here and now – against which we must erect defences.

3 Dichotomized discourse

Claims to authenticity are always ideological, and always imply a contrast between two entities or states of affairs. Strictly, authenticity draws a contrast both internally between a present reality and some imagined or lost original or ideal (e.g. the supposed original purity of the national speech community; or the language competence of the "native speaker"; or how I would like to be, and so on), and externally, between the upholders of this ideal and the inauthenticity of those whose beliefs or practices appear to deviate from it or threaten it – a category it calls into being for exactly this purpose. Both contrasts are evident in Cameron's speech: on the one hand, between a shifting present and the supposed traditions of local communities, and on the other between "us", who appreciate these things as intrinsically "ours", and "them", who don't.

Authenticity figures regularly in the dichotomizing discourses by which a disfavoured category is banished from association with "us", leaving "our" integrity assured. Such discourses have been instrumental in many contexts in legitimizing preferred forms of knowledge and identity in the Western tradition, and excluding others (see, for example, Lloyd 1990: 43; Creutz-Kämppi 2008). Its features become naturalized when projected on to apparently more basic, objective or salient dichotomies – speech vs. writing; vernacular vs. standard; male vs. female; normal vs. deviant; native vs. non-native, and so forth, with strong presupposition of greater legitimacy for the practices, the forms of life, it designates, providing them with a moral finality that requires no further justification (cf. Rorty 1989: 73), with regard to which individuals may have a great deal at stake. Who indeed could doubt that it is better to be authentic than inauthentic, or that this reflects the natural order of things? In the discourse of language and national identity, including the data discussed here, "the language" itself becomes a key feature of this kind (something one speaks / does not speak). Conjoined with a Herderian concept of national identity, authenticity thus acquires a central role in national self-understanding, and the question of who has a legitimate claim to membership.

4 Establishment and vernacular authenticity

As Cameron's text implies, authenticity and vernacularity seem naturally to go hand in hand. "Real" communities are above all ordinary ones. The long-held orthodoxy in sociolinguistics that the most spontaneous, vernacular language, least under the influence of public norms or deliberate stylistic choices, the most coherent speech community, the densest social network, is also the most "natural" specimen, hence most worthy of study, has treated the connection between them as self-evident. The same idea is in Orwell, and is recycled in Major's 1993 speech: the real strength of the British is not military or economic power or global influence (although these may be what appear to count at a macro level); what is "really" authentic, and their key to survival, is ordinary people and the humdrum muddle of vernacular life.

Here, significantly, Cameron's emphasis is different. Despite its fleeting rhetorical evocation of the "real" mundane world of the school run and the pub, his 2011 speech – a calculated appeal to anti-immigration sentiments on the right of his party, as well as in society more generally – uses this vision of vernacular authenticity to justify the imposition of conformity on those arriving "in our neighbourhoods". It is not a vernacular defence of (harmless, miscellaneous) "us" against (menacing, monolithic) "them", but a motive for concerted state action to ensure that "they" fit in. As such, it displays the features of "establishment authenticities" described by Coupland (2003: 420): it is "oppressive and ... statist" rather than egalitarian, concerned with conformity rather than diversity, with "'what is proper, for you as well as for us'"; and manifests itself in concrete form in legislation requiring immigrants to Britain to demonstrate proficiency in English.

These are expressions of the kinds of mainstream norm enforcement that, in most contexts, seem to be just the opposite of authentic. As Coupland notes, sociolinguists, whose sympathies have, quite properly, been with vernacular communities, and those marginalized by the state and its "hygienist, exclusionary obsessions" (2003: 420), are likely to find these concerns less appealing. Yet, he reminds us, the quest for authenticity, and notions of "authentic language" and the authentic speech community are no less resonant in establishment contexts. Indeed, illiberal state discourses of authenticity require special attention, since they provide a rich medium for the naturalization of language ideologies.

Needless to say, language is not always the main focus (cf. Blackledge 2005: 88). For language, in most contexts, we could read race: language covers the impossibility now of framing such discussions in racial terms. Underlying Cameron's text is an assumption that "real community" is monoglot and exclusive, and that "the language" (treated as a unitary, clearly-delimited entity) defines the moral, cultural, and historical space in which "our" community has created its sense of authentic belonging, now being dislocated by uncontrolled intrusion of non-English-speaking others. According to the conventions of "language and citizenship" discussion, to which Cameron is able to allude, "to be fully English (or British) is to speak English. To speak other languages is to be incompletely English (or British)" (Blackledge 2005: 89).[1] Their use by Cameron to construct the boundaries of "local neighbourhoods" reflects their unproblematic status in contemporary political ideology. His image of a pristine English speech-world is sketched in just a few stylized strokes, yet these suffice to summon up a whole mythology; a rhetorical gesture made possible by an already well-established indexical order in which English speaking is held to stand for a set of desirable, historically situated, native qualities – of decency, fairness, unfussy vernacular tolerance.

The process at work here, a strategy typical of ideological contexts, is one that can be described as "indexical inversion" (Inoue 2004: 43). Already naturalized meanings are imposed on speakers' linguistic behaviour, so that they are seen to conform to a particular ideological narrative, thereby at once creating and confirming the reality they purport to identify: in this case about the history and positive characteristics of English speakers. Ultimately, it is implied, what makes English English is its association with this imagined (not to say imaginary) group of speakers and their native qualities. Conversely, it is the supposed nature of the language that serves to guarantee the peculiarly distinctive character of its native

---

1 The emphasis on norms of linguistic behaviour is centrally concerned here with the definition and production of authentic Britishness; however, the phenomenon is far from uniquely British. For example, this is the then German Interior Minister Wolfgang Schäuble, interviewed in *Frankfurter Allgemeine Zeitung*, 13th March 2006:
Q: Was können wir von Ausländern erwarten, die dauerhaft hier leben?
A: Wir können erwarten, daß sie mit uns hier leben wollen. Sie sollten Deutsch lernen und am zivilgesellschaftlichen Leben in seiner Vielfalt teilnehmen. Sie sollten nicht so leben wollen, als wären sie nicht hier.
Q: What can we expect from foreigners who live here permanently?
A: We can expect that they want to live here with us. They should learn German and take part in the diversity of civil society. They should not want to live as if they weren't here.
(http://m.faz.net/aktuell/politik/inland/interview-schaeuble-der-islam-ist-keine-bedrohung-fuer-uns-1302682.html)

speakers, and to normalize the boundary – more accurately, the great divide – that separates them from non-English-speakers.

5 Constructing rhetorical borders

It will come as no surprise that, when presented for online debate, questions about English language learning for immigrants to Britain should prompt the expression of hostile – often xenophobic – attitudes. These have a long pedigree in the British (more particularly English) context, and have formed an explicit part of the narrative within which standard English has defined itself, repetition of which has established the "common sense" ground of stock argument for popular discussions of this kind, and for the conformity required of foreigners coming to England. In a study of English grammarians of the 17th and 18th centuries, Mitchell sketches the already clear lines of this position (2012: 123; cf. also Bauman and Briggs 2003: 300):

> Qualities such as good character and good citizenship were associated with using the English language correctly. [...] If foreigners wanted to be accepted, they had to learn the English language idiomatically and prove they had some degree of language competency. There could be no hint that they would corrupt the vernacular or remain isolated in their own native language. Foreigners coming to England were expected to learn the rules of grammar and pronunciation. It is these rules that helped regulate who rose in society and who was excluded.

More recently, a similar role has been played by the "native speaker", whose ideal English language competence has most often been (and in many cases still is) held up as the goal for second language learners (cf. Gill 2012). This "native speaker" is an idealization that both creates and excludes its complement, but constant elision of the idealized category with actual first language users of English has been instrumental in naturalizing the apparently common sense boundaries of nativeness, in relation to which the "non-native speaker" is inevitably positioned (and disadvantaged). Where the "native speaker" is fluent, authoritative, in full control of the standard language, the "non-native" is inevitably less so, always at some intermediate point along the interlanguage trajectory towards the "native speaker" ideal, never likely to arrive. A development that seems to confirm the logic of this argument is the recuperation now occurring of the "non-native", often in terms that merely reverse the polarity of the dichotomy and reconstruct the "native speaker" as in fact the inauthentic one (conservative, prescriptive, intolerant, etc.), this time in relation to a non-Anglocentric set of linguistic norms and practices (creative, flexible, accommodating, etc.).

As examples of this kind suggest, rhetorical boundaries are more rigid and absolute than "natural" ones: this attempted realignment has cost great rhetorical effort, but is still far from secure; and while the challenge to "native speaker" hegemony is well-motivated, using the dichotomous / exclusive authentication strategy to achieve it is not an advance towards a less ideological state of affairs, but an almost exact parallel of that previously used on behalf of the "native speaker".

By contrast, even (or perhaps especially) in "rigid" cases where group belonging is regarded by members themselves as categorical, self-definition need not imply rhetorical work to exclude outsiders. In the case of the Old Order Amish, for instance, a community for whom domain-specific language choice (among "Deitsch", "Hochdeitsch" and English) is just one of a well-defined set of practices indexing Amish identity and beliefs, authenticity and belonging are powerfully experienced, and the inside/outside distinction is strictly – at times even severely – enforced (see, for example, Johnson-Weiner 1998). Nonetheless, this is not accompanied by rhetorical exclusion of the "English", but rather by pragmatic accommodation, and (surprisingly, in the light of the relentless spread of new "English" technologies) no fully articulated perception of threat to the community's linguistic integrity. It would seem that, in the absence of major anxiety over identity, rhetorical borders are superfluous.[2]

6 Defending the border online

If mobility and hybridity, the global "flows"[3] of goods, messages, languages and populations, in patterns shaped in large part by global inequalities, are defining characteristics of late modern social experience, so are resistance, points of contest, protectiveness towards vanishing resources (material but also – among other things – linguistic), both as apparently stable communities and values find themselves under pressure and as political measures are deployed by governments to regulate the processes of change.

---

2 For first-hand insights into the practices of the Old Order Amish, I am indebted to Johanna Jansson, research student at Åbo Akademi University, who has spent extended periods living in an Old Order community.

3 It is hard not to agree with Mary Louise Pratt (2010), who has questioned talk of "flows" of populations as falsifying the human experience of those involved, since this is more often than not rough, traumatic, full of friction and obstruction.

The obverse of the mobile modern speaker, attuned to inflections of meaning and indexical potential in complex social environments, is the "local" defender of the "old" order, of the stable sense of reality and community, and the essential characteristics of prevailing social and linguistic norms. For groups in these circumstances, authentic national identity counts; not as a particular deployment of indexical resources or "knowing" social positioning, but non-negotiably and absolutely. Such views are well represented in the corpus discussed here.

The BBC data consists of posts gathered in 2007 and 2010 from a BBC online discussion forum that invites responses from readers on issues occasioned by current news stories, both of them in this case clearly provocative. The first had the headline: "Unemployed 'must learn English'" (BBC 2007) – a curious formulation, referring to a government plan to require unemployed people "who cannot speak English" to prove that they are learning it or face loss of benefits (partly justified as a way to save money on translation services), and reframed by most responses to refer explicitly to the immigration of non-English speaking people to Britain. The second, "English rules tightened for immigrant partners" (BBC 2010), concerned proposed legislation to require those applying for a UK visa to join a British spouse or partner to prove that they have some proficiency in English.

There are of course many things to be said about these issues and the way in which they are presented, and many things that the contributors to the forum do say. Like Cameron's speech, both belong to the more assertive approach adopted by recent governments on either side in British politics towards limiting numbers of immigrants and requiring active commitment to British culture/society by those admitted. Both are sensitive and complex, and had already been subject of extensive discussion at various levels of sophistication in the media; like Cameron, both foreground English language proficiency as the site for potential action; and, needless to say, both elicited a lively response: the first received 149 posts; the second 1026 in the space of two days, many very different in tone and content from the articles that prompted them, many willing to exclude non-English speaking immigrants of any kind.

It is relevant to consider the nature of the "Have Your Say" format, in which a news story written by BBC journalists, and framed according to their priorities, is presented and responses are then invited to a specific set of related questions. Those wishing to comment must register on the web site, but are free to post pseudonymously; writers for the most part adopt nicknames proclaiming stylized identities, often semi-humorous or indexing a political stance (Often rejected, Go Away Gordon Brown, Leftie Agitator, ruffled feathers, Confuciousfred, etc.) – indeed, these are the only signs of overt identity stylization that occur more or less generally here. Posts are both pre-moderated and reactively moderated, according to a set of house rules which, among other things, forbid offensive comments.

While the genre shares some of the features of debate, with sometimes extended interaction between participants, usually involving citation of the message being replied to, many posts are one-off responses to the original questions, often a reframing of the issue or incidental comment addressed to the forum's audience in general. Very few take up the discursive frame proposed by the original articles. Moreover, the asynchronous character of the posts tends to inhibit the extended development of themes, or engagement with further issues as they emerge. Inevitably, as readers enter the forum continuously, there is a wearying reiteration of similar points, each time as if new to the discussion, raising the question of how such texts are read: is there, in fact, anyone who reads consecutively through all of them? On the evidence of the present data, it appears that "officially" authoritative, expert contributors do not post there (in contrast to the radio version of the same forum, where participants' own names are used and there is strong editorial control), message senders do not overtly claim expert status, and their positions are not responded to or reframed by any further commentator outside the HYS forum itself, or editorially shaped by the use of formatting, or graphics, etc. within the medium of the web pages (unlike similar debates in the press, cf. Milani 2007: 117); hence there is no disengaged perspective from which to understand the main points that arise or relate them to one another. Indeed, the only overt editorial intervention, beyond that of moderation, is the decision to close the discussion.

Two further questions call for comment. One is the nature and status of language ideological debate in a computer-mediated context, where "here" is a key term ("coming over here", "moving here", "live here", "work here", "this country", etc.), but posts are detached from any particular location, in effect from anywhere. If these are voices from Cameron's "real" communities, they are also apparently at home in this much more transient, impromptu, late modern space. The other concerns how authority is claimed in a context dominated by participants who themselves mostly speak from a position of relative powerlessness, features of whose posts index lack of public prestige, and who are likely, on this evidence, to have little access to the production of authoritative "mainstream" discourses. I will return to the second point below.

What results is an emergent collection of broadly identifiable topic categories, around which individual posts seem to circulate. Here it is possible to do no more than indicate their range (see Table 1): among the most prominent are a variety of policy recommendations, hostility to the then Labour government, the status of English in relation to Welsh, Scots, and Gaelic, accusations and denials of racism, the linguistic chauvinism of the English abroad, the (mis)use of tax payers' money, the provision of translation, resources for language learning, political correctness and media bias. Common to a great majority, however, is a

POLICY	LANGUAGE
Make them learn	Practical communication needs
Labour opened the flood gates	English is easy
No English - no entry	Level of 5–7 year old
Common sense	What about Welsh, Gaelic, Scots?
What about being fair to us?	What is the language?
Should cut benefits	
Taxpayers' money	
Translation costs	
Britain is full / large numbers	
Where else would be so lax?	
Government policy at fault / in a mess	
Political correctness to blame	

Good for women / forced marriage	
Prevents alienation	
Provision for English classes	
Help them learn	
Don't stigmatize / penalize	
Learners need support	
No jobs to find	
Same should apply to British	

US	THEM
Not racist	Lazy / arrogant foreigners
Show individual effort / motivation	Why come here?
Common courtesy / good manners	Here from choice / can always leave
We would learn their language	Expect too much
Experiences in other countries	Get unfair advantages
English is part of who we are	Need to integrate
Treated unfairly	Should show us respect
-------------------------	Not much to ask
British hypocrisy	Isolated from community
	Live in ghettos of non-English speakers

	Immigrants want to learn

Table 1: Main topoi in the Have Your Say data

discourse in which speaking / knowing / understanding English is treated as an all-or-nothing category, and taken to index a spectrum of supposedly authentic "British" traits – linguistic, moral, social, economic – including diligence, respect for the law, self-reliance, willingness to make an effort, especially the effort to learn "others'" languages when in "their" countries, that legitimate speakers as members of the "British" ethnolinguistic community, and mark them off unambiguously from the foreigner who rejects or disregards them. For example:

> This should be rolled out across the board in my opinion and should apply to everyone that wishes to settle in this country. In Holland, if you don't speak the language (or read) then you are going to have problems. I do not see why the Tax Payers of this country should fund a service that provides translators for those that will not make the effort to assimilate. You only have to walk into a doctors surgery to see how many notices/leaflets are published in foreign languages. Benefit Offices provide Translators and so does the legal system all at the expense of the Tax Payer, where else does this happen?
> Data set 2, post 95

Or again:

> Yes, Yes and Yes. I realise campaigners on any issue, but especially immigration, will always cry 'unfair'. How on earth can it be discriminatory to demand immigrants into the UK should have a command of the English language? It is about time strong laws were made on immigration. We, the British people, are being asked to make painful cuts and wage restraint. Government Departments are being squeezed of cash so why not immigration? The only way we can get around immigration problems is for immigrants to integrate into the general community. This will be achieved much easier if they spoke the language of the Country - English. Those of us who have lived in another country know the disadvantage of not speaking the local language. So - we make the effort to learn it.
> Data set 2, post 129

As already noted, the construction of an authentic "us" involves two separate contrasts; in this case they are inherently contradictory: first, between the present indulgent "pc" British policy of government funded translation services and assistance for immigrants and the natural order that prevails elsewhere, in which you are left to survive by your own efforts; and then between "those of us" who make the effort to learn others' languages when abroad and show respect to our host societies, and foreigners who expect special treatment.

The dice are inevitably loaded. If, as constantly asserted, the only acceptable way for "them" to cross this boundary is through hard work and an active effort to integrate, the rhetorical structure affords them no scope to do so. Meanwhile, their own language repertoires and competences are either ignored completely or presented as an obstacle to integration. Here again, as for Cameron, agency is always theirs – hence also responsibility for the situation in which they have chosen to place themselves. If efforts or compromises are to be made, it is they who must be prepared to make them. If there are failures of recognition or understanding, or unrealistic expectations, those too are theirs alone. One of the worst is not to understand the "common sense" realities of British life:

> These campaign groups seem to be under the delusion that Britain some kind of magical paradise that everyone in the world has a RIGHT to move to. They don't. We have our own language and our own customs, if you want to move here then you have to adapt to them. If you don't want to learn the language or don't want to adapt to British customs and culture, then maybe you should reconsider if this is really the country you want to move to. Maybe another one would suit you better?
> Just seems like common sense to me!
> [Data set 2, post 24]

The use of stylized second person address here, "as if" to the migrant, but in fact talking past them to an implied sympathetic audience is a common feature in posts of this kind, reinforcing the assumption of shared in-group attitudes. Overt racism is forbidden by BBC house rules (although there are frequent pre-emptive denials of racism); but, while xenophobic comments are widespread, many posts prefer to emphasize the "common sense" of the requirements under discussion – it is just a minor question of language proficiency, after all, and English is an easy language to learn – and express surprise that anyone could dissent from this, or find it excessive: if immigrants object, that merely confirms their laziness, lack of courtesy or serious intentions.

> Why do people keep going on about Brits moving abroad? We are talking about this government and learning the native language here! And most Brits that I know who go abroad to live do learn the basics they need to get by and do most of their further learning there it's just common courtesy!
> I don't see a problem with it and English is a good language to learn as it is a universal language so surely this is a good thing?
> Data set 2, post 228

7 The legitimacy of vernacular voices

News editors in "responsible" media such as the BBC may be inclined to take the view expressed by the editors of *The Times Online* and *Independent.co.uk* (both quoted in Thurman 2008: 144–5) that such forums are "anchors for crackpots", "… a bunch of bigots … shouting from one side of the room to the other and back again". But how exactly are these voices positioned, and how are they authorized?

While the presence of user-generated content may seem in one sense to underwrite the democratic accountability of the medium and authenticity of its messages, even the invitation to "Have your say" already implies management by editorial gatekeepers and a contrast with the producers of more powerful media discourses, a point underlined by the placing of the forum behind a link in a separate section of the web site, disengaged from the BBC's officially authorized and authoritative news and opinion sections, at once actively solicited and firmly excluded. Topics are chosen by BBC journalists, so in this sense, too, the discussion is already fixed, as some contributors point out. Perhaps its real motive (as one of them suggests) is to generate a spectacle to titillate an audience of non-participants. Nonetheless, the topics here are journalistically framed to open up the discussion to alternative voices and positions, including a positive orientation towards the provision of work opportunities for migrants and ways to enable them to acquire skills, with coverage of the views of groups committed to migrant welfare and rights. Yet while alternative voices are also raised in the forum, a majority of participants engage in it in ways that effectively close it down again. In particular, the "common sense" trope is deployed repeatedly, to clinch and stifle argument, often to dispute the need for any debate at all; implying the obtuseness of others' inability to see the obvious.

However, within the rhetorical economy of the whole news story, the same features that delegitimize and disqualify most participants from access to mainstream sources of authority and opinion-forming also invest them with authenticity as the voices of "ordinary people" with "real" opinions. From this perspective, editorial decisions about whether to normalize spelling, or clean up the language in forum posts are not merely about technical aspects of acceptability, but about how they are to be positioned in relation to these particular indices of vernacular authenticity. In opposition to the liberal journalistic frame in which the issues are presented, their voices from the margins, often vocally opposed to what they see as dominant, "pc", "caring" attitudes, and the non-ethnolinguistic discourses of rights and entitlements, create a context in which the "unsayable" finds authorized public expression; not a "mainstream" or establishment voice, but vernacular – and, as such, a voice to which political interests regularly defer.

8 Conclusion

In April 2012, the following article appeared in the Daily Express – a newspaper known for its robust, conservative opinions – accompanied by a large photograph of the union jack (Widdicombe 2012).

> **IMMIGRANTS SHOULD LEARN OUR LANGUAGE**
> **It is impossible to have true diversity without integration**
> **By Ann Widdecombe**
>
> **IF EVER I were to choose to live in another country I would simply take it for granted that I would try to learn its language and respect its laws.**

> Of course it would be wonderful to find a British expat community but that is not at all the same as expecting the country itself to preserve my Britishness.
>
> Yet cash-strapped councils are spending money teaching the children of immigrants the language of the country they have left instead of expecting them to learn English to as high a standard as possible and leaving their parents' language to be learned at home.
>
> The excuse – you could never call it a reason – for this madness is "diversity". Yet it is impossible to have true diversity without integration.

Its author, Ann Widdecombe, a former Conservative government minister, regular Express columnist and media "personality", went on to praise "successful immigrant communities", notably Jewish, as well as "Asian families" she knows, who have achieved this with positive results. However:

> By contrast where "ghettos" have developed and immigrants have shunned their new world the results have been disaffection and poverty.
>
> The antidote is to make sure the children have a good command of English and are encouraged to aspire and compete with the indigenous population, not to shut them off into a world where they speak principally a language for which 95 per cent of the population has no use.
>
> To be bilingual is a major asset, which is why children whose parents come from two different countries begin with a big advantage.
>
> Not only are they fluent in two tongues from an early age but they develop a feel for languages which stands them in good stead in their education.

> So I do not believe for one moment that another language should not be spoken at home but that is down to the parents not the local council whose emphasis should be firmly on English, which is native not only to here but also to half the world.

It would be hard to distinguish this article from many of the posts to the HYS forum. Its conjunction of English proficiency and respect for the law, and unwarranted implication that non-English speakers lack this; its voicing of immigrants' unreasonable expectations by reference to what the writer herself would not expect when living abroad; its foregrounding of entextualized "integration"; its attribution of agency to immigrants who have "shunned their new world" and live in ghettos (and here she is likely to be understood to mean Muslim immigrants); its exclusion of their own linguistic repertoire from public life and utility, and emphasis on the global "nativeness" of English – all belong to the "authentic", "common-sense" vernacular discourse of British ethnolinguistic self-definition and boundary maintenance, further indexed (for anyone who may have missed the point) by the photograph of the British flag.

Common to the contexts I have discussed is a conception of national boundaries in essentialized linguistic terms, and a willingness to construct an absolute linguistic divide between insiders and outsiders. For both David Cameron and many of the HYS contributors, these define the space in which Britain is authentically itself, requiring constant vigilance against erosion caused by non-English speaking incomers and lax state policies. What legitimizes state action is the defence of authenticity, in particular, the vernacular authenticity of "real" communities. Cameron's calculated "establishment" rhetoric seeks to motivate the tough, legislative consequences he has in mind by means of glancing intertextual reference to a literary/political tradition promoting the timeless virtues of vernacular Britishness; Widdecombe's piece of populist journalism adopts a clearly vernacular voice to assert the priority of "native" British qualities expressed in "our language". Despite their claims to oppose divisiveness in society, both work in dialogue with popular discourses such as those found in the HYS data to reinforce an image of the British nation state that is divisive and unaccommodating.

These are current issues with serious human consequences. The fact that such views can be maintained, not only by "crackpots" but within mainstream political discourses courting popular approval, in the face of an everyday reality in which multilingual and multiethnic identities are increasingly and unproblematically the norm, suggests that what is needed here is not merely more evidence of unfairness or a more persuasive presentation of the issues, but a critically informed challenge to the basis of entrenched "common sense" discourses themselves, especially illiberal discourses of authenticity.

References

Bauman, Richard & Charles Briggs 2003: *Voices of Modernity: Language Ideologies and the Politics of Inequality*. Cambridge: Cambridge University Press.

BBC 2007: Unemployed must learn English. BBC News website. http://news.bbc.co.uk/2/hi/uk_news/6352793.stm.

BBC 2010: English rules tightened for immigrant partners. BBC News web site. http://www.bbc.co.uk/news/10270797.

Bendix, Ruth 1997: *In search of Authenticity: the Formation of Folklore Studies*. Madison: University of Wisconsin Press.

Blackledge, Adrian 2005: *Discourse and Power in a Multilingual World*. Amsterdam/ Philadelphia: John Benjamins.

Blackledge, Adrian 2009: Lost in translation? Racialization of a debate about language in a BBC news item. In Sally Johnson and Tommaso M. Milani (eds.), *Language Ideologies and Media Discourse: Texts, Practices, Politics,* 143–161. London: Continuum.

Blommaert, Jan 2009: Language, asylum and the national order. *Current Anthropology* 50(4): 415–441.

Blommaert, Jan, Helen Kelly-Holmes, Pia Lane, Sirpa Leppänen, Máiréad Moriarty, Sari Pietikäinen & Arja Piirainen-Marsh 2009: Media, multilingualism and language policing: An introduction. *Language Policy* 8: 203–207.

Blommaert, Jan & Jef Verschueren 1992: The role of languages in European nationalist ideologies. *Pragmatics* 2(3): 355–375.

Blommaert, Jan & Jef Verschueren 1998: *Debating Diversity: Analyzing the Rhetoric of Tolerance*. London: Routledge.

Bucholtz, Mary 2003: Sociolinguistic nostalgia and the authentication of identity. *Journal of Sociolinguistics* 7(3): 398–416.

Cameron, David 2011a: Prime Minister's address to Conservative party members on the government's immigration policy. Guardian (online edition). http://www.guardian.co.uk/politics/2011/apr/14/david-cameron-immigration-speech-full-text.

Cameron, David 2011b: PM's speech at Munich Security Conference. http://www.number10.gov.uk/news/pms-speech-at-munich-security-conference/.

Coupland, Nikolas 2003: Sociolinguistic authenticities. *Journal of Sociolinguistics* 7(3): 417–431.

Creutz-Kämppi, Karin 2008: The othering of Islam in a European context: Polarizing discourses in Swedish-language dailies in Finland. *Nordicom Review* 29 (2): 295–308.

Eckert, Penelope 2003: Elephants in the room. *Journal of Sociolinguistics* 7(3): 392–397.

Eckert, Penelope 2009: Three waves of variation study: the emergence of meaning in the study of variation. http://www.stanford.edu/~eckert/PDF/ThreeWavesofVariation.pdf.

Frankfurter Allgemeine Zeitung 2006: Interview: Schäuble: „Der Islam ist keine Bedrohung für uns." http://m.faz.net/aktuell/politik/inland/interview-schaeuble-der-islam-ist-keine-bedrohung-fuer-uns-1302682.html.

Gill, Martin 2011: Authenticity. In Jan-Ola Östman and Jef Verschueren (eds.), *Pragmatics in Practice: Handbook of Pragmatics Highlights*, Vol. 9, 46–65. Amsterdam/Philadelphia: John Benjamins.

Gill, Martin 2012: Nativeness, authority, authenticity: the construction of belonging and exclusion in debates about English language proficiency and immigration in Britain. In Carol Percy and Mary Catherine Davidson (eds.), *Languages and Nation: Attitudes and Norms,* 271–291. Bristol: Multilingual Matters.

Inoue, Miyako 2004: What does language remember? Indexical inversion and the naturalized history of Japanese women. *Journal of Linguistic Anthropology* 14(1): 39–56.

Lindholm, Charles 2008: *Culture and Authenticity*. Oxford: Blackwell.

Lloyd, Geoffrey 1990: *Demystifying Mentalities*. Cambridge: Cambridge University Press.

Major, John 1993: Speech to the Conservative group for Europe. http://www.johnmajor.co.uk/page1086.html.

Martin, Daniel 2010: Nation states are dead: EU chief says the belief that countries can stand alone is "a lie and an illusion". Mail Online. http://www.dailymail.co.uk/news/article-1328568/Nation-states-dead-EU-chief-says-belief-countries-stand-lie.html.

Milani, Tommaso 2007: Voices of authority in conflict: The making of the expert in a language debate in Sweden. *Linguistics and Education* 18: 99–120.

Mitchell, Linda 2012: Language and national identity in 17th- and 18th-century England. In Carol Percy and Mary Catherine Davidson (eds.), *Languages and Nation: Attitudes and Norms,* 123–140. Bristol: Multilingual Matters.

Orwell, George 1954: *England Your England and Other Essays*. London: Secker and Warburg. [First published 1941.]

Pratt, Marie-Louise 2010: You don't understand the system: reflections on language and globalization. Plenary lecture. Sociolinguistics Symposium 18, University of Southampton.

Rorty, Richard 1989: *Contingency, Irony and Solidarity*. Cambridge: Cambridge University Press.

Taylor, Charles 1991: *The Ethics of Authenticity*. Cambridge, MA: Harvard University Press.

Thurman, Neil 2008: Forums for citizen journalists? Adoption of user generated content initiatives by online news media. *New Media and Society* 10: 139–157.

Widdicombe, Ann 2012: Immigrants should learn our language. Express (online edition). http://www.express.co.uk/posts/view/315082/Immigrants-should-learn-our-language/.

Johanna Sprondel and Tilman Haug

What's in a *promesse authentique?*
Doubting and confirming authenticity in
17th-century French diplomacy

Die Falschheit mit gutem Gewissen; die Lust an der Verstellung als Macht herausbrechend,
den sogenannten ‚Charakter' beiseite schiebend, überflutend, mitunter auslöschend; das
innere Verlangen in eine Rolle und Maske, in einen *Schein* hinein; ein Überschuß von
Anpassungs-Fähigkeiten aller Art, welche sich nicht mehr im Dienste des nächsten engsten
Nutzens zu befriedigen wissen: alles das ist vielleicht nicht *nur* der Schauspieler an sich?
Friedrich Nietzsche, *Die Fröhliche Wissenschaft*

1 Introduction

What does indexing authenticity indicate? According to concepts of authenticity predominant among sociolinguists, we may define authenticity as marking
adherence to a locally and/or socially defined community using speech acts that
presumably indicate a shared set of norms and are accepted as "original in some
important social or cultural matrix" (Coupland 2003: 419). "Speech style" thus
serves, as Nikolas Coupland continues, as an "anchor for solidarity and local
affiliation" (Coupland 2003: 430). Therefore the indexing of authenticity would
depend just as much on the person making a speech as on those who receive the
speech as authentic or inauthentic, which would at the same time include extensions that lead to the "construction of social meaning" (Eckert 2005), making
authenticity a term that serves not only to describe a(n) (speech)act itself but also
give it a dialectic level: in order to be accepted and considered authentic within a
'matrix' the rules of a 'matrix' have to be accepted, adopted and applied, leading
to a reading of authenticity that blurs the normative borders of authenticity as a
behavioural act and an expression of personhood. Because even though sociolinguistic definitions already provide a viable guideline for empirical research, such
a reading of authenticity does not necessarily satisfy the conceptual ideas of philosophers and historians. Firstly, one might ask whether this concept of authenticity as marking one's geographical situation, social status, political affinity,
ethical values, etc. does not miss something essential.

Is authenticity merely a means of social inclusion in a speech community
founded on a projection of (allegedly) shared values and norms? Have we not, at

least from a philosophical point of view, come to associate a broader concept of personhood with the term authenticity? Indeed, the very notion of what can be understood as authenticity from a philosophical perspective appears to be much more than aligning oneself by means of certain acts. As Hegel, Smith, Nietzsche, Heidegger, Marcuse, Adorno, Charles Taylor and others have shown, it is rather a normative concept of personhood including (or at least requiring) personal intentions, truthfulness, genuineness and sincerity to oneself than a matrix that can be easily deciphered by a social group. This does not only concern the question of what authenticity comprises or should comprise from an ethical point of view, ascribing authenticity to a person or to what he or she is saying. If we embrace the idea that by acting authentic one indicates an affiliation to a 'class' or 'place' and is therefore accepted as a credible member of a speech community, this still leaves a more important question unanswered: What comes next, once we have identified ourselves and have been identified by others as such speakers? Can deepened social, political, and economic relationships ensue from such speech acts? What do they mean in the ascription of sincerity, and sociologically more important, in terms of trust or trustworthiness?

Secondly, from the point of view of the history of ideas, questions emerge regarding how and when a notion of authenticity came into being and since when the concept and the term authenticity have been associated with notions of a 'true', 'original' personality unaltered by things foreign to his or her 'true identity'. This seems to be all the more interesting as a diachronic analysis, albeit rather provisional, of the history of the concept shows that what the term refers to practically throughout the Modern Period is something slightly other than that. Back then, there is neither a concept of an authentic personality, nor a notion of authenticity concerning a piece of art that refers to an authenticity of its author or an object that would 'authenticate' itself as an expression of the 'culture' it originated from. And as Lionel Trilling stated (Trilling 1972: 3ff), it is only around the middle of the 18th century that the concept of authenticity as a normative discourse of itself emerged, in which authenticity and an authentic behaviour led to a fulfilled, uncompromising life and where the difference between being received as authentic and being authentic emerged – where Polonius would no more be asking for authenticity but for sincerity and thus a social attitude when he proclaims "This above all: to thine ownself be true, // And it must follow, as the night the day, // Thou canst not then be false to any man." (Shakespeare, *Hamlet*, 1.3.78–80)

In the following, we would like to reflect on concepts of authenticity that do not only build on the 'indexical' and socially inclusive function of speech acts, but also take into account the broader notion of sincerity, genuineness, credibility and trustworthiness indicated as well as the notion of sovereign governmental authority implied in the Early Modern semantics of the term 'authenticus' resp. 'authentique'. By doing so, we hope to elucidate how a sociolinguistic model of authenticity can actually be rooted in a political sphere that was much less about an individual pursuit of authenticity (Lévi-Strauss 1976). Rather it was the case, as we shall see, that the different notions of authenticity were in a constant interplay with each other and could require seemingly contradictory styles of behaviour, turning the individual into an actor instead of allowing him or her to be an authentic agent. Therefore we shall begin our analysis from the early modern semantics of the term, without limiting our analysis to the usage of the term 'authentique'. Rather, in what Reinhart Koselleck called "controlled terminology", we would like to describe instances where actors reassured each other or themselves of their authenticity in the aspects laid out above (Koselleck 2006: 375).

2 Authenticity as a matter of authority

The reading of authenticity within the field of 'genuineness' or 'originality' in an aesthetic sense can be traced back to the 18th century. 'Authentica', according to Zedler's *Universallexicon, the* early modern German Dictionary, refers to "the original of a text body or a testament [...] as opposed to the copy" (Zedler 1732: 1167). And it is in this sense that the term has entered discussions of *Quellenforschung*. Interestingly, while the English language knows the term in the same meaning, the *Oxford English Dictionary* also offers an example of a different use of the word that bridges two meanings of the term: John Trapp noted that in his commentary on the Book of Job he was "sufficiently asserting the authenticity and authority of this Book" (Trapp 1657). It is this interweaving of authority and authenticity that can be seen as a core aspect of authenticity before[1] the enlightenment and that Zedler proposes for the term 'authenticus': "glaubwürdig, das von ansehenlichen glaubwürdigen Leuten gestellet, und für gut angesehen ist, was gilt und angenommen wird" ["credible, which is stated by esteemed credible people and regarded for good, which is valid and accepted"] (Zedler 1732: 1167). The term

---

1 One might even argue that the reference to authority in the field of authenticity stays one of the core aspects throughout the Enlightenment. Not only argues Kant (though opposing the doctrinaire) that the authenticity of interpretations of biblical texts falls to the "Gott in uns" (Kant 1968 and 1977), but – as one might argue – even a matrix, a social network, a community can be considered authoritative, even though the individual is acknowledged a self-autonomy that can be a blessing or a burden.

(here mainly referring to written objects, ancient texts, the Bible and the law) is here clearly linked to a judgement by an *authority* that, so we may say, is credible in itself by her or his (surely rather his, back then) social status and thus authentic. But the importance of the term reaches far beyond the philological or theological exegesis, which the cited passages refer to. This becomes perfectly clear as Zedler's article continues: "authentica interpretatio wird genennet, da weiter zu widersprechen oder darinne zu critisiren, niemand erlaubt". ["An authentic interpretation is one which no one is allowed to criticize or to dissent from"]. The need for such authoritative interpretations mainly comes about "wenn weder der Iudex noch ein I(uris)C(onsul)tus die Gesetze erklären kan, wenn der Verstand zweydeutig und obscur, in welchem Fall es dem Landes-Herrn allein zukommt, daß er das Rätsel auflöse, und ist ein Verbrechen der beleidigten Majestät, wenn ein Unterthan oder sonst jemand sich dessen ohne dessen Auctorität unterfangen würde" ["when neither a judge nor an attorney can interpret the Law, when the sense is ambiguous and obscure, in which case it is left solely to the sovereign prince, to solve the mystery, and it is a crime of lèse majesté, in case a subject or anyone would dare to do so without his authority"] (Zedler 1732: 1167). Here the term appears closely linked to the sphere of law and government: an 'authentic interpretation' is in itself an act of governing authority. It represents nothing less than 'maiestas', the very sovereign power of the prince itself. Up to this point, we may thus note that the term has been associated with acts of philological, judicial and, perhaps most importantly, of governing authority.

But as already implied, the above does not only hold true for the early modern German semantics of the term. Contemporary French dictionaries are even clearer about this: 'authentique' in the famous *Encyclopédie* is defined as "une chose d'autorité reçue" ["a thing deriving from an accepted authority"]. This could refer to sovereign, i.e. monarchic political authority, which was the reason why it could be used synonymously with the terms 'solennel' or 'célèbre'. But it could also describe claims "attestés par des personnes qui sont régulièrement de foi. C'est dans ce sens que nous disons: les vérités de la religion chrétienne sont fondées sur des témoignages authentiques, actes, papiers authentiques" ["made by persons that are generally credible. It is in this sense that we say: The truth of Christian Religion is founded upon authentic testimony, authentic acts and papers"] (Encyclopédie 1751: 895)[2]. In this respect, authenticity in the sense of

---

2 Interestingly enough, the entries both in Furetière's *Dictionnaire* and in the *Encyclopédie* refer to a link between 'authentique' and personal traits in the wider sense, stating "The nobility and other persons of distinguished rank formerly had the privilege of being called authentic, because

greater credibility was ascribed to an upper stratum of society as a whole. It was not to be found in *personal* traits but more generally ascribed as one of the insignia of a higher position within a stratified society. And as a piece in the documentation of the Peace of Ryswyck indicates, some actors like the Papal *camerlengo*, the head of the papal treasury (Apostolic Chamber), even used 'authenticus' as one of his titles (Moetjens 1707, 5: 686). The truth and genuineness referred to by the term then was one of received authority and referred to as acts and objects, rather than 'personal' identity: someone who was authentic was a 'persona' who fulfilled an important social position; it was part of the qualities ascribed to an officeholder, in whose words and actions one could and should have 'faith'. This already shines a light on a discourse of authenticity that, although its framing cannot be compared to that we started out with in this essay, nevertheless bears the normative discursive structure of acceptance due to a constructed, authoritative nomination.

3 Deceived by authenticity

To clarify this point we have chosen a historical example that may, at first glance, appear slightly odd: French diplomats and their practices in the later 17th century. Around that time, the French moralist Jean de la Bruyère defined the diplomat of his age as follows: "Toutes ses vues, toutes ses maximes, tous les raffinemens de sa politique tendent à une seule fin, qui est de n'être point trompé, et de tromper les autres". ["All his views, all his principles, all the refinement of his behavior are directed to one single goal, which is to be not deceived, while deceiving all the others"] (Oeuvres de La Bruyère 1886: 266). According to a fake book of rules for French statesmanship, which was in fact a vitriolic pamphlet written in the midst of a wave of aggressive Francophobia in the Holy Roman Empire (see Schillinger 1999; Wrede 2004: 424–545) by an anonymous German author in the 1670s and viciously named *Machiavellus Gallicus*, it was the aim of French foreign policy "Fremder Potentaten und Fürsten consilia zu verwirren/ gute zu hintertreiben/böse einzusickern (…) ihre Residenten als honorable Instrumenten aller Französischer Bosheit halten" ["to perturb the advice given to foreign leaders and princes, to hinder good ones, to promote bad ones [...] to employ their envoys as honourable instruments of all French vices."] Therefore their profession has

---

they were supposed to be more worthy of having faith in them than the others" ("La noblesse, & les personnes d'un rang distingué avoient autrefois le privilège d'être appellées authentiques, parce qu'on les présumoit plus dignes de foi que les autres" (Encyclopédie 1751: 895).

been "ehrliche Spionen abzugeben/ Aller Orten Uneinigkeit zu streuen / was ver-
eingt zu zertheilen / was zusammen hängt / zu trennen / umb dazwischen das
Französische interesse zu säen" ["to make honorable spies, to promote discord
everywhere, to separate what is united to sew the French particular interest
everywhere in between." ([Anonymus] 1675: 48). It is hardly surprising that the
'patriots' during the French Revolution referred to the Ancien Régime diplomacy
as "L'école du mensonge et du secret", the school of lying and secrecy', which
they explicitly turned against (Kugeler 2006: 128) and which was perceived as an
epitome of the whole decadence and 'rotten politics' of Ancien Régime France
(Bélissa 1999: 300). So from this we may conclude that it appears that France in
the 17th century was not exactly the home of authenticity.

But the study of the normative literature on early modern diplomacy as well
as an analysis of the practice of early modern diplomats can show how a different
notion of authenticity, in fact one that might be fruitful for answering the question of what indexing authenticity indicates itself, may be deduced. In French
diplomacy, or so we assume, the notion of authenticity consisted of the mastery
of switching between different patterns of speech and behaviour according to the
situational requirements rather than an invariability of the same. A good, authentic diplomat would rapidly change his manners – thereby forgetting about the
individual agency and turning into an actor on the stage of politics.

In order to demonstrate how such authenticity (and we might even consider
speaking of authenticit*ies* in this case) was not only displayed and perceived differently in various situational frameworks but also referred to as different parts
and role requirements within an ambassador's identity, we propose a threefold
concept of authenticity for the following analysis:
–   an authenticity of political representation, which takes into account the his-
    torical semantics of the term we laid out above;
–   an authenticity of social identity, which serves the purpose of indicating
    social identity and affiliation and the implicit as well as explicit communica-
    tion of shared norms and values;
–   an authenticity in the sense of sincerity, truthfulness and credibility.

If we begin our analysis from the contemporary use of the word 'authentique', it
becomes clear that it seldom relates to a diplomat's attitude. It only concerns official pieces of writing, declaration, legitimate claims and other formal objects. The
term was not so much used in describing behaviour in diplomatic practice guides
concerning the 'parfait ambassadeur' or the daily business of observing the other
in diplomatic correspondence, but rather in the collections of official documents
and 'actes publics' following the great 17th- and 18th- century peace congresses.
(Moetjens 1694, 1: 197, 338, 437), (Moetjens 1694, 3; 284, 313), (Moetjens 1694, 4:

495, 701); 1; (Moetjens 1699, 3: 107, 349). For instance, the documentation of the 1713 Peace Congress of Utrecht, settling a Conflict amongst all major European powers, promised 'authentic pieces' to its readers in its title (Freschot 1714).

However, when ambassadors like Hugues de Lionne or the Duc de Gramont were sent to Frankfurt to influence the Imperial Election and to look out for possible Alliances with German Princes, they were explicitly ordered to act in an 'authentique' fashion. Concerning proposals of a mediation of Peace with Spain on the part of the Elector of Mayence, Cardinal Mazarin, the overall powerful French first minister at the time, instructed Lionne and Gramont explicitly:

> je crois que vous pourriez dans le dernier secret convenir avec lui des conditions de la paix, et après en être tombés d'accord, lui faire une promesse authentique que le Roi y donnera les mains aux conditions que vous aurez ajustées.

> [I think you could settle the peace terms with him in extreme secrecy, and after having reached an agreement, make an authentic promise that the King will give his consent on the conditions you will have set out] (Mazarin 1657: 255 recto).

Obviously Mazarin was not so much concerned about 'authentic' behaviour by the ambassadors as individuals. Rather an 'authentic promise' should make a direct link between what they proposed and negotiated to the French King and his authority and the 'carte blanche' they were given to act in his name, so as to render it credible to their counterpart and to ensure that they acted as immediate 'proxies' of the king. In what respect, then, is this formalized role of the ambassador also a problem of personal authenticity? Isn't representing one's master and in this sense fulfilling an assignment a practice in which personal traits are replaced by playing a purely professional role?

Matters were much more complicated for Early Modern diplomats, at least for the highest-ranking ones, the ambassadors (Krischer 2011: 201–206). The Early modern ambassador had a special relationship to the authority he represented. Representation was more than a professional role to fulfil. Instead the 'ambassadeur' had to be the virtual 'embodiment' of the Prince and the *maiestas* he represented, a relationship that was expressed through terms such as *image sacrée* or *umbra domini*, or "their masters' mirror" (Wieland 2004: 359). The logic of ambassadorial representation was thus designed to make him in a way indistinguishable from his master. This representational paradigm stayed in place well into the later 18th century. As late as 1769, the philosopher of law Johann Christian Wolff stated, that not only "dervorstellende Character eines Gesandten" ["the representative character of a diplomat"], gave him the right to act as proxy; for Wolff "macht ein Gesandter nach dem Naturgesetz gleichsam einerley moralische Person mit dem, der ihn abgeschickt hat, aus, so daß es eben so viel ist, als wenn dieser selbst gegenwärtig wäre, und derjenige, an welchen er verschickt wird, ihn als eine ihm gleiche Person ansehen muss" ["according to natural justice a diplomat forms one and the same person with the one who has dispatched him, so that whoever receives him is required to treat him as such"] (Wolff 1769: 853). This in part explains the fact that ceremonial matters were such a prominent field of conflict that could block actual diplomatic negotiations for months, even years. Only by the correct ceremonial treatment of the Ambassador the political identity of his master could be expressed, only the "fiction of presence" expressed in the ceremonial would finally legitimize the decisions made by the princely proxies (Stollberg-Rilinger 2001: 22). Prior to official negotiations, ceremonial matters had to be sorted out in order to avoid conflicts (Stollberg-Rilinger 2011: 157–158). Any ceremonial disadvantage was considered to relate to the person of the Prince himself and his rank and status in an environment that was still seen as a 'Society of Princes' with a strong sense of rank and hierarchy rather than as a balanced 'International System' (Bély 2000).

Representation in this case did not simply mean that diplomats acted on behalf of their absent master, it ideally meant a real substitution of the latter's presence by means of a virtual embodiment of the Prince. In order to be regarded 'authentic' in the sense of his function as *ministre public* he did not have to be genuinely himself but was required to assume the identity of the person he represented. The first notion of authenticity thus sums up one basic requirement for the *parfait ambassadeur*: assuming an identity as credible *ministre public* by virtually impersonating one's master. The question is hence one of being *received* as authentic rather than of *being* authentic. Therefore it is no surprise that Early Modern diplomatic theory made abundant use of the omnipresent contemporary 'theatrum' semantics (Weller 2008: 379 – 382). Not only was the diplomatic world a stage, where Kings and Princes were engaged in a *theatrum praecedentiae*. The term describing the very substance of the *ministre-public*-function was a theatrical metaphor as well: *caractère*. Representational authenticity referred primarily to the credibility of an ambassador's 'stage performance' and thus to the success of assuming and performing the identity of the represented prince. It was, as paradoxical as it may sound from a modern perspective, *mimesis* of another person, very much so in the sense of Plato's acting "hós tis állos ón" ["as if one was someone else"] – which in the Republic is stigmatized as *mimesis* in the sense of deceiving (Shorey 1969). Renaissance diplomats were inclined to take the semantics of the theatrical world quite literally: to assume the *caractère* of a diplomat would mean to imitate known traits of the ruler such as voice, posture, etc. (Mattingly 1955: 217). The Spanish author Juan Vera y Zuñiga went even a step further in exploiting this metaphor in his treatise *El Enbaxador* (Vera 1620). He established, relying on terms of the theatrical world, a distinction between two personae of the ambassador and employed the theatrum-metaphor:

> Dos personas son las que representa el Enbaxador: una la de su Rei, otra la suia propria, i assi tiene dos diferentes modos de negociar, i portarse, que como en la tragedia, el que a Alexandro, Iason, o Ciro representa, mientras està en el teatro con ornamentos reales, procura imitar en palabras i aciones a aquella persona que supone; mas luego que se retira al vestuario, si bien de los orname[n]tos no se despoja, porque espera bolver a salir al teatro, con todo obra, i habla en su figura, privada, i particular; tal el Enbaxador en las solenidades publicas, en las audiencias, en las juntas que se halla, como ministro deve satisfazer la autoridad, i decoro de su Principe, i de su oficio, mas fuera de alli en el trato domestico, en las visitas privadas, en los conbites familiares, en los razonamientos ordinarios, bien que el mismo Enbaxador se queda, deve tenplar el decoro publico, con la llaneza particular, desseando mas parecer el que es, que el que parece

> [An ambassador represents two persons all together, the first one is that of his king; the other his own; and subsequently he has to have two courses of actions. And just like in a tragedy, where he who represents Alexander, Jason or Cyrus tries to imitate in words and in actions the person he impersonates while he is on stage; but when he goes backstage, while not taking off his costume, since he hopes to re-enter the scene, he nevertheless acts and talks like a private and single person, very similarly the Ambassador has to keep, as a minister, his gravitas and the authority and decorum of his Prince and his position at all public celebrations, and at the Audiences and solemn festivities he is called to attend; but out of that amongst his own people, at private visits, banquets and ordinary conversation, he has – even though he is still the ambassador – to temper the serious style he uses at official events with private frankness, trying to seem much more who he is himself, than who he seems to be] (Vera 1620, 2: 117r/v).

But who precisely was the ambassador when he stepped out of or 'toned down' his role? Abraham de Wicquefort's treatise *L'Ambassadeur et ses fonctions*, first published in 1681, went further into again establishing a distinction between the two personae of an Ambassador. Making use of the familiar metaphor, Wicquefort drew an even more precise distinction between the two 'identities' of a diplomat, distinguishing on the one hand the ambassador as a function (*ministre public*), on the other hand the ambassador as a person (*honnête homme*).

> un bon Ambassadeur est aussy un grand personnage de théatre, & que pour réussir en cette profession, il faut être un peu Comédien. 'Il n'y a point de comédie, où les acteurs parois-sent moins ce qu'ils sont en effet, que les Ambassadeurs sont dans la negociation, & il n'y en a point qui représentent de plus importants personnages. Mais comme le plus habile acteur n'est pas toujours sur le théatre, & change de manière d'agir après que le Rideau est tiré; ainsi l'Ambassadeur, qui a bien joué son rolle dans les fonctions de son caractère, doit faire l'honneste homme, lors qu'il ne joue plus la comédie.

[A good ambassador is also a great theatrical personality, and in order to achieve in this profession, one has to be sort of a comedian [...] There is no other comedy, where the actors display less of who they really are, than ambassadors during a negotiation, and there is no other, where more important personalities are displayed. But just as the capable actor is not always on stage and changes his manner of conduct after the curtain has been drawn, the same way the ambassador, who has played well his role while he exercised his character, must conduct himself as the *honnête homme*, while he is no longer acting]. (Wicquefort 1681, 2: 3).

Wicquefort claimed that continuously sticking to the *caractère* of an authentic *ministre public* would violate the requirements of a 'parfait ambassadeur': An ambassador, who never stepped out of character would turn a *pedant politique*, an abhorrent social persona any self-respecting *honnête homme* diplomat would by no means like to be confused with (Wicquefort 1681, 2: 4).

4 Matrices and castes

In practice, though, the social setting of early modern diplomacy was even more complicated than what Wicquefort's distinction between a political and a social persona suggests. While theorists like Wicquefort or Vera tended to emphasize that the ambassador's sole loyalty lay with his master and he had to fulfil his ambassadorial role without taking into account his personal interests, during the 17th century diplomacy in most European states was in fact rarely an exclusive matter of princely service or serving a state. Rather diplomats had to cope with a large scope of different roles and identities. Ambassadors were not only servants to a prince, but also for instance patrons to a group of people in their home country, maybe clients to higher nobles or to a *ministre favori* such as Cardinal Richelieu or Mazarin. Furthermore, they were members of a noble house and as such concerned with expanding the fortunes of their relatives and their offspring, or at least preventing their family from the short-term economic hardships that often went along with costly diplomatic service (von Thiessen 2010). Above all, most of them were part of a society of nobles or a society that was defined by a 'quasi-noble life style'. All these dispositions required role-switching and balancing between social and political norms. Thus a second form of 'social authenticity' was required that went beyond the representative function and that could be summed up by the ideal of the quasi-noble *honnête homme* (Höfer & Reichhardt 1986; Scheffers 1980). An *honnête homme* had to engage in practices of noble sociability, creating parallel identities of purely acting as a political entity tied to the body politic, and as Vera pointed out, the physical body of the Prince. Being an *honnête homme* would imply behavioural practices and rhetorical styles that were so clearly defined that ambassadors could easily identify each other as members of this group – simply by identifying the other as an authentic speaker and performer within the matrix of the caste. While the cited writings drew a clear distinction between acting as negotiator / *ministre public* and acting as a polite social individual, in practice the line between both styles of interaction was blurred and often deliberately crossed. This was not only a consequence of a lack of differentiation of political and social systems and their respective norms, it also served political purposes, because ambassadors could offer personal cooperation based on a common code of politeness and a style of speech shared among a European upper stratum of society, broadening the scope of possible interactions where their agency as *ministre public* was limited or even non-existent.

Employing codes of 'civility' and 'politeness' was an important technique of initiating any form of communication in early modern diplomacy, as in every other type of upscale social interaction throughout the early modern period (Watts 2003: 140–165; Beetz 1990; Chartier 1986; Brown & Levinson 1987). And it could not do without a great deal of exaggeration. Early modern upscale interactants promised each other all the world. Superfluous to mention: they rarely quite meant it precisely that way. Obviously they were not inclined to. Politeness was a mode of speech and gesture that was often confined to ritualized sequences of communication, for example the opening of a negotiation. It was not considered to contain meaningful literal 'information'. Polite speech had not to be scrutinized for honesty and sincerity: it made it possible to communicate about relationships between the speakers and further possibilities of communication. *Civilités* only made it clear that the speakers were willing and able to pursue further communication according to social norms and could, in principle, cooperate with one another in a meaningful way later on (Köhler 2009: 387 - 397). The commonplace polite exaggeration served to establish a common ground of allegedly shared norms and values between speakers.[3] The function that *civilités* had in diplomacy then seems very similar to what modern sociolinguistics see as authentic. Communication about a shared set of norms had the mutual assurance of the value of the latter as its purpose, thereby indicating that one was part of a 'legitimate' group of speakers – a community of *honnêtes hommes*, which included the nobility and leant toward their ideal, but was not necessarily identical with it. Moreover speakers made it clear that that they were inclined to pursue

---

3 When, for example, French 17th-century noblemen assured each other all sorts of help and service in rituals of politeness, they did not actually communicate their unbounded desire to assist each other, rather they made it clear that they communicated on the basis of a shared value: noble-style generosity of (in contemporary French) *largesse* (Kühner 2009).

rules of *honnête-homme* interaction. Socio-professional authenticity was generated by modes of speech that were rather indifferent to personal authenticity in the sense of being sincere or genuine. Nevertheless, some contemporary theorists of politeness were more concerned with the gap between the social function of politeness and the authentic attitude of the speakers. Antoine de Courtin, himself a former diplomat, proposed in his 1671 *Nouveau traité de la civilité* to fill that gap by techniques of 'autosuggestion' of the truthfulness of what was said, to render them more authentic, which by modern standards ultimately meant resorting to hypocrisy (Courtin 1671: 137).

These practices came to importance when for example negotiating peace treaties. Apart from rather ritualized practices of politeness that loosely defined the possibilities of mutual understanding, *honnête-homme* diplomats could also exploit the fact that most participants in a peace congress usually were members of a broader European Noble Society, which was 'in nuce' reinstated at a peace congress and its social environment to render political understanding easier. For example the Peace Congress of Nimègue[4] started from a point where no formal contacts between the two main parties, the Dutch and the French, were possible. The first propositions of peace could only be made in instances of purely social, informal interaction, not in a regular negotiation process where diplomats would have acted in their capacity as *ministres publics* (Köhler 2011: 271). So it required a certain style of speech that had to be brought out in an informal manner, and eventually had to be marked by a semantics of informality. These were for example emphasized as *conversation* in a clear distinction to processes of 'meaningful' negotiation. Diplomats could highlight the personal level upon which they communicated, for example by stating that they spoke to each other *en ami* (Köhler 2011: 272). It is important to note that in these cases speech acts were semantically disguised as if they had almost nothing to do with the negotiation itself, when they in fact were an effective means to set off negotiations or revive stalled communications. Contrary to techniques of politeness, *honnête-homme* speech styles (or speech that was marked as such) could be ascribed a meaningful political function. Diplomats could then even be explicitly advised to speak in their own right, 'purely as themselves' and stripped of their official role (see also: Mignet 1835, 1: 233). In that sense, they were 'authentic' at a representational level: representing themselves and their personal ties to one another, as well as their inclusion in a respectable society of *honnêtes hommes*. Defining social situ-

---

4 The Peace Congress was held from 1674 to 1679 to end an all-out European War that Louis XIV had provoked (Köhler 2011; Ekberg 1979).

ations as informal and employing a semantics of informality here was key to their separation from more official negotiations.

But *honnête-homme* styles of speech and interaction also defined one of the core duties of every diplomat: the negotiation process. Contemporary theorists of diplomacy both agreed on the fact that, technically, good negotiating did not differ much from practices of *conversation*. And even though Wicquefort drew an analytical distinction between *conversation* and *négociation*, he admitted that when it came to describe the good style of negotiation, his advice focussed on conversation, and aimed at forming an 'honnête homme'. So formal and informal styles of speech and interaction hardly differed and "on peut estendre la Maxime jusques à la Politique" ("one could extend the principle to politics") (Wicquefort 1681: 28). According to Wicquefort, the secret of good negotiation was neither persuasion by better argument nor a formalized rhetorical technique. Instead, the objective of conversational style in negotiation towards the other was "d'entreprendre de l'entraisner (...) le ramener par une violence douce & insinuante" ("to try to drag him along" (...) 'by a sweet and intriguing force"), manipulating him into agreement with one's proposals (Wicquefort 1681: 33). The apparent lack of a clear-cut distinction of political and social spheres in the Early Modern period did not so much lead Early Modern theorists to a failure to 'realize' the modern distinction between 'arguing' and 'bargaining' in political theory; they merely saw it as useless and inoperative.

Francois de Callières in his extraordinarily influential treatise *L'Art de Négocier avec les Princes* (1716) went even further in emphasizing this manipulative dimension of conversation as an *honnête-homme* style of negotiation (Callières 1716), creating emotional commitment with the counterpart. The primary skill of Callières' negotiator was an "art de plaire" (Waquet 2005: 138–142). Even though Callières had recognized *conversation* as a strategical means of manipulation by politeness, in negotiations, there was a strong moral sense that absolutely forbade blunt lying and deception of the other. Therefore Early Modern ethics sought ways to employ *civilité* to one's personal advantage without hurting the societal virtue of 'bienséance'. Instead, they differentiated between certain styles of inauthenticity, for which the famous distinction between 'simulation', lying and deceiving, and an indirect style, not telling the truth, hiding certain facts, etc., stood; in short, 'dissimulation' was established (Snyder 2009; Cavaillé 2002; Geitner 1992). Polite conversation that only worked with a high degree of 'indirectness' and 'avoidance', for example the avoidance of a direct rejection of proposals was a means of successful dissimulation and could comply to ethical standards of the time. Early modern political ethics 'backed up' such spaces of legitimate inauthenticity.

Where these norms and the ethics from which they emanated were fully applied to the practice of diplomatic negotiations, speakers clearly ran the risk of being trapped in what Niklas Luhmann has called a "Paradox der politischen Kommunikation" ("paradox of political communication"). The fact that one's intentions, even if they were completely sincere, became incommunicable for the very reason that actors employed certain speech styles focused on creating cooperation on a personal level by facilitating further communication (Luhmann 2008: 166). When the gap between polite and affirmative conversation and meaningful negotiation could no longer be bridged, French diplomats frequently resorted to accusing their interlocutors of adapting their speech to whomever they were talking to, saying ultimately nothing and behaving "comme un Prothée [sic]" ("like a Proteus") (de Gravel 1657: 491 verso).

5 Symbols and indices

The "paradox of political communication" has serious consequences for the relation between the styles of authenticity we have laid out. Here a conflict emerges between one style of authenticity, as a mode to qualify oneself as a legitimate speaker and actor in a community made up of *honnêtes hommes* employing styles of speech and behaviour that enable communication and cooperation at a low level of commitment on the basis of shared norms, values, and modes of interaction, and the third mode of authenticity, which entails sincerity, reliability, and trust in meaningful communication and committed political cooperation. The ensuing problem for political communication can be summed up very well by a distinction introduced by the American sociologist and student of Erving Goffman, Robert Jervis. For Jervis, there are two different degrees of sincerity of political intention: signals and indices. A 'signal' can be identified "as statements or actions the meanings of which are established by tacit or explicit understandings among the actors" [...]. "Both the sender and the perceiver realize that signals can be as easily issued by a deceiver as by an honest actor. The cost of issuing deceptive signals, if any are deferred, to the time when it is shown that the signals were misleading." Indices on the other hand Jervis defines as:

> statements or actions that carry some inherent evidence that the image projected is correct because they are believed to be inextricably linked to the actor's capabilities or intentions. Behaviour that constitutes an index is believed by the perceiver to tap dimensions and characteristics that will influence or predict an actor's later behaviour and to be beyond the ability of the actor to control for the purpose of projecting a misleading image (Jervis 1970: 18–19).

If we consider Jervis's distinction, it easily becomes clear that acts of politeness and *honnête-homme* style interaction contained signals that were powerful tools to communicate about relationships and further communication according to conventionalized styles of speech, but were at the same time no means for actually committing anyone to deeper political and social relationships or for preventing deception and misunderstanding. But how, then, were early modern diplomats able to issue 'indices' in the sense proposed by Robert Jervis?

First of all, an 'index' should not at all be misunderstood as a fixed, predefined code of speech or behaviour. In contrast to signals they can only rarely be of use as conventions. If words and actions were regarded as expressions of true intentions beyond the capability to deceive, they had to be identified as such according to situations or dynamics of communication within a group of observers. In one of the very few works concerning early modern concepts of sincerity, Claudia Benthien and Steffen Marthus point out that sincerity required powerful 'dramatizations' to separate it from other modes of speech (Benthien & Martus 2006: 10–11). Conventional speech between diplomats could often hardly meet these requirements. The most likely solution to these problems that early modern diplomats came up with, was 'widening the field' in terms of styles of speech and interaction, media and the number of participants in such interactions.

In the following, we will point out two ways of how such solutions could be brought about. The *first possibility* considers the extension of spaces of communication beyond face-to-face-communication between two parties and partial abandonment of civil and polite codes of interaction. These very often took the form of what Erving Goffman once named acts of 'ceremonial profanation' (Goffman 1982: 85–89). Actors 'turned around' social situations and spaces, where they were expected to profess politeness and civility and acted in a blunt and openly confrontational manner instead. The effects of such behaviour on the perception of political actors become clear in the following example. During the imperial election in Frankfurt 1657/58, as we already mentioned above, Baron Johann Christian von Boineburg, a minister of the overall influential Elector of Mayence Johann Philipp von Schönborn and self-professed adherent of the French party in the Empire and as such in Opposition to the ruling House of Habsburg, put up a harsh dispute with one of the Ministers of the Archduke Leopold, the Habsburg candidate to the imperial throne, who was eventually elected. He did so while he stayed with others in the Emperor's *antichambre*, the 'waiting room' of his temporary residence in the city of Frankfurt (de Gramont and de Lionne 1658a: 16 verso). Boineburg's behaviour made an impression on both sides. Soon afterwards he was informed by the imperial officials that they would avoid any further contact with him and cut him off from any information concerning the Imperial embassy. French diplomats in turn were now inclined to regard Boineburg as the 'good Frenchman' he claimed to be, given the fact that now his ties to the Habsburgs were effectively severed. Boineburg could now be trusted by the French and given the regular payments that French diplomats had promised him (de Gramont and de Lionne 1658b: 69 recto).

The whole set of interactions required more than a conventional 'one-on-one' communication between two actors. It necessarily involved the participation of a third party, the political enemy and its representatives, who were defied by these bold breaks of codes of politeness, and, ideally, a group of spectators that these 'dramatizations' were put on display for. All in all, these demonstrations of trust-worthiness and authenticity call for an enlarged triadic model of the trust-building process. Nevertheless, the case just cited can only be properly explained if we take into account French diplomats' general perception that they acted in a dual system of Habsburg and Bourbon 'spheres of influence' in the Empire, leaving German Princes and their ministers basically no alternative choice but to join one party or the other. While this perception was actually misleading, the observation of impoliteness would suffice to convince French diplomats that their German clients were truly 'bon français' and trustworthy for further interaction.

There was still a *second possibility* for actors to 'authenticate' themselves and their speeches in the sense of sincerity and trustworthiness. This involved first of all a shift of the type of media employed in practices of negotiation from orality to letters. By the exchange of written proposals and arguments, the whole nego-tiation process would go on record, a marked difference compared to face-to-face negotiations with one another. For instance, during the Westphalian Peace nego-tiations set out to end the Thirty Years War, the almighty Cardinal Mazarin and the Queen Mother Anne d'Autriche clearly demonstrated the 'dangers' that went along with written statements. Writing, though it might support the progress of negotiations, was clearly seen as a form of creating commitment and authentic-ity – which explains their initial rejection of the proposal made by the envoys in Munster to negotiate in written form: "La plus forte raison [...] c'est que les déclarations que l'on fait par escript engagent trop, ce qui n'arrive pas quand les instances se font de vive voix, parce que [...] on peut se relâcher sans déchet de réputation" ("The most powerful reason [...] is that the declarations one gives in writing are too committing, this doesn't happen when the proposals are done in oral speech. That is because one could withdraw them without loss of reputa-tion") (Bosbach et al. 1986: 3). Here the Queen Mother and her minister showed *ex negativo* that the permanence of scripture in opposition to the spoken word had the capacity to force the actors to render their claims and intentions credible and thus tied them in a way to their own claims of their intentions to seek peace. Such procedure could force all the negotiating parties to lay down their claims clearly, without the ambiguities and the possibilities for non-commitment entailed in the spoken language of negotiation.

So while one focus of authenticity after the 18th century lay on the question of the reliability of sources and texts, in late-17th-century diplomatic culture, the act of writing itself was of great importance. But not only did writing 'authenticate' in the official, political sense, it was also a technique for rendering credible claims made in negotiation processes. This claim to credibility here could be achieved by putting the process of negotiation on record, exchanging written proposals rather than negotiating 'face-to-face' with one another. Nevertheless, the protocol as an instance of diplomats' actual words and proposals 'going on record' should not be overestimated, since protocols were often heavily edited before becoming official documentation. That this was common practice in the later 19th century, is for example readily admitted by Prussian diplomat and former chief of staff in the foreign ministry Joseph Maria von Radowitz in his memoirs (Radowitz 1925: 48).

A second stage of creating reliability and thus making proposals authentic by inflicting pressure to act following them was publishing political pamphlets containing these promises. During the above-mentioned Congress of Nimègue the French clearly stated their intentions to make peace with England. At first Louis XIV laid out his ideas of such a peace towards a third-party institution, the mediators of peace. Then he ordered for those ideas to be published to a small but then already important political public sphere of readers. While Jürgen Habermas had reduced the early modern public sphere to a "representative publicness", where Princes merely displayed their power through public ceremonies towards a passive public (Habermas 1991: 5–14), more recent studies have shown that there was a discursive public sphere, with politically knowledgeable and interested readers, in place by the late 17th century (Gestrich 1994). Thus, the peace aims of the Crown became known to a larger public. In doing so he did not only commit himself (and his diplomats) in terms of what was and what was not negotiable. In it, he aimed to show that French ambassadors actually meant what they said, because by having published those aims first, nothing more and nothing less than the king's honour and reputation were coupled to sticking to his own aims (Köhler 2010: 422–426). Here the credibility of the self-commitment by the king and his diplomats was relegated to the involvement of a rather anonymous public sphere outside the very localized "culture of presence" at a diplomatic Congress. It is important to underline that publicly announced goals of peace negotiation actually worked rather for the reason of the 'enlarged' display of monarchical honour or the possibility of dishonour than for fear of criticism by the subjects. Furthermore, the involvement of the public under these circumstances could have a tremendous adverse effect during peace-making processes, since the public announcement of goals for peace also severely limited a Prince's ability to compromise (Kampmann 2010: 153–156).

This again seems to defy the modern emphatic sense of authenticity, where the 'truthfulness' in authentic behaviour is linked to a notion of immediacy and presence that only a 'face-to-face'culture could provide. Claude Lévi-Strauss's classical account of authenticity, for example, plays a sense of oral face-to-face authenticity prevalent in pre-modern, 'primitive' societies against mediated inauthenticity as falsehood and inoriginality (Lévi-Strauss 1976). It would seem that early modern diplomatic actors were much more distrustful of their oral face-to-face culture than we are today and could regard writing and the involvement of the public via a 'media system' as a legitimate space of communication for the expression of authenticity in the sense of sincerity and credibility.

6 Conclusion

As it appears, maybe the most remarkable feature of indexing authenticity in early modern diplomacy is that, due to the political culture it was embedded in, adhering to one consistent set of speech styles and behavioural codes, the diplomat could not have possibly coped with the scope of multiple authenticities he had to refer to. So from a modern perspective we could not possibly speak of authenticity when referring to early modern diplomacy. In fact we find the exact opposite of what we find with e.g. Charles Taylor (Taylor 1992), Hegel (1969, 1970) and others – and with Heidegger (1927) we may even speak of 'Gerede' of the 'Man' (§35) that we find in 17th century diplomacy, and that is not only in-authentic, but moreover disguising authenticity. But still it seems too easy to simply speak of a turning point somewhere in the mid 18th century from where we may differ between authenticity and sincerity, as Trilling did (Trilling 1972). Not only because it seems to be a graduate change that took place – but also because the multiple meanings of authenticity seem to be intertwined in a certain way.

As we have seen, reducing authentic acts of speech and behaviour to their function as indicators for 'class' and 'place' as indicating affiliation to a certain social group leaves some important aspects of the concept unaddressed. The development of the semantic field 'authentic/authenticity' and the genesis of the modern use of the term and its implications show that the concept of authenticity in the early modern period was markedly different from what has come to be understood as 'authentic' during in the modern age. As we have seen, the early modern semantics of the term points to the fact that the term was exclusively used to describe acts and statements deriving from an authority – be it in serving an authority by so-called authentic behaviour, or an authority implying authenticity. It could refer to acts and decrees of the political sovereign or to philological expertise and theological doctrine.

But while judging from contemporary accounts 17th diplomacy seems at first glance to be little more but a thriving hotbed for lying, deceit and hypocrisy; a more thorough analysis of its contemporary theory and practice actually points to the interrelatedness of different 'authenticities' in early modern diplomacy, indexed by the different styles of speech and behaviour. First of all, diplomats had to be authentic in the authority-related sense of the term, by 'authenticating' themselves as immediate proxies for their principals through ceremonial representation, or, even, by exact imitation of their masters. Acting on behalf of one's master and thereby renouncing to one's 'genuine' identity was often described in theatrical metaphors, which were commonplace in 17th century culture. Accordingly, the political authenticity of an early modern ambassador has to be seen in terms very different from any notion of personal authenticity, in the sense of being genuine and true to oneself.

Interestingly enough, the lack of a political sphere, apart from the social identities of its mostly noble actors, led theorists of diplomacy to emphasize the necessity of displaying a second social identity as an *honnête homme*, by which social bonds and agreement on shared values and life-styles were established. These eventually could even create incentives for communication on a personal level, where it was impossible for the ambassadors as *ministres publics*. Authenticity here was required as an indicator for social identity. Indexing social authenticity and authenticity in the sense of sincerity and genuineness of political intentions were very different from one another – they even could contradict each other. The importance of authenticity here though, like the public display of politeness and impoliteness, was needed to 'authenticate' political affiliation, which might well be seen as a way of 'modern' seeking for being authentic, following the intention to be accepted in a 'class' or 'place'.

References

[Anonymous] 1675: *Machiavellus Gallicus. Das ist: Verwandelung und Versetzung der Seele des Machiavelli in Ludovicum XIV.dem König von Franckreich/ Vorgestellet durch hundert Politische Frantzösische Axiomata* [Unknown]: unknown Publisher.

Beetz, Manfred 1990: *Frühmoderne Höflichkeit. Komplimentierkunst und Gesellschaftsrituale im altdeutschen Sprachraum* .Stuttgart: J.B. Metzler.

Bélissa, Marc 1999: La diplomatie et les traités dans la pensée des Lumières: ‚Négociation universelle' ou ‚école du mensonge'? *Revue d'Histoire Diplomatique* 113: 291–317.

Bély, Lucien 2000: *La Société des Princes. XVIe–XVIIIe siècle.* Paris: Fayard.

Benthien, Claudia & Steffen Martus : 2006 : Einleitung. Aufrichtigkeit – zum historischen Stellenwert einer Verhaltenskategorie. In Clausia Benthien and Steffen Martus (eds.), *Die Kunst der Aufrichtigkeit im 17. Jahrhundert,* 1–16. Tübingen: Niemeyer.

Bosbach, Franz, Kriemhild Goronzy & Rita Bohlen (eds.) 1986: Acta Pacis Westphalicae. Serie II, Abteilung B, Die Französischen Korrespondenzen, Bd. 2, 1645, Münster: Aschendorff.

Brown, Penelope & Stephen C. Levinson 1987: *Politeness: Some Universals in Language Usage.* Cambridge: Cambridge University Press.

Callières, François 1716: *De la Manière de négocier avec les souverains, de l'utilité des négociations, du choix des ambassadeurs et des envoyez, et des qualitez nécessaires pour réussir dans ces employs.* Amsterdam: "pour la Compagnie".

Cavaillé, Pierre 2002: *Dis-simulations. Jules-César Vanini, François La Mothe Le Vayer, Gabriel Naudé, Louis Machon et Torquato Accetto; religion, morale et politique au XVIIe siècle,* Paris: H. Champion.

Chartier, Roger 1986: Civilité. In Rolf Reichardt and Eberhard Schmitt (eds.), *Handbuch politisch-sozialer Grundbegriffe in Frankreich 1680 – 1820,* 7–50, Heft 4, München: Oldenbourg.

Coupland, Nik 2003 : Sociolinguistic Authenticities. *Journal of Sociolinguistics* 7: 417–431.

Courtin, Antoine de 1671: *Nouveau traité de civilité, qui se pratique en France parmi les honnêtes gens.* Paris: Hélie Josset.

Diderot, Denis: (ed.): 1751: *Encyclopédie ou dictionnaire raisonné des sciences, des arts et des métiers par une société de gens de lettres, mis en ordre et publié par Diderot et quant à la partie mathématique par d'Alembert,* vol. 1. Paris: Briasson.

Eckert, Penelope 2005: Variation, convention, and social meaning. Paper presented at the Annual Meeting of he Linguistics Society of America, Oakland, CA, USA, 7 January 2005. Available online at http://www.stanford.edu/~eckert/EckertLSA2005.pdf.

Ekberg, Carl J. 1979: *The Failure of Louis XIV's Dutch War.* Chapel Hill: University of North Carolina Press.

Freschot, Casimir (ed.) 1714: *Actes, mémoires et autres pièces authentiques concernant la paix d'Utrecht,* vol. 1. Utrecht: de Water & van Poolsen.

Geitner, Ursula 1992: *Die Sprache der Verstellung. Studien zum rhetorischen und anthropologischen Wissen im 17. und 18. Jahrhundert.* Tübingen: Niemeyer.

Gestrich, Andreas 1994: *Absolutismus und Öffentlichkeit: Politische Kommunikation in Deutschland zu Beginn des 18. Jahrhunderts.* Vandenhoeck & Ruprecht: Göttingen.

Goffman, Erving 1982: *Interaction Ritual: Essays on Face-to-face Behavior.* New York: Pantheon Books.

Gramont, Antoine de & Hugues de Lionne 1658a: Report to Mazarin, 4/16, Frankfurt. In *Affaires au Ministère des Affaires Etrangères,* Série: Correspondance politique, Allemagne 142.

Gramont, Antoine de & Hugues de Lionne 1658b: Report to Mazarin, 4/16, Frankfurt. In *Affaires au Ministère des Affaires Etrangères,* Série: Correspondance politique, Allemagne 142.

Gravel, Robert de 1657: Report to Mazarin, Frankfurt 7/31. In *Archives au Ministère des Affaires Etrangères,* Série: Correspondance politique, Allemagne, vol. 137.

Habermas, Jürgen 1991: *The Structural Transformation of the Public Sphere: An Inquiry Into a Category of Bourgeois Society.* Boston: MIT Press.

Hegel, Georg Wilhelm Friedrich 1969: *Wissenschaft der Logik. Theorie Werkausgabe,* Bd. 5 und 6. Ed. by Eva Moldenhauer and Karl Markus Michel. Frankfurt a. M.: Suhrkamp.

Hegel, Georg Wilhelm Friedrich 1970: *Phänomenologie des Geistes. Theorie Werkausgabe,* Bd. 3. Ed. by Eva Moldenhauer and Karl Markus Michel. Frankfurt a. M.: Suhrkamp.

Heidegger, Martin1927: *Sein und Zeit.* Halle a.d.S.: M. Niemeyer.

Höfer, Anette & Rolf Reichhardt 1986: Honnête homme, Honnêteté, honnêtes gens. In Rolf
  Reichhardt (ed.): *Handbuch politisch-sozialer Grundbegriffe in Frankreich 1680–1820*, Heft
  7, 7–73. München: Oldenbourg.
Jervis, Robert 1970: *The Logic of Images in International Relations*. Princeton: Princeton
  University Press.
Kampmann, Christoph 2010: Der Ehrenvolle Friede als Friedenshindernis: Alte Fragen und
  neue Ergebnisse zur Mächtepolitik im Dreißigjährigen Krieg. In Inken Schmidt-Voges et
  al. (eds.), *Pax perpetua. Neuere Forschungen zum Frieden in der Frühen Neuzeit,* 141–156.
  München: Oldenbourg.
Kant, Immanuel 1968: *Kritik der reinen Vernunft. Werke*, Bd. 3f. Ed. by Wihelm Weischedel,
  2 Bde. Frankfurt a. M.: Suhrkamp.
Kant, Immanuel 1977: Die Metaphysik der Sitten. *Werke*, Bd. 8. Ed. by Wihelm Weischedel .
  Frankfurt a. M.: Suhrkamp 1977.
Köhler, Matthias 2009: Höflichkeit, Strategie und Kommunikation. Friedensverhandlungen
  an der Wende vom 17. zum 18. Jahrhundert. In Gisela Engel (ed.). *Konjunkturen der
  Höflichkeit*, 379–401. Frankfurt a. M.: Klostermann.
Köhler, Matthias 2010: Verhandlungen, Verfahren und Verstrickung auf dem Kongress von
  Nimwegen 1676–1679. In Barbara Stollberg-Rilinger and André Krischer (eds.), *Herstellung
  und Darstellung von Entscheidungen. Verfahren, Verwalten und Verhandeln in der
  Vormoderne,* 411–440. Berlin: Duncker & Humblot.
Köhler, Matthias 2011: *Strategie und Symbolik. Verhandeln auf dem Kongress von Nimwegen*.
  Köln/Weimar/Wien: Böhlau.
Koselleck, Reinhart 2006: Begriffsgeschichtliche Probleme der Verfassungsgeschichte. In
  Idem: *Begriffsgeschicht(en). Studien zur Semantik und Pragmatik der politischen und
  sozialen Sprache,* 365–401. Frankfurt a. M.: Suhrkamp.
Krischer, André 2011: Das Gesandtschaftswesen und das moderne Völkerrecht. In Martin
  Kintzinger et al. (eds.), *Rechtsformen internationaler Politik. Theorie, Norm und Praxis vom
  12. bis 18. Jahrhundert,* 197–239. Berlin: Duncker & Humblot.
Kühner, Christian 2009: Freundschaft im französischen Adel des 17. Jahrhunderts. In
  Discussions 2 [perspektivia.net; 27.2.2012].
Kugeler, Heidrun 2006: 'Ehrenhafte Spione'. Geheimnis, Verstellung und Offenheit in der
  Diplomatie des 17. Jahrhunderts. In: Claudia Benthien and Steffen Martus (eds.), *Die Kunst
  der Aufrichtigkeit im 17. Jahrhundert,* 127–148. Tübingen: Niemeyer.
Lévi-Strauss, Claude 1976: *Structural Anthropology. Vol 2*. New York. Basic Books.
Lionne, Hugues de 1658: Report to Mazarin, Frankfurt, 1/8. In *Archives au Ministère des Affaires
  Étrangères*, Série Correspondance politique, Allemagne 142.
Luhmann, Niklas 200: Die Ehrlichkeit der Politiker und die höhere Amoralität der Politik. In
  Niklas Luhmann, *Die Moral der Gesellschaft*, 163–174, Frankfurt a. M.: Suhrkamp.
Mattingly, Garrett 1955: *Renaissance diplomacy*. London. Cape.
Mazarin, Jules de 1657: Dispatch to Gramont and Lionne, Frankfurt, 9/15. In *Archives au
  Ministère des Affaires Etrangères*, Série: Mémoires et Documents, France, vol. 272.
Mignet, François-Auguste-Marie-Alexis 1835 : *Négociations relatives à la succession d'Espagne
  sous Louis XIV ou correspondances, mémoires et actes diplomatiques concernant
  l'avènement de la maison de Bourbon au trône d'Espagne; accompagnés d'un texte
  historique et précédés d'une introduction par M. Mignet*, vol I., Paris: Imprimerie Royale.
Moetjens, Adrian (ed.) 1694: *Actes et mémoires des négociations de la paix de Nimègue,* vol. 1.
  Amsterdam/The Hague: Wolfgangk & Moetjens.

Moetjens, Adrian (ed.) 1695: *Actes et mémoires des négociations de la paix de Nimègue,* vol. 3. Amsterdam/The Hague: Wolfgangk & Moetjens.

Moetjens, Adrian (ed.) 1699: *Actes et mémoires des négociations de la Paix de Ryswick,* vol. 5. The Hague: Moetjens.

Moetjens, Adrian (ed.) 1707: *Actes et mémoires des négociations de la Paix de Ryswick,* vol. 5. The Hague: Moetjens.

Nietzsche, Friedrich 1973: *Werke.* Abteilung 5: Werke, Kritische Gesamtausgabe, Abt.5, Bd.2, Idyllen aus Messina; Die fröhliche Wissenschaft; Nachgelassene Fragmente Frühjahr 1881–Sommer 1882. Ed. by Giorgio Colli, Mazzino Montinari, Wolfgang Müller-Lauter, Karl Pestalozzi. Berlin: De Gruyter.

Radowitz, Joseph Maria von 1925 *Aufzeichnungen und Erinnerungen aus dem Leben des Botschafters Joseph Maria von Radowitz.* Bd. 1, 1839–1877. Ed. by Hajo Holborn. Stuttgart: Deutsche Verlagsanstalt.

Scheffers, Henning 1980: *Höfische Konvention und die Aufklärung: Wandlungen des Honnête-homme-Ideals im 17. u. 18. Jahrhundert.* Bonn: Bouvier.

Schillinger, Jean 1999: *Les pamphlétaires allemands et la France de Louis XIV.* Bern et.al.: Peter Lang.

Servois, Gustave (ed.) 1886: *Oeuvres de La Bruyère: Les caractères.* Paris: Hachette.

Shakespeare, William 1985: *Hamlet, Prince of Denmark.* New Cambridge Shakespeare ser. Ed. by Phillip Edwards, Phillip. Cambridge: Cambridge University Press.

Shorey, Paul 1969: *Plato. The Republic,* vol. I, books I–V. Cambridge, MA: Harvard University Press.

Snyder, Jon 2009: *Dissimulation and the Culture of Secrecy in Early Modern Europe.* Berkeley: University of California Press.

Stollberg-Rilinger, Barbara 2001: Einleitung. In Barbara Stollberg-Rilinger (ed.), *Vormoderne politische Verfahren,* 9–24. Berlin: Duncker & Humblot.

Stollberg-Rilinger, Barbara 2011: Völkerrechtlicher Status und zeremonielle Praxis auf dem Westfälischen Friedenskongress. In Martin Kintzinger et al. (eds.), *Rechtsformen internationaler Politik. Theorie, Norm und Praxis vom 12. bis zum 18. Jahrhundert,* 147–164. Berlin: Duncker & Humblot.

Taylor, Charles 1992: *The Ethics of Authenticity.* Cambridge, MA: Harvard University Press.

Trapp, John 1657: *A Commentary or Exposition upon the Books of Ezra, Nehemiah, Esther, Job and Psalms.* London: Printed by T.R. and E.M. for Thomas Newberry and Joseph Barber.

Trilling, Lionel 1972: *On Sincerity and Authenticity.* Cambridge, MA: Harvard University Press.

Vera y Zuñiga, Juan Antonio De 1620: *El Enbaxador.* Sevilla: Francisco de Lyra.

von Thiessen, Hillard 2010: Switching Roles in Negotiation: Levels of Diplomatic Communication between Pope Paul V Borghese (1605–1621) and the Ambassadors of Philip III. In Stefano Andretta, Jean-Claude Waquet and Christian Windler (eds.), *Paroles de négociateurs: l'entretien dans la pratique diplomatique de la fin du Moyen Age à la fin du XIXᵉ siècle* 151–172. Rome: Ecole française de Rome.

Waquet, Jean-Claude 2005: *François de Callières: l'art de négocier en France sous Louis XIV.* Paris: Editions Rue d'Ulm.

Watts, Richard J. 2003: *Politeness.* Cambridge: Cambridge University Press.

Weller, Thomas 2008: Kein Schauplatz der Eitelkeiten. Das frühneuzeitliche Theatrum Praecedentiae zwischen gelehrtem Diskurs und sozialer Praxis. In Oswald Bauer, Ariane Koller and Flemming Schock (eds.), *Dimensionen der Theatrum-Metapher in der frühen Neuzeit. Ordnung und Repräsentation von Wissen,* 379–403. Hannover: Werhahn.

Wicquefort, Abraham de 1681: *L'Ambassadeur et ses fonctions*, vol. 2. The Hague: Jean & Daniel Steucker.

Wieland, Christian 2004: Diplomaten als Spiegel ihrer Herren? Römische und florentinische Diplomatie zu Beginn des 17. Jahrhunderts. *Zeitschrift für historische Forschung 31*: 359–379.

Wolff, Christian 1769: *Grundsätze des Natur- und Völkerrechts, worin alle Verbindlichkeiten und alle Rechte aus der Natur des Menschen in einem beständigen Zusammenhange hergeleitet werden*. Halle: Renger.

Wrede, Martin 2004: *Das Reich und seine Feinde. Politische Feindbilder in der reichspatriotischen Publizistik zwischen Westfälischem Frieden und Siebenjährigem Krieg*. Mainz: Zabern.

Zedler, Johann Heinrich (ed.) 1732: *Großes vollständiges Universal-Lexicon aller Wissenschaften und Künste*, vol. 2. Halle/Leipzig: Zedler.

Index